Nikon

D3300™

Digital Field Guide

Nikon® D3300™

Digital Field Guide

J. Dennis Thomas

WILEY

Nikon® D3300™ Digital Field Guide

Published by
John Wiley & Sons, Inc.
10475 Crosspoint Boulevard
Indianapolis, IN 46256
www.wiley.com

Credits

Acquisitions Editor
Aaron Black

Project Editor
Cricket Krengel

Technical Editor
George Maginnis

Copy Editor
Marylouise Wiack

**Senior Content Development &
Assembly Manager**
Mary Corder

**Vice President and Executive Group
Publisher**
Richard Swadley

Project Coordinator
Patrick Redmond

Quality Control Technician
Shannon Ramsey

Proofreading and Indexing
BIM Indexing & Proofreading Services

About the Author

J. Dennis Thomas is an Austin, Texas-based photographer and the author of 20 Nikon *Digital Field Guides* by Wiley Publishing, as well as the author of *Concert and Live Music Photography: Pro Tips from the Pit* and *Urban and Rural Decay Photography: Finding the Beauty in the Blight*, published by Focal Press. He is also a frequent author of articles on photographic theory and technique for *Digital Photo Magazine*, MasteringPhoto.com, and his own website, the Nikon Digital Field Guide Online (http://NikonDFG.com).

He is represented by Corbis Images and has done freelance photography for *Rolling Stone*, *SPIN*, and *Veri.Live* magazines. His photographs have been featured in many notable publications including *Rolling Stone*, *SPIN*, *People*, *Us Weekly*, *Elle*, *W magazine*, *Thrasher*, *Ebony*, *New York Post*, *Veri.Live*, and many more.

When not out photographing or in front of his computer writing about photography, he can be found gracing the stages of the Live Music Capital of the World and popping up randomly in films and television shows.

Acknowledgments

I'd like to thank all of the people behind the scenes at Wiley that help make these books as good as they are. My name is on the front, but I couldn't do it without the Wiley team behind me. I'd specifically like to thank Cricket for being a kind and patient Project Editor and lending a helping hand whenever needed.

I'd also like to thank Precision Camera in Austin TX — owner Jerry Sullivan and staff members Sarah, Robert, Noel, and everyone else there.

Contents

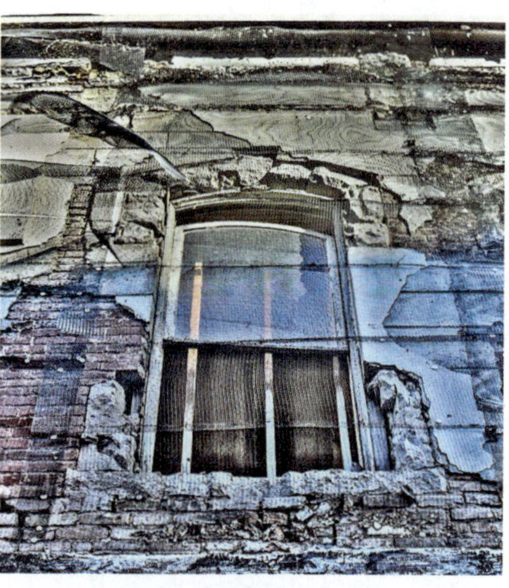

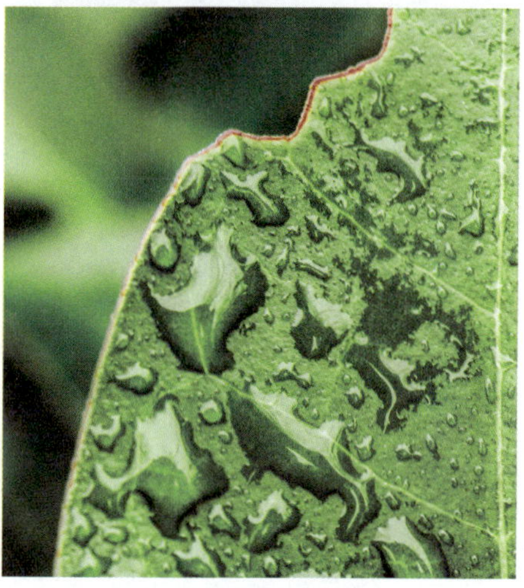

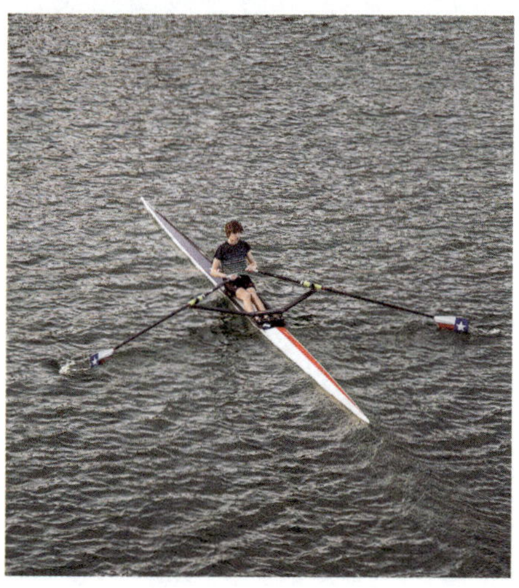

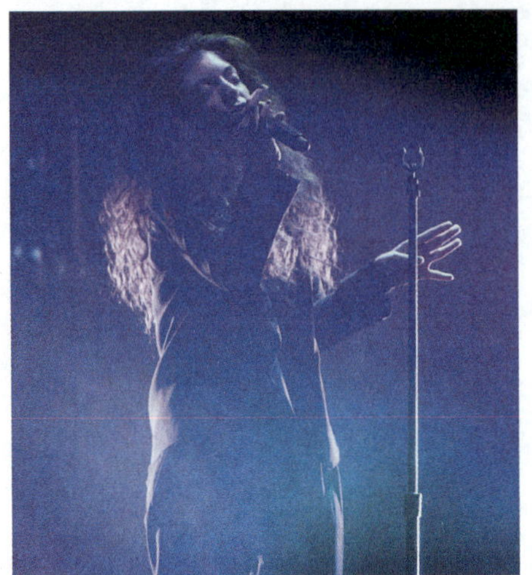

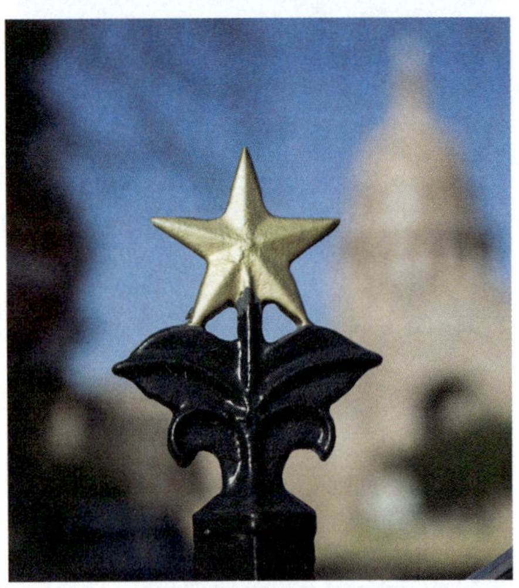

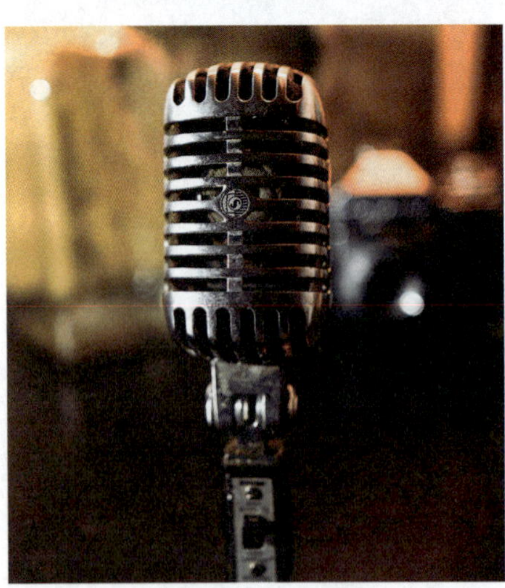

CHAPTER 3
Setting up the Nikon D3300   67

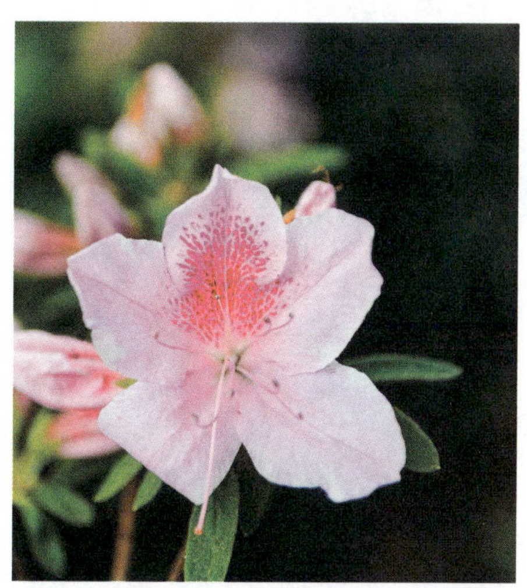

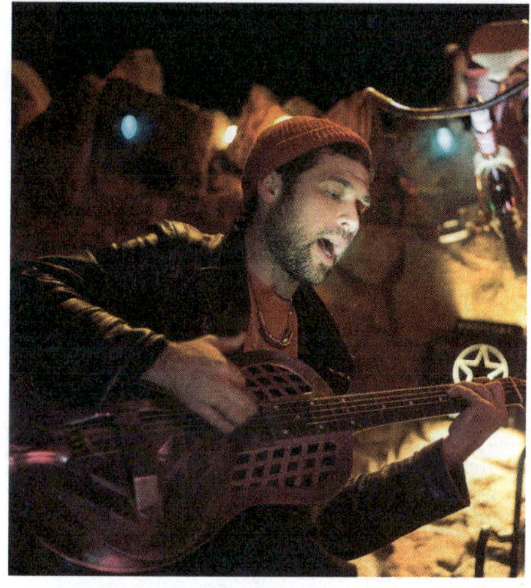

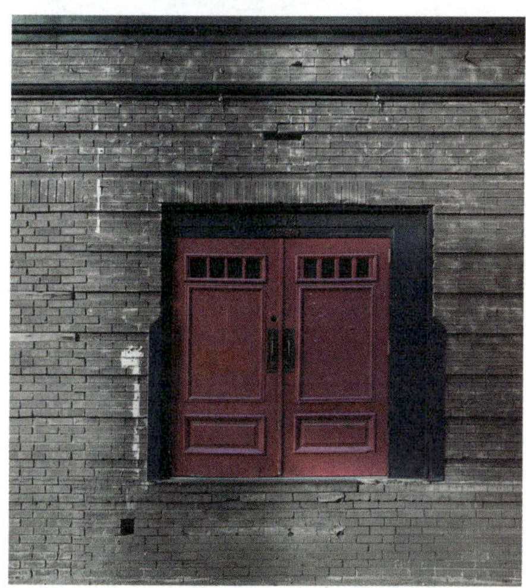

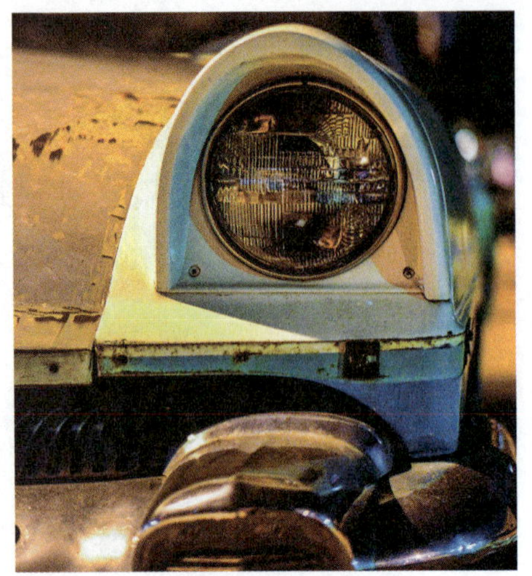

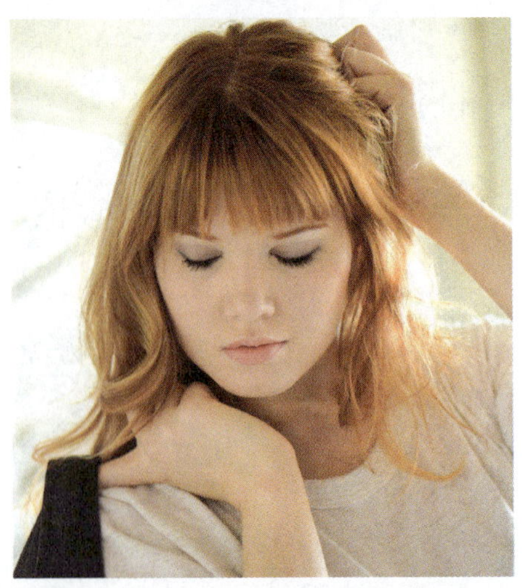

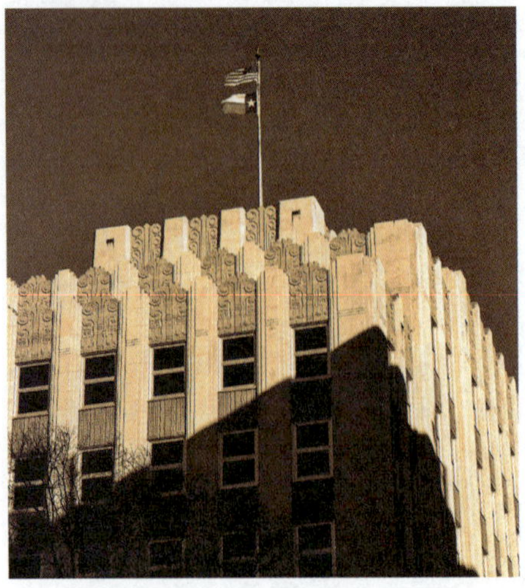

CHAPTER 4
Selecting and Using Lenses
with the Nikon D3300   107

CHAPTER 5
Controlling Exposure   129

CHAPTER 6
Working with Light 145

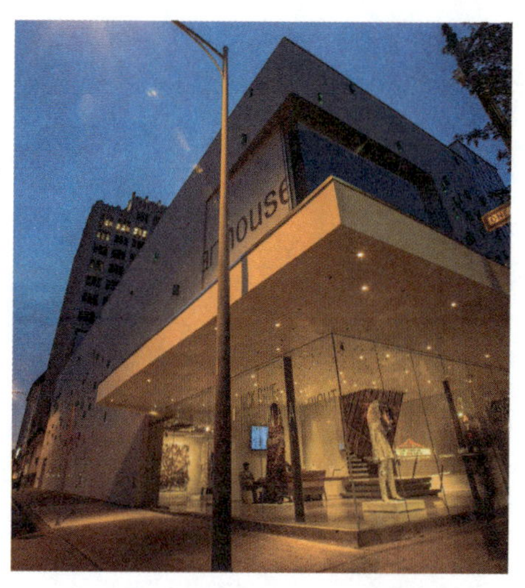

CHAPTER 7
Working with the Live View and Video Modes 163

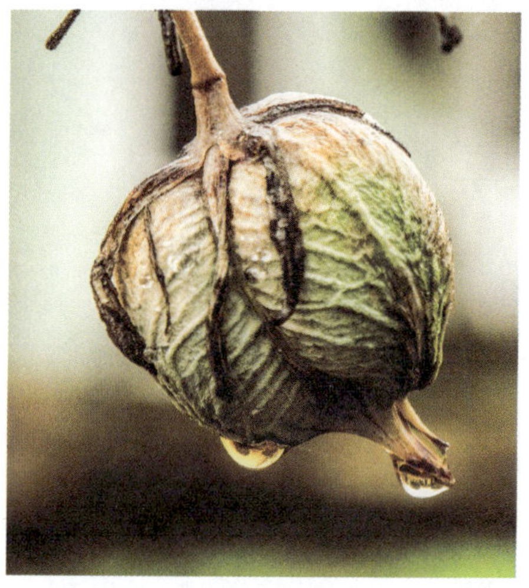

CHAPTER 8
Real-World Applications 179

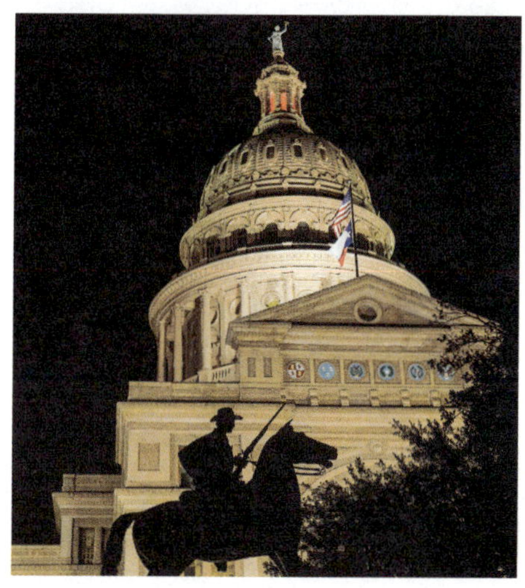

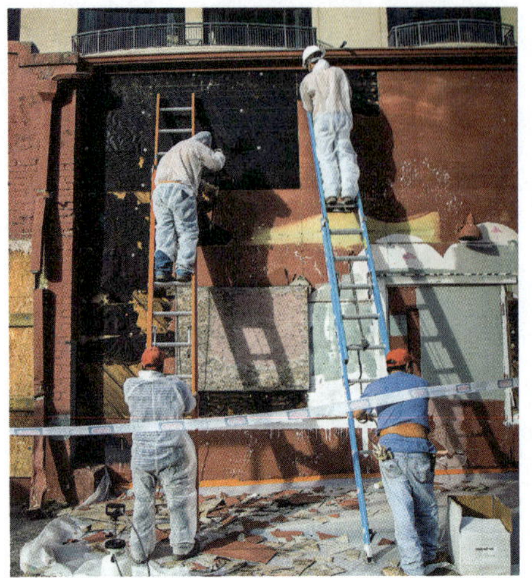

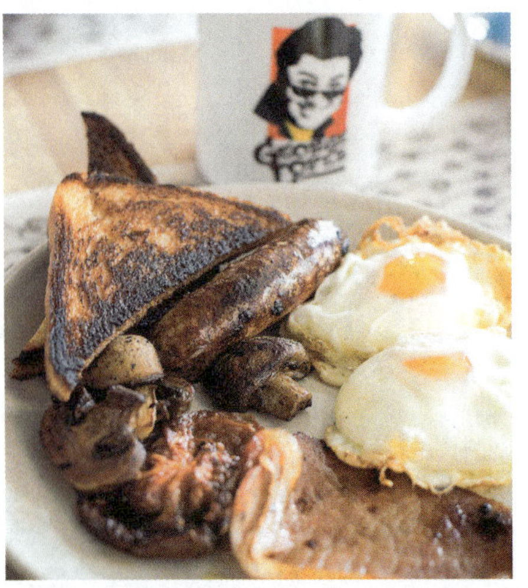

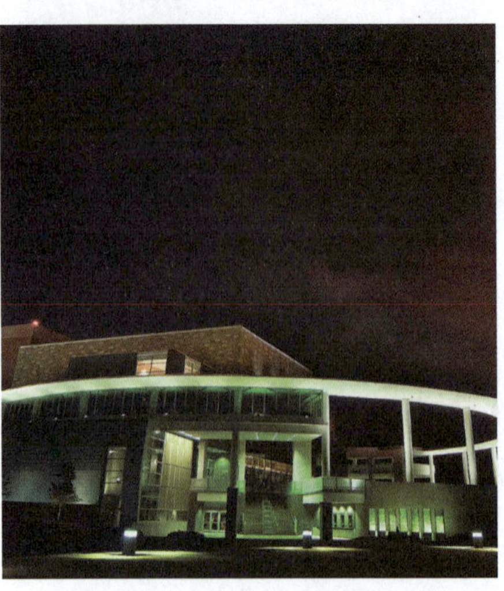

CHAPTER 9
After Capture   219

APPENDIX A
General Composition Tips   231

APPENDIX B
Accessories   237

Glossary   243

Index   253

Introduction

The D3300 is the culmination of many generations of Nikon cameras. One of the nicest things about the entry-level cameras these days is that they contain all of the technology that made Nikon's best cameras so successful. When the D3000 was announced it was a nice, if unremarkable, little camera that worked well for snap-shooters. Of course as technology marches on the upgrades eventually find their way from the professional cameras down to the junior models. By the time the D3200 was released it was a pretty good camera, but with the D3300, in a small package you get a camera that performs nearly as well, and in some respects even better, than the top of the line Nikon DX camera, the D7100.

If you take a look at the spec sheet of the D3200 as compared to the D3300, at first glance it doesn't look like much of an upgrade. But, the devil is in the details as they say. First, the D3300 has a lighter, more compact, yet sturdier body with a monocoque design borrowed from the D5300. Another thing that separates the D3300 from any other Nikon camera kit is the new collapsible lens that when closed down reduces the lenses size about 1/3, making it a great travel camera. The optical viewfinder magnification of the D3300 is also upped from 0.78x to 0.85x, which makes it easier on your eyes for composing. These are some the external changes, but the guts of the camera have a few upgrades that make much more of a difference.

One of the key differences of the D3300 from the D3200 is the removal of the Optical Low-Pass Filter (OLPF). Removing this filter allows the camera to resolve more fine detail, making images appear sharper and more crisp. Another often overlooked, but very important part of the camera is the image processor. This controls how fast the data from the sensor can be processed. The D3300 has the EXPEED 4 processor, which is Nikon's newest processor and is used in the top-of-the-line D4s. The EXPEED 4 processor allows for a number of key changes that include an increase in continuous shooting speed up to 5 fps, the ability to shoot HD video at 60fps, and an increase of base ISO from 100-6400 to 100-12800. It also gives much cleaner images at higher ISO settings than either the D5300 or the D7100, both of which are already very good at high ISOs.

The D3300 also offers a new panorama mode, a special effects shooting mode, and an improved battery that allows you to shoot many more frames on single charge.

When it's all said and done, the D3300 can produce images with quality that rivals that of the D7100 (which costs about twice as much). The D3300 is an ideal camera for someone who wants professional image quality, but doesn't need the all the extra features of a more expensive camera. Hiding in that small D3300 body is a feature-rich camera with all the oomph to capture beautiful, high-quality images.

About the Digital Field Guide

The Nikon Digital Field Guide book series is intended to act as an adjunct to the manual that comes with your camera. While the manual gives you a great overview of the camera, a photographer didn't write it. The *Nikon D3300 Digital Field Guide* gives you all the information you need about the camera from a working photographer's perspective.

The goal of this guide is to help photographers — from novice to advanced amateur — grasp all of the features of their new camera. It includes tips learned from working with the camera in the field, as well as some basic information to help newer photographers get up to speed quickly.

This full-color guide walks you through setting up your camera, offers insight about which settings to use, and tells you why each setting is useful in particular situations. Full-color images demonstrate different photography concepts, and show you some of the things the D3300 is able to accomplish.

The *Nikon D3300 Digital Field Guide* will help you familiarize yourself with your camera more quickly, so that you can not only navigate and handle it better, but also more easily achieve your photographic vision.

CHAPTER 1

Exploring the Nikon D3300

The 3000 series of cameras are the smallest dSLRs in the Nikon lineup. The D3300 body was redesigned using the monocoque structure, which first appeared in the D5300. The design allows the camera to be smaller and lighter than the D3200 while gaining a stronger structural integrity.

Because these cameras are much more compact than the Nikon professional series cameras, by necessity they have fewer buttons with which to change the myriad combinations of settings. That being said, the D3300 does have its fair share of buttons and dials, many of which have more than one function depending on the way the camera is programmed and which mode the camera is in. It's important to become familiar with the camera and all of its buttons and dials first, so that you can quickly change the necessary settings to adapt to your shooting environment.

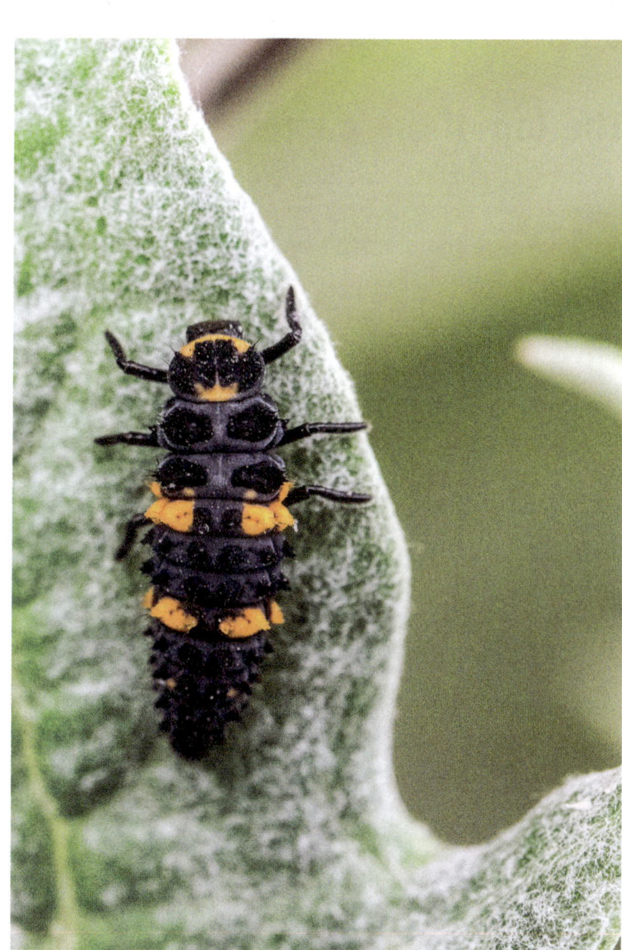

Knowing where the buttons are and what they do allows you to change your settings without taking your eye from the viewfinder so you don't miss a shot.

Key Components of the D3300

As I mentioned previously, the D3300 doesn't have the multitudes of buttons and dials that some of the other Nikon camera models do, so the few controls the camera does have are very important. Most of them perform numerous duties depending on the camera mode, so understanding how each control functions is key to controlling your camera quickly so that you don't miss a shot.

The following sections break the camera features down into segments and describe each control.

The top of the camera

Most of the important buttons are on the top of the D3300. This makes it easier to find them, especially when you have your eye to the viewfinder. This is where you find the dial to change the shooting modes, as well as the all-important shutter-release button and the movie-record button.

The following list includes the controls and buttons on top of the camera:

▶ **Movie-record button.** When the camera is in Live View mode (**Lv**), you press this button (which is labeled with a red dot) to start recording video. Press it a second time to stop recording.

▶ **Shutter-release button.** This is the most important button on the camera. It is a two-stage button: pressing it halfway activates the camera's autofocus and light meter; fully depressing it releases the shutter, and a photograph is taken. When the camera has been idle, and has "gone to sleep," lightly pressing the shutter-release button wakes it up. When the Auto Info display is set to On, half-pressing and holding it turns the Information display off, while releasing it turns the Information display on. When the image review is on, lightly pressing the shutter-release button turns off the LCD screen and prepares the camera for another shot.

NOTE The Auto Info display settings is in the Setup Menu (**Y**).

▶ **On/Off switch.** Located concentric to the shutter-release button, this switch turns the camera on and off. Pull the switch to the right to turn the camera on and push it to the left to turn the camera off.

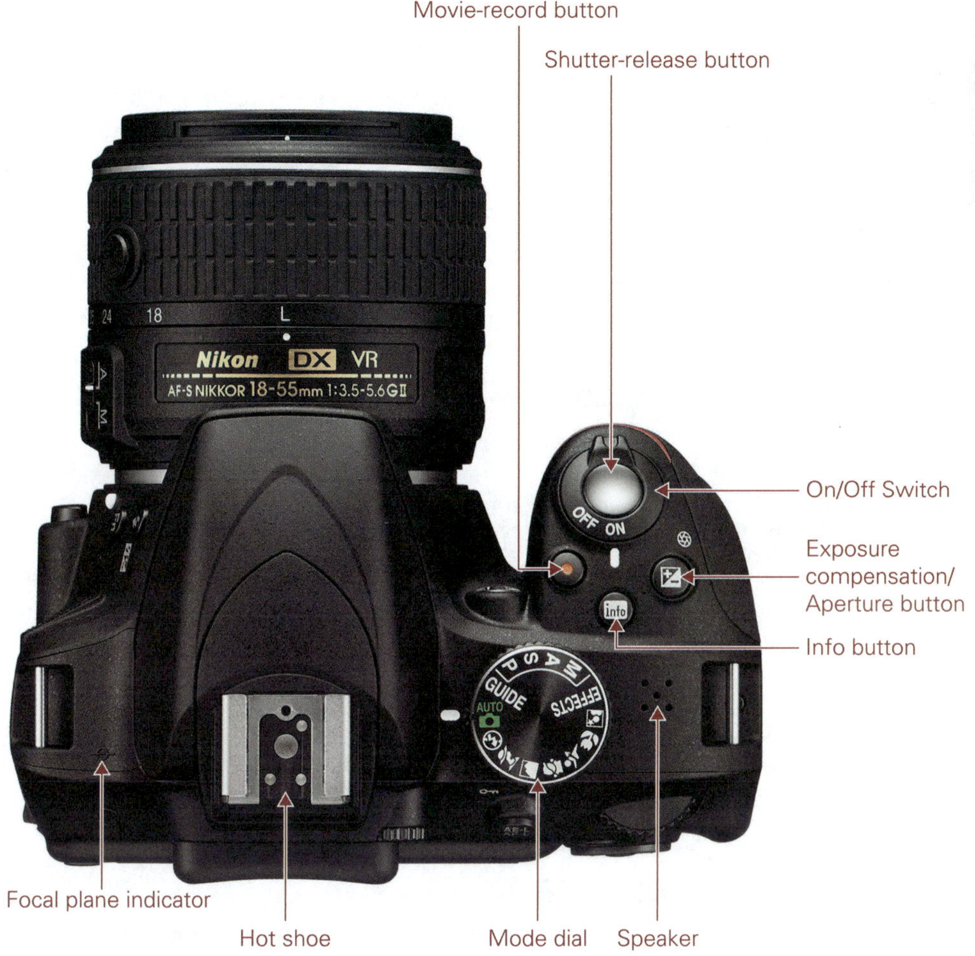

Image courtesy of Nikon, Inc.

1.1 The controls on top of the camera.

▶ **Exposure compensation (☒)/Aperture (⊚) button.** Press this button while rotating the Command dial to modify the exposure set by the D3300 light meter when it is in the Programmed auto (**P**), Shutter-priority auto (**S**), or Aperture-priority auto (**A**) modes. Turning the Command dial to the right increases the exposure, while turning the dial to the left decreases the exposure. When the camera is set to Manual exposure mode (**M**), you can press this button and rotate the Command dial to adjust the aperture settings.

▶ **Info button (Info).** Press this button to display information on the LCD screen. The information display shows all of the exposure and camera setting options.

▶ **Speaker.** This small speaker allows you to hear the sound of the video playback. The fidelity isn't very good, but it gives you a close approximation of what you will hear during playback.

▶ **Mode dial.** This is an important dial. Rotating the Mode dial allows you to change your shooting mode quickly. You can choose one of the scene modes, the Special Effects mode, one of the semiautomatic modes, or Manual exposure mode, which lets you pick the exposure settings.

CROSS REF For a detailed description of all exposure modes, see Chapter 2.

▶ **Hot shoe.** This is where you attach an accessory flash to the camera body. The hot shoe has an electronic contact that tells the flash to fire when the shutter is released. A number of other electronic contacts allow the camera to communicate with the flash, enabling the automated features of a dedicated flash unit such as the SB-700.

▶ **Focal plane indicator.** This marks the plane where the front of the sensor lies. Nikon uses this as the mark of the closest focusing distance of a lens, and when measuring distances for manual flash calculations, this is where the measurement to the subject from the camera should start.

The back of the camera

The back of the camera is where you find the buttons that mainly control playback and menu options, although a few buttons control some of the shooting functions. Most of the buttons have more than one function. Additionally, you use many of the buttons in conjunction with the Command dial or multi-selector. On the back of the camera, you also find several key features, including the all-important LCD screen and viewfinder.

The following are the elements on the back of the camera:

▶ **Rear infrared receiver.** This receiver picks up the infrared signal from the optional ML-L3 wireless remote.

▶ **Viewfinder.** This is what you look through to compose your photographs. Light coming through the lens is reflected from a series of five mirrors (called a *pentam-irror*), enabling you to see exactly what you're shooting. The rubber eyepiece around the viewfinder gives you a soft place to rest your eye and blocks any extra light from entering the viewfinder as you compose and shoot your images.

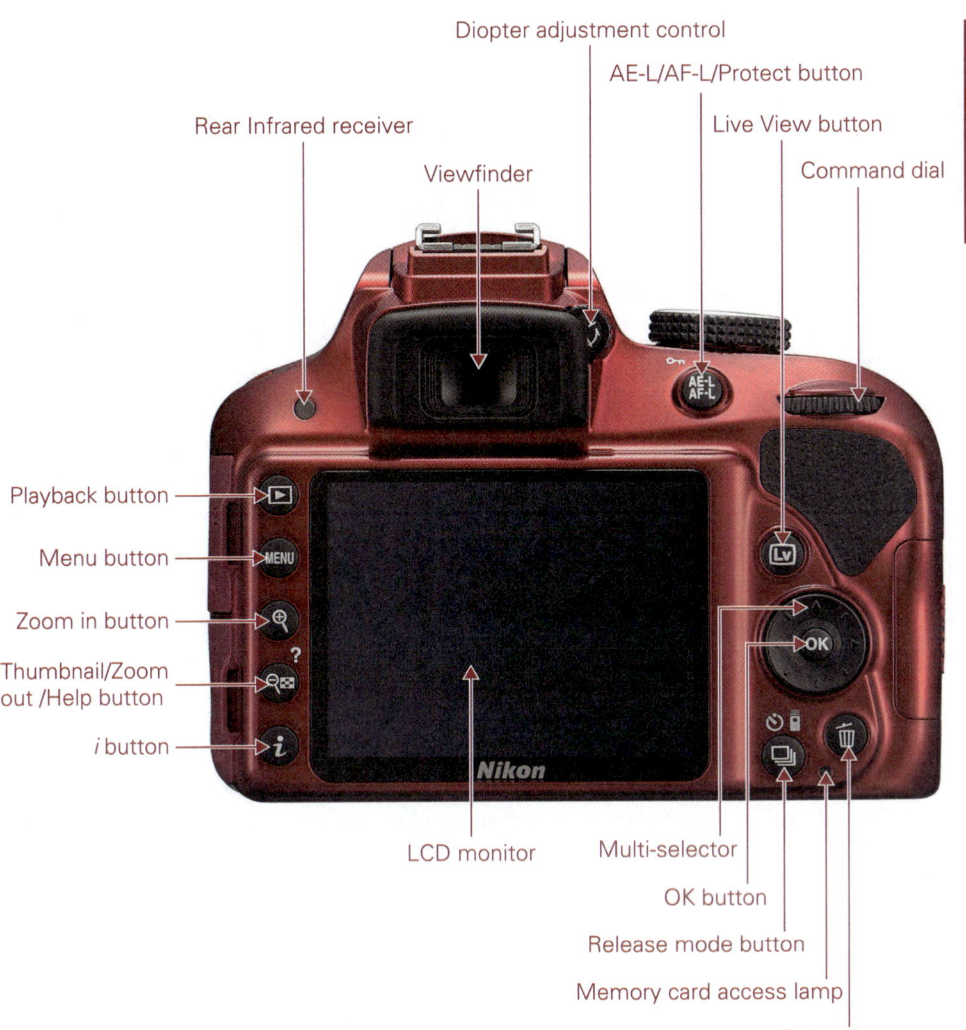

Image courtesy of Nikon, Inc.

1.2 The controls on the back of the camera.

▶ **Diopter adjustment control.** Just to the right of the viewfinder (hidden behind the eyecup) is the diopter adjustment control. Use this control to adjust the viewfinder lens to suit your individual vision strength (not everyone's eyesight is the same). The best way to do this is to look at the viewfinder display and rotate the dial until the information in the viewfinder display is sharp.

▶ **AE-L/AF-L ( )/Protect ( ) button.** The Auto Exposure/Autofocus Lock ( )/Protect ( ) button locks the Auto Exposure (AE) and Autofocus (AF). You can customize this button in the Setup menu (Y) under the Buttons option.

The button can be set to provide AE/AF Lock (default), AE Lock only, AE Lock (hold), AF Lock only, or AF-ON. AE Lock (hold) locks the exposure when you press the shutter-release button once; the exposure remains locked until you press the button again or the shutter releases. AF-ON engages the AF in the same way that half-pressing the shutter-release button does. When the camera displays an image in Playback mode, press this button to lock the image and protect it from being deleted.

▶ **Live View button (LV).** A quick press of the Live View button (LV) puts the camera in Live View mode, so you can shoot stills or videos using the LCD monitor as a viewfinder.

▶ **Command dial.** You use this dial to change a variety of settings, depending on the button with which you are using it. By default, it changes the shutter speed when the camera is in Shutter-priority auto (S), Programmed auto (P), and Manual exposure (M) modes. When shooting in Aperture-priority auto mode (A), it changes the aperture setting. It can also adjust exposure compensation and change the flash mode.

▶ **Playback button (▶).** Press this button to activate playback. By default, it displays the most recently taken photograph. You can also view other pictures by pressing the multi-selector left (◀) and right (▶).

▶ **Menu button (MENU).** Press this button to access the D3300 menu options, including Playback (▶), Shooting (📷), Custom Setting (✐), and Retouch (🖾). Use the multi-selector to choose the menu you want to view, and then press the OK button (OK) to enter the specific menu screen.

▶ **Zoom in button (🔍).** When reviewing your images or using the Live View option (LV), you can press the Zoom in button (🔍) to get a closer look at the details of your image. This is a handy feature for checking the sharpness and focus of your shot. When the camera is zoomed in, use the multi-selector to navigate around within the image. To view your other images at the same zoom ratio, you can rotate the Command dial. To return to full-frame playback, press the Thumbnail/Zoom out button (🔍). You may have to press the Thumbnail/Zoom out button (🔍) multiple times, depending on how much you zoomed in previously.

▶ **Thumbnail/Zoom out/Help button (🔍) (❓).** When reviewing images, press this button to switch from full-frame playback (that is, viewing the whole image) to viewing thumbnails. The thumbnail view displays 4, 9, or 72 images. You can also view images by calendar date. When you're viewing the menu options, press this button to display a help screen that explains the functions of that particular menu option. This button also zooms out of an image on which you have zoomed. If the Help icon (**?**) is flashing on the LCD, pressing this button brings up a dialog box that explains a little more about the selected menu item.

▶ *i* **button (ⓘ).** Press this button once to bring up the information edit display on the LCD screen and use the multi-selector to adjust the camera settings. When in Playback mode, pressing this button brings up options for rating, entering the Retouch menu, or selecting and deselecting the image to send to a smart device (if the WU-1a is connected).

▶ **LCD monitor.** This is the most prominent feature on the back of the camera. This 3.2-inch, liquid crystal display (LCD) is a very bright, high-resolution screen with 921,000 dots. The LCD is where you view all of the current camera settings and review your images after shooting. It also displays the video feed for Live View mode (**Lv**) and video recording.

▶ **Multi-selector.** This is another button that serves several purposes. When playing back images, you use it to scroll through the photographs you've taken or to view image information, such as histograms and shooting settings. When the D3300 is in Single-point AF (⌷) or Dynamic-area AF (⊞) mode, you can use the multi-selector to change the active focus point. You can also use the multi-selector to navigate through the menu options.

▶ **OK button (OK).** When viewing menus, press the OK button (OK) to select the highlighted menu item. In Playback mode (▶), press the OK button (OK) to display thumbnails. When actively shooting, press the OK button (OK) to reset the active focus point to the center.

▶ **Release mode button (⊚).** Press this button to display the release mode options on the LCD screen. Use the multi-selector to choose an option, and then press the OK button (⊚) to set it.

▶ **Memory card access lamp.** This light blinks when the memory card is in use. Under no circumstances should you remove the memory card when this light is on or blinking. You could damage the card or your camera, and lose any information in the camera's buffer. If the buffer is full when you switch the camera off, the camera stays powered on and this lamp continues blinking until the data finishes transferring from the buffer to the memory card.

▶ **Delete button (🗑).** If you are reviewing your pictures and find some that you don't want to keep, press this button to delete them. To prevent you from accidentally deleting images, the camera displays a dialog box asking you to confirm that you want to erase the picture. Press the Delete button (🗑) a second time to erase an image permanently.

The front of the camera

While this is the business end of the camera, there really aren't many controls here. The most important part is pointed right at you — the lens.

The features are as follows:

► **Front infrared receiver.** This receiver picks up the infrared signal from the optional wireless remote, the ML-L3.

► **AF-assist illuminator.** This is an LED that shines on the subject to help the camera focus when the lighting is dim. The AF-assist illuminator only lights up when in Single-servo AF mode (**AF-S**) or Full-time-servo mode (**AF-F**) and the center AF point is selected. This LED also lights up when you set the camera to Red-Eye Reduction flash (**⚡◉**) using the camera's built-in flash.

► **Microphone.** The D3300 has a small built-in condenser microphone for recording sound with your videos.

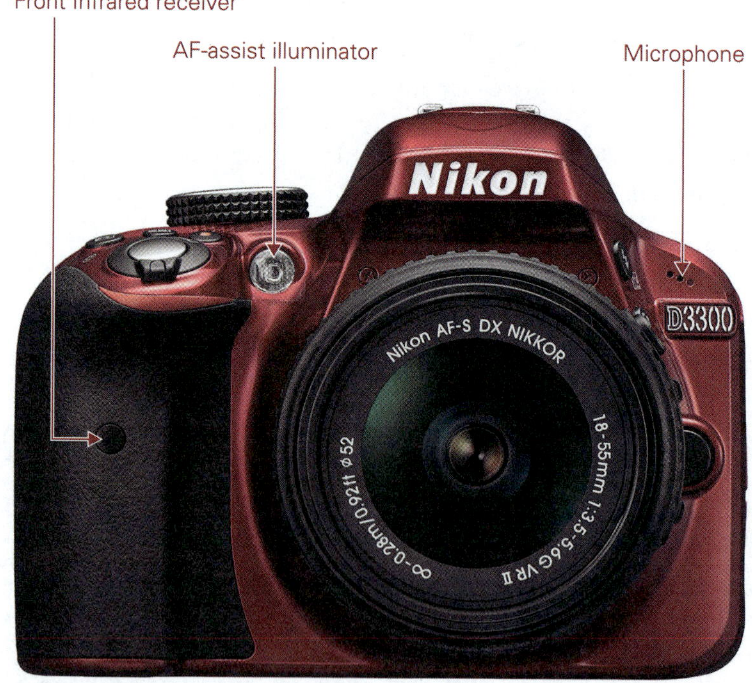

Image courtesy of Nikon, Inc.

1.3 The front of the Nikon D3300.

The left side of the camera

On the left side of the camera (with the lens facing away from you, as you would normally hold it), you find the output terminals and a few other important buttons. The terminals connect accessories or link your camera to a computer or other external source for viewing. The terminals are hidden under a rubber cover that helps keep out dust and moisture.

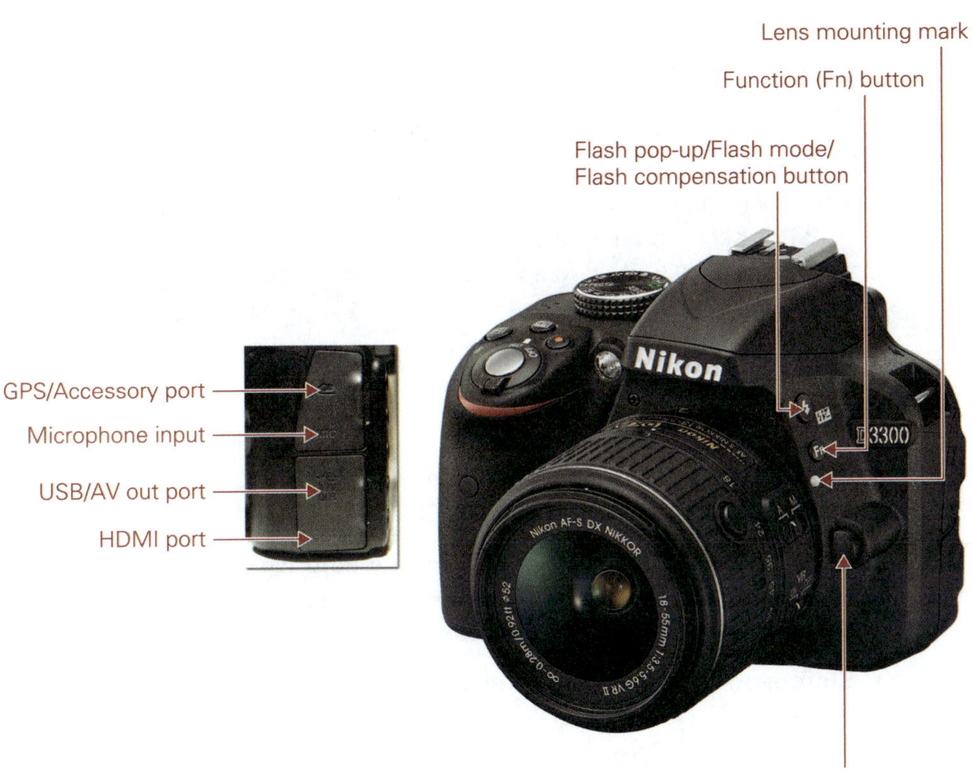

Image courtesy of Nikon, Inc.

1.4 The left side of the Nikon D3300.

The features are as follows:

▶ **Flash pop-up/Flash mode (⚡)/Flash compensation button (⚡✦).** When you're using the Programmed auto (**P**), Shutter-priority auto (**S**), Aperture-priority auto (**A**), or Manual (**M**) exposure modes, press this button to open and activate the built-in flash. Pressing this button and rotating the Command dial on the rear of the camera allows you to choose a flash mode. Depending on the Shooting mode (📷), you can choose from among the default Front curtain sync (⚡), Red-eye reduction (⚡◉), Red-eye reduction with slow sync (⚡), Slow sync (⚡ SLOW), Rear-curtain sync (⚡ REAR), and Rear-curtain slow sync (⚡ SLOW REAR) modes. After the flash pops up, press this button in conjunction with the Exposure Compensation button (✦), while rotating the Command dial to adjust the Flash Compensation (⚡✦). This enables you to adjust the flash output to make the flash brighter or dimmer depending on your needs. When you shoot in the Automatic point-and-shoot (📷) or scene modes, the flash automatically activates, but some flash sync modes aren't available in some scene modes. The following flash modes are available when using the scene modes:

- **Automatic (📷), Portrait (🎭), Child (👶), and Close-up (🌷).** In these flash modes, you can use the default, Auto-flash (⚡ AUTO), Auto with red-eye reduction (⚡◉AUTO), or set it to Off.

- **Night portrait scene mode (🌃).** In this mode, you can select Red-eye reduction (⚡◉SLOW), the default, Auto with slow sync (⚡ SLOW), or Off (⚡).

- **Programmed auto (P), Aperture-priority auto (A).** In these modes, you can select Red-eye reduction (⚡◉), Red-eye reduction with slow sync (⚡), Slow sync (⚡ SLOW), or Rear-curtain slow sync (⚡ SLOW REAR).

- **Shutter-priority auto (S), Manual (M).** These modes allow you to use Red-eye reduction (⚡◉) or Rear-curtain sync (⚡ REAR).

▶ **Function (Fn) button (Fn).** You can set the Function button (Fn) to a number of settings so that you can access them quickly, rather than searching through the menu options manually. You can set the button to change the ISO sensitivity (default), image quality, white balance, or Active D-Lighting. Depending on which option you select, you can press the Function button (Fn) and rotate the Command dial to change the settings. You can change the setting options in the Setup menu (🔧) under the Buttons option.

CROSS REF For the complete list of options you can control with the Function button (**Fn**), see Chapter 3.

► **Lens mounting mark.** Most lenses have a white or red mark to help you align them, so you can then rotate and lock them into place. Use this white mark to line up with the mounting mark on the lens.

► **Lens release button.** This button disengages the locking mechanism of the lens, allowing the lens to be rotated and removed from the lens mount.

► **GPS/Accessory port.** This accessory port allows you to connect an accessory remote, such as the Nikon GP-1/GP-1a, MC-DC2, and the WR-1 or WR-R10 wireless remote control.

► **Microphone input.** You can use this port to connect an external microphone, which records sound for your videos at a better quality than you can get from the built-in microphone.

► **USB/AV out port.** This is where you plug in the USB cable to attach the camera to your computer, and transfer images directly from the camera to the computer. Using the included EG-CP16 A/V cable, you can also use this port to connect your camera to a standard-definition TV. This is also where the WU-1a Wi-Fi adapter is connected as well as a printer if using Pict-Bridge to print images directly from the camera.

► **HDMI port.** This terminal is for connecting your camera to a high-definition (HD) TV or monitor. It requires a type C mini-pin HDMI cable, which is available at any electronics store.

NOTE On the right side of the camera you find the cover for the memory card slot. To open the cover and insert or remove a memory card, slide it toward the back of the camera and it springs open.

The Viewfinder Display

The viewfinder display is kind of like the heads-up display in a jet plane. It allows you to see a lot of useful information about the settings of the camera. This helps you set up the shot without taking your eye away from the viewfinder to check on your settings. Most of the information also appears in the Information display, but it is less handy when you are looking through the viewfinder composing a shot.

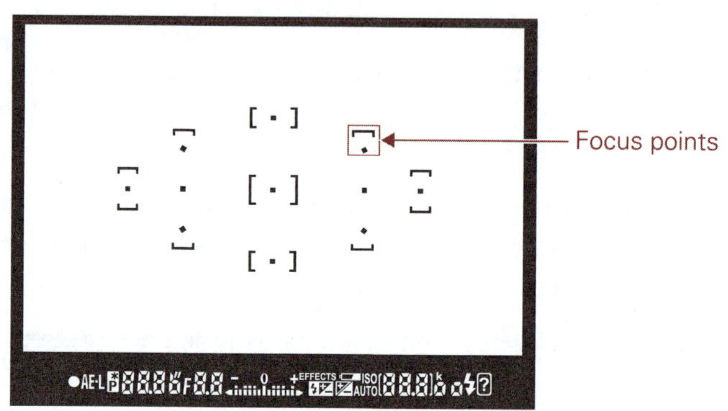

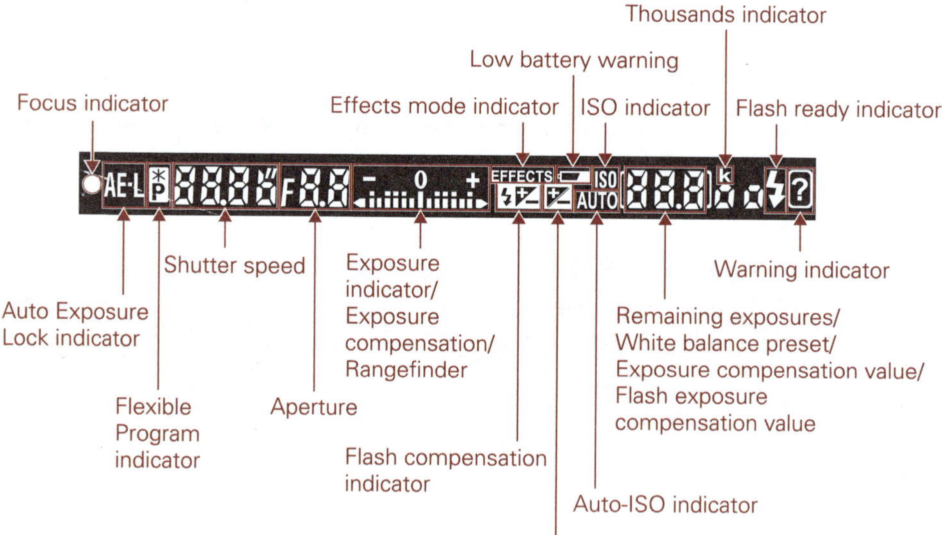

1.5 The viewfinder display.

Here is a complete list of the information you find in the viewfinder display:

▶ **Focus points.** The first thing you are likely to notice when looking through the viewfinder is a small rectangle near the center of the frame. This is your active focus point. Note that only the active focus point is shown full time when you use the Single-point ([□]), Dynamic-area ([⊡]), or 3-D tracking ([3D]) autofocus settings. When you set the camera to Auto area AF mode ([■]), you don't see the focus point until you press the shutter-release button halfway and the camera achieves focus.

▶ **Focus indicator.** This green dot lets you know whether a scene is in focus. When the camera achieves focus, the green dot lights up; if the camera is not in focus, the dot isn't displayed. If the camera is unable to achieve focus after a few seconds the indicator will blink.

▶ **Auto Exposure Lock indicator (AE-L).** When this indicator lights up, you know that the Auto Exposure is locked.

▶ **Flexible Program indicator (P*).** This indicator appears when you use the Programmed auto mode (P) and Flexible program (P*) mode is activated.

▶ **Shutter speed.** This indicator shows how long the shutter is set to stay open, from 30 seconds (30") up to 1/4000 (4000) second.

▶ **Aperture.** This indicator shows the current aperture setting. The words *aperture* and *f-stop* are used interchangeably. The aperture setting indicates the width of the lens opening and appears as a number (1.4, 2, 2.8, 4, 5.6, and so on).

▶ **Exposure Indicator/Exposure compensation display/Rangefinder.** When the bars are in the center, the camera is at the proper settings to get a good exposure. By default, when the bars are to the left, the image is underexposed, and when they are to the right, the image is overexposed. This option only appears when in Manual (M) mode, when Exposure compensation (⊡) is applied, or if the camera is under- or overexposing at the current settings. This display also doubles as a digital rangefinder to help you when manually focusing lenses. If the indicator bars are on the left, the focus is falling in front of the subject; if the indicator bars are on the right, the focus is behind the subject. Rotate the focus ring until a single indicator bar is centered and you see a 0 above the innermost two rangefinder lines. The focus indicator also appears when the camera achieves focus.

▶ **Flash compensation indicator (⚡⊡).** When this indicator appears, Flash exposure compensation is on. You adjust Flash compensation by pressing the Flash Mode button (⚡) in conjunction with the Exposure Compensation button (⊡) and rotating the Command dial.

- **Effects mode indicator (EFFECTS).** This indicator appears when the mode dial is set to Effects.

- **Low battery warning (▭).** When the camera's battery is nearly depleted, this icon appears. If it is flashing, the battery is completely exhausted and you can't take any more pictures.

- **Exposure compensation indicator (🗷).** When you see this icon, exposure compensation is applied to the exposure setting. To set exposure compensation, press the Exposure Compensation button (🗷) and rotate the Command dial.

- **ISO indicator (ISO).** If you set the Function button (Fn) to ISO (the default), this indicator appears when you press the button to let you know that the numbers you see are the ISO numbers.

- **Auto ISO indicator (AUTO).** This indicator appears when you activate Auto ISO (AUTO) to let you know that the camera is controlling the ISO settings. You can turn on Auto ISO (AUTO) in the ISO sensitivity settings, located in the Shooting menu (📷).

- **Remaining exposures/White balance preset/Exposure compensation value/Flash exposure compensation value.** By default, this set of numbers lets you know how many more exposures can fit on the memory card. The actual number of exposures may vary according to file information and compression. When you press the shutter-release button halfway, the display shows how many exposures can fit in the camera's buffer before it is full and the frame rate slows down. The *buffer* is in-camera RAM that stores your image data while that data is written to the memory card. This also shows the White balance preset recording indicator (**PRE**), as well as the Exposure compensation (🗷) and Flash compensation (⚡🗷) values. When you connect the camera to a computer, *PC* appears here.

- **Thousands indicator (K).** This indicator lets you know that there are more than 1,000 exposures remaining on your memory card.

- **Flash ready indicator (⚡).** When this indicator appears, the flash, whether it is the built-in flash or an external Speedlight attached to the hot shoe, is fully charged and ready to fire at full power.

- **Warning indicator (❓).** When an error occurs with the camera, this icon flashes. Press the Help button (❓).

The Information Display

The Information display shows all of the relevant shooting and camera information. You can also change some of the most important camera settings quickly in the Information display without entering the camera menu system, which can take up important time when shooting.

You activate the Information display by pressing the Info button (Info), located on top of the camera directly behind the shutter-release button. Once the Information display is activated and appears on the monitor, press the *i* button (*i*) to enter the Info edit menu, which allows you to change some key settings on the camera (see figure 1.7). By default, when the Info edit display is active, using the multi-selector highlights the setting you want to change and the D3300 displays the Screen tips to guide you through what each setting does. Once the setting you want to access is highlighted, press the OK button (**OK**) to view the options for that specific setting.

The information remains on display until no buttons have been pushed for about 10 seconds (the default), or you can press the shutter-release or Info (Info) buttons. This display shows you everything you need to know about your camera settings. Additionally, the camera has a sensor built in that tells it when you are holding it vertically, and the Information display is shown upright, regardless of which way you are holding your camera.

The main display area shows the following important settings:

► **Shooting mode.** This indicator displays the Shooting mode that your camera is currently set to. This can be one of the scene modes (in which case it displays the appropriate icon), or one of the semiautomatic modes, such as Programmed auto (**P**), Shutter-priority auto (**S**), Aperture-priority auto (**A**), or Manual (**M**), in which case it displays the corresponding letter. This display changes when you rotate the Mode dial.

► **Aperture.** The terms *aperture* and *f-stop* are used interchangeably. Aperture is the opening in the lens that allows light into the camera. This indicator displays the aperture at which the camera is set. Lower numbers indicate wider openings that let in more light, and higher numbers indicate smaller openings that let in less light. As a visual aid, this displays what the aperture might look like if you were looking inside the lens.

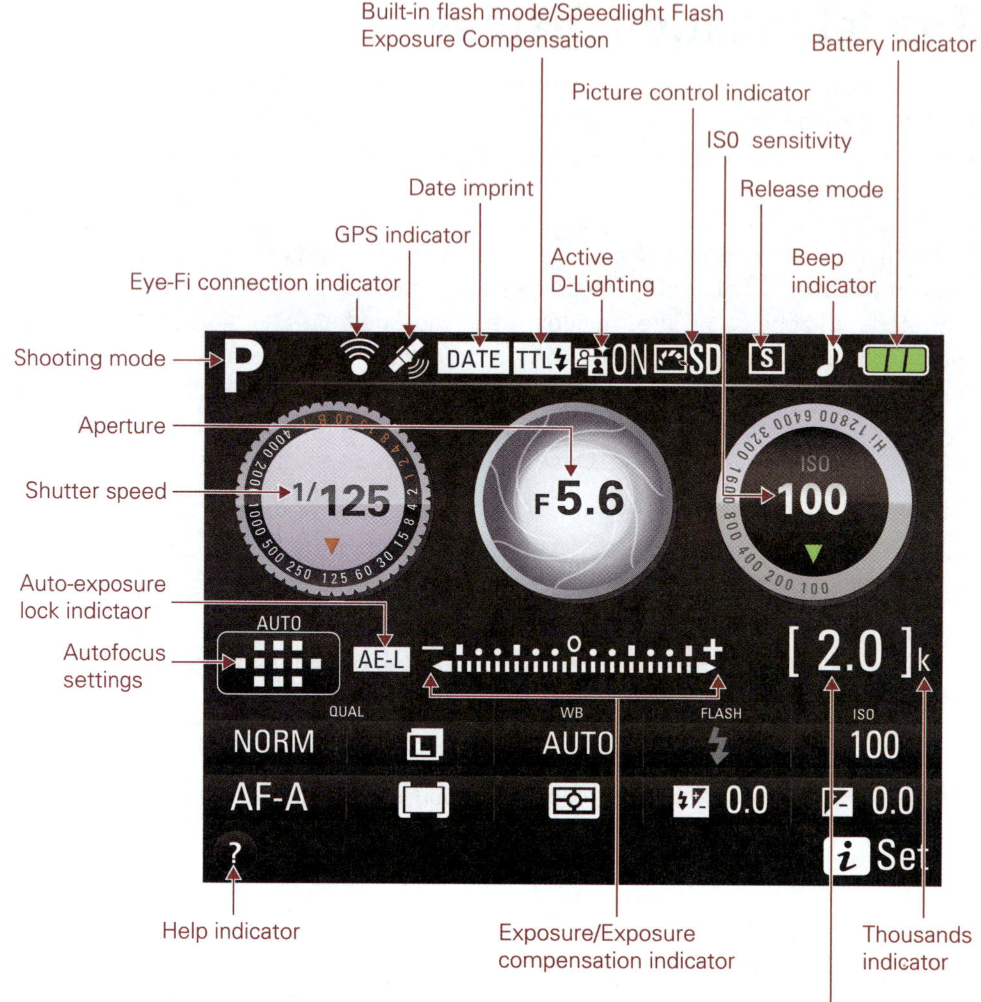

1.6 **The Information display on the Nikon D3300.**

▶ **Shutter speed.** This shows the length of time that the shutter remains open
during the exposure. This indicator displays the shutter speed setting using a
graphic similar to what you might see on a vintage film camera. As the shutter
speed changes, the dial appears to move as well.

▶ **Auto-exposure lock indicator.** This indicator is shown when the autoexposure
setting is locked by using the AE-L/AF-L lock button ( ).

▶ **Autofocus settings.** This area displays information about the autofocus settings, the Auto area AF mode (▣), and the active focus point when the camera is in Single servo AF mode (**AF-S**). It also displays the active focus and surrounding points when in the Dynamic-area AF (⊡) and 3-D tracking (**3D**) modes.

▶ **Help indicator.** This icon is shown when there is additional information available about a particular setting. Pressing the Help button (**?**) brings up a dialog box that explains the setting in further detail.

▶ **Exposure/Exposure compensation indicator.** When shooting in Manual exposure mode (**M**), this is displayed and used as a light meter to assess your exposure. When in any other mode, including scene and effects modes, this is only displayed if the settings indicate an under- or overexposure. When in Programmed auto (**P**), Shutter-priority auto (**S**), or Aperture-priority auto (**A**) mode, this icon only appears when exposure compensation (**⊠**) is applied.

▶ **Exposures remaining/White balance recording (PRE)/Capture mode indicator (PC).** By default, this displays the approximate number of photos that can be recorded to the memory card. When the camera is making a White balance preset, this area displays that icon (PRE).

▶ **Thousands indicator (K).** When a memory card is inserted that allows more than 1,000 images to be recorded, this icon appears.

On the top bar of the Information display, the following indicators display some of the less critical settings, as well as some options related to additional accessories:

▶ **Eye-fi connection indicator.** This indicator is displayed when an optional Eye-Fi wireless SD card is being used.

▶ **GPS Indicator.** When an optional GPS unit such as the Nikon GP-1 is activated this indicator is shown. When the indicator is flashing, the GPS unit is searching for a signal. If a signal connection is being maintained, the indicator stays on.

▶ **Date imprint.** When the camera is set to add the time and date to the image, this indicator is shown. The date option is turned on in the Setup menu (**Y**).

▶ **Built-in flash mode/Speedlight Flash Exposure compensation.** When the built-in flash is activated, the exposure mode, Manual (**M⚡**) or TTL (**TTL⚡**), is displayed here. It also appears if you attach a Speedlight and apply Flash compensation with the controls on the Speedlight, rather than with those on the camera.

▶ **Active D-Lighting.** This indicator is displayed when the Active D-Lighting is turned on.

▶ **Picture control indicator.** This indicator shows the Picture Control setting that is currently active. The options are Standard (SD), Neutral (NL), Vivid (VI), Monochrome (MC), and Landscape (▨). The Picture Controls are set in the Shooting Menu.

▶ **ISO sensitivity.** This indicator shows you the ISO sensitivity settings. If the camera is set to ISO-Auto, you notice that ISO-A blinks above the sensitivity number.

▶ **Release mode.** This area shows the icon for the currently set Release mode. The options are Single frame (**s**), Continuous (◉), Quiet (**Q**), Self-timer (☉), Delayed remote (2s), Quick-response remote (▯).

▶ **Beep indicator.** This icon has two versions: Beep on (♪) and Beep off (⊗). One or the other appears at all times.

▶ **Battery indicator.** This indicator shows the amount of power left in the battery, but lacks any other in-depth information.

> **TIP** The Information edit display is where you go to change your most commonly used settings. Press the *i* button (ⓘ) to access these settings and change them quickly. Use the multi-selector to highlight the desired option, and then press the OK button (**OK**) to view the settings options.

The following options are available in the Info edit menu:

▶ **Image quality.** This is where you set the image quality file type. You can set the camera to record RAW files, JPEG files, or RAW+JPEG Fine simultaneously. This is also where you set the JPEG compression. The JPEG compression options are Fine, Normal, and Basic.

▶ **Image size.** When you record JPEGs, you can set the camera to record different file sizes. This option isn't available when shooting RAW files only.

▶ **White balance.** This is where you select the white balance settings.

▶ **Flash mode.** This is where the flash mode options are set. The options differ depending on the selected exposure mode.

▶ **ISO sensitivity.** This option changes the ISO sensitivity settings.

▶ **Focus mode.** Use this menu option to change the focus mode from Auto servo AF (**AF-A**), Single servo AF (**AF-S**), Continuous servo AF (**AF-C**) mode, or Manual focus (**M**).

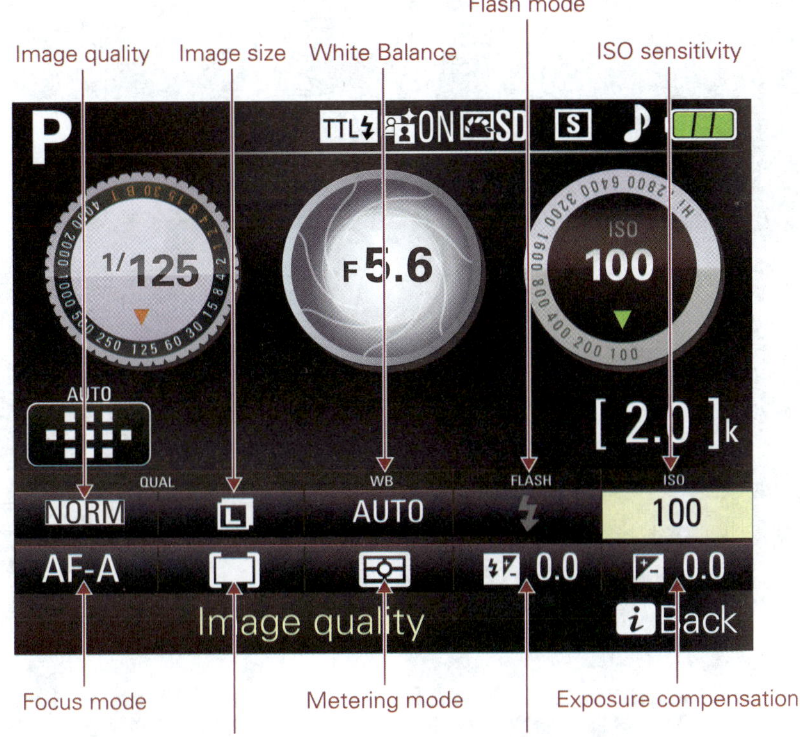

1.7 The Info edit display.

▶ **Autofocus area mode.** This option changes the autofocus area mode. You can choose from the following options when the Focus mode is set to Auto servo AF (AF-A) or Continuous servo AF (AF-C) mode: Single-point AF ([□]), Dynamic-area AF ([⊡]), 3-D tracking ([3D]), or Auto-area AF (■). If the Focus mode is set to Single servo AF (AF-S) the options are Single-point AF ([□]) or Auto-area AF (■).

▶ **Metering mode.** You change the metering options here. You have the following three options: Matrix (▨), Center-weighted (◉), or Spot (⊡) metering.

▶ **Flash compensation.** You can set the Flash compensation (⚡🗲) here. Flash compensation increases or decreases the amount of light emitted by the flash. This option is only available in the Programmed auto (P), Shutter-priority auto (S), Aperture-priority auto (A), or Manual (M) exposure modes.

▶ **Exposure compensation.** This is where you can adjust the exposure compensation (🗲) to fine-tune the exposure. This option is only available in the Programmed auto (P), Shutter-priority auto (S), Aperture-priority auto (A), or Manual (M) exposure modes.

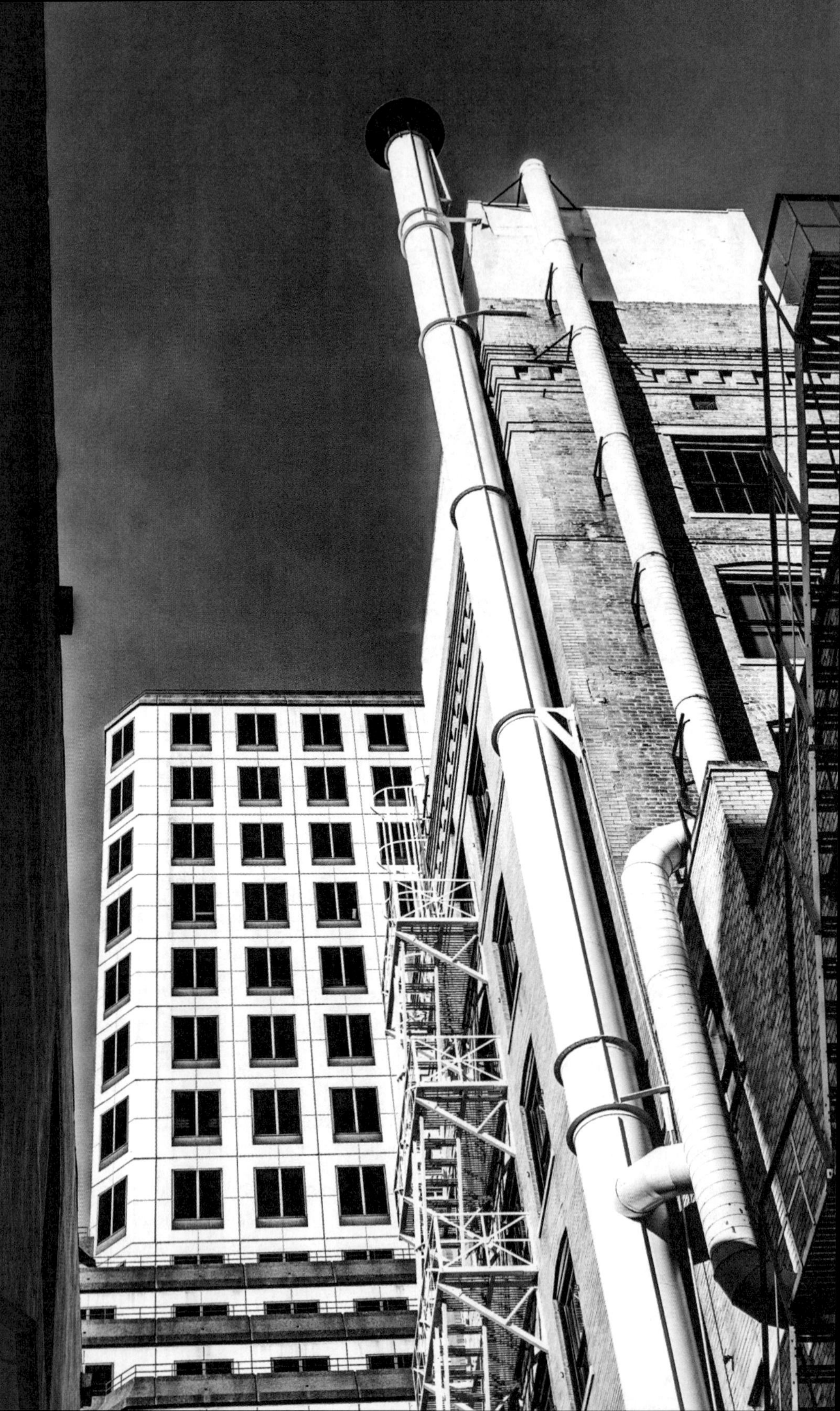

CHAPTER 2

Nikon D3300 Essentials

After familiarizing yourself with the basic layout of the various controls on your Nikon D3300, you are ready to explore what all of these buttons, switches, and dials do. The essentials are the most important parts of the camera system. There are a lot of modes, menus, and settings to get acquainted with, and that's where I go in this chapter. There's also quite a bit of information packed in here, so I suggest that you grab your camera, sit down, and read this chapter thoroughly with the camera in your hand so you can become comfortable with where the important features are located on your camera.

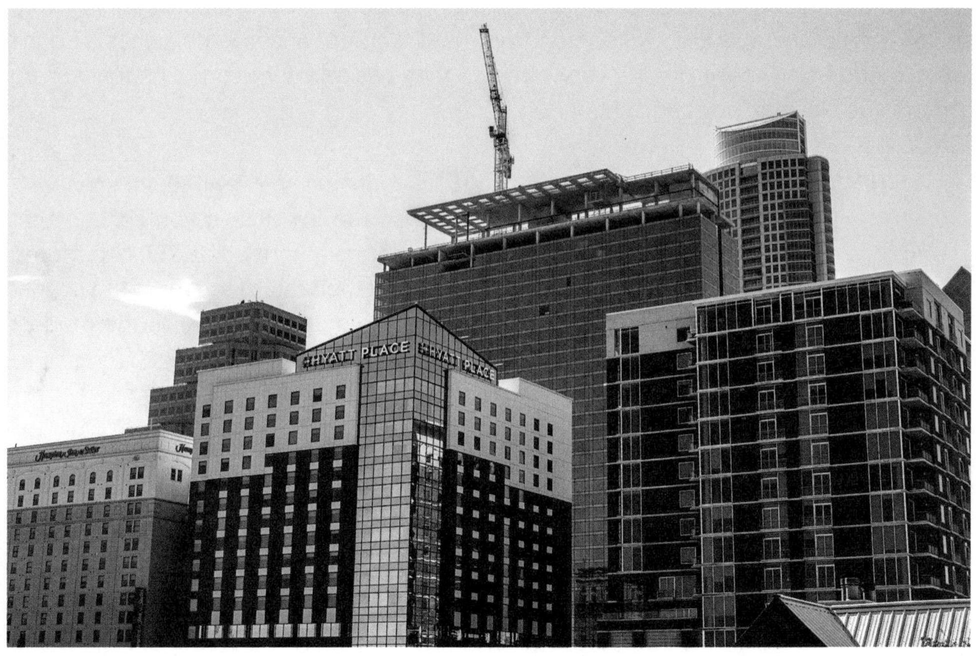

Knowing which modes and features to use in any given situation allows you to get a good exposure, no matter what.

Exposure Modes

The *exposure modes* are the functions that dictate how the aperture and shutter speed are selected. There are four main exposure modes: Programmed auto (**P**), Aperture-priority auto (**A**), Shutter-priority auto (**S**), and Manual (**M**). These four modes are all you really need to set exposures, but for simplicity and ease of use, especially for beginning photographers, Nikon also offers scene modes.

When you use scene modes, the camera chooses the correct settings for different types of shooting situations. Scene modes designate everything from autofocus and Picture Controls, to flash and ISO settings (although you are able to adjust some of these). To switch among the exposure modes, simply rotate the Mode dial on top of the camera.

Automatic modes

The D3300 has two fully automatic, or Auto, modes that do all the work for you. These are simple grab-and-go camera settings to use when you're in a hurry or you just don't want to be bothered with changing the settings. The Auto modes control everything from shutter speed and aperture to ISO sensitivity and white balance. To be honest, I don't recommend using these modes very often as they basically turn your high-functioning camera into a simple point and shoot.

> **TIP** To override the Auto ISO setting (**AUTO**), you can change ISO sensitivity in the Info settings. The override remains in effect unless you change the camera to the Programmed auto (**P**), Shutter-priority auto (**S**), Aperture-priority auto (**A**), or Manual (**M**) mode, and then return to one of the scene modes. When you change back to a scene mode from any of the modes just mentioned, the Auto ISO function (**AUTO**) reactivates.

> **CAUTION** Auto-ISO cannot be overridden in the Panorama or Night Vision Effects modes.

In Auto mode (**AUTO**), the camera takes complete control of the exposure. The camera's meter reads the light, color, and brightness of the scene and runs the information through an algorithm. This information is used by the camera's Expeed 4 imaging processor to determine what type of scene you are photographing, and the D3300 then chooses the settings it deems appropriate for the scene.

If there isn't enough light to make a proper exposure, the camera's built-in flash pops up when you half-press the shutter-release button for focus. The flash fires when the shutter is released, resulting in a properly exposed image. This mode is ideal for taking snapshots because you can concentrate on capturing the image and let the camera determine the proper settings.

The Auto Flash off mode (⊛) functions in the same way as Auto mode (📷), except that it disables the flash, even in low-light situations. In instances where the lighting is poor, the camera's AF-assist illuminator provides sufficient light to achieve focus. The camera uses the focus area of the closest subject to focus on.

This setting is preferable when you want to use natural or ambient light for your subject or in situations where you aren't allowed to use flash, such as in museums, or at events where the flash may cause a distraction, such as weddings.

Programmed auto mode

Programmed auto (**P**) is similar to the automatic mode covered previously, but it's much more useful because the camera isn't completely in charge of setting all the parameters. This leaves you in control of many of the important settings, but also frees you from having to be in control of every aspect of the exposure settings.

When the camera is in Programmed auto (**P**), it decides the shutter speed and aperture settings for you based on a set of algorithms. The camera does its best to select a shutter speed that allows you to shoot handheld without suffering from camera shake while also adjusting your aperture so that you get sufficient depth of field to ensure everything is in focus. When the camera body is coupled with a lens that has a CPU built in (all Nikon AF lenses have a CPU), the camera automatically knows what focal length and aperture range the lens has. The camera then uses this lens information to determine the optimal settings.

This exposure mode chooses the widest aperture possible until it reaches the optimal shutter speed for the specific lens. Then the camera chooses a smaller f-stop and increases the shutter speed as light levels increase. For example, when you use the kit lens at the 24mm setting, the camera keeps the aperture wide open until the shutter speed reaches about 1/30 second (just above minimum shutter speed to avoid camera shake). Upon reaching 1/30 second, the camera adjusts the aperture to increase depth of field.

CAUTION When you use the Auto ISO setting (**AUTO**) in Programmed auto mode (**P**), the camera tries to hold the shutter speed at the number specified in the Auto ISO (**AUTO**) sensitivity settings.

The exposure settings selected by the camera appear in both the Information display and the viewfinder display. Although the camera chooses what it thinks are the optimal settings, it does not know your specific needs. For example, you may want a wider or smaller aperture for selective focus. Fortunately, you aren't stuck with the camera's exposure choice. You can engage what is known as *Flexible Program* (**P***). Flexible Program allows you to deviate from the camera's selected aperture and shutter speed in Programmed auto mode (**P**). You can automatically engage this feature by simply rotating the Command dial until you get the desired shutter speed or aperture. This allows you to choose a wider aperture or faster shutter speed when you rotate the dial to the right, or a smaller aperture or slower shutter speed when you rotate the dial to the left. With Flexible Program (**P***), you can maintain the metered exposure, while still having some control over the shutter speed and aperture settings.

For example, say that you're shooting a portrait and you want a wider aperture to throw the background out of focus, and the camera has set the shutter speed at 1/60 second with an aperture of f/8.0. If you rotate the Command dial to the right, you can open the aperture to f/4.0, which increases the shutter speed to 1/250 second. This is an *equivalent exposure,* meaning that you get the same amount of light reaching the sensor but the settings are different.

When Flexible Program (**P***) is on, an asterisk appears next to the Programmed auto mode icon (**P**). Rotate the Command dial until the asterisk disappears to return to the default Programmed auto settings (**P**), or turn the camera off and back on.

NOTE Programmed auto mode (**P**) is not available when you use non-CPU lenses.

Aperture-priority auto mode

Aperture-priority auto (**A**) is a semiautomatic mode. In this mode, you decide which aperture to use by rotating the Command dial, and the camera sets the shutter speed for the best exposure based on your selection. A situation in which you may want to select the aperture is when shooting a portrait and you want a large aperture (small f-stop number) to blur out the background by minimizing depth of field. You can also use Aperture-priority auto (**A**) when shooting a landscape and you want a small aperture (large f-stop number) to ensure the entire scene is in focus by increasing depth of field.

Choosing the aperture to control depth of field is one of the most important aspects of photography. It allows you to control selectively which areas of your image, from foreground to background, are in sharp focus and which are blurred. Controlling depth of field enables you to draw the viewer's eye to a specific part of the image, which can make your images more dynamic and interesting to the viewer.

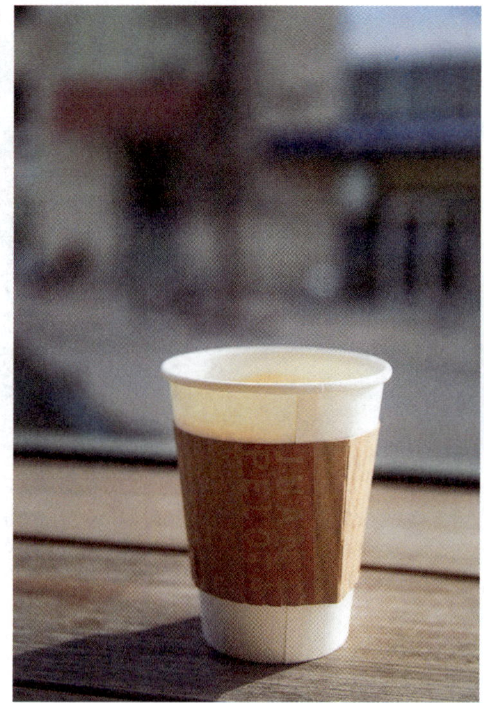

2.1 Shooting in Aperture-priority auto mode is great when you need to set a particular aperture for effect. For this shot I used a wide aperture of f/1.4 to make the background a nice blur, isolating the cup so it stands out as the main subject. Exposure: ISO 100, f/1.4, 1/500 second using a Sigma 35mm f/1.4 | A.

Shutter-priority auto mode

Shutter-priority auto (**S**) is another semiautomatic mode. In this mode, you choose the shutter speed by rotating the Command dial and the camera automatically sets the aperture. You can choose shutter speeds from as long as 30 seconds to as short as 1/4000 second.

You generally use Shutter-priority auto (**S**) to capture moving subjects or action scenes. Choosing a fast shutter speed allows you to freeze the action of a fast-moving subject, such as when shooting sports. Running athletes or bicyclists move extremely fast, so you need to use a shutter speed of about 1/250 second or faster to freeze the motion and prevent blur. This allows you to capture the details of the subject with sharp definition.

You can also use Shutter-priority auto mode (**S**) to set a slow shutter speed. A slow shutter speed allows you to introduce many creative effects into your photography. Selecting a slow shutter speed of about 1/15 second to 4 seconds allows you to create a motion blur from any subjects that may be moving in the frame. Shooting flowing water with a slow shutter speed gives it a smooth, glassy appearance, while shooting a scene with moving automobiles creates cool light trails from the head- and taillights. Of course, to be able to achieve a slow shutter speed, the lower the light the better; also keep in mind that it's best to use a tripod when attempting long exposures.

Even when you shoot quick action, you may sometimes want to use a slower shutter speed. If you use a slow shutter speed while panning on a moving subject, it blurs the background while keeping the subject in relatively sharp focus. A blurred background is an extremely effective way of portraying motion in a still photograph.

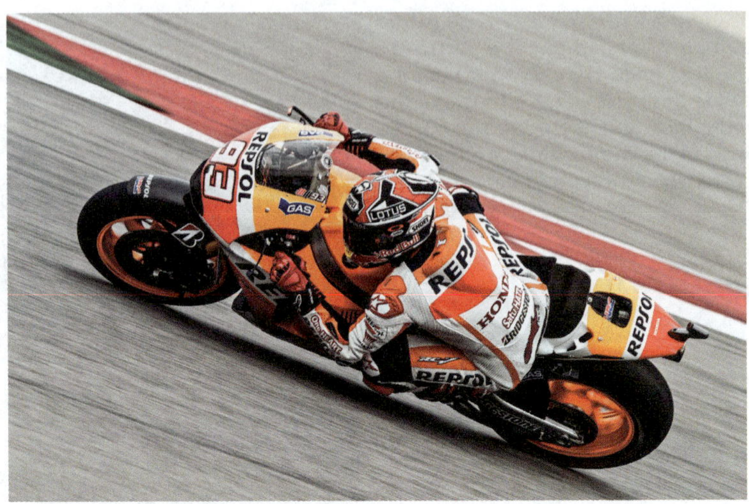

2.2 I used a relatively slow shutter speed and panning to capture the background movement of this motorcycle racing along the track. Exposure: ISO 100, f/8, 1/320 second using a Sigma 120–300mm f/2.8 | S at 300mm.

Manual mode

When in Manual mode (M), you set both the aperture and shutter speed. You can use the electronic analog exposure display (located in the viewfinder or on the LCD monitor in Live View) on the D3300 to determine the exposure needed, or if you're using a non-CPU lens you can estimate the exposure or use a handheld light meter. There are smartphone apps that allow you to use your iPhone or similar device as a light meter.

The following are a few situations in which you might want to set the exposure manually:

▶ **When you want complete control over exposure.** Usually, the camera decides the optimal exposure based on technical algorithms and an internal database of image information. However, what the camera decides is optimal may not necessarily be optimal in your mind. You may want to underexpose the image to make it dark and foreboding, or you may want to overexpose it to make the colors pop (making them bright and contrasty). When you set your camera to Manual mode (M), you can choose the settings and place your image in whatever tonal range you want without having to waste time on exposure compensation settings.

TIP When using Manual exposure (M), you can always view the exposure meter in the viewfinder to see where the actual exposure is at.

NOTE When using Auto-ISO and Manual exposure (**M**), exposure compensation can be activated.

▶ **When you use studio flash.** If you use studio strobes or external, undedicated flash units, you don't need the camera's metering system. When using external strobes, you need a flash meter or manual calculation to determine the proper exposure. In Manual mode (**M**), you can quickly set the aperture and shutter speed to the proper exposure; just be sure not to set the shutter speed above the rated sync speed of 1/200 second.

▶ **When you use non-CPU lenses.** The D3300 only functions in Manual mode (**M**) with these older lenses.

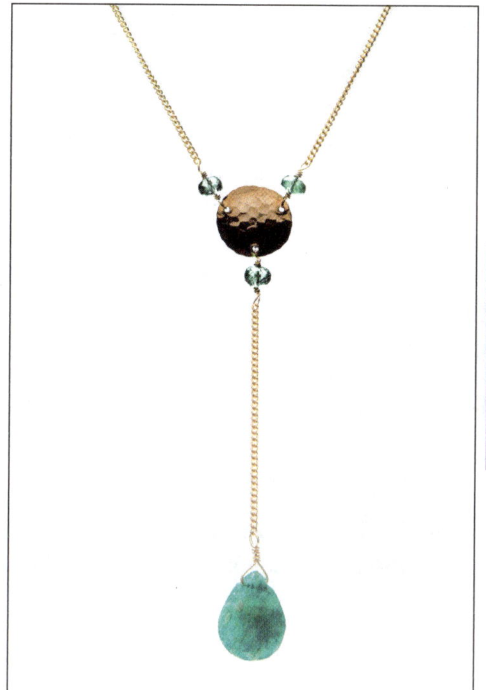

2.3 I used Manual mode for this product shot lit with studio strobes. Exposure: ISO 200, f/11, 1/200 second using a 28–70mm f/2.8D AF-S.

Guide Mode

Guide mode is a feature that is available only in Nikon 3000-series cameras such as the D3300. The Guide mode feature is intended to walk an absolute beginner through the photo-taking process using graphics and simple explanations that aren't heavy with photographic jargon. Guide mode has been redesigned from the D3200 and has a few different features.

In this section I'm only going to touch on the features of Guide mode; because the ultimate goal of Guide mode is to make it simple and easy to use, going into detail on the features would be somewhat redundant.

To enter Guide mode, simply rotate the Mode dial of the camera to the Guide mode setting (**GUIDE**). The Guide Mode menu appears on the LCD monitor, displaying four options to choose from.

Shoot

This option walks you through taking photos using specific examples as guidelines so you can get an idea of the effect you will achieve. These options are sometimes similar to, if not exactly the same as, a few select Scene and Effects modes. You can also create artistic photographs with effects that can only be made by using specific camera settings. Additionally, there are two options to choose from which are quite apparent from their naming conventions. You select these options by using the multi-selector up (▲) or down (▼) to highlight the setting. You can then press the multi-selector right (▶) or the OK button (**OK**) to view the settings. The options are as follows:

- ▶ **Easy operation.** This option gives you choices from a variety of everyday shooting scenarios. The options are Auto, No flash, Distant subjects, Close-ups, Sleeping faces, Moving subjects, Landscapes, Portraits, Night portrait, and Photograph night landscapes.

- ▶ **Advanced operation.** This gives you options that deal with how to make certain effects that involve using particular camera settings. You can choose from Soften backgrounds, Bring more into focus, Freeze motion (people), Freeze motion (vehicles), Show water flowing, Capture reds in sunsets, Take bright photos, Take dark (low key) photos, and Reduce blur.

View/delete

True to its name, this option allows you to view and delete your images. This is the Guide mode version of using the Playback menu (▶). You select these options by using the multi-selector up (▲) or down (▼) to highlight the setting. You can then press the multi-selector right (▶) or the OK button (**OK**) to view the settings. There are five options to choose from here.

- ▶ **View single photos.** This option allows you to view each individual photo fullscreen on the LCD monitor. You can use the Zoom in button (🔍) or the Thumbnail/Zoom out button (▦) to view closer or to zoom out to thumbnail view.

- ▶ **View multiple photos.** When this option is selected, the playback defaults to thumbnail view and you can use the Zoom in button (🔍) or the Thumbnail/Zoom out button (▦) to view closer or to zoom out to thumbnail view.

- ▶ **Choose a date.** This option brings up a calendar view and allows you to view only the photographs you took on a specific date.

- ▶ **View a slide show.** Using this option plays back the images stored on the memory card sequentially without you having to press any buttons.

- ▶ **Delete photos.** This option is used to erase any photos that you don't want to keep.

Retouch

This option in Guide mode gives you access to six of the more popular retouching tools: Trim, Filter effects (cross screen), Filter effects (soft), Photo illustration, Miniature effect, and Selective color.

Setup

The Setup choice takes some of the more useful options of all the menus and puts them in one spot for you to set easily. The options are Image quality, Image size, Auto off timers, Print date, Display and sound settings, Movie settings, Playback folder, Playback display options, DPOF print order, Clock and language, Format memory card, Output settings, Wireless mobile adapter, and Slot empty release lock.

NOTE All of the settings discussed in the Guide mode section are discussed in greater detail in the sections that pertain to them specifically.

▶ While Guide mode is great for jumping in and getting the types of photographs you picture in your mind, it doesn't really explain what settings it uses and why they create the effects that they do. It simply holds your hand. This is okay if you want to take snapshots, but if you really want to become a photographer, you need to understand what each setting does and why it causes different effects. So although using Guide mode in the absolute beginning can help, it's best not to rely on it as a crutch once you start to grasp the basic tenets of photography.

Scene Modes

If you've been using the fully Automatic modes — Auto (📷) and Auto flash off (⚡) — you may have noticed, especially when shooting in difficult lighting situations or other special circumstances, that these modes may not give you the results you desired. The D3300 scene modes take into account different lighting situations and desired outcomes and modify the way the camera sets the exposure to create specific effects. Scene modes also control the autofocus settings, the flash settings, and the aperture, shutter speed, Picture Controls, and ISO sensitivity settings.

When you use scene modes, you cannot adjust the white balance (**WB**), Picture Controls, or Active D-Lighting (**ADL**) settings. Each scene mode has default settings for ISO, AF-area, autofocus, and flash modes, but you can change them. These settings return to the default when you turn the camera off or turn the Mode dial to another setting.

The camera may also determine whether there is enough light to make an exposure, and then activate the built-in flash if the light is insufficient. Conversely, in some scene modes such as Landscape (⛰), the camera also makes sure that the flash is not used, even in low-light situations.

The D3300 has six scene modes to cover the most common shooting scenarios, so that you can focus on capturing the image without worrying about the camera settings. Although the scene modes are great for starting out, as you develop as a photographer, you won't need to rely on these modes to make creative exposures.

You can choose the following scene modes directly from the Mode dial on your D3300:

▶ **Portrait mode (▨).** This mode is for taking pictures of people. The camera automatically adjusts the colors to provide natural-looking skin tones. It focuses on the closest subject and, if possible, attempts to use a wide aperture to reduce the depth of field. This draws attention to the subject of the portrait, leaving distracting background details out of focus. The built-in flash and AF-assist illuminator automatically activate in low-light situations. Picture Control is set to Portrait (▨PT).

▶ **Landscape mode (⛰).** When taking photos of far-off vistas, you want to use this mode. The camera automatically adjusts the colors to apply brighter greens and blues to foliage and skies. The camera also automatically focuses on the closest subject and uses a smaller aperture to provide a greater depth of field to ensure focus throughout the entire image. In this mode, the camera automatically disables the AF-assist illuminator and the flash. Picture Control is set to Landscape (▨LS).

▶ **Child mode (▨).** This mode is ideal for taking portraits or candid shots of children. The camera automatically adjusts the colors to provide more saturation while still providing a natural skin tone. It automatically focuses on the

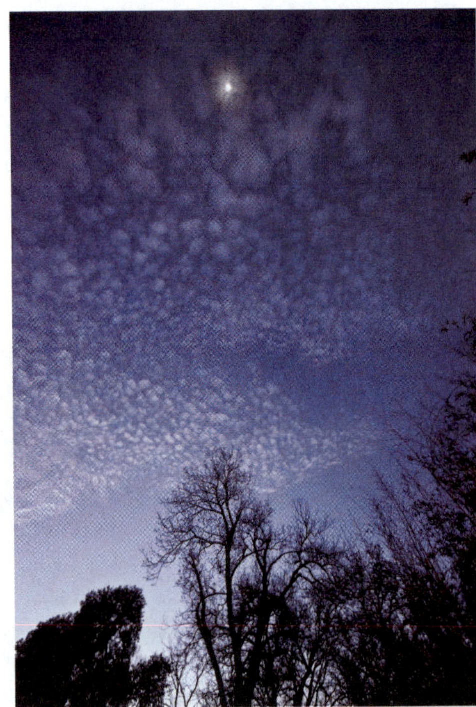

2.4 This image was taken with the Landscape mode. Exposure: ISO 800, f/10, 1/30 second using a Sigma 10–20mm f/3.5 DC HSM at 10mm.

closest subject and uses a fairly small aperture to capture background details. The built-in flash is automatically activated when the light is low. Picture Control is set to Standard (⬚SD).

▶ **Sports mode (⬚).** A fast shutter speed freezes the action of moving subjects when the camera is set to this mode. The camera focuses continuously as long as the shutter-release button is half-pressed. The camera also uses Predictive Focus Tracking based on information from all the focus areas in case the main subject moves from the selected focus point. The camera disables the built-in flash and AF-assist illuminator when you select this mode. Picture Control is set to Standard (⬚SD).

> **TIP** To capture a quick-sequence shot, set the Release mode (⬤) to one of the two Continuous shooting modes: Continuous high-speed (⬚H) or Continuous low-speed (⬚L).

▶ **Close-up mode (⬚).** Use this mode for close-up or macro shots. It uses a fairly wide aperture to provide a soft background while giving the main subject a sharp focus. In this mode, the camera focuses on the subject in the center of the frame, although you can use the multi-selector to choose one of the other focus points to create an off-center composition. When light is low, the camera automatically activates the built-in flash. Be sure to remove your lens hood when using the flash on close-up subjects because the lens hood can cast a shadow on your subject by blocking the light from the flash. Picture Control is set to Standard (⬚SD).

> **CROSS REF** It's best to use the Close-up scene mode (⬚) in conjunction with a macro lens or close-up filter. See Chapter 4 for more details on macro lenses and Chapter 8 for general macro shooting advice.

▶ **Night portrait mode (⬚).** This mode is ideal for taking portraits in low-light situations. The camera automatically activates the flash and uses a longer shutter speed (Slow sync) to capture the ambient light from the background. This balances the ambient light and the light from the flash, giving you a more natural effect. You may want to use a tripod when you use this mode to prevent blurring from camera shake that can occur during longer exposure times. Picture Control is set to Portrait (⬚PT).

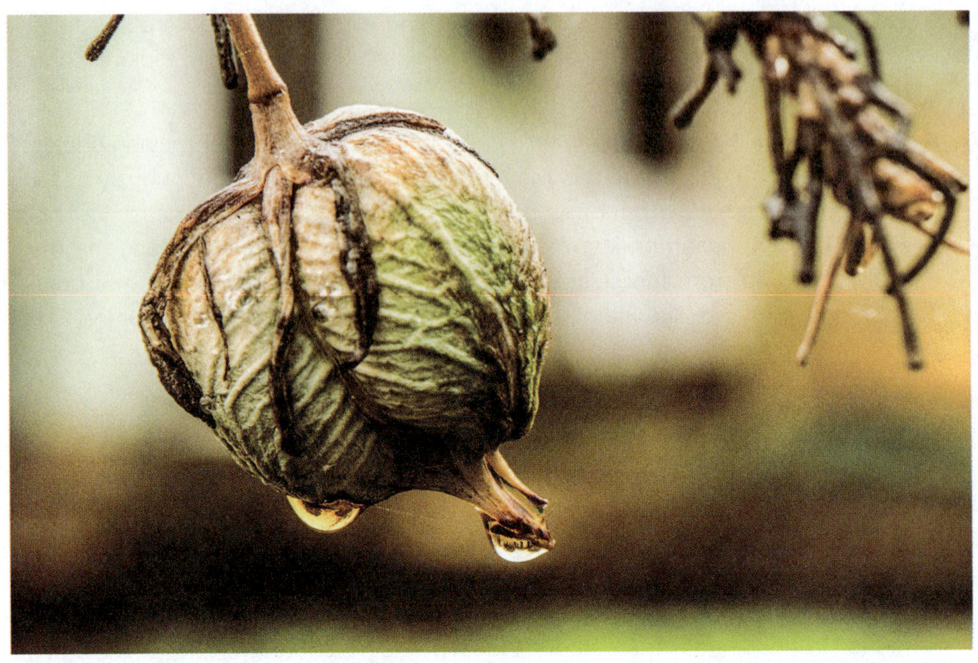

2.5 This shot was taken using the Close-up scene mode. Exposure: ISO 6400, f/16, 1/80 second using a Nikon 60mm f/2.8G macro lens.

Special Effects Modes

Special effects modes, once found only on the D5000 series of cameras, are now available on the D3300. Some of the options are similar to scene modes, but there are key differences. Most of the options add special effects similar to what you may add using image-editing software on your computer.

Many of these effects are best utilized when shooting in Live View mode (**Lv**) so that you are able to preview the effect (you won't be able to see the effect in the optical viewfinder).

NOTE When using Color illustration, Color sketch, and Miniature effect modes, the camera's processor is slowed somewhat and the video refresh rate is reduced significantly, making the Live View appear slow and jerky.

In addition, each of the effects has different caveats; some will only autofocus in Live View (**Lv**), and some won't autofocus at all. Some of the effects must first be set up using Live View (**Lv**) before you can use them when shooting through the viewfinder. These are all covered in their specific sections.

To use these Effects settings, rotate the Mode dial to Special effects (**EFFECTS**), and then rotate the Command dial to select an effect. Press the OK button (**OK**) to display any optional settings for an effect.

> **NOTE** When using most of the Special effects modes, the camera automatically switches to JPEG. RAW images are *only* recorded when shooting in the High key (**Hi**), Low key (**Lo**), and Silhouette (**A**) modes.

Night vision

Night vision mode (**A**) is intended for use only in very low light. It's a monochromatic mode that allows the camera to expand the ISO sensitivity up to the equivalent of 102400. This mode doesn't produce optimal image quality, but the effect can be interesting. Keep in mind that there is no High ISO Noise Reduction and the images will typically have an extreme amount of noise and banding. Autofocus is only available in Live View mode (**Lv**). I recommend that you use this option sparingly.

Super vivid

This option cranks up the color saturation and contrast to extra-high levels, which results in intense colors, deep shadows, and bright highlights. Use this option on scenes that have a lot of brightly colored objects for a nice effect. I don't recommend using this option with scenes that have people in them, as the skin tones will look unnatural.

Pop

This effect is close to the Super vivid effect, but the color saturation is slightly less and the contrast isn't quite as high. This gives your photo an added boost of color without going overboard, which allows it to maintain a certain amount of realism.

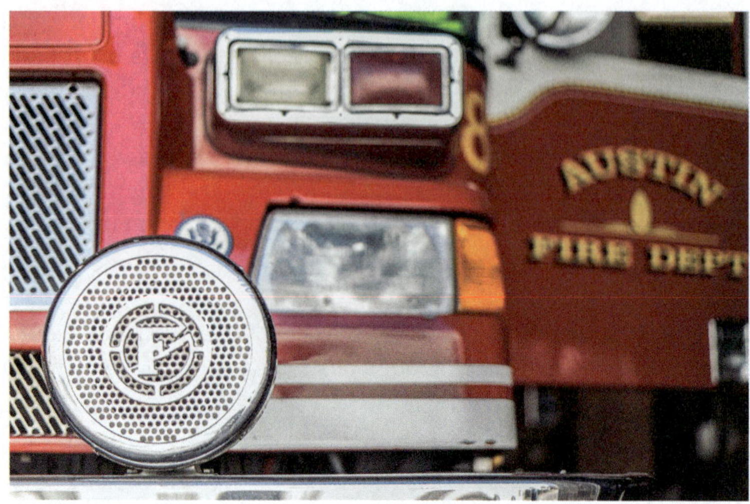

2.6 This image was taken using the Pop effect. Exposure: ISO 100, f/1.8, 1/250 second using a Nikon 35mm f/1.8G.

Photo illustration

The Photo illustration effect makes a photograph appear similar to a painted sign or poster. This is one of the effects that are best used in Live View so that you can preview the scene before capturing it. This effect should be set up prior to shooting. After selecting the option, activate Live View by pressing the Live View button (**Lv**) and press the OK button (**OK**) to bring up the effect setting, which is called Thickness. This determines the width of the outlines. Use the multi-selector right (▶) to make the outlines thicker (+) or multi-selector left (◀) to make them thinner (-). Press the OK button (**OK**) to set.

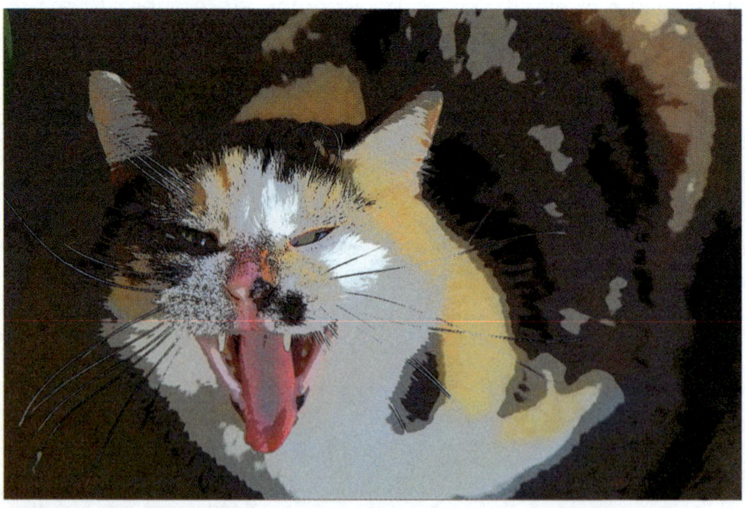

2.7 This image was taken using the Photo illustration effect. Exposure: ISO 400, f/5.6, 1/1235 second using the kit lens at 55mm.

Color sketch

Color sketch mode (⟐) gives an image a cartoon-like appearance. This effect should also be set up first in Live View mode (**Lv**) before you can use it to shoot stills through the viewfinder. After you select Color sketch mode (⟐) from the Special effects menu (**EFFECTS**), press the Live View button (**Lv**), and then press the OK button (**OK**) to adjust the settings. You can then select one of the following choices by pressing the multi-selector up (▲) or down (▼):

▶ **Vividness.** Press the multi-selector right (▶) to make the colors super saturated. Press the multi-selector left (◀) to mute the colors for an almost black-and-white effect.

▶ **Outlines.** This option controls how thick the lines appear. Press the multi-selector left (◀) to make them appear as if they were drawn by a very fine pen; press the multi-selector right (▶) to make them appear as if they were drawn by a thick, black marker. You may notice that as the outline thickens, the colors become more saturated.

After you select your settings, press the OK button (**OK**) to set them. You can then continue to shoot in Live View mode (**Lv**), or you can exit and shoot using the viewfinder while retaining the Color sketch settings (⟐).

Toy camera effect

If you aren't familiar with toy cameras, they are cheap, plastic film cameras that were mass-produced in the 1970s and '80s. Because the quality of the cameras and lenses was so low, the images similarly suffered from poor quality and were known for *vignetting* (darkening of the image corners) and bright colors with a lot of contrast.

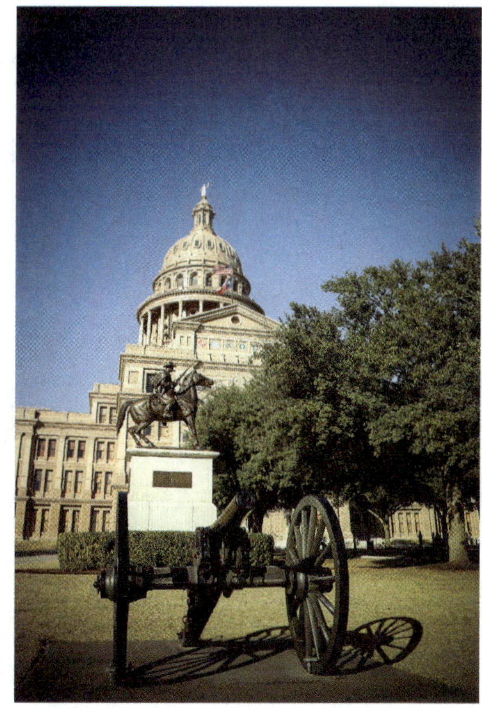

2.8 This image was taken using the Toy camera effect. Exposure: ISO 200, f/10, 1/400 second using the kit lens at 18mm.

You have probably seen these effects before in smartphone apps such as Instagram or Hipstamatic. This is actually one of the few effects modes that I find works quite well at adding an interesting effect.

Once you set the Toy camera effect (by choosing it using the multi-selector), activate Live View (**Lv**) and then press the OK button (⊙) to adjust the setting options. There are two options: Vividness and Vignetting. The first option controls how colorful and saturated the image is, and the second option controls how pronounced the darkening of the edges of the frame is. Use the multi-selector up (▲) and down (▼) to switch between the Vividness and Vignetting options. Use the multi-selector left (◄) to lessen the effect, or right (►) to increase the effect.

Miniature effect

The Miniature effect (🏞) applies what is commonly called the Tilt/Shift effect. This effect applies a simulated shallow depth of field to an image by blurring selected parts of it, and keeping others in sharp focus. This tricks the eye and brain, and causes the subject in the image to appear much smaller than it actually is. This effect works best on images taken from an overhead perspective.

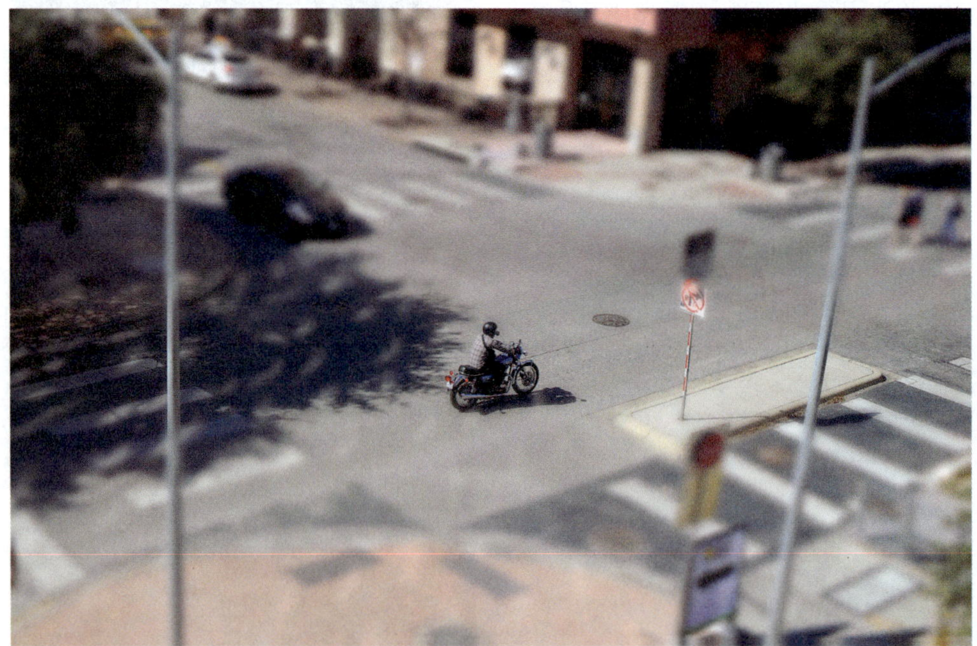

2.9 An example of the Miniature effect. Exposure ISO 100, f/11, 1/200 second with a Sigma 35mm f/1.4 | A.

It's best to set this effect up in Live View mode (**Lv**) before you use it. Select Miniature effect (🖼) from the Special effects mode (**EFFECTS**), and then press the Live View button (**Lv**). Use the multi-selector to position the focus point, and then press the shutter-release button halfway to focus.

> **TIP** To confirm focus, press the Zoom in button (🔍). To return to Miniature effect (🖼), press the Thumbnail/Zoom out button (🔍).

Once you select your focus point and focus, press the OK button (**OK**) to display the effect options. Press the multi-selector up (▲) or down (▼) to adjust the width of the area you want to remain in focus. Press the multi-selector left (◄) or right (►) to choose whether the in-focus area is horizontal or vertical. This effect works best when applied horizontally. Press the OK button (**OK**) to save your settings. You can then continue to shoot in Live View mode (**Lv**), or you can exit and use the viewfinder to compose your shots. Just remember that you cannot preview the effect in the viewfinder. The line of focus moves as you move the focus area.

One very odd feature about this effect is that when you record video, the camera compresses the video and plays it back at high speed. According to the manual, 30 to 45 minutes of actual recording yields a movie that is only about 3 minutes in length when played back. Also, be aware that autofocus and sound recording are disabled when you use the Miniature effect (🖼) while recording. You can also apply the Miniature effect (🖼) to existing still images in the Retouch menu (🖊).

Selective color

The Selective color mode (🖋) allows you to choose up to three colors to keep in the image. The camera then automatically turns the remaining colors to black and white. It can give your images an interesting effect that was once only possible using image-editing software such as Adobe Photoshop. Now, you can do it in-camera and preview the effect in Live View mode (**Lv**). Once again, this option *must* be set in Live View mode (**Lv**) before you can use it while shooting through the viewfinder.

After you choose the Selective color mode (🖋) from the Special effects menu (**EFFECTS**), press the Live View button (**Lv**) to enter Live View mode. Press the OK button (**OK**) to display the options. The first thing you want to do is decide which color to select. It's best to choose a bright color, such as a deep red, blue, green, or yellow. The camera's sensor can have difficulty in detecting dull colors, especially grays, tans, and skin tones.

You will notice a white, square cursor in the center of the monitor image (similar to the Live View focus point, but smaller and white). Use the multi-selector to move the cursor over the top of the color you want to select. Once the cursor is over the desired color, press the multi-selector up (▲) to select the color.

> **TIP** If you want to be more meticulous about the selected color, use the Zoom in button (🔍) to get a more detailed look. Press the Thumbnail/ Zoom out button (🔍) to return to full-screen view.

After you select the color, look at the top-right corner of the screen and you see three boxes, one of which contains the selected color. You also see numbers directly to the right of each box. Using the multi-selector up (▲) or down (▼), you can choose from 1 to 7; the default is 3. You can increase the color range (4 to 7) to include similar colors, or you can decrease the range (1 to 2) so that the selected color is more specific.

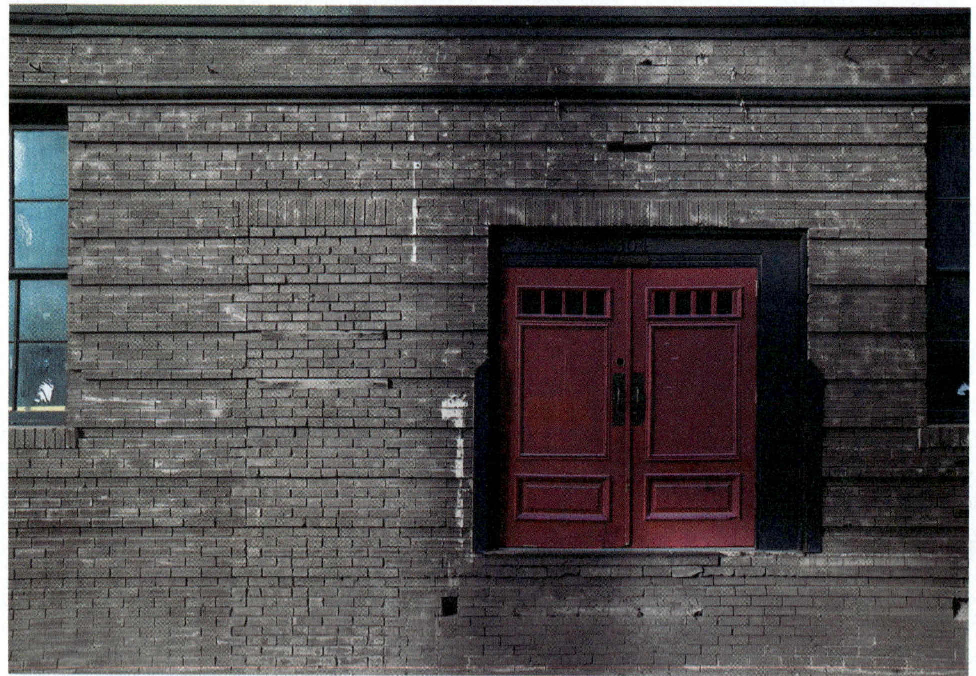

2.10 The Selective color mode. Exposure: ISO 100, f/7.1, 1/60 second using a Sigma 17–70mm f/2.8–4 DC HSM OS at 17mm.

As I mentioned before, you can select up to three colors. Use the Command dial to select one of the other boxes and repeat the process if you want. You do not have to select three colors; you can choose only one if you prefer. To deselect a color, simply use the Command dial to select a box, and then press the Delete button (🗑). To delete all selected colors, press and hold the Delete button (🗑).

Silhouette

In Silhouette mode (🌋), the camera sets the exposure for the bright part of the scene to silhouette the dark subject against a bright background. This option looks best when shooting at dusk or dawn. Flash is turned off to avoid lighting the subject and the AF-assist illuminator is disabled.

High key

Use the High key setting (Hi) when shooting a light subject against a light background. The camera applies some exposure compensation to slightly overexpose and add some brightness to the scene.

Low key

Use the Low key setting (Lo) when photographing dark subjects on a dark background. This mode also punches up the highlights just a bit to get good definition between the shadows and highlights.

HDR painting

This is a brand-new feature making its debut in the D3300. Similar to the standard HDR mode, the camera makes two exposures and combines them to increase the dynamic range or range of tonality in the image. Using the standard HDR setting yields a more natural look. The HDR painting effect gives the images the surreal look that most people think of when the term HDR is used. While this mode can be used for fun at times, be careful not to overuse the effect as it can appear garish.

Keep in mind that, as with all HDR photos, the images should be taken using a tripod to ensure that the images line up perfectly, or the photo may appear blurry. If there is movement in the frame, you may see ghost-like artifacts in your HDR painting image.

Because this effect requires two exposures and processing by the camera, you cannot preview it when using Live View (Lv). Similarly, you cannot use flash or continuous shooting, and the HDR painting mode cannot be used when shooting movies.

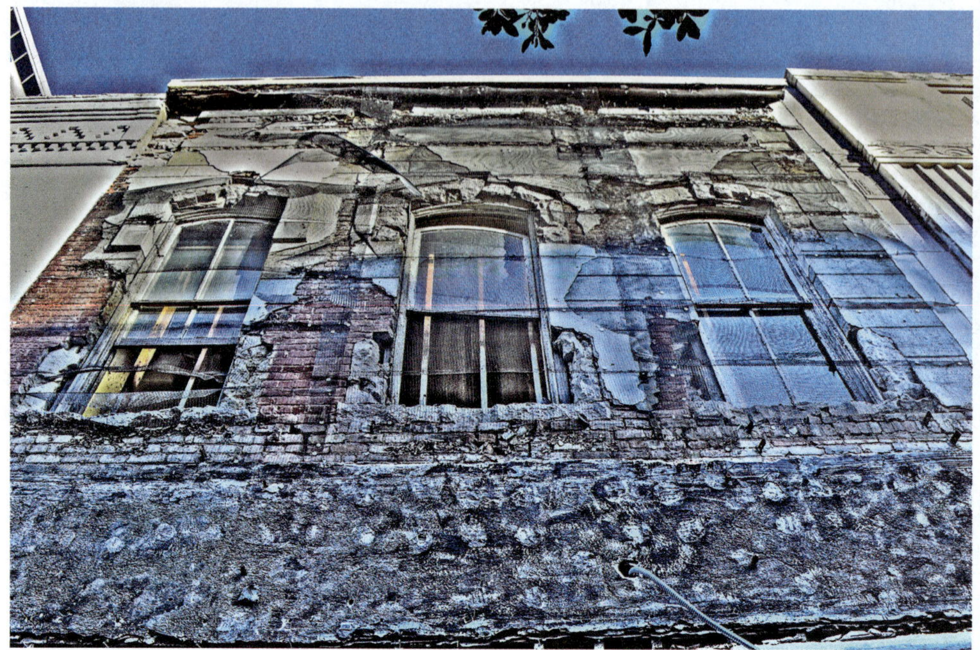

2.11 An example of an image using HDR painting. Exposure: ISO 640, f/2.8, 1/10 second using a Tamron 17–50mm f/2.8 VC at 40mm.

NOTE When the camera is set to HDR painting and the move-record button is pressed, the video will not display the HDR effect.

Easy panorama

Easy panorama mode is a new feature on Nikon cameras that allows you to photograph expansive vistas with a wide, sweeping view by using Live View and tracking the camera along a path. When the mode is selected, a camera dialog box tells you to activate Live View to start. After entering Live View, focus and press the shutter-release button to start. Once you start, you can pan the camera horizontally or vertically with a slow, even pace. You can hold the camera horizontally to get a taller image.

CAUTION If you move too quickly or erratically, the panorama recording stops and you have to start over again.

Once you're finished, you can play back the motion of the camera in review, but when you download it from the memory card, the image is stored as a JPEG.

NOTE Easy panorama mode doesn't record full 24MP files. The images sizes for panoramas are as follows: Normal (horizontal pan) 4800 x 1080; normal (vertical pan) 1632 x 4800; wide (horizontal pan) 9600 x 1080; wide (vertical pan) 1632 x 9600

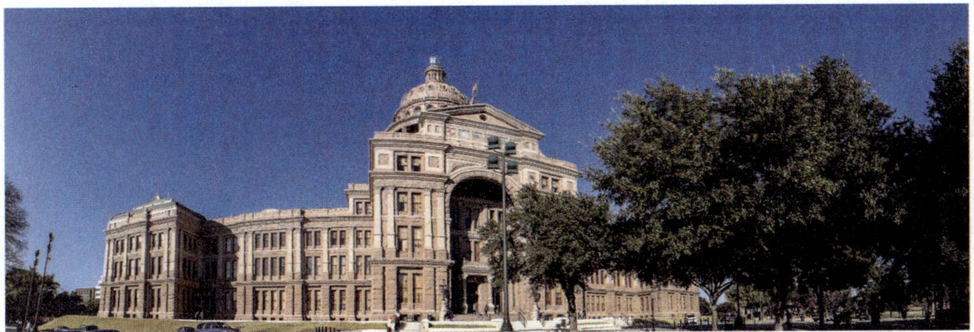

2.12 An image taken using the Easy panorama setting. Exposure: ISO 640, f/2.8, 1/10 second using a Tamron 17–50mm f/2.8 VC at 40mm.

Metering Modes

The D3300 has three metering modes — Matrix (▨), Center-weighted (◉), and Spot (⊡) — to help you get the best exposure for your image. You can change the modes in the Info display menu. Metering modes determine how the camera's light metering sensor collects and processes the information used to determine exposure. Each of these modes is useful for different types of lighting situations.

Matrix metering mode

The default metering system that Nikon cameras use is a proprietary system called 3D Color Matrix metering II, or just Matrix metering for short. Matrix metering mode (▨) uses the 420-pixel RGB (Red, Green, Blue) sensor on the D3300 to read a wide area of the frame, and sets the exposure based on the light intensity, contrast, color, and composition of the scene as well as the focus distance (for current Nikon lenses). Then the camera runs the data through sophisticated algorithms, compares it to information from 30,000 images stored in its database, and determines the proper exposure for the scene.

In simple terms, it works like this: You're photographing a landscape. The metering sensor detects a bright area near the top of the frame and a darker area near the bottom. The camera takes this information and adds in the fact that the focus is set at or near infinity, which indicates a far-off subject. The RGB sensor also reads the quantity of the colors (for example, a lot of blues in the sky and greens in the foreground) and uses that information as well. Running all of this data through the Expeed 4 processing system, the camera determines that this is a landscape scene. It then compares the data with information from the 30,000+ images mentioned earlier and uses all of these details to make a pretty accurate assessment of what the proper exposure should be.

The D3300 automatically chooses a Matrix metering system based on the type of Nikon lens that you use. Here are the options:

- **3D Color matrix metering II.** All current Nikon DX lenses use this metering type. When you use Matrix metering mode (▣), the camera decides the exposure setting based mainly on the brightness and contrast of the overall scene, and the colors of the subject matter, as well as other data. It also considers the distance to the subject, which focus point is used, and the lens focal length to determine which areas of the image are important to get the proper exposure. For example, if you're using a wide-angle lens with a distant subject and a bright area at the top of the frame, the meter considers this when setting the exposure, so the sky and clouds don't lose critical detail.

- **Color matrix metering II.** This type of metering is used when an older Nikon AI-P lens (which has a CPU) is attached to the camera. Nikon only offers three of these lenses and they are quite rare, with the 45mm f/2.8 AI-P being the most common. The Matrix metering recognizes that an AI-P lens is attached and the camera uses only brightness, subject color, and the focus point to determine the right exposure.

Matrix metering mode (▣) is suitable for most subjects, especially when you're dealing with a complex lighting situation. Given the large amount of image data in the Matrix metering mode (▣) database, the camera can make a fairly accurate assessment of what type of image you are shooting and adjust the exposure accordingly. For example, for an image with a high amount of contrast and brightness across the top of the frame, the camera tries to expose for the scene so that the highlights retain detail. Paired with Nikon Active D-Lighting (**ADL**), your exposure will have good dynamic range throughout the image.

Center-weighted metering mode

When you switch the camera's metering mode to Center-weighted (⊙), the meter takes a light reading of the whole scene, but bases the exposure settings mostly on the light falling on the center of the scene. The camera determines about 75 percent of the exposure from an 8mm circle in the center of the frame and 25 percent from the area around the center.

Center-weighted metering mode (⬚) is a very useful option, especially when you shoot photos with the main subject in the middle of the frame. This metering mode is useful when photographing a dark subject against a bright background, or a light subject against a dark background. It works especially well for three-quarter to close-up portraits, where you want to preserve the background detail while exposing correctly for the subject.

When there may be small areas of extreme brightness or darkness near the edge of the frame, you can get consistent results using Center-weighted metering mode (⬚) without worrying about the fluctuations in exposure settings that sometimes result when using Matrix metering mode (⬚).

Spot metering mode

In Spot metering mode (⬚), the camera does just that: meters only a spot. This spot is only 3.5mm in diameter and only accounts for 2.5 percent of the frame. The spot is linked to the active focus point, so you can focus and meter your subject at the same time, instead of metering the subject, pressing the Auto-Exposure Lock button (⬚), and then recomposing the photo. The D3300 has 11 focus points, so it's like having 11 spot meters to choose from throughout the scene.

Choose Spot metering mode (⬚) when the subject is the only thing in the frame for which you want the camera to expose. You select the spot meter to measure a precise area of tone or brightness within the scene. For example, when you photograph a subject on a completely white or black background, you might not be concerned with preserving detail in the background; therefore, exposing just for the subject works out perfectly. This mode works well for concert photography, when the musician or singer is lit with a bright spotlight. You can capture every detail of the subject and just let the shadow areas go black.

Autofocus

The D3300 offers the Multi-CAM 1000, which has been standard since the introduction of the 3000-series, and has proven itself to be a time tested and accurate focusing system. The Multi-CAM 1000 autofocus reads contrast values from a sensor inside the camera's viewing system to determine proper focus.

Autofocus Sensors

The D3300 has two autofocus sensor types: cross and horizontal. As you may have guessed, cross-type sensors are shaped like a cross while horizontal sensors appear as horizontal lines. You can think of them like plus and minus signs. Cross-type sensors are able to read the contrast horizontally and vertically. Horizontal sensors can only interpret contrast in one direction. (When you position the camera in portrait orientation, the horizontal sensors are positioned vertically.)

Cross-type sensors can evaluate for focus more accurately than horizontal sensors, but horizontal sensors can do it more quickly (provided that the contrasting elements run perpendicular to the sensor). The D3300 has one cross-type sensor in the center AF point, while the surrounding ten AF points are horizontal type.

Phase detection

The autofocus system on the D3300 uses *phase detection*, which is determined by a sensor in the camera body. To achieve phase detection, a beam splitter diverts the light coming from the lens into two optical prisms that send the light as two separate images to the AF sensor in the D3300. This creates a type of rangefinder in which the base is the same size as the diameter or aperture of the lens. The larger the length of the base (or the wider the aperture), the easier it is for the rangefinder to determine whether the two images are "in phase," or in focus.

This is why lenses with wider maximum apertures, such as f/2.8, often focus faster than lenses with smaller maximum apertures, especially in low light. This is also why the autofocus usually can't work with slower lenses coupled with a teleconverter, which reduces the effective aperture of the lens. The base length of the rangefinder images is simply too small to allow the autofocus system to determine the proper focusing distance. The autofocus sensor reads the contrast or phase difference between the two images that are projected onto it. This is the primary way in which the D3300 autofocus system works. This type of focus is also referred to as Secondary Image Registration Through-the-Lens (SIR-TTL) because the autofocus sensor relies on a secondary image, as opposed to the primary image projected into the viewfinder from the reflex mirror.

Contrast detection

The D3300 only uses contrast detection focus when you use the Live View (Lv) and Live View video (📹) modes. This is the same method that smaller compact digital cameras use to focus. Contrast detection focus is a bit slower and uses the image sensor to determine whether the subject is in focus. In a relatively simple operation, the sensor detects the contrast between different segments of the scene on a pixel level. The camera does this by moving the lens elements until it achieves sufficient contrast between the pixels that lie under the selected focus point. With contrast detection, you can focus on a greater area of the frame, meaning you can set the focus area to anywhere within the scene.

Contrast detection focus is highly accurate. Because you can pinpoint the focus point more accurately, I highly recommend using Live View mode (**Lv**) when using a tripod, whether you are in the field or a studio. On the other hand, because contrast detection focus takes longer, I don't recommend using it for moving subjects or action shots.

Focus Modes

Focus modes simply control how the camera achieves focus when you press the shutter-release button halfway. You can choose from the following four settings: Auto servo AF (**AF-A**), Continuous servo AF (**AF-C**), Single servo AF (**AF-S**), and Manual focus (**MF**). Each of these is useful in different situations, which I discuss in the following sections.

CAUTION When the lens autofocus switch is set to Manual (**MF**), you cannot select an autofocus mode.

To change the focus mode, you must enter the Info display edit menu. Press the *i* button (**ⓘ**) to view the Info display, and then press it again to display the cursor and edit the settings. Use the multi-selector to navigate to the focus mode option on the display, and then press the OK button (**OK**). You can then use the multi-selector left (◀) and right (▶) to scroll through the focus mode options. After you select the focus mode, press the OK button (**OK**) to set it.

Auto servo AF mode

When you use the Auto servo AF mode (**AF-A**), the D3300 autofocus system determines whether the subject is moving and automatically selects the Continuous servo AF (**AF-C**) or Single servo AF (**AF-S**) mode. The shutter is only released when the camera detects that the scene is in focus. This mode is adequate for shooting snapshots, but I wouldn't count on it to work perfectly in situations in which focus is critical.

Continuous servo AF mode

The Continuous servo AF mode (**AF-C**) is the autofocus mode you want to use when shooting sports, or in any other situation in which the subject is moving. When you set the camera to Continuous servo AF mode (**AF-C**), it continues to focus as long as you press the shutter-release button halfway, or if the AE-L/AF-L button (AE-L/AF-L) is set to On (**AF-ON**) in the Setup menu (Y). If the subject moves, the camera activates Predictive Focus Tracking. Predictive Focus allows the camera to track the subject and maintain focus by attempting to predict where the subject will be when the shutter is released. By default, when the camera is in Continuous servo AF mode (AF-C), it fires when you fully depress the shutter-release button, but only if the subject is in focus. This is called Focus Priority, and it allows you to get more images in focus when photographing moving subjects.

Single servo AF mode

In Single servo AF mode (AF-S) — which is not to be confused with the AF-S lens designation — the camera focuses when you press the shutter-release button halfway. When the camera achieves focus, the focus locks, and it remains so until the shutter is released or the shutter-release button is no longer depressed. Again, by default, the camera does not fire unless it achieves focus. Single servo AF (AF-S) is the best mode to use when shooting portraits, landscapes, or other photos in which the subject is relatively static. Using this mode also helps ensure that you have fewer out-of-focus images.

Manual focus mode

When you select Manual focus mode (MF), the D3300 disables the autofocus system. To achieve focus, you rotate the focus ring of the lens until the subject appears sharp when you look through the viewfinder. You can use Manual focus mode (MF) when shooting still-life photographs or other still subjects with which you want total control of the focus, or when you are using a non-autofocus lens. Keep in mind that the camera shutter releases, regardless of whether the scene is in focus.

When using Manual focus mode (MF), the D3300 offers some assistance in the form of an electronic rangefinder that can be turned on in the Setup menu (Y). When the camera or lens is switched to Manual focus (MF), the exposure meter display becomes the electronic rangefinder. If the indicator shows to the right, the focus is behind the subject; an arrow to the left indicates that the focus is in front of the subject. Keep in mind that you still need to choose a focus point so that the camera can determine where the subject is in the frame so that the rangefinder can work properly. You can use Manual focus mode (MF) when shooting close-ups and macros, as well as portraits when you need to focus on a specific area.

I find that manual focusing is much easier when using Live View (Lv) because you can see exactly what the camera is seeing. The viewfinders of modern dSLR cameras are not optimized for manual focusing (hence the rangefinder/focus confirmation option). When using Live View, you can also zoom in on the subject to get a closer look at the area you are focusing on without actually zooming the lens.

Autofocus Area Modes

The D3300 has the following four AF-area modes: Single-point AF ([□]), Dynamic-area AF ([⋮]), 3-D tracking ([3D]), and Auto-area AF ([■]). Each mode is useful in different situations, and each can be modified to suit a variety of shooting needs. Note that AF-area modes aren't available to change when using certain scene and effects modes.

You can set AF-area modes in the Info display edit menu. Press the *i* button (*i*), and then use the multi-selector to navigate to the AF-area mode option (next to the Autofocus mode option). Press the multi-selector left (◀) and right (▶) to scroll through the options. Press the OK button (**OK**) when the desired setting is displayed.

The D3300 3-D tracking mode ([3D]) enables the camera to automatically switch focus points and maintain sharp focus on a moving subject as it crosses the frame. In 3-D tracking mode ([3D]), the camera recognizes color and light information, and uses it to track the subject.

Auto-area AF mode

Auto-area AF mode ([■]) is exactly what it sounds like: the camera automatically determines the subject and chooses one or more autofocus points to lock focus. When used with NIKKOR G-type AF-S lenses like the kit lens, the D3300 Scene Recognition System is able to recognize human subjects. This means that the camera has a better chance of focusing where you want rather than accidentally focusing on the background when shooting a portrait. I tend not to use a fully automatic setting such as this, but I find it works reasonably well for snapshots with a relatively deep depth of field. When you set the camera to Single servo AF mode (**AF-S**), the active autofocus points light up in the viewfinder for about 1 second when the camera attains focus; when you set it to Continuous servo AF mode (**AF-C**), you can see the active point tracking the subject as it moves through the frame.

Single-point AF mode

Single-point AF ([□]) is the easiest mode to use when you shoot slow-moving or completely still subjects. You can press the multi-selector up (▲), down (▼), left (◀), or right (▶) to choose one of the autofocus points. The camera only focuses on the subject if it is in the selected autofocus area. By default, Single-point AF mode ([□]) allows you to choose from any one of the 11 autofocus area points.

Dynamic-area AF mode

Dynamic-area AF mode (⊡) also allows you to select the autofocus point manually, but unlike Single-point AF mode (⬚), some or all of the surrounding unselected points remain active; this way, if the subject happens to move out of the selected focus area, the camera's highly sophisticated autofocus system can track it and adjust the focus for the movement.

When you set the focus to Single servo AF mode (**AF-S**), it operates the same as Single-point AF mode (⬚). To take advantage of Dynamic-area AF mode (⊡), you must set the camera to Continuous servo AF mode (**AF-C**).

You can then choose from the following two options:

- **Dynamic-area AF (⊡).** When you set your D3300 to Dynamic-area AF mode (⊡), you can select any one of the camera's 11 autofocus points to be the primary one. If your subject moves out of the selected focus area, the autofocus system uses the other ten autofocus points to determine focus. Use this setting when you shoot subjects that move predictably. For example, baseball players typically run in a straight line, so you don't need many points for autofocus coverage as you track along with the subject.

- **3-D tracking (3D).** In this mode, all 11 autofocus points are active. You select the primary autofocus point, but if the subject moves, the camera uses 3-D tracking to select a new primary autofocus point automatically. With 3-D tracking, the camera uses distance and color information from the area immediately surrounding the focus point to determine what the subject is. If the subject moves, the camera selects a new focus point. This mode works very well for subjects that move unpredictably; however, you need to be sure that the subject and the background aren't similar in color. When you photograph a subject that has a color similar to the background, the camera may lock focus on the wrong area, so use this mode carefully. This mode is best for situations where a lone subject is against a plain, contrasting background; for example, it is useful when capturing a bird, or even an airplane, against a plain, blue sky.

Release Modes

Shutter release modes (◉) control how the shutter release operates. A number of options are useful in many shooting situations. To change the release mode, press the Shutter release mode button (◉). Use the multi-selector to highlight one of the following options on the LCD screen, and then press the OK button (**OK**) to set it:

▶ **Single-frame shooting mode (S).** When you select the Single-frame shooting mode (S), the camera takes one picture when you fully depress the shutter-release button. Even if you hold the button down, only one frame is captured. The shutter-release button must be completely unpressed to reset it. You can use this mode when shooting portraits, still-life compositions, products, or any other static or still subjects.

▶ **Continuous low-speed shooting mode (⧉L).** In this mode, the camera shoots at up to 3 frames per second (fps) repeatedly while you hold down the shutter-release button. This is a good mode to use when trying to capture subjects that are not moving too quickly.

▶ **Continuous high-speed shooting mode (⧉H).** When you select this mode, the D3300 shoots up to 5 fps while you press and hold the shutter-release button. This mode is for shooting fast action and sequence shots, or trying to capture a fleeting moment that may never happen again. For best results, you should set the shutter speed to at least 1/250 second and use a fast memory card. Shooting at 1/250 or faster allows you to be sure that you get the full frame-rate speed. Once the buffer is full, the frame rate drops, and then resumes after the buffer flushes and the data has been written to the card. Using a faster-rated memory card allows the camera to clear the buffer more quickly.

▶ **Quiet shutter release mode (Q).** This mode operates similar to Single-frame shooting mode (S), except that when you hold down the shutter-release button, the reflex mirror is held up in place until you release the button. Normally, the shutter sound emits when the mirror flips up, the shutter opens and closes, and the mirror flips down. In Quiet shutter release mode (**Q**), you can split the noise into two distinct sounds: one when the mirror flips up and the shutter opens, and another when the mirror flips down when you release the shutter-release button. In theory, this makes the shutter-release button half as noisy. The idea behind Quiet shutter release mode (**Q**) is that the photographer can snap a photo and move to another area before releasing the reflex mirror to the down position. In practice, however, the Quiet shutter release mode (**Q**) isn't much quieter than Single-frame mode (S).

▶ **Self-timer release mode (☉).** The self-timer is a handy option that allows a delay between the pressing of the shutter-release button and the actual release of the shutter. This allows you to quickly jump into the frame for self-portraits or to join in on group shots. This feature is also useful when capturing timed exposures, as it reduces camera shake caused by pressing the shutter-release button when the camera is on a tripod. Here, you can select the length of the delay (2, 5, 10, or 20 seconds), and the number of shots (1 through 9). If the number of shots is more than 1, the camera shoots the selected number of frames at 4-second intervals.

▶ **Remote mode (⬛◎)))).** You use this mode with the ML-L3 wireless remote, available separately from Nikon. This inexpensive remote uses infrared (IR) signals sent to infrared receivers, on the front and rear of the D3300. This eliminates the need to press the shutter-release button on the camera. You can then choose one of the following options:

- **Delayed remote mode (◎2s).** This provides a 2-second delay from the time that you press the ML-L3 button before the shutter releases.

- **Quick response remote mode (◎).** This immediately releases the shutter when you press the ML-L3 button. The shutter releases, regardless of whether the camera is in focus.

ISO Sensitivity

ISO, which stands for *International Organization for Standardization,* is the rating for the speed of film or, in digital terms, the sensitivity of the sensor. Because they are standardized, ISO numbers allow you to be sure that when you shoot at ISO 100, you get the same exposure, no matter which camera you are using.

The D3300 doesn't have a dedicated button to change the ISO setting, but by default the Function button (**Fn**) is set to change the ISO sensitivity when you press it and rotate the Command dial. Alternately, you change the ISO sensitivity in the Info display's Edit menu screen. To access it, press the *i* button (*i*), and then use the multi-selector to navigate to the ISO sensitivity option that you want. Press the multi-selector left (◀) or right (▶) to change the settings. When you finish, press the OK button (**OK**). A third way to adjust the ISO is in the Shooting menu (◻) under the ISO sensitivity settings option.

The D3300 has a native ISO range of 100 to 12,800. In addition to these standard ISO settings, the D3300 also offers a setting that extends the available range of the ISO so you can shoot in the darkest of settings. This option is labeled with an H for high speed. The high-speed ISO option is Hi1. This setting gives you up to ISO 25,600.

It should be noted that using the Hi1 setting does not produce optimal results. You will notice a large amount of grain and noise in your images. When set to the Hi1 option, the camera uses the processor to increase exposure (as opposed to amplifying the signal from the sensor). You can perform these same operations manually in your favorite RAW convertor with better accuracy. For this reason, I don't recommend using the extended ISO settings unless you are shooting JPEGs and capturing the image is of the utmost importance.

Auto ISO

The Auto ISO setting (**AUTO**) automatically adjusts the ISO for you in locations in which the light changes, giving you one less setting to worry about. Nikon has made the Auto ISO feature available for a few years now, and I am a big proponent of it. I find that this setting results in many more low-noise images when shooting in conditions where the lighting is changing rapidly.

Auto ISO (**AUTO**) is more intuitive and smarter than it was when first introduced. To turn on Auto ISO (**AUTO**), go to the Shooting menu (**📷**), select ISO sensitivity settings, and then set the Auto ISO sensitivity control to On. There is an Auto setting that selects the threshold for shutter speed versus ISO based on focal length, which is especially handy when using a zoom lens (which most people do these days).

Be sure to set the following options in the Shooting menu (**📷**) under the ISO sensitivity settings option:

- ▶ **Maximum sensitivity.** Choose an ISO setting that allows you to get an acceptable amount of noise in your image. If you're not concerned about noisy images, then you can set it all the way up to Hi1. If you need your images to have less noise, you can choose a lower ISO; the choices are from ISO 200 to Hi1 in 1-stop increments.

- ▶ **Minimum shutter speed.** This setting determines when the camera adjusts the ISO to a higher level. At the default, the camera increases the ISO when the shutter speed falls below 1/30 second. If you're using a longer lens or you're photographing moving subjects, you may need a faster shutter speed. In that case, you can set the minimum shutter speed up to 1/2000 second. On the other hand, if you're not concerned about camera shake, or if you're using a tripod, you can set a shutter speed as slow as 1 second. When using the Auto ISO setting (**AUTO**), the camera chooses the shutter speed based on the focal length of the lens (provided the lens has a CPU). When you use Auto ISO (**AUTO**), you can specify whether the camera gives priority to shutter speed or ISO sensitivity. Slower prioritizes shutter speed and faster prioritizes ISO sensitivity.

Noise reduction

Noise starts becoming noticeable in images taken with the D3300 when you shoot above ISO 1600 or use long exposure times. To solve the problem of image noise, most camera manufacturers have built-in noise reduction (NR) features. Noise reduction is turned on in the Shooting menu (**📷**). The D3300 applies Noise Reduction at all ISO settings, but until the ISO sensitivity is cranked up substantially it's generally unnoticeable.

The camera applies a noise reduction algorithm to any shot taken with a long exposure (1 second or more). Basically, the camera takes another exposure, this time with the shutter closed, and compares the noise from this dark image to the original one. The camera then applies the noise reduction, which takes about the same amount of time to process as the length of the shutter speed; therefore, you can expect it to take about double the amount of time it takes to make one exposure. This is referred to as *dark frame noise reduction.*

While the camera applies noise reduction, the viewfinder displays the blinking Noise Reduction icon (Job nr). You cannot take additional images until this process is finished. If you switch the camera off before the NR is finished, noise reduction is not applied.

> **NOTE** You can turn Long exposure Noise Reduction on or off in the Shooting menu.

When photographing at high ISO sensitivity, the camera runs any image shot at ISO 800 or higher through the noise reduction algorithm. This feature works by reducing the coloring in the chrominance of the noise and slightly softening the image to reduce the luminance noise.

> **NOTE** *Chrominance* refers to the color of noise and usually appears more prominently in the shadow areas as colored dots, and *luminance* refers to the size and shape of the noise and is typically visible throughout the image as speckles.

You should also keep in mind that Noise Reduction slows down the processing of your images. This can reduce the capacity of the buffer, causing the frame rate to slow down when you shoot in the Continuous high-speed (⊒H) or Continuous low-speed (⊒L) shooting modes.

When you turn off Noise Reduction, the camera still applies noise reduction to images shot at ISO 2500 and higher, although the amount is less than when you set the camera to Low with Noise Reduction on.

> **NOTE** When shooting in NEF (RAW), the camera doesn't apply any noise reduction to the data, but NR is tagged in the file. To apply the in-camera noise reduction to the final image, you must open and edit the RAW file in Nikon software.

For the most part, I do not use in-camera noise reduction. In my opinion, even at the lowest setting, the camera is very aggressive when applying noise reduction, and for that reason, there is a loss of detail. For most people, this is a minor quibble and not very noticeable, but I'd rather keep all available detail in my images and apply noise reduction in post-processing. This way, I can decide how much to reduce the chrominance and luminance rather than letting the camera do it. One thing to note, however, is that even when the in-camera noise reduction is set to Off, a small amount of noise reduction is applied. This NR is much less than the amount applied if the option is turned on.

NOTE Adobe Camera Raw and other image-editing software include proprietary noise reduction.

White Balance

Light, whether from sunlight, a light bulb, a fluorescent light, or a flash, has a specific color. The Kelvin scale is used to measure these colors. A color's measurement is its *color temperature.* The white balance (**WB**) allows you to adjust the camera so your images look natural, regardless of the light source. Given that white is most dramatically affected by the color temperature of a light source, this is what you base your settings on — hence the term *white balance.* You can change the white balance in the Shooting or Info edit menus.

You may still wonder how a color can have a temperature. Once you understand the Kelvin scale, things will make a little more sense.

The Kelvin scale

Kelvin is a temperature scale, normally used in the fields of physics and astronomy, where absolute zero (0K) denotes the absence of all heat energy. The concept is based on a theoretical object called a *black body radiator.* As this black body radiator is heated, it starts to glow. When it reaches a certain temperature, it glows a specific color. It is akin to heating a bar of iron with a torch. As the iron gets hotter it turns red, then yellow, and then eventually white before it reaches its melting point (although the theoretical black body does not have a melting point).

The concept of Kelvin and color temperature is tricky as it is the opposite of what you likely think of as *warm* and *cool* colors. For example, on the Kelvin scale, red is the lowest temperature, increasing through orange, yellow, white, and to shades of blue, which are the highest temperatures. Humans tend to perceive reds, oranges, and yellows as warmer, and white and bluish colors as colder. However, physically speaking, as defined by the Kelvin scale, the opposite is true.

White balance settings

Now that you know a little about the Kelvin scale, you can begin to explore the white balance settings. White balance is so important because it helps ensure that your images have a natural look. When you deal with different lighting sources, the color temperature of the source can have a drastic effect on the coloring of the subject. For example, a standard light bulb casts a very yellow light; if the camera doesn't add a bluish cast to compensate for the color temperature of the light bulb, the subject can look overly yellow or amber.

To adjust for the colorcast of the light source, the camera introduces a colorcast of the complete opposite color temperature. For example, to combat the green color of a fluorescent lamp, the camera introduces a slight magenta cast to neutralize the green. Here are the white balance settings on the D3300:

▶ **Automatic white balance setting (AUTO).** This setting is good for most circumstances. The camera takes a reading of the ambient light and makes an automatic adjustment. This setting also works well when you use a Nikon CLS-compatible Speedlight because the camera calculates the color temperature to match the flash output.

▶ **Incandescent white balance setting (✹).** Use this setting when the lighting comes from a standard household light bulb with a tungsten filament. In 2012, the United States began phasing out the production of higher wattage light bulbs (75 to 100W), and as of January 2014, the production of 40 to 60W bulbs has ceased, so this setting will likely become less necessary as supplies dwindle.

▶ **Fluorescent white balance setting (✵).** This setting is ideal when the lighting is coming from a fluorescent-type lamp or compact fluorescent light bulb. You can also adjust for different types of fluorescents, including high-pressure sodium and mercury-vapor lamps. To make this adjustment, go to the Shooting menu (⬛), choose White balance, and then choose Fluorescent. From there, use the multi-selector to choose one of the seven types of lamps.

▶ **Direct sunlight white balance setting (☀).** Use this setting when shooting outdoors in the sunlight.

▶ **Flash white balance setting (⚡).** This setting is ideal when using the built-in flash, a hot-shoe Speedlight, or external strobes.

▶ **Cloudy white balance setting (☁).** Use this white balance setting under overcast skies.

▶ **Shade white balance setting (⌂).** When you shoot in the shade of a tree, a building, an overhang, a bridge, or any location in which the sun is out but blocked, use this setting.

▶ **Preset manual white balance setting (PrE).** When you use this setting, you choose a neutral object to measure for the white balance. It's best to choose an object that is either white or light gray. There are some accessories, such as a gray card (which is included in this book) and the ExpoDisc, that you can use to set the white balance. To use the gray card, simply place it in the scene and take the reading from it. To use the ExpoDisc, attach it to the front of the lens like a filter, and then point the lens at the light source to set your white balance (**WB**). The Preset manual white balance setting (PrE) works best in difficult lighting situations, such as mixed lighting. *Mixed lighting* means there are two sources lighting a scene. I usually use this setting when photographing with my studio strobes.

Figure 2.13 and figure 2.14 show the difference that white balance settings can make to your images.

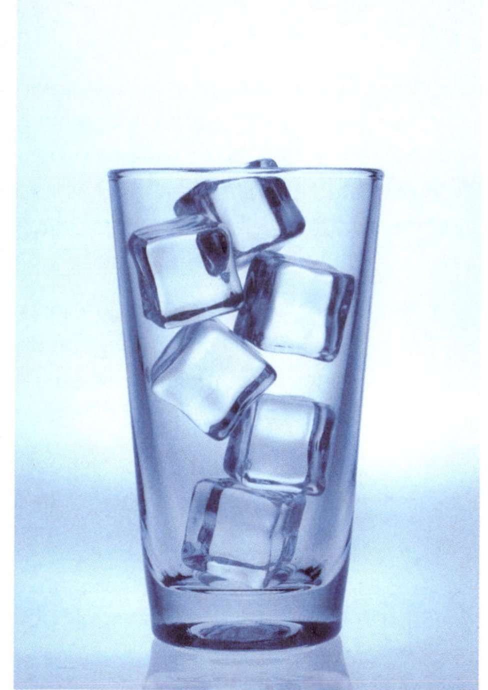

2.13 This shot was taken using the Incandescent white balance setting. Exposure: ISO 200, f/22, 1/200 second using a Nikon 28–70mm f/2.8 D AF-S.

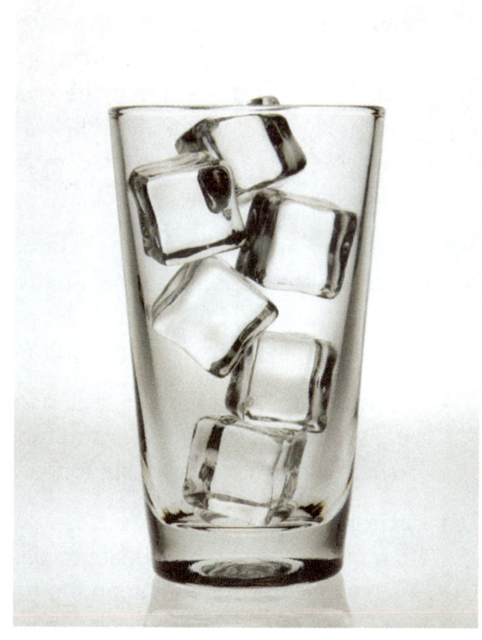

2.14 This shot was taken using a custom white balance set to the white backdrop using the Preset Manual white balance setting. Exposure: ISO 200, f/22, 1/200 second using a Nikon 28–70mm f/2.8 D AF-S.

Picture Controls

The Picture Control feature allows you to adjust your image settings quickly, including sharpening, contrast, brightness, saturation, and hue, based on your shooting needs. Picture Controls are only adjustable when using the Programmed auto (**P**), Shutter-priority auto (**S**), Aperture-priority auto (**A**), or Manual (**M**) modes because they are set automatically in the scene modes. To set Picture Controls, press the *i* button (**i**) to display the Info edit menu, and then use the multi-selector to navigate to the Picture Control option.

The D3300 comes with the following six Picture Controls:

- **Standard (SD).** This setting applies slight sharpening, and a small boost of contrast and saturation. This is the recommended setting for most shooting situations.

- **Neutral (NL).** The Neutral setting (NL) applies a small amount of sharpening and no other modifications to the image. This setting is preferable if you apply extensive post-processing to your images.

- **Vivid (VI).** Use this setting to give your image a fair amount of sharpening and boost the contrast and saturation. This setting is recommended for printing directly from the camera or memory card, as well as for shooting landscapes. Personally, I feel that this mode is a little too saturated and often results in unnatural color tones. It is not ideal for portraits because it usually doesn't reproduce skin tones accurately.

- **Monochrome (MC).** As the name implies, this option makes an image monochrome. This doesn't simply mean black and white; you can also simulate photo filters and toned images such as sepia, cyanotype, and more. You can also adjust the settings for sharpening, contrast, and brightness.

- **Portrait (PT).** The Portrait setting (PT) gives you just a small amount of sharpening, which gives the skin a smoother appearance. The colors are slightly muted to help achieve realistic skin tones.

- **Landscape (LS).** The Landscape setting (LS) is ideal for shooting landscapes and natural vistas. It appears to be very similar to the Vivid Picture Control (VI) with a little more boost added to the blues and greens.

You can customize all of the original Picture Controls to suit your personal preferences. There are myriad options, such as giving the images more sharpening and less contrast.

NOTE Although you can adjust the original Picture Controls, you cannot save over them, so there is no need to worry about losing them.

You can choose from the following customizations:

- **Quick adjust.** This option works with the Standard (⊡SD), Vivid (⊡VI), Portrait (⊡PT), and Landscape (⊡LS) Picture Controls. It exaggerates or de-emphasizes the effect of the Picture Control in use. You can set Quick adjust from −2 to +2.

- **Sharpness.** This setting controls the apparent sharpness of your images. You can adjust this setting from 0 to 9, with 9 being the highest level of sharpness. You can also set this option to Auto (A) to allow the camera's imaging processor to decide how much sharpening to apply.

- **Contrast.** This setting controls the amount of contrast applied to your images. In photos of scenes with high contrast (sunny days), you may want to adjust the contrast down; in scenes with low contrast, you may want to add some contrast by adjusting the settings up. You can set the Contrast from −3 to +3, or to A.

- **Brightness.** This setting adds or subtracts from the overall brightness of your image. You can choose 0 (default), +, or −.

- **Saturation.** This setting controls how vivid or bright the colors are in your images. You can set it between −3 and +3, or to A. This option is not available in the Monochrome Picture Control setting (⊡MC).

> **NOTE** The Brightness and Saturation options are unavailable when you turn on Active D-Lighting (**ADL**).

- **Hue.** This setting controls how your colors look. You can choose from −3 to +3. Positive numbers make the reds look more orange, the blues look more purple, and the greens look more blue. Negative numbers make the reds look more purple, the greens look more yellow, and the blues look more green. This setting is not available in the Monochrome Picture Control setting (⊡MC). I highly recommend leaving it at the default setting of zero.

- **Filter effects.** This setting is only available when you set your D3300 to the Monochrome Picture Control setting (⊡MC). The monochrome filters approximate those traditionally used with black-and-white film, and increase contrast or create special effects. The following are the available Monochrome filter effects:
  - **Yellow.** This adds a low level of contrast. It causes the sky to appear slightly darker than normal and anything yellow to appear lighter. It is also used to optimize contrast for brighter skin tones.
  - **Orange.** This adds a medium amount of contrast. The sky appears darker, giving greater separation between the clouds. Orange objects appear light gray.

- **Red.** This adds a large amount of contrast, drastically darkening the sky while allowing the clouds to remain white. Red objects appear lighter than normal.

- **Green.** This darkens the sky and lightens any green plant life. You can use this color filter for portraits as it softens skin tones.

▶ **Toning.** Toning adds a color tint to your monochrome images. The following toning options are available:

- **B&W.** The black-and-white option simulates the traditional black-and-white film prints developed in a darkroom. The camera records the image in black, white, and shades of gray. This mode is suitable when the color of the subject is not important. You can use it for artistic purposes or, as with the Sepia option, to give your image an antique or vintage look.

- **Sepia.** The Sepia color option duplicates a photographic toning process that is based on a traditional darkroom technique using silver-based black-and-white prints. Sepia-toning a photographic image requires replacing the silver in the emulsion of the photo paper with a different silver compound, thus changing the color, or *tone,* of the photograph. Antique photographs generally underwent this type of toning; therefore, the sepia color option makes the images look reddish-brown, giving them an antique look. You may want to use this option to convey a feeling of antiquity or nostalgia in your photograph. This option works well with portraits, as well as still life and architectural images. You can also adjust the saturation of the toning from 1 to 7, with 4 being the default and the middle ground.

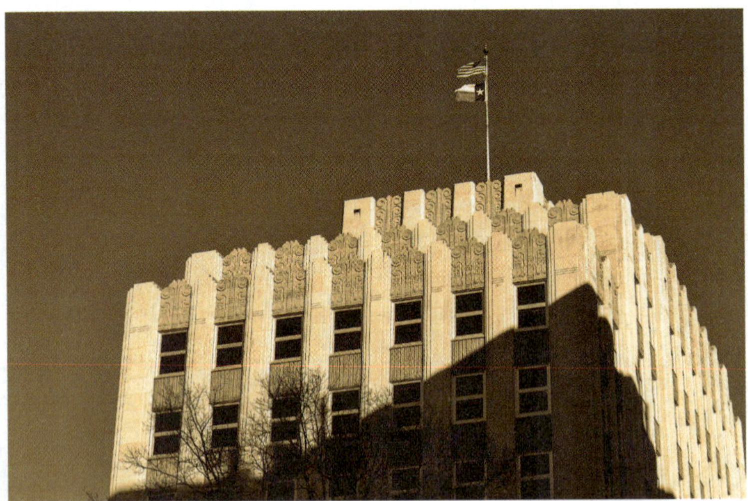

2.15 A Sepia-toned image. Exposure: ISO 400, f/13, 1/800 second using a Sigma 30mm f/1.4 | A.

- **Cyanotype.** The cyanotype is another old photographic printing process. When the image is exposed to the light, the chemicals that make up the cyanotype turn deep blue. This method was used to create the first blueprints and was later adapted to photography. The images you take in this setting are in shades of cyan. Because cyan is considered a cool color, this mode is also referred to as cool. You can use this mode to make very interesting and artistic images. You can also adjust the saturation of the toning from 1 to 7, with 4 being the default setting.

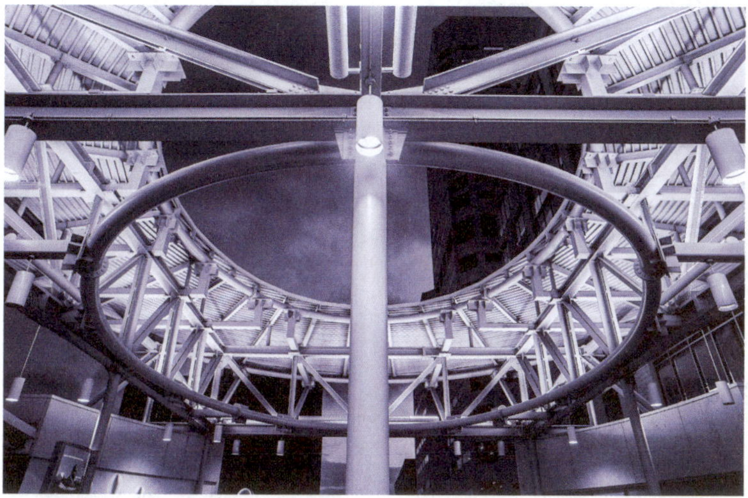

2.16 An image with Cyanotype applied. Exposure: ISO 400, f/13, 1/800 second using a Sigma 30mm f/1.4 | A.

- **Color toning.** You can also choose to add colors to your monochrome images. Although color toning is similar to the Sepia and Cyanotype toning options, it isn't based on traditional photographic processes. It simply involves adding a colorcast to a black-and-white image. You can choose from seven color options: red, yellow, green, blue-green, blue, purple-blue, and red-purple. As with Sepia and Cyanotype, you can adjust the saturation of these colors.

To customize an original Picture Control, follow these steps:

1. **Go to the Set Picture Control option in the Shooting menu (⬛), and then press the multi-selector right (▶).**

2. **Choose the Picture Control that you want to adjust.** Choose the Neutral (⬛NL) or Standard (⬛SD) Picture Control settings if you want to make smaller changes, because these have relatively low settings (contrast, saturation, and so on). To

make bigger changes to color and sharpness, select the Vivid Picture Control setting (⌸VI). To adjust monochrome images, choose the Monochrome Picture
Control setting (⌸MC), and then press the multi-selector right (▶).

3. **Press the multi-selector up (▲) or down (▼) to highlight the setting that
   you want to adjust (such as sharpening, contrast, brightness, and so on).**
   When the desired setting is highlighted, press the multi-selector left (◀) or right
   (▶) to adjust it. Repeat this step until you've adjusted all settings to suit your
   preference.

4. **Press the OK button (OK) to save the settings.**

To return the Picture Control to the default setting, follow steps 1 and 2, and then
press Delete (🗑). A dialog box appears asking for confirmation. Select Yes to return to
the default setting or No to continue to use the Picture Control with the current
settings.

> **NOTE** When you alter an original Picture Control setting, an asterisk appears
> next to it, such as SD*, VI*, and so on.

File Formats, Size, and Compression

The D3300 creates and stores image data in two types of files: NEF (or RAW) and
JPEG. You can choose to shoot one or the other or both at the same time. Each file
type has its own strengths and weaknesses although neither type is the absolute correct type to shoot. For ease of use, more manageable file sizes, and compatibility with
image-editing software (especially older software), JPEGs are great. The drawback is
that you lose a lot of image information when the raw data from the sensor is converted into a JPEG file.

On the other side of the equation is the NEF or RAW file. This file format stores all of
the image data recorded by the sensor as the exposure is made. The imaging processor makes note of the camera settings, but doesn't make any final or lasting changes
to the sensor data. This gives you more flexibility during the editing process. RAW files
are much larger than JPEGs because they contain more information. A major drawback is that each camera's RAW files are proprietary and you may need to upgrade
your image-editing software to the latest version to use the RAW file.

Each file type has compression algorithms applied to keep file sizes as small as possible, but with JPEGs, you can also set the camera to record a smaller image size by
downsampling. I cover all of this and more in the following sections.

NEF (RAW)

Nikon RAW files are referred to as NEF, which stands for *Nikon Electronic Format*. RAW files contain all the image data acquired by the camera's sensor. When a JPEG is created, the camera applies different settings to the image, such as white balance, sharpness, noise reduction, and so on. When you save the JPEG, the rest of the unused image data is discarded to help reduce the file size. With a RAW file, this image data is saved so it can be used more extensively in post-processing. In some ways a RAW file is like a *digital negative* because you use it in the same way as a traditional photographic negative; that is, you take the RAW information and process it to create your final image.

Although some of the same settings are tagged to the RAW file (white balance, sharpening, saturation, and so on), these settings aren't fixed and applied as they are in a JPEG file. This way, when you import the RAW file into your favorite RAW converter, you can make changes to these settings without detrimental effects. Capturing your images in RAW format allows you to be more flexible when post-processing them, and generally gives you more control over the quality of the images.

JPEG

JPEG, which stands for *Joint Photographic Experts Group,* is a method of compressing photographic files, as well as the name of the file format that supports this type of compression. The JPEG is the most common type of file used to save images on digital cameras. Due to the small size of the file that is created and the relatively good image quality it produces, JPEG has become the default file format for most digital cameras.

The JPEG compression format was developed because of the immense file sizes that digital images produce. Photographic files contain millions of separate colors, and each individual color is assigned a number; therefore, the files contain vast amounts of data, which makes them quite large.

JPEG Compression Explained

In the early days of digital imaging, the huge file sizes and relatively small storage capacity of computers made it almost impossible for most people to store images. Not terribly long ago, a standard laptop hard drive was only about 5GB. For people to efficiently store images, they needed a file format that could be compressed without losing too much of the image data during reconstruction. Enter the Joint Photographic Experts Group. This group of experts came in and designed what is now known as the JPEG.

continued

---

continued

JPEG compression is a very complicated process involving many mathematical equations, but the steps involved can be explained quite simply. The first thing the JPEG process does is break down the image into 8-x-8–pixel blocks. and the RGB values are changed to represent luminance and chrominance values. The luminance value describes the brightness of the color while the chrominance value describes the hue.

Once the luminance and chrominance values have been established, the data is run through what is known as the *Discrete Cosine Transform* (DCT). This is the basis of the compression algorithm. Essentially, the DCT takes the information for the 8-x-8 block of pixels and assigns it an average number because, for the most part, the changes in the luminance and chrominance values will not be drastic in such a small part of the image.

The next step involves quantizing the coefficient numbers that were derived from the luminance and chrominance values by the DCT. *Quantizing* is the process of rounding off numbers. This is where file compression comes in. How much the file is compressed depends on the quantization matrix. The *quantization matrix* defines how much the information is compressed by dividing the coefficients by a quantizing factor. The larger the number of the quantizing factor, the higher the quality (and therefore, the less compression). This is what is going on in Photoshop when you save a file as a JPEG and the program asks you to set the quality; you are simply defining the quantizing factor.

Once the numbers are quantized, they are run through a binary encoder that converts the numbers to the 1s and 0s our computers love so much. You now have a compressed file that is on average about one-quarter of the size of an uncompressed file.

JPEG compression is known as a *lossy* compression because when the files are closed and compressed, they lose information. For the most part, this loss of information is imperceptible to the human eye. A bigger issue to consider with JPEGs comes from what is known as *generation loss*. Every time you open, alter, and save a JPEG, it loses a small amount of detail. After doing this multiple times, the image's quality starts to deteriorate, as less and less information becomes available. Eventually the image may start to look pixelated or jagged (this is known as a *JPEG artifact*). Obviously, this can be a problem, but you would have to open, alter, and resave the JPEG many hundreds of times before you would notice a reduction in image quality, provided you save at high-quality settings.

Image size

When saving to JPEG format, the D3300 allows you to choose an image size. Reducing the image size is like reducing the resolution on your camera; it allows you to fit more images on the memory card. The size you choose depends on what your output is going to be. If you know you will be printing your images at a large size, you definitely want to record large JPEGs. If you're going to print at a smaller size (8 × 10 or 5 × 7), you can get away with recording at the Medium or Small setting. Image size is expressed in pixel dimensions. The large JPEG setting records your images at 6000 × 4000 pixels; this gives you a file that is equivalent to about 24 megapixels. Medium size gives you an image of 4496 × 3000 pixels, which is in effect the same as a 13.5-megapixel image. The small size gives you a dimension of 2992 × 2000 pixels, which gives you about a 6-megapixel image.

To determine what size print you can make from your file, you need to do a little math. Simply divide the pixel height and width of the file size by the intended output resolution in pixels-per-inch (ppi). Higher ppi numbers give more detailed prints. Most photo-quality printers print from 240ppi to 300ppi, the latter being the most common and the best setting to use for just about all of your photo printing needs. So, for example, at the largest size, the D3300 gives you a 24MP image at 6000 × 4000 pixels. Divide 6000 by 300 and 4000 by 300 and you get approximately 20 × 13 inches. See Table 2.1 for actual print sizes for each resolution, as well as the closest common print sizes that correspond to the nearest actual measurements. Keep in mind that these sizes are at 300ppi.

Table 2.1 Print Sizes

Size	Actual print size (inches)	Common print size (inches)
Large 6000 × 4000	20 × 13	17 × 11
Medium 4496 × 3000	15 × 10	14 × 11
Small 2992 × 2000	10 × 6.7	10 × 8

You can select the Image size using the Info edit option by pressing the *i* button (🛈) or alternatively in the Shooting menu (📷).

> **NOTE** You can only change the image size when you shoot in the JPEG file format; RAW files record only at the largest size.

Image quality

With JPEGs, in addition to the size setting, which changes the pixel dimension, you have the Quality setting, which determines the compression ratio that is applied to your JPEG image. Your choices are Fine, Normal, and Basic. JPEG Fine files are compressed to approximately 1:4, Normal files are compressed to about 1:8, and Basic files are compressed to about 1:16.

RAW versus JPEG

Choosing RAW or JPEG files depends on the final output of the file. You don't have to choose one file format and stick with it. You can change the settings to suit your needs, or you can choose to record both RAW and JPEG simultaneously.

Here are some reasons to shoot JPEGs:

▶ **Small file size.** JPEGs are much smaller than RAW files; therefore, you can fit many more of them on your memory card and later on your computer's hard drive. If space limitations are a problem, shooting JPEG allows you to get more images in less space.

▶ **Printing straight from the camera.** RAW files can't be printed without first being converted to JPEG (which you can do in-camera with the D3300).

▶ **Continuous shooting.** JPEG files are smaller than RAW files, so they don't fill up the camera's buffer as quickly, allowing you longer bursts without slowing the frame rate.

▶ **Less post-processing.** If you're confident in your ability to get the image perfect at capture, you can save time by not having to process the image in a RAW converter and go straight to JPEG.

Here are some reasons to shoot RAW files:

▶ **More detail and exposure latitude.** The sensor captures more highlight and shadow detail in RAW files, which can be retrieved during post-processing, if needed.

▶ **16-bit images.** The D3300 captures RAW images in 12 bits. When converting a file using Adobe Camera Raw (ACR) or Nikon Capture NX 2, you can save your images as 16-bit files. When the information is written to JPEG in the camera, the JPEG is saved as an 8-bit file. RAW gives you the option of working with more colors in post-processing.

▶ **White balance.** The white balance setting is tagged in the RAW file, but it isn't fixed in the image data. Changing the white balance on a JPEG image can cause posterization, and usually doesn't yield the best results. Changing the white balance settings of a RAW file doesn't degrade the image.

▶ **Sharpening and saturation.** These settings are also tagged in the RAW file, but not applied to the actual image data. You can add these settings in post-processing to your own specifications.

▶ **Image quality.** Because the RAW file is unfinished, you can make many changes to the details of the image without any degradation of quality.

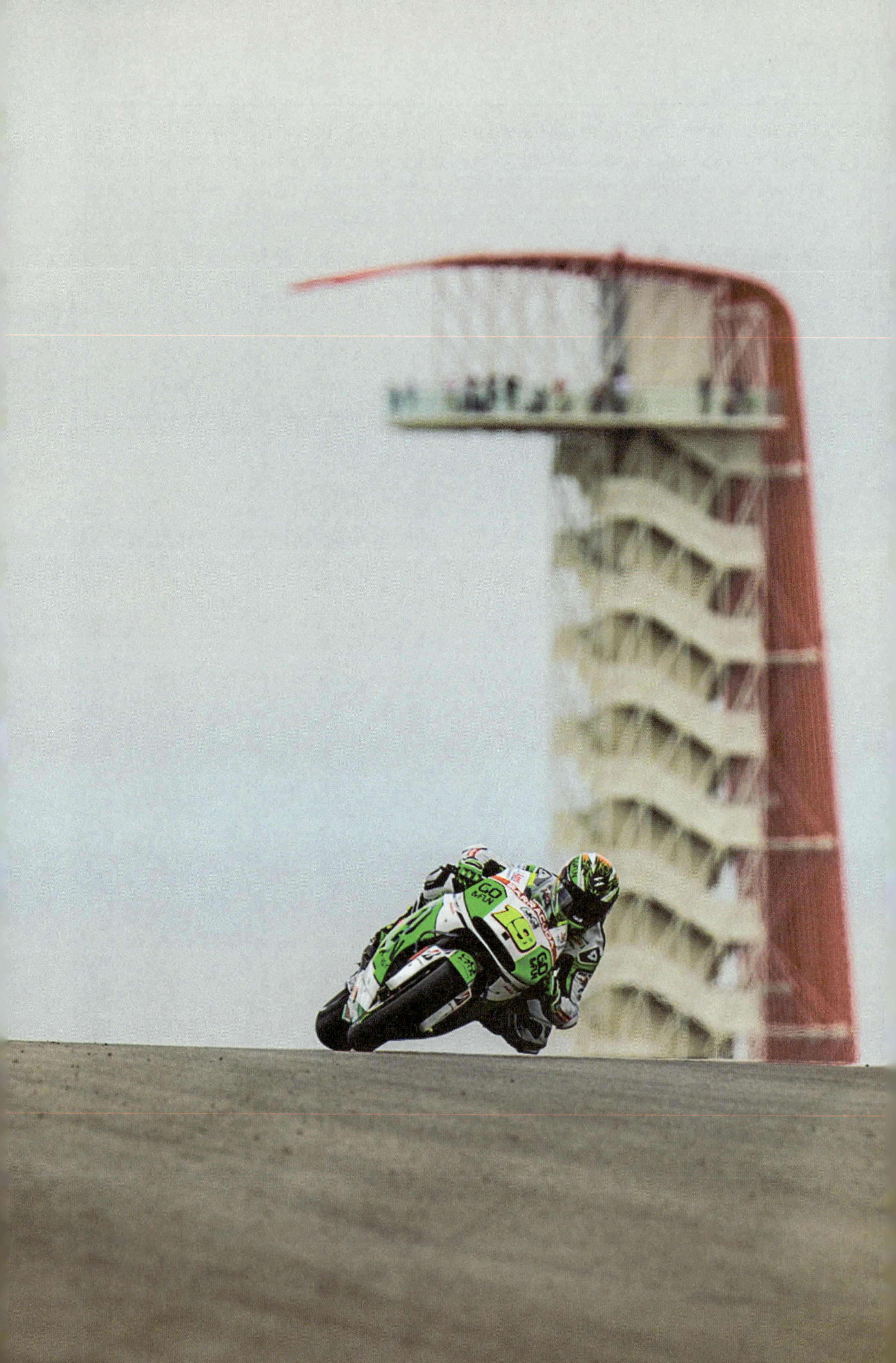

CHAPTER 3

Setting up the Nikon D3300

The D3300 is a small camera, but it has quite a few buttons that are used for setting some of the most frequently accessed options. The D3300 also has several settings that can only be accessed by the menu system. You need to become familiar with the menu if you want to change important settings on the fly. If you're constantly searching through the menu for the right settings, you risk losing shots.

Luckily, many of the most important settings are available quickly with a press of the *i* button (*i*), but there are many options that you can set to create a camera experience that is much more intuitive to you personally.

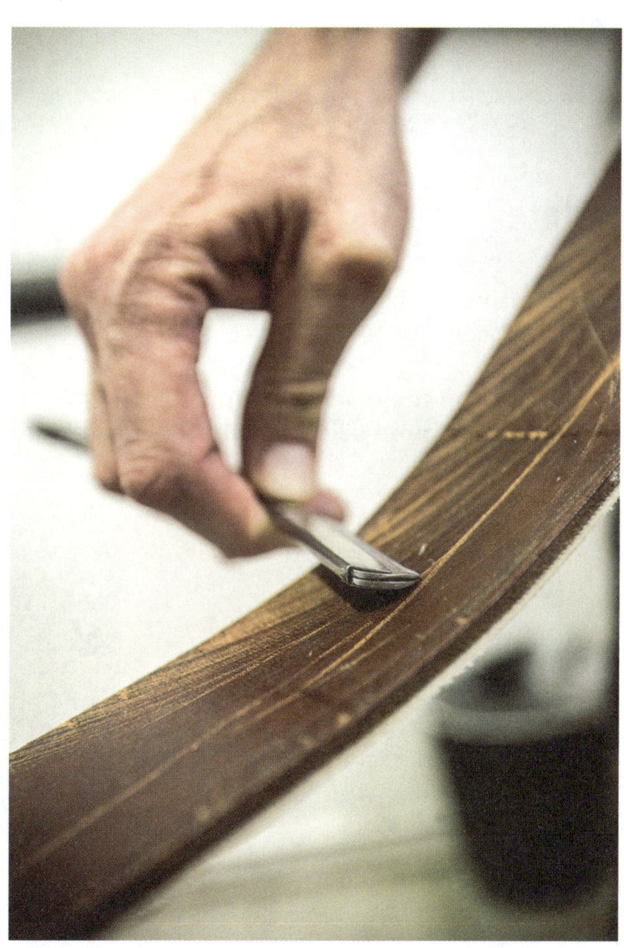

Setting up your camera effectively allows you to focus on your art.

The Playback Menu

The Playback menu (▶) displays options that allow you to control how your images are stored and reviewed. You can also select how the camera displays the images during image review, and what information is displayed while reviewing your images. Press the Menu button (MENU), and then use the multi-selector up (▲) or down (▼) to highlight the Playback menu (▶). Then press the OK button (OK) or multi-selector right (▶) to access the options.

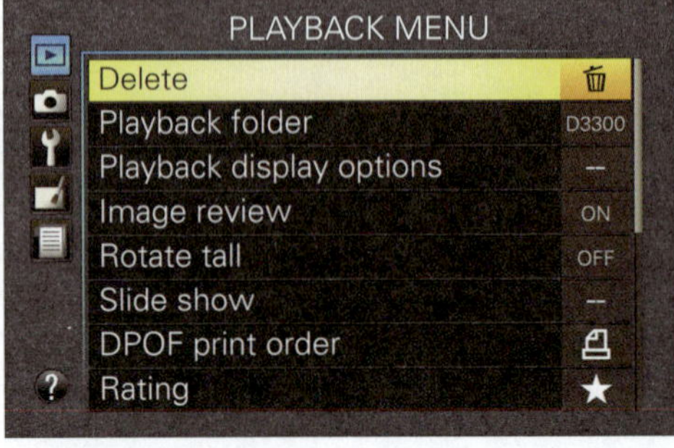

3.1 The Playback menu.

Delete

The Delete option allows you to delete selected images from your memory card, delete images from a certain date, or delete all of the images at once. To delete selected images, follow these steps:

1. **Press the multi-selector right (▶), highlight Selected (default), and then press the multi-selector right (▶) again.** The camera displays an image selection screen.

2. **Press the Thumbnail button (▦) to set the image or images that you want to delete.** You can also press the Zoom in button (🔍) to review an image close up before deleting it. When you select the image for deletion, the trash can symbol (🗑) appears in the upper-right corner of the thumbnail.

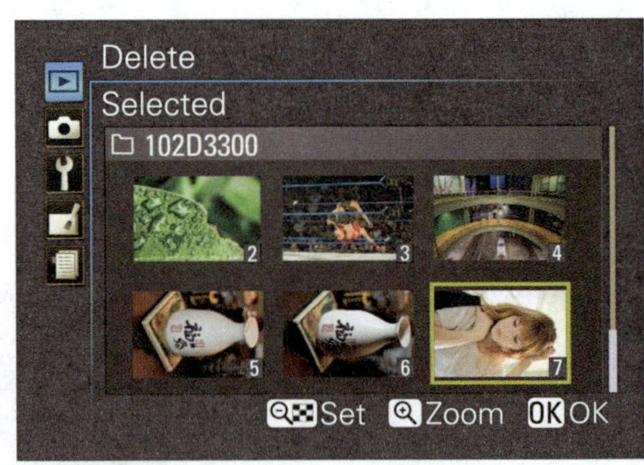

3.2 Selecting images to delete.

3. **Press the OK button (OK) to erase the selected images.** The camera asks you for confirmation before deleting the images.

4. **Select Yes, and then press the OK button (OK) to delete.** To cancel the deletion, highlight No (default), and then press the OK button (OK).

To delete images from a specific date, use the multi-selector to highlight Select date, and then press the multi-selector right (▶) or the OK button (OK). A list of dates (or a single date if you've only shot for one day on a card) appears; use the multi-selector to highlight a date, and then press the multi-selector right (▶) to select the date of the images for deletion. A check mark appears in the box next to the date of the images that will be deleted. You can press the Thumbnail button (🔍) to view the images taken on that date to confirm that you want to delete them. Press the OK button (**OK**) to set the date range for deletion. When you're ready to delete the images, press the OK button (**OK**) again; a dialog box appears, asking for confirmation. Select Yes to delete or No to cancel, and then press the OK button (**OK**).

To delete all images, use the multi-selector to highlight All, and then press the OK button (**OK**). Select Yes when asked to confirm the deletion, and then press the OK button (**OK**) to delete. To cancel the deletion, highlight No (default), and then press the OK button (**OK**).

Playback folder

The Nikon D3300 automatically creates folders in which to store your images. The main folder that the camera creates is called DCIM, and within this folder the camera creates a subfolder to store the images; the first subfolder the camera creates is labeled 100ND3300. After shooting 999 images, the camera automatically creates another folder, 101ND3300, and so on. If you have used the memory card in another camera and have not formatted it in the D3300, there will be additional folders on the card (ND3200, ND5300, and so on).

You can change the current folder using the Storage folder option in the Shooting menu. You have the following two folder choices:

- ▶ **Current.** This option displays images only from the folder to which the camera is currently saving. This feature is useful when you have multiple folders from different sessions. Using this setting allows you to preview only the most current images.

- ▶ **All.** This option plays back images from all folders that are on the memory card.

Playback display options

A lot of information is available when you review images, and the Playback display options allow you to customize that information. By default, playback displays the photo with some basic information (storage folder, file number, date and time, Image quality, and size) in a letterbox below.

There are two options from the main Playback display options. The first option is Additional photo info. Pressing the OK button (**OK**) brings up a submenu with the following options. You can select one, all, or any combination of the following options to change the information that is displayed.

► **None (image only).** As indicated, this shows the full-size image only, with no information at all.

► **Highlights.** When you activate this option, any highlights that are blown out will blink. If this happens, you may want to apply some exposure compensation or adjust your exposure to be sure to capture highlight detail.

► **RGB Histogram.** When you activate this option, you can view the separate histograms for the Red, Green, and Blue channels along with a standard luminance histogram.

► **Shooting Data.** This option allows you to review the shooting data (metering, exposure, lens focal length, and so on).

► **Overview.** This option shows a thumbnail version of the image with the luminance histogram, as well as general shooting data: shutter speed, aperture, ISO, and so on.

When you select any of these options, you can toggle through them by pressing the multi-selector up (▲) and/or down (▼).

> **NOTE** If GPS data has been obtained and applied, the camera displays an additional GPS data screen, which shows the Latitude, Longitude, Altitude, and Time.

The second option is much simpler. It's called Transition effects. You can set this option to On or Off. Setting the option to On causes the images to slide into place when scrolling through the images during playback. Turning it Off simply causes the next image to immediately appear.

Image review

The Image review option (refer to Figure 3.1) allows you to choose whether the image is shown on the LCD monitor immediately after you shoot it. When you turn this option off, you can view the image by pressing the Playback button (▶). Keeping this option off conserves battery power because the LCD monitor is actually the biggest drain on your battery. When shooting events with a lot of quickly changing action, such as sporting events and concerts, you may want to keep this option off. I have found that when shooting fast subjects, leaving the review on causes the camera to scroll through the image data instead of moving the focus point. This can cause you to lose important shots.

If you're shooting portraits or other shots where you are shooting single images, you can turn this option on. This allows you a chance to immediately review the image to check the exposure, framing, and focus.

Rotate tall

The D3300 has a built-in sensor that can tell whether the camera was rotated while you took the image. The Rotate tall option rotates images that you have shot in portrait orientation to display upright on the LCD screen. I usually keep this option set to Off because the portrait orientation image appears substantially smaller when displayed upright on the LCD screen.

The options are:

▶ **On.** The camera automatically rotates the image to be viewed while holding the camera in the standard upright position. When you turn this option on (and you set the Auto image rotation setting to On in the Setup menu [**Ψ**]), the camera orientation is recorded for use in image-editing software.

▶ **Off (default).** When you turn the auto-rotating function off, images taken in portrait orientation display sideways on the LCD screen in landscape orientation.

Slide show

The Slide show option allows you to display a slide show of images from the current active folder. You can use this feature to review the images that you have shot without having to use the multi-selector. This is also a good way to show friends or clients your images. You can connect the camera to an HDTV to view the slide show on a big screen. The following options are available:

▶ **Start.** This option simply starts the slide show. It plays back both still images and movies.

▶ **Image type.** This option allows you to select what kinds of files are played back. You can select Still images and movies, Still images only, Movies only, or by Rating.

▶ **Frame interval.** This option allows you to select how long the still images display. The options are 2, 3, 5, or 10 seconds.

▶ **Transition effects.** Setting the option to On causes the images to slide into place similar to the effect that you would see using a traditional slide projector.

While the slide show is in progress, you can press the multi-selector right(▶) to skip forward or left (◀) to skip back. Press the multi-selector up (▲) or down (▼) to view shooting information or histograms. You can also press the Menu button (MENU) to return to the Playback menu (▶), press the Playback button (▶) to end the slide show, or tap the shutter-release button lightly to ready the camera for shooting.

If you press the OK button (**OK**) while the slide show is in progress, the slide show pauses and offers options for restarting, changing the frame rate, or exiting the slide show. Press the multi-selector up (▲) or down (▼) to make your selection, and then press the OK button (**OK**).

DPOF print order

DPOF stands for Digital Print Order Format. This option allows you to select images to be printed directly from the camera. You can use this feature with DPOF-compatible printers or devices such as a photo kiosk at your local photo printing shop. This is a handy feature if you don't have a printer at home and you want to have prints made quickly, or if you do have a printer and want to print your photos without downloading them to your computer.

CAUTION DPOF can only be used with JPEG files. If there are no JPEGs on the card, this option is not available. If you shoot RAW files, you can use the RAW editing features in the Retouch menu (✐) to create a JPEG copy.

Follow these steps to create a print set:

1. **Use the multi-selector to choose the DPOF print order option, and then press the multi-selector right (▶) to enter the menu.**

2. **Use the multi-selector to highlight Select/Set, and then press the multi-selector right (▶) to view thumbnails.** You can press the Zoom in button (🔍) to view a larger preview of the selected image.

3. **Press the multi-selector right (▶) or left (◀) to highlight an image to print, and then press the Thumbnail button (▦) and multi-selector up (▲) to set the image and choose the number of prints.** You can choose from 1 to 99. The number of prints and a small printer icon appear on the thumbnail. Continue this procedure until you have selected all of the images that you want to print. Press the multi-selector down (▼) to reduce the number of prints and remove the image from the print set.

4. **Press the OK button (OK).** An imprint options menu appears with the following two options:

   - **Print shooting data.** Press the multi-selector right (▶) to set. Press the multi-selector right (▶) again to unset. A check mark appears in the box next to the menu option when the option is set. When you select this option, the shutter speed and aperture setting appear on the print.

- **Print date.** Press the multi-selector right (▶) to set. Press the multi-selector right (▶) again to unset. A check mark appears in the box next to the menu option when the option is set. When you select this option, the date the image was taken appears on the print.

5. **Press the OK button (OK).** This saves the Print order.

Rating

This is a feature that is new with the introduction of the D3300. It allows you to rate your images from 1 to 5 stars. Choosing this option from the menu screen brings up the image selection screen. Use the multi-selector to highlight the image you want to rate, press the Zoom in button (🔍) to inspect the image closer, press the OK button (OK) to select the image then use the multi-selector up (▲) or down (▼) to rate the image.

Once the image is rated, when it is imported to certain software such as Nikon's ViewNX2 or Lightroom, you can quickly find the images that you like the most.

Select to send to smart device

This option is only available if you're using the optional WU-1a Wi-Fi adapter. You can use the Nikon WMU app to send images to your smart device; this allows you to browse through the images on your camera and select the ones you want uploaded to your smart device instead of browsing the images on your smart device using the app. This way the images are immediately ready for transfer when you open the app on your device. This is done through the selection screen, which is similar to deleting and rating the image. If you have not attached a WU-1a adapter, then this option appears grayed out and cannot be accessed.

> **NOTE** When in Playback mode, you can quickly Rate, Retouch, or Select images to send to a smart device. To view an image full-size in Playback mode, press the *i* button (ℹ).

The Shooting Menu

The Shooting menu (📷) allows you to control how images are captured on your D3300. This includes ISO, image quality, white balance, Picture Controls, and more. In short, anything that affects the file or how the image is captured is set here. Some of the options in this menu, such as Image quality (**QUAL**), White balance (**WB**), ISO (**ISO**), and Picture Control (**⌷**), can also be set using external buttons, so you don't have to enter this menu to change them.

Reset shooting menu

Simply put, the Reset shooting menu option resets all of the Shooting Menu options covered in this section to their defaults. To do this, select this option, and then press the OK button (**OK**) or the multi-selector right (**▶**). Two options then appear: Yes and No. Select Yes to reset or No to cancel, and then press the OK button (**OK**) again.

Image quality

Select Image quality (see Figure 3.3) to change the image quality of a file. You can choose from the following options:

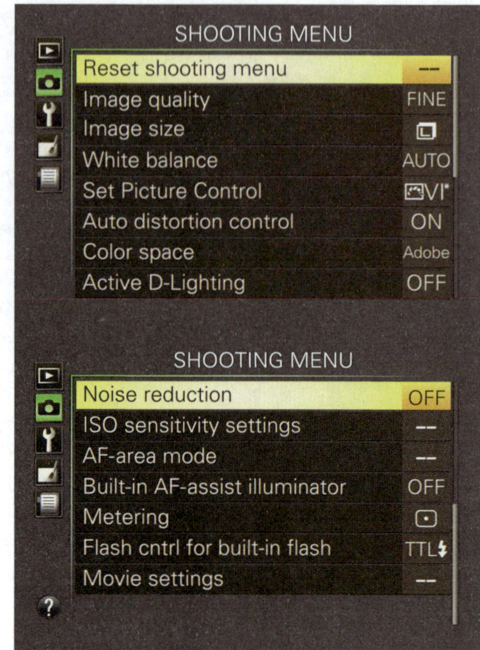

3.3 **The Shooting menu, shown in two screens.**

▶ **NEF (RAW) + JPEG fine.** This option saves two copies of the same image, one in RAW format and one in JPEG format with minimal compression.

▶ **NEF (RAW).** This option saves the images in RAW format with all of the 14-bit data from the sensor. You can adjust the RAW recording settings in the NEF (RAW) recording option in the Shooting menu (**◻**).

▶ **JPEG fine.** This option saves the images in JPEG format with minimal compression of about 1:4.

▶ **JPEG normal.** This option saves the images in JPEG format with standard compression of about 1:8.

▶ **JPEG basic.** This option saves the images in JPEG format with high compression of about 1:16.

CROSS REF For more detailed information on image quality, compression, and file formats, see Chapter 2.

Image size

The Image size option allows you to choose the size of JPEG files. You can change the image size depending on the intended output of the file. Choose from the following sizes:

- ▶ **Large.** This setting gives you a high-resolution image of 6000 × 4000 pixels, or 24 megapixels.

- ▶ **Medium.** This setting gives you a resolution of 4496 × 3000 pixels, or 13.5 megapixels.

- ▶ **Small.** This setting gives you a resolution of 2992 × 2000 pixels, or 6 megapixels.

Note that when the Image Quality is set to RAW only, this option is "grayed out" and not available because RAW files can only be recorded at the highest resolution.

White balance

You can change the white balance settings using this menu option. Select a white balance setting from the standard settings: Auto (**AUTO**), Incandescent (✷), Fluorescent (▦), Direct Sunlight (☀), Flash (⚡), Cloudy (☁), and Shade (🏠). You can also set a custom white balance using the Preset manual option (PrE).

CROSS REF For more detailed information on white balance settings and color temperature, see Chapter 2.

To select one of the standard settings, choose the White balance option (see Figure 3.3) from the Shooting menu (📷), use the multi-selector to highlight the preferred setting, and then press the multi-selector right (▶) or the OK button (**OK**). This displays a new screen that gives you the option to fine-tune the standard setting. This screen displays a grid that allows you to adjust the color tint of the selected white balance setting.

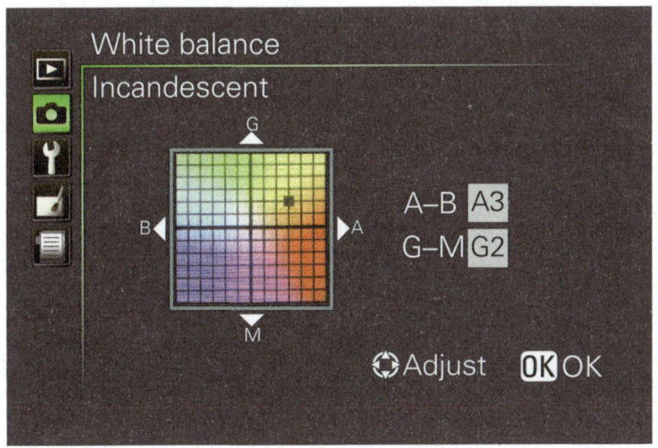

3.4 The White balance fine-tuning grid.

The horizontal axis of the grid allows you to adjust the color from amber to blue, making the image warmer or cooler, while the vertical axis of the grid allows you to change the tint by adding a magenta or green cast to the image. Using the multi-selector, you can choose a setting from 1 to 6 in either direction; additionally, you can add points along the horizontal and vertical axes simultaneously. For example, you can add 4 points of amber to give it a warmer tone and also add 2 points of green, shifting the amber tone more toward yellow.

Choose the Fluorescent setting (▦) to display the following menu options:

- **Sodium-vapor.** These types of lights are often found in streetlights and parking lots. They emit a distinct, deep-yellow color.

- **Warm-white fluorescent.** These types of lamps give a white light with a slight amber cast to add some warmth to the scene. They burn at around 3000K, similar to an incandescent bulb.

- **White fluorescent.** These lamps cast a very neutral, white light at around 5200K.

- **Cool white fluorescent.** As the name suggests, this type of lamp is a bit cooler than a white fluorescent lamp and has a color temperature of 4200K.

- **Day white fluorescent.** This lamp approximates sunlight at about 5500K.

- **Daylight fluorescent.** This type of lamp gives you about the same color as daylight. This lamp burns at about 6300K.

- **High temp. mercury-vapor.** These lights vary in temperature, depending on the manufacturer, and usually run between 4200 and 6000K.

This menu is handy if you know the specific type of lighting fixture that is being used. For example, most outdoor sporting arenas use mercury-vapor lights to light the field at night. If you select the Fluorescent white balance setting (▦) from the Shooting menu (▣), and then choose the last option, High temp. mercury-vapor, you get a more accurate and consistent white balance, allowing you to more accurately assess the histogram.

The Preset manual white balance option (`PrE`) allows you to make your own custom white balance settings. You can use this option when shooting in mixed lighting, such as a room with an incandescent bulb and sunlight coming through a window, or when the camera's Automatic white balance (**AUTO**) isn't quite getting the correct color.

You can set a custom white balance in two ways: using direct measurement, where you take a reading from a neutral-colored object (a gray card works best for this) under the light source; or copying it from an existing photograph, which allows you to choose a white balance setting directly from an image stored on the memory card.

To preset the white balance manually, select Measure from the Preset manual white balance menu option (PrE), and then press the OK button (OK). The camera displays a blinking white balance preset icon (PrE). Next, aim the camera at a neutral subject and take a photo. If the preset was successful, the White balance good icon (Gd PrE) flashes in the viewfinder. If the White balance no good icon (no Gd PrE) flashes in the viewfinder, you need to shoot another photo. You need an ample amount of light to get a proper white balance setting.

You can also copy the white balance setting from any photo that is saved on the memory card that's in your camera. There are two options to select from: Measure or Use photo. Select Use photo from the Preset manual submenu. This displays two options: This image or Select image. Use the This image option to set the white balance to the image that you selected for the Preset manual (PrE). To use the Select image option, press the multi-selector right (▶). The menu then displays a list of available folders. Press the multi-selector up (▲) or down (▼) to choose a folder, and then press the multi-selector right (▶). This displays thumbnails of the images in the folder. Use the multi-selector to navigate through the images.

When you find a suitable image, press the OK button (OK) to select it. Use the Zoom in button (🔍) if you want to take a closer look at the image. After you select an image, you again see the This image and Select image options. However, for the This image option, you now see a thumbnail of the image you selected. Make sure that This image is highlighted, and then press the OK button (OK).

Set Picture Control

Picture Controls allow you to choose how the images are processed, and you can also use them in the Nikon ViewNX 2 and Nikon Capture NX 2 image-editing software. Picture Controls allow you to get the same results when using different cameras that are compatible with the Nikon Picture Control System.

NOTE When you save images as NEF (RAW files), Picture Controls are embedded in the metadata, and only Nikon software can use these settings. When you open RAW files in a third-party program, such as Lightroom or Adobe Camera RAW in Photoshop, Picture Controls are not applied.

When the D3300 is set to a color mode — Standard (⊡SD), Neutral (⊡NL), Vivid (⊡VI), Portrait (⊡PT), Landscape (⊡LS) — you can adjust the sharpening, contrast, brightness, hue, and saturation. If the camera is in Monochrome mode (⊡MC), you can adjust the filter effects and toning.

Select Set Picture Control (⊡) (see Figure 3.3) from the Shooting menu (📷) to adjust all of the Picture Controls to suit your specific needs or tastes. The D3300 also allows you to view a grid graph that shows you how the Picture Controls relate to each other in terms of contrast and saturation. Each Picture Control is represented on the graph by a square icon with the letter of the Picture Control to which it corresponds. Picture Controls that you have modified display with an asterisk next to the letter.

To view the Picture Control grid, select the Set Picture Control option from the Shooting menu (📷). Press the OK button (**OK**), and the Picture Control list appears: Select one of the Picture Control settings. Press the Zoom in button (🔍) to view the grid.

Once the Picture Control grid appears (see Figure 3.5), you can use the multiselector to scroll though the different Picture Control settings. After you highlight a setting, press the multiselector right (▶) to adjust the settings or the OK button (**OK**) to set the Picture Control. Press the Menu button (**MENU**) to exit back to the Shooting menu (📷), or tap the shutter-release button to prepare the camera for shooting.

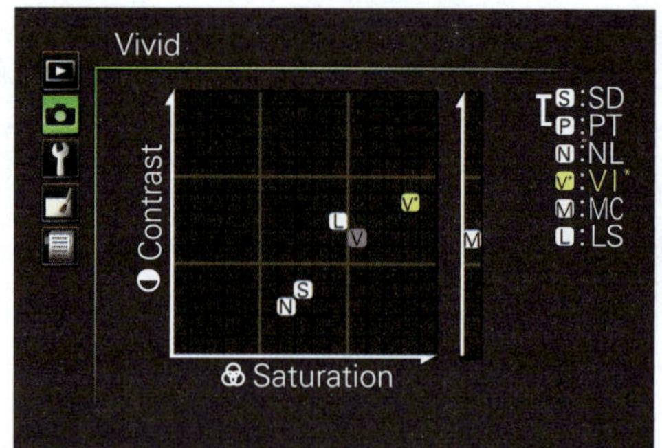

3.5 The Picture Control grid.

Auto distortion control

Each lens has its own specific distortion characteristics, and Nikon has built-in software that automatically corrects it on NIKKOR D- and G-type lenses only. It also only applies to JPEG or NEF files opened in Nikon software. Auto distortion control doesn't work with NIKKOR Perspective Control and fisheye lenses, or when shooting video. Nikon also does not guarantee that this feature will work with third-party lenses.

Color space

Color space (see Figure 3.3) simply describes the range of colors (also known as the *gamut*) that a device can reproduce. With the D3300, you have two choices of color spaces: sRGB and Adobe RGB. The color space you choose depends on what the final output of your images will be. The options are:

▶ **sRGB.** This is a narrow color space, meaning that it deals with fewer colors and also more saturated colors than the larger Adobe RGB color space. The sRGB color space is designed to mimic the colors that most midrange to low-end computer monitors can reproduce.

▶ **Adobe RGB.** This color space has a much broader color spectrum than is available with sRGB. The Adobe gamut was designed for dealing with the color spectrum that can be reproduced with most mid to high-end printer equipment.

This leads to the question of which color space you should use. If you take pictures, download them straight to your computer, and typically only view them on your monitor or upload them for viewing on the web, then sRGB is fine. The sRGB color space is also useful when printing directly from the camera or memory card with no post-processing.

If you are going to have your photos printed professionally or you intend to do a bit of post-processing to your images, using the Adobe RGB color space is recommended. This allows you to have subtler control over the colors than is possible using a narrower color space like sRGB.

I generally capture my images using the Adobe RGB color space. I then do my post-processing and make a decision on the output. If I know that I will be posting an image to the web, I convert it to sRGB; any images destined for my printer are saved as Adobe RGB. I usually end up with two identical images saved with two different color spaces. Because most web browsers don't recognize the Adobe RGB color space, any images saved as Adobe RGB and posted on the Internet usually appear dull and flat.

NOTE Some photo printing labs also require sRGB files. Consult with the lab to see what its requirements are before sending a file.

Active D-Lighting

Active D-Lighting (ADL) is designed to help you retain shadow and highlight detail when shooting in a high-contrast situation — such as direct sunlight — which can cause dark shadows and bright highlight areas. The exact nature of how this works is a proprietary Nikon feature encoded into the EXPEED 4 image processor.

Using Active D-Lighting (ADL) changes all of the Picture Control (⊡) brightness and contrast settings to Auto. This setting can be thought of as a more subdued form of High Dynamic Range (HDR); even though the processing is very different, the final goal is the same: to expand the dynamic range of the image. In my experience, I've found that Active D-Lighting works well enough, but I prefer to shoot in RAW and although the settings are saved to the metadata for use with Nikon software, I would rather do the adjustment myself in Adobe Photoshop, so I turn this feature off.

When using Active D-Lighting, the camera needs some extra time to process the images. Your buffer fills up faster when shooting continuously, so expect shorter burst rates.

Noise reduction

When using high ISO sensitivity settings or capturing long exposures, you may notice a splotchy or grainy appearance in your images. This is an artifact called digital noise, or just noise for short. It is the result of either the amplification of the signal (high ISO) or the heat generated by the sensor during long exposures.

Turning this option on allows the camera to reduce the noise at the expense of some of the fine detail in the image.

The D3300 employs a technique for long exposures called dark frame noise reduction. It is calculated by making an exposure of the same time with the shutter closed; the camera then analyzes the noise and bases the noise reduction on this second exposure.

CAUTION Using the dark frame noise reduction feature doubles the processing time and doesn't allow you to shoot any more photographs until the noise reduction is finished.

ISO sensitivity settings

The ISO sensitivity settings (see Figure 3.3) allow you to set the ISO sensitivity and Auto ISO. You can also change the ISO sensitivity using the Info edit menu. The options go from ISO 100 on up to ISO 25,600 (Hi1) in 1 stop increments. The base settings are ISO 100 to ISO 12800. It's recommended that you stick with the base settings rather than Hi1 setting. The Hi1 setting may cause excessive noise and banding.

CROSS REF ISO settings are covered in detail in Chapter 2.

AF-area mode

The AF-area mode either tells the camera how to select the active focus point or tells the camera that you are controlling the active focus point. There are different AF-area modes for Viewfinder shooting or Live view and movie shooting.

When you select the Viewfinder option, the D3300 offers the following four AF-area modes: Single-point AF ([□]), Dynamic-area AF ([⬚]), 3-D tracking (11-point) ([3D]), and Auto-area AF ([■]). Each mode is useful in different situations, and each can be modified to suit a variety of shooting needs. Note that AF-area modes aren't available to change when using certain scene and effects modes.

CROSS REF For more information on AF-area modes, see Chapter 2.

For Live view and movie recording, you can select from four options that are different than the Viewfinder shooting options. These include Face-priority AF (☺), Wide-area AF (WIDE), Normal-area AF (NORM), and Subject-tracking AF (⊕).

CROSS REF For more information about Live view and movie AF-area modes, see Chapter 7.

Built-in AF-assist illuminator

The AF-assist illuminator is a small, white LED lamp on the front of the camera that lights up when there isn't enough light for the camera to focus properly (when using the viewfinder only). In certain instances, you may want to turn this option off, such as when shooting faraway subjects, or in dim settings, like concerts or plays, where the light from the camera may be a distraction. When set to On, the AF-assist illuminator lights up in low-light situations only if the Single Servo AF (AF-S) and Auto-area AF (■) modes are selected. When in Single-point AF mode ([□]) or when Dynamic-area AF mode ([⬚]) is chosen, the center autofocus point must be active. When set to Off, the AF-assist illuminator does not light at all.

> **CAUTION** The AF-assist illuminator is not available when using 3D-tracking.

Metering

Metering modes determine how the camera's light metering sensor collects and processes the information used to determine exposure. Each of these modes is useful for different types of lighting situations. There are three options in this setting: Matrix (▨), Center-weighted (⊙), and Spot (▱).

> **CROSS REF** For more information on metering modes and how they work, see Chapter 2.

Flash cntrl for built-in flash

Essentially, the flash control option controls how your built-in flash operates. The two options are

- **TTL (TTL⚡).** This is the fully automatic flash mode. You can make minor adjustments using Flash compensation (⚡🄵).

- **Manual (M⚡).** You choose the power output in this mode. You can choose from full power down to 1/32 power.

> **CROSS REF** For more information on flash photography and the Nikon Creative Lighting System, see Chapter 6.

Movie settings

The Movie settings on the D3300 allow you to adjust the size, frame rate, and quality of the videos you record. You can choose from the following options:

- **Frame size/frame rate.** This option allows you to set the size of the HD video and select the frame rate that is appropriate for your output. The following options are available:

  - **1920 × 1080; 60p** (1080₆₀★/1080₆₀)
  - **1920 × 1080; 30p** (1080₆₀★/1080₃₀)
  - **1920 × 1080; 24p** (1080₂₄★/1080₂₄)
  - **1280 × 720; 60p** (720₆₀★/720₆₀)
  - **640 × 424; 30p** (424₃₀★/424₃₀)

CROSS REF For in-depth information about recording video and bit rates, see Chapter 7.

▶ **Movie quality.** There are two options here: High quality and Normal. These options set the maximum bit rate at which the video records.

▶ **Microphone.** This option allows you to adjust the volume of the recording using the built-in microphone or an external microphone. There are three easy options:

  • **Auto sensitivity.** This simple option automatically adjusts the volume level so that the audio levels don't clip. This works well enough for most general video usage.

  • **Manual Sensitivity.** This option allows you to set the microphone to record at a specified volume. This option is best for recording sound in a controlled environment.

  • **Microphone off.** This turns off the audio recording. You may want to select this option if you are recording audio for your video project using an external recorder. This is what most professional videographers do.

▶ **Wind noise reduction.** Setting this option to On engages a low-cut filter that helps to stop the microphone from recording the frequencies of sound that are created when the wind blows over the microphone. This option is okay for using the built-in mic, but if you're using an external mic, I suggest getting a special wind reduction accessory.

▶ **Manual movie settings.** Set this option to On if you want to adjust the shutter speed and ISO sensitivity manually. This gives you more creative control over your videos. When Manual movie settings are turned Off, the camera sets the ISO and shutter speed automatically, although you can still control the aperture.

NOTE To use Manual movie settings, the camera must be in Manual mode (M).

The Setup Menu

The Setup menu (Y) contains a smattering of options, most of which aren't changed very frequently, including the time and date. A couple of other options are Clean image sensor and Format memory card, which you may need to access from time to time.

Reset setup options

This option allows you to reset all of the menu options to the camera default settings, with the exception of Time zone and date, Language, Storage folder, and Video mode.

Format memory card

If you select the Format memory card option, it erases everything on the memory card. It's a good idea to format your card every time you download the images to your computer (just be sure all of the files are successfully transferred before formatting). Formatting the card helps protect against corrupt data.

Monitor brightness

The Monitor brightness menu sets the brightness of the LCD monitor. You may want to make it brighter when viewing images in bright sunlight, or dimmer when viewing images indoors or to save battery power. You can adjust the brightness of the LCD monitor ± 5 levels. The menu shows a graph with ten bars ranging from black to gray to white. The optimal setting is where you can see a distinct change in color tone in each of the ten bars. If the last two bars on the right side blend, the LCD monitor is too bright; if the last two bars on the left side blend, the LCD monitor is too dark.

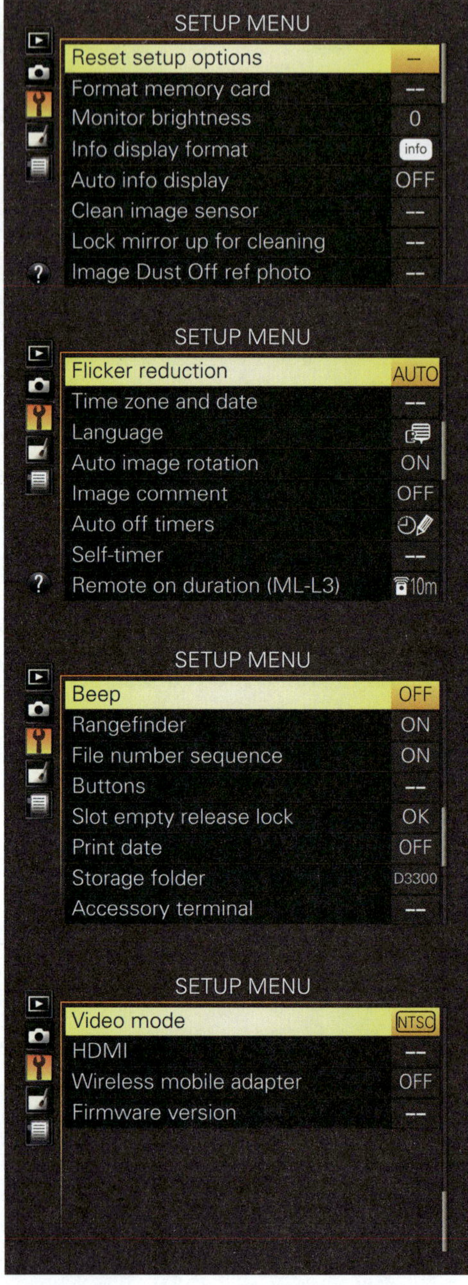

3.6 The Setup menu, shown in four parts.

Info display format

Select the Info display format option to choose how the Info display menu appears. You can choose the classic display, which shows the exposure settings simply as numbers, or you can choose the graphic interface, which can help you visualize the exposure settings so that you can have an easier grasp of what's going on with the settings.

In addition, you can choose different display options for the Scene and Effects (**EFFECTS**) shooting modes, as well as the Programmed auto (**P**), Shutter-priority auto (**S**), Aperture-priority auto (**A**), and Manual (**M**) modes. On top of that, both the graphic and classic displays allow three choices of color and background: Light on dark, blue, and dark on light.

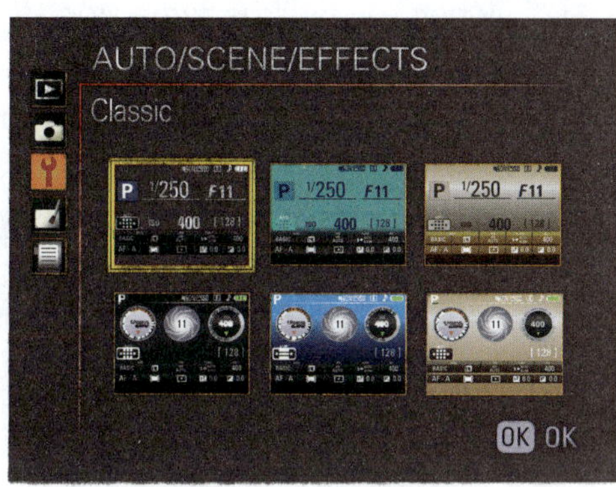

3.7 The Classic (top) and Graphic (bottom) Info display options.

Auto info display

Set the Auto info display option to On, and you can view the Info display by simply tapping the shutter-release button. You can turn the display off again by pressing the Info button (Info). If Auto info display is set Off you can call up the shooting info by pressing the Info button (Info). This is my preference.

Clean image sensor

The camera uses ultrasonic vibration to remove dust from the filter in front of the sensor. This helps keep most dust off the sensor, but it is not going to keep it dust-free forever. You may need to have the sensor professionally cleaned periodically.

After you select the Clean image sensor option from the Setup menu (**Y**), you can highlight the Clean now option, which cleans the image sensor immediately when you press the OK button (**OK**). Selecting the Clean at startup/shutdown option displays a submenu that includes the following options:

- ▶ **Clean now.** The camera goes through the cleaning process immediately after you select this option and press the OK button (**OK**).

- ▶ **Clean at startup and shutdown.** Choosing this option brings up another submenu with the following four items on it.

- **Clean at startup.** The camera cleans the image sensor when you turn the camera on.

- **Clean at shutdown.** The camera cleans the sensor when you power the camera down. This is my preferred setting because it doesn't interfere with the start-up time.

- **Clean at startup and shutdown.** The camera cleans the image sensor when you turn the camera on and also when you power it down.

- **Cleaning off.** This option disables the dust reduction function when you turn the camera on and off. You can still use the Clean now option when this is set.

Lock mirror up for cleaning

When you select the Lock mirror up for cleaning option the mirror flips up and remains in that position so you can inspect or clean the image sensor. The sensor is also powered down to reduce any static charge that may attract dust. The easiest way to clean the sensor is with a blower designed to blow puffs of air onto the sensor and remove any loose dust particles. This, combined with using the Clean image sensor feature regularly, should keep sensor dust to a minimum.

Sometimes, dust or dirt adheres to the filter that covers the sensor and it may need a wet cleaning. This involves a special swab and sensor cleaning fluid. Some people prefer to wet clean or swab the sensor themselves, but I recommend that you take your camera to an authorized Nikon service center for this during the initial factory warranty period. Any damage caused by improper cleaning is not covered by warranty, and can lead to a very expensive repair bill.

That being said, learning to swab the sensor on your own is not difficult. It can also save you a lot of time and expense. You can remove the lens before or after locking up the mirror, but typically, it's easier to remove the lens beforehand. Follow these steps to lock up the mirror:

1. **Press the Menu button (MENU) and use the multi-selector to enter the Setup menu (Y).** Use the multi-selector to navigate to the Lock mirror up for cleaning option.

2. **Press the OK button (OK) or the multi-selector right (▶).** This brings up the Start menu option. Press the OK button (OK). This shows a dialog box with instructions for raising the mirror.

> **NOTE** The mirror will not raise and lock if the battery power is too low.

3. **Press the shutter-release button to open the shutter, and then raise and lock the mirror.** You now have access to the sensor, and can inspect or clean it.

4. **Turn off the camera.** This closes the shutter and lowers the mirror to the resting position.

> **CAUTION** Make sure that nothing is in the way of the shutter or mirror before you turn off the camera. If a blower nozzle or swab is in the way, it will severely damage the shutter curtain, and possibly, the mirror. Also, make sure that the battery has plenty of charge. If it is depleted, the shutter closes and the mirror drops without warning.

Image Dust Off ref photo

The Image Dust Off ref photo option takes a photo that shows any dust or debris that may be stuck to the sensor. Nikon Capture NX 2 then uses the image to retouch any subsequent photos where the specks appear automatically.

To use this feature, select either Start or Clean sensor and then start. Next, you are instructed by a dialog box to take a photo of a bright, featureless, white object about four inches (10cm) from the lens. The camera automatically sets the focus to infinity. A Dust Off reference photo can only be taken when using a CPU lens. It's recommended to use at least a 50mm lens, and when using a zoom lens, you should zoom all the way in to the longest focal length. The reference image, however, can be used for images taken at any focal length.

Flicker reduction

Some light sources, such as older fluorescent and mercury-vapor lights, can cause a video to flicker, depending on the local AC power grid. There are three options: Auto, 50 Hz, and 60 Hz. In the United States, the frequency is 60Hz; in Europe, 50Hz is the standard. The Auto option generally takes care of the problem, but if you aren't getting good results, try adjusting to a smaller aperture. Note that when the camera is set to Manual movie settings and you are shooting in Manual exposure, Flicker reduction is not available so setting the shutter speed to 1/60 or faster may be required to control the problem.

Time zone and date

Select Time zone and date to set the camera's internal clock. You can then choose from the following options:

- ▶ **Time zone.** Use the multi-selector to choose your time zone using the map display.

- ▶ **Date and time.** This is where you set the clock. It's pretty self-explanatory.

- ▶ **Date format.** You can set the order in which the date appears: Year/Month/Date, Month/Date/Year, or Date/Month/Year.

- ▶ **Daylight saving time.** If you turn this option on when Daylight saving time is in effect, then the time is changed by one hour.

Language

When you select the Language option, you can set the language in which the menus and dialog boxes are displayed.

Auto image rotation

When you select the Auto image rotation option, the camera records its orientation when you shoot a photo (portrait or landscape). This allows the camera (and image-editing software) to show the photo in the proper orientation. This way, you don't have to take the time in post-processing to rotate images.

Image comment

When you select Image comment, you can attach comments to the images you take with your D3300. You enter the text using the Input Comment menu. You can then view the comments in Nikon Capture NX 2 or ViewNX 2 software, or you can view them in the photo information on the camera. Setting the attach comment option applies the comment to all images you take until you disable this setting.

NOTE Image comments are limited to 36 characters.

Auto off timers

This option controls how long the LCD monitor displays remain on when you do not push any buttons. Because the LCD monitor is the primary drain on power consumption for any digital camera, choosing a shorter delay time is usually preferable. You can choose Short, Normal, or Long, or you can set each type differently in the Custom menu. The Custom options are:

> ▶ **Playback/menus – 8s, 20s, 1min, 5min, 10min**

> ▶ **Image review – 4s, 8s, 20s, 1min, 10min**

> ▶ **Live view – 5min, 10min, 15min, 20min, 30min**

> ▶ **Standby timer – 4s, 8s, 20s, 1min, 30min**

Self-timer

This setting puts a delay on when the shutter is released after you press the shutter-release button. This is handy when you want to take a self-portrait and you need some time to get yourself into the frame. You can also use the Self-timer release mode (⟳) to reduce camera shake caused by pressing the shutter-release button on long exposures. You can adjust the following settings:

> ▶ **Self-timer delay.** You can set the delay to 2, 5, 10, or 20 seconds.

> ▶ **Number of shots.** You can press the multi-selector up (▲) or down (▼) to set the camera to take from one to nine photos taken at 4 second intervals.

Remote on duration (ML-L3)

This setting controls how long the camera stays active while waiting for a signal from the ML-L3 wireless remote. You can set it to 1, 5, 10, or 15 minutes. After the preset amount of time has passed, the camera's exposure meter is turned off. To reactivate the camera, tap the shutter-release button.

Beep

When this option is on, the camera emits a beep when the self-timer is counting down or when the autofocus locks in Single-servo AF mode (**AF-S**). You can choose High, Low, or Off. Although the beep can be useful when in Self-timer mode (⟳), it can also be an annoying feature, especially if you are photographing in a relatively quiet area. The beep does not sound when using Live View or when shooting in Quiet shutter release mode (**Q**). The default setting is Low.

Rangefinder

Setting this option to On causes the exposure indicator in the viewfinder to act as an electronic rangefinder to help with focus when the lens or camera is set to manual focus. If the indicator is showing to the left, the focus is in front of the subject; if it shows to the right, the focus is falling behind the subject. When the camera is set to Manual exposure (**M**), the camera automatically defaults to displaying the exposure meter.

File number sequence

The D3300 names files by sequentially numbering them. This option controls how the sequence is handled. When set to Off, the file numbers reset to 0001 when you format a memory card, create a new folder, or insert a new memory card. When you set the option to On, the camera continues to count from the last number until it reaches 9999; it then returns to 0001 and counts up from there. When you set this option to Reset, the camera starts at 0001 when the current folder is empty. If the current folder contains images, the camera starts at one number higher than the last image in the folder. I always set this option to On when setting up my camera. It reduces the risk of creating files with the same name, which can cause problems with file management. It also helps me keep track of approximately how many shutter releases my camera has made.

Buttons

This option allows you to customize some buttons on the D3300 for functions that you may find more useful than the default settings.

- ▶ **Assign Fn button.** The Assign Fn button menu allows you to choose what the Function button (**Fn**) does when you press it.

  - **Image quality/size.** Pressing the Function button (**Fn**) and rotating the Command dial allows you to set the image quality and size.

  - **ISO sensitivity.** Pressing the Function button (**Fn**) and rotating the Command dial allows you to change the ISO sensitivity settings.

  - **White balance.** Pressing the Function button (**Fn**)and rotating the Command dial allows you to change the white balance options.

  - **Active D-Lighting.** This option allows you to adjust the Active D-Lighting (**ADL**) settings quickly by pressing the Function button (**Fn**) and rotating the Command dial.

> **CAUTION** White balance and Active D-Lighting options aren't functional in Scene or Effects modes when programmed to the Function button (**Fn**)

- ▶ **Assign AE-L/AF-L button.** The Assign AE-L/AF-L button option allows you to assign a function to the AE-L/AF-L button (**AE-L/AF-L**). Choose from the following options:

  - **AE/AF Lock.** The focus and exposure is locked when you press and hold the AE-L/AF-L button (**AE-L/AF-L**).

- **AE lock only.** The exposure locks when you press and hold the AE-L/AF-L button (AE-L/AF-L). Focus continues to function normally.

- **AE Lock (hold).** The exposure locks until you press the AE-L/AF-L button (AE-L/AF-L) a second time or the exposure meter is turned off when the camera goes to sleep or is switched off.

- **AF Lock only.** The focus locks while you press and hold the AE-L/AF-L button (AE-L/AF-L). The AE continues as normal.

- **AF-ON.** This option activates the camera's autofocus system.

Slot empty release lock

The Slot empty release lock controls whether the shutter releases when there isn't a memory card in the camera. When you set it to Enable release, the shutter fires, and any image displayed on the monitor is saved temporarily. When you set it to Release locked, the shutter does not fire

Print date

This option only works with JPEGs, not RAW files. It allows you to add the following data to your JPEG image files:

▶ **Off.** No data is imprinted on the image.

▶ **Date.** The month, day, and year are imprinted.

▶ **Date and time.** The month, day, and year are imprinted, along with the time.

▶ **Date counter.** This option displays the number of days remaining or the number of days that have passed from the selected date. You can set the date to start counting from in this menu as well.

Storage folder

Use the Storage folder option to select the folder in which your images should be saved as you shoot. You can also create new folders, rename existing folders, or delete folders that you no longer need. By default, the camera creates a folder numbered 100D3300. When the folder has 999 photos in it or contains a photo with the file number 9999, the D3300 creates a new folder with a number that is one higher (101D3300, and so on).

The Storage folder options are

▶ **Select folder.** The default folder is D3300, and there's another pre-existing folder simply called Nikon. When you enter the Select folder submenu, the current active folder appears on top and all subsequent folders follow in alphabetical order. Simply use the multi-selector to highlight the desired folder, and then press the OK button (**OK**) to select it.

▶ **New.** By selecting the New option, you can create a folder with your own designation. Simply choose a five-character, alphanumeric name for your folder, and then enter the name using the text entry menu that appears when you enter the New folder submenu. Use the multi-selector to scroll around in the keyboard text area at the top of the screen and highlight the letter or number that you want to input. When the correct character is highlighted in the keyboard area, press the OK button (**OK**). You can use the Command dial to move the cursor within the name area at the bottom to select the space where you want to place the character. To delete a character, move the cursor over the top of the letter and then press the Delete button (🗑) to erase. After you input the text, press the Zoom in button (🔍) to create the folder. The folder then becomes the active storage folder.

▶ **Rename.** You can also rename an existing folder. You may want to rename a folder instead of creating a new one, especially if you already have a folder that contains images. You can rename the folder so that you can easily remember what photos are in the folder to help with file management.

▶ **Delete.** Navigating to this option and selecting Yes deletes the empty folder on the memory card. The camera asks you for confirmation so that you don't accidentally erase any folders.

Accessory terminal

The Accessory terminal menu is where you set options related to certain accessories such as a remote control or GPS unit.

▶ **Remote control.** This section is where you set up the control features for the ML-L3 or the new Nikon wireless remotes, the WR-1 and WR-T10. Although the ML-L3 wireless remote doesn't technically plug in here, this is where you set the option for the button press.

  • **Remote shutter release.** This option allows you to set the main button to take still photos or to start the camera recording movies (both ML-L3 and WR-T10).

- **Assign Fn button.** The WR-T10 has a Function button (**Fn**) that the ML-L3 doesn't have, so this option obviously doesn't apply to the ML-L3. You can set the Function button (**Fn**) to perform the same action as the AE-L/AF-L button (AE-L/AF-L), or you can set it to activate Live View.

▶ **Location data.** The Location data menu is where you access the settings for an optional GPS unit. There are a few options to choose from.

- **Standby timer.** The standby timer turns off the camera display and light meter when not in use (go to sleep). Setting this option to Enable allows the camera to go to sleep (thus terminating the GPS connection). Setting this option to Disable turns the standby timer off so that the camera does not go to sleep. This keeps the GPS connections active, but drains the battery much quicker.

- **Position.** If the camera is successfully connected to a GPS satellite, this option will display the GPS coordinates.

- **Set clock from satellite.** Setting this option to Yes sets the time that is recorded to the metadata from the UTC, as opposed to the time from the camera's internal clock.

Video mode

Select the Video mode option to set the video playback mode. There are two options: NTSC and PAL. If you are in North America, use the NTSC option; if you are in Europe, set it to PAL.

HDMI

The D3300 has an HDMI (high-definition multimedia interface) output that allows you to connect your camera to a high-definition TV (HDTV) to review your images. The first option is Output resolution. There are five settings: Auto, 1080p (progressive), 1080i (interlaced), 720p (progressive), 576p (progressive), and 480p (progressive). The default is Auto, which selects the appropriate setting for your TV automatically. I recommend leaving the Output resolution set to Auto. See the manual for your TV to find the correct resolution if you decide to set it manually.

The second option in this menu is Device Control. This setting is important because, if it's not set right, it could disable the Live View feed for the HDMI device. After you select Device Control, you can choose from the following options:

▶ **On.** Select this option only when you want to use your HDTV to view image playback as you would see it on your camera's LCD screen. If your HDTV is HDMI-CEC capable, you can use the TV remote control as you would the multi-selector. Be aware that if this option is set to On, you will not be able to use Live View.

▶ **Off.** Use this option if you want to use the HDTV as a monitor to view Live View for shooting video or stills. This enables the camera to display what is on the LCD screen directly to your HDTV or HDMI device.

NOTE If you want to change the HDMI settings, you must first disconnect the camera from the HD device.

Wireless mobile adapter

If the WU-1a Wi-Fi adapter is connected to the accessory terminal, this is where you enable it so that you can transfer images or see Live View on your smart device when using the Nikon Wireless Mobile Utility (WMU) app.

Firmware version

Select Firmware version from the menu to display the firmware version your camera is using. Firmware is a computer program embedded in the camera that tells it how to function. Camera manufacturers routinely update the firmware to correct for any bugs or to make improvements on the camera's functions. Nikon posts firmware updates on its website at www.nikonusa.com.

The Retouch Menu

The Retouch menu (✍) allows you to make changes and corrections to your images without using imaging-editing software. As a matter of fact, you don't even need to download your images to a computer. You can make all of the changes in-camera using the LCD screen preview (or hooked up to an HDTV if you prefer). The Retouch menu (✍) only makes *copies* of the images, so you don't need to worry about doing any destructive editing to your actual files.

There are two ways to access the Retouch menu (✍). This first one is the quickest, but it doesn't display all of the options that are available in the full menu. Follow these steps:

1. **Press the Playback button (▶) to enter Playback mode.** Your most recent image appears on the LCD screen.

2. **Use the multi-selector to review your images.**

3. **When you see an image you want to retouch, press the *i* button (ⓘ).** Select Retouch from the menu and press the multi-selector right (▶) to view the options.

4. **Use the multi-selector to high-light the Retouch option you want to use.** Depending on the Retouch option you choose, you may have to select additional settings.

5. **Make adjustments if necessary.**

6. **Press the OK button ([OK]) to save.**

This is the second method for entering the Retouch menu (✍). Using this method will get you access to all of the options available. Follow these steps:

1. **Press the Menu button ([MENU]) to view the menu options.**

2. **Press the multi-selector down (▼) to move to the Retouch menu (✍).**

3. **Press the multi-selector right (▶), and then press the multi-selector up (▲) or down (▼) to highlight the Retouch option you want.** Depending on the Retouch option you select, you may have to select additional settings. Once you select your option(s), thumbnails appear.

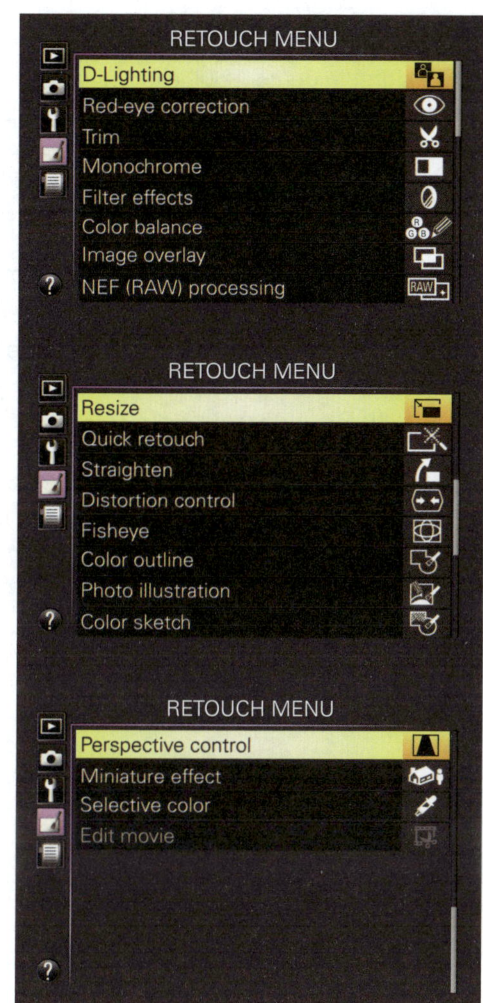

3.8 **The Retouch menu, shown in three parts.**

4. **Use the multi-selector to select the image to retouch, and then press the OK button ([OK]).**

5. **Make the necessary adjustments.**

6. **Press the OK button ([OK]) to save.**

D-Lighting

The D-Lighting option (▣ON) allows you to adjust the image by brightening the shadows without losing the highlight details. This is not the same as Active D-Lighting (ADL). D-Lighting uses a curves adjustment to help bring out details in the shadow areas of an image. This option is for use with backlit subjects or images that may be slightly underexposed.

When you select the D-Lighting option (▣ON) from the Retouch menu (✎), you can use the multi-selector to choose a thumbnail, and then press the Zoom in button (🔍) to get a closer look at the image. Press the OK button (**OK**) to choose the image to retouch, and two thumbnails appear: one is the original image, and the other is the image with D-Lighting applied.

You can press the multi-selector up (▲) or down (▼) to select the amount of D-Lighting: Lo, Hi, or an unlabeled setting in between. You can view the results in real time and compare them with the original before saving. Press the OK button (**OK**) to save, the Playback button (▶) to cancel, or the Zoom in button (🔍) to view the full-frame image.

If the camera detects a face in the photo, you also have the option to set the D-Lighting to Portrait subjects. This option tones down bright highlights and increases the level of shadow detail by brightening the shadows more than it does using the standard mode. I find the effect to be a little heavy at times, which can cause excessive noise in the shadow area. I suggest using the Portrait mode with a Lo setting and looking at the shadow areas closely to monitor the noise levels.

Red-eye correction

Select the Red-eye correction option if you want the camera to automatically correct for the red-eye effect that can sometimes be caused when you use the flash to take pictures of people. This option is only available on photos taken with flash. When you choose images to retouch from the Playback menu (▶) by pressing the OK button (**OK**) during preview, this option is grayed out and cannot be selected if the camera detects that a flash was not used. When you attempt to choose an image directly from the Retouch menu (✎), a message appears, stating that this image cannot be used.

Once you select the image, press the OK button (**OK**); the camera then automatically corrects the red-eye and saves a copy of the image to the memory card. If you select an image on which flash was used but there is no red-eye present, the camera displays a message stating that red-eye is not detected in the image and no retouching will be done.

Trim

Select the Trim option to crop your image to remove distracting elements, or crop closer to the subject. Use the multi-selector to find the image to crop and press the OK button (**OK**) to select it. You can also use the Zoom in button (🔍) and the Zoom out button (🔍) to adjust the size of the crop. This allows you to crop closer in, or back it out if you find that you've zoomed in too much.

Use the multi-selector to move the crop around the image so you can center the crop on the part of the image that you think is most important. When you are happy with the crop you've selected, press the OK button (**OK**) to save a copy of the image, or press the Playback button (▶) to return to the main menu without saving.

Rotating the Command dial allows you to choose different aspect ratios for your crop. You can choose the aspect ratio to conform the crop to the following sizes:

- ▶ **3:2.** This is the default crop size. It is good for prints that are 4 × 6, 8 × 12, and 12 × 18.

- ▶ **4:3.** This ratio is for 6 × 8 or 12 × 16 prints.

- ▶ **5:4.** This is the standard size for 8 × 10 prints.

- ▶ **1:1.** Select this ratio for a square crop.

- ▶ **16:9.** This is what's known as a *cinematic crop*. Movie screens and widescreen televisions use this ratio.

Monochrome

The Monochrome option (see Figure 3.9) allows you to make a copy of your color image in a monochrome format. You can select from the following three options:

- ▶ **Black-and-white.** This option changes your image to shades of black, white, and gray.

- ▶ **Sepia.** Select this option to give your image the look of a black-and-white photo that has been sepia toned. Sepia toning is a traditional photographic process that gives the photo a reddish-brown tint.

- ▶ **Cyanotype.** This option gives your photos a blue or cyan tint. Cyanotypes are a result of processing film-based photographic images.

When using the Sepia or Cyanotype options, you can press the multi-selector up (▲) or down (▼) to adjust the lightness or darkness of the effect. Press the OK button (**OK**) to save a copy of the image or press the Playback button (▶) to cancel without saving.

Filter effects

The Filter effects option allows you to simulate the effects of using certain filters over your lens to subtly modify the colors of your image. You can choose from the following seven filter effects:

- ▶ **Skylight.** A skylight filter is used to absorb some of the UV rays emitted by the sun. The UV rays can give your image a slightly bluish tint. Using the skylight filter effect causes your image to be less blue.

- ▶ **Warm filter.** A warming filter adds a little orange to your image to give it a warmer hue. This filter effect can sometimes be useful when using flash because flash can sometimes cause your images to feel a little too cool.

- ▶ **Red intensifier.** This filter boosts the saturation of reds in the image. Press the multi-selector up (▲) or down (▼) to lighten or darken the effect.

- ▶ **Green intensifier.** This filter boosts the saturation of greens in the image. Press the multi-selector up (▲) or down (▼) to lighten or darken the effect.

- ▶ **Blue intensifier.** This filter boosts the saturation of blues in the image. Press the multi-selector up (▲) or down (▼) to lighten or darken the effect.

- ▶ **Cross screen.** This effect simulates the use of a star filter, creating a star-shaped pattern on the bright highlights in your image. If your image doesn't have any bright highlights, the effect is not apparent. Once you select an image for the Cross screen filter, you see a submenu with a few options that you can adjust. You can choose the number of points on the stars: 4, 6, or 8. You can also choose the amount; there are three settings that give you more or fewer stars. You can choose three angle settings that control the angle at which the star is tilted. You also have three settings that control the length of the points on the stars.

- ▶ **Soft.** This filter applies a soft glow to your images. This effect is mostly used for portraiture but can also be used effectively for landscapes.

After choosing the desired filter effect, press the OK button (**OK**) to save a copy of your image with the effect added.

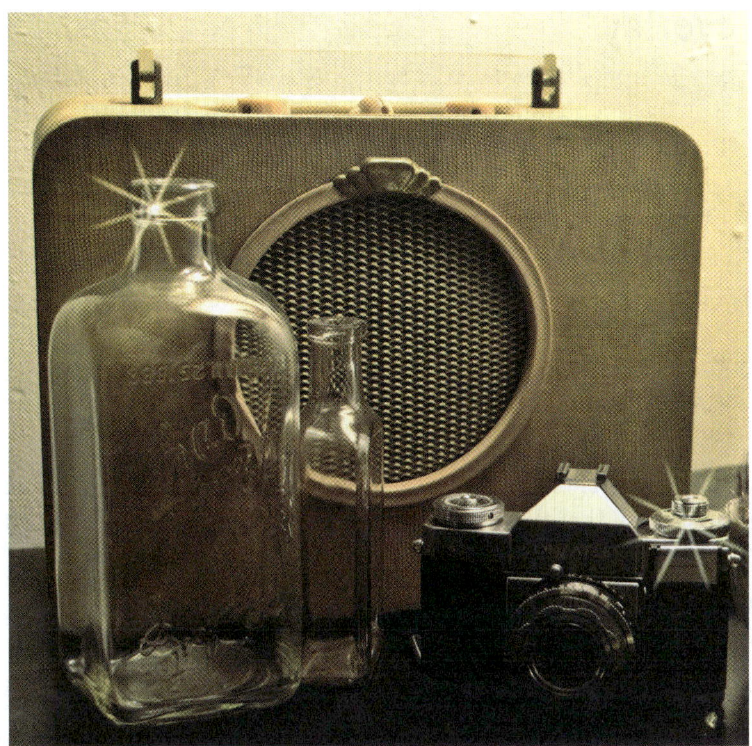

3.9 The Cross screen filter has been applied to this image. Exposure: ISO 4500, f/4.5, 1/60 second with the 18–55 kit lens.

Color balance

You can use the Color balance option to create a copy of an image on which you have adjusted the color balance. Using this option, you can use the multi-selector to add a color tint to your image. You can use this effect to neutralize an existing color tint or to add a color tint for artistic purposes.

Press the multi-selector up (▲) to increase the amount of green, down (▼) to increase the amount of magenta, left (◄) to add blue, or right (►) to add amber.

A color chart and color histograms are displayed along with an image preview so you can see how the color balance affects your image. When you are satisfied with your image, press the OK button (**OK**) to save a copy.

CAUTION If you adjust the color balance using the LCD monitor as a reference, it may not yield the most accurate results.

Image overlay

The Image overlay option allows you to combine two RAW images and save them as one. You access this menu option by entering the Retouch menu (✎),

> **NOTE** To use this option, you must have at least two RAW images saved to the memory card. This option is not available for use with JPEGs.

Follow these steps to create an image overlay:

1. **Press the Menu button (MENU) to view the menu options.** Use the multi-selector to scroll down to the Retouch menu (✎), and then press the multi-selector right (▶) to enter it.

2. **Press the multi-selector up (▲) or down (▼) to highlight Image Overlay, and then press the multi-selector right (▶).** This displays the Image Overlay menu.

3. **Press the OK button (OK) to view RAW image thumbnails.**

4. **Use the multi-selector to highlight the first RAW image to be used in the overlay, and then press the OK button (OK) to select it.**

5. **Adjust the exposure of Image 1 by pressing the multi-selector up (▲) or down (▼), and then press the OK button (OK) when the image is adjusted to your liking.**

6. **Press the multi-selector right (▶) to switch to Image 2.**

7. **Press the OK button (OK) to view RAW image thumbnails.**

8. **Use the multi-selector to highlight the second RAW image to be used in the overlay, and then press the OK button (OK) to select it.**

9. **Adjust the exposure of Image 2 by pressing the multi-selector up (▲) or down (▼), and then press the OK button (OK) when the image is adjusted to your liking.**

10. **Press the multi-selector right (▶) to highlight the Preview window.**

11. **Press the multi-selector up (▲) or down (▼) to highlight Overlay to preview the image.** Use the multi-selector to highlight Save if you want to save the image without previewing it.

NEF (RAW) processing

The NEF (RAW) processing option allows you to do some basic editing to images saved in the RAW format, without downloading them to a computer and using image-editing software. This option is limited in its function but allows you to fine-tune your image more precisely when printing straight from the camera or memory card.

You can save a copy of your image in JPEG format, choose the image quality and size at which to save the copy, adjust the white balance settings, fine-tune the exposure compensation, and select a Picture Control setting (⊡) to apply.

To apply RAW processing, follow these steps:

1. **Enter the NEF (RAW) Processing menu through the Retouch menu (✑).**

2. **Press the OK button (OK) or multi-selector right (▶) to view thumbnails of the images stored on your card.** Only images saved in RAW format appear.

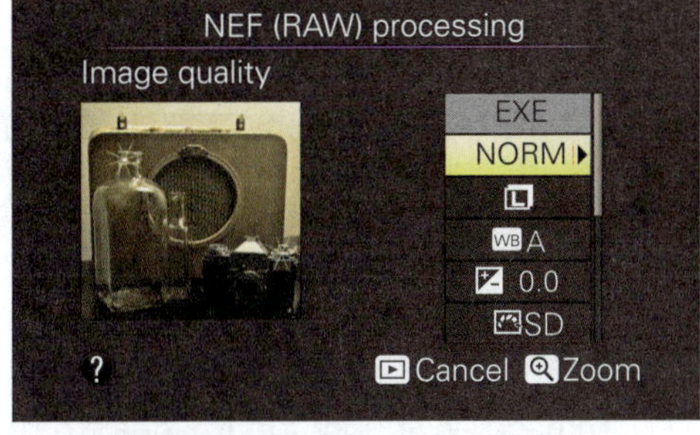

3.10 **The NEF (RAW) processing option in the Retouch menu.**

3. **Use the multi-selector to scroll through the thumbnails, and then press the OK button (OK) to select the highlighted image.** This displays a screen with the image adjustment submenu located to the right of the image you selected.

4. **Press the multi-selector up (▲) or down (▼) to highlight the adjustment you want to make.** You can set image quality, image size, white balance, exposure compensation, Picture Control, Hi ISO NR, Color space, and D-Lighting. You can also press the Zoom in button (🔍) to view a full-screen preview.

5. **After you make your adjustments, use the multi-selector to highlight EXE, and then press the OK button (OK) to save the changes.** Press the Playback button (▶) to cancel without saving. EXE sets the changes, and saves a copy of the image in JPEG format at the size and quality that you select. The camera default saves the image as a Large, Fine JPEG.

CROSS REF For more information on image size, quality, white balance, and exposure compensation, see Chapter 2.

Resize

The Resize option is handy because it allows you to make smaller-sized copies of your images. Smaller pictures are more suitable for making small prints and web-sized images, and for e-mailing to friends and family. The first thing you need to do when creating a resized image is to select the Choose size option from the submenu. You then have the following options:

- ▶ **2.5M.** 1920 × 1280 pixels.

- ▶ **1.1M.** 1280 × 856 pixels.

- ▶ **0.6M.** 960 × 640 pixels.

- ▶ **0.3M.** 640 × 424 pixels.

After you decide the size at which you want your small pictures copied, go to the Select image option. When the Select image option is chosen, the LCD screen displays thumbnails of all of the images in the current folder. To scroll through your images, press the multi-selector right (▶), left (◀), up (▲), or down (▼). Use the Zoomout/thumbnail button (⊟) to select the images. You can select as many images as you have on your memory card (videos cannot be selected). Selected images show a small icon in the top-right corner. Press the Zoom in button (⊕) to take a closer look at the image. When all the images from which you want to make a resized copy are selected, press the OK button (**OK**). A dialog box pops up asking you to confirm. Select Yes and press the OK button to make the copies.

Quick retouch

The Quick retouch option is the easiest one to use in the Retouch menu (✐). The camera automatically adjusts the contrast and saturation, making your image brighter and more colorful, perfect for printing straight from the camera or memory card. In the event that your image is dark or backlit, the camera also automatically applies D-Lighting to help bring out details in the shadow areas of your picture.

Once you select an image for Quick retouch, you can choose how much of the effect to apply: High, Normal, or Low. The LCD screen displays a side-by-side comparison between the image as shot and the retouched image to give you a better idea of what the effect looks like.

Once you decide how much of the effect you want, press the OK button (**OK**) to save a copy of the retouched image, or you can press the Playback button (▶) to cancel without making any changes to your picture.

Straighten

The Straighten feature fixes images that were shot at a slight angle, which is another nice feature to have available when printing directly from the camera. When you select an image, press the multi-selector right (▶) and left (◀) to adjust the tilt amount. A grid overlay is displayed over the image. You can use it to align with the horizon or another straight object in the photo.

Distortion control

As discussed in Chapter 4, some lenses are prone to distortion. The Distortion control option allows you to make in-camera corrections for lens distortion. There are two options: Auto and Manual. Auto automatically applies any needed corrections, and Manual allows you to apply the effect yourself using the multi-selector. Press the multi-selector right (▶) to reduce barrel distortion (wide-angle), or press the multi-selector left (◀) to reduce pincushion distortion (telephoto).

CAUTION The Distortion control Auto setting is recommended for use with NIKKOR G- and D-type lenses only. If the Auto distortion control is set to ON in the shooting menu the Auto setting is unavailable.

NOTE With lenses that have excessive distortion, a small amount of the image area may be cropped out when the distortion corrections are applied.

Fisheye

The Fisheye option adds barrel distortion to the image to make it appear as if it were taken with a fisheye lens. Press the multi-selector right (▶) to increase the effect or left (◀) to decrease it. To be honest, this effect isn't that great, so use it at your own peril.

Color outline

The Color outline feature takes the selected image and creates an outline copy that you can open in image-editing software, such as Adobe Photoshop or Corel Paintshop Pro, and color in manually. This option works best when used on an image with high contrast.

Photo illustration

This option darkens and thickens the edges of the elements of the image and breaks the colors down to the basics, making the photo appear as if were a silk-screened poster. You can adjust the thickness of the lines in the menu options.

Color sketch

Select Color sketch to make your image appear as if it were drawn with colored pencils. Selecting Vividness allows you to increase the color saturation of the effect. The Outlines option allows you to change the thickness of the outlines of the sketch.

Perspective control

The Perspective control option allows you to correct problems with perspective caused when you point the camera upward, or shoot at an angle instead of straight on. Think of shooting a tall building; when you tilt the camera up at the building, it causes the base to look larger than the top of the building. You can correct for this by using the Perspective control option.

Press the multi-selector up (▲) or down (▼) to adjust the vertical perspective. Press the multi-selector left (◄) or right (►) to adjust the horizontal perspective.

If you plan on using the Perspective control feature, it's best to use a very loose composition in order to leave room for the image corrections, which can cause parts of the image to be cropped out.

Miniature effect

The Miniature effect (🎥) is modeled after a technique that some people call the *tilt-shift effect* because it can be achieved optically with a tilt-shift lens. Quite simply, what this effect does is simulate the shallow depth of field normally present in macro shots. This tricks the eye by making a large subject appear very tiny. The effect only works with very far-off subjects, and works better when the vantage point is looking down. It's a cool effect, but it only works with limited subjects, so keep that in mind.

Once an image is selected for use with the Miniature effect (🎥), you can use the multi-selector up (▲) or down (▼) to move the sharpness zone up or down in the image. Use the multi-selector left (◄) or right (►) to adjust the width of the sharpness zone. Press the Zoom out/Thumbnail button (🔍) to turn the sharpness zone from horizontal to vertical. You can then use the multi-selector up (▲) or down (▼) to adjust the width of the sharpness zone in the image. Press the multi-selector left (◄) or right (►) to move the sharpness zone left or right.

Press the Playback/Zoom in button (🔍) to preview the effect. Press the OK button (**OK**) to save a copy of the image with the effect added, or press the Playback button (▶) to cancel.

Selective color

Use the Selective color option to turn your image black and white, while retaining up to three colors. After selecting the image, use the multi-selector to maneuver the cursor over an object of a particular color. Once the cursor is over the color, press the AE-L/AF-L button (AE-L/AF-L) to select the color. Press the multi-selector up (▲) or down (▼) to adjust the purity of the color. Lower numbers are more specific with the color; higher numbers select a broader range of the color selection.

Rotate the Main Command dial right to select the other color options and follow the same procedures. For more precise color selection, use the Zoom in button (🔍) to magnify the image. To reset the image, press and hold the Delete button (🗑). Press the OK button (**OK**) to save the image.

Edit movie

The Edit movie option allows you to make basic edits to videos that you shoot with the D3300. You have three options: choose the Start frame, choose the End frame, and grab a still image from the video. Each edit you make is saved as a new file, so there's no need to worry about making any permanent changes to your original file. To edit your video, follow these steps:

1. **Press the Menu button (MENU), and then use the multi-selector to select the Retouch menu (✐).**

2. **Select Edit Movie and press the OK button (OK) or the multi-selector right (▶) to view menu options.**

3. **Choose the edit you want to make and press the OK button (OK) or the multi-selector right (▶).** The options are Choose start point, Choose end point, or Save selected frame. A menu appears with all videos saved to the current card.

4. **Use the multi-selector to scroll through the available videos and select one to edit.** The selected video is highlighted in yellow. Press the OK button (OK) when your video is selected.

5. **Press the OK button (OK) to begin playback.** Press the multi-selector up (▲) at the point in the video where you want to make the edit. You can press the multi-selector down (▼) to stop playback. Press the multi-selector left (◀) and right (▶) to go backward or forward in the video clip.

6. **Press the multi-selector up (▲) to make the edit.** I prefer to press the multi-selector down (▼) to pause the movie first, and make sure that's where I want to make the cut. I then make the edit and the movie saves automatically.

> **TIP** You can access the Edit movie option by pressing the *i* button (**ⓘ**) during playback.

Recent Settings

The last menu on the camera is Recent Settings. This option stores the last 20 settings you used so that you can go back and access them. Each time you use a setting, it's placed at the top of the list, moving the others down and knocking the last one off.

CHAPTER 4

Selecting and Using Lenses with the Nikon D3300

I always stress that lenses are one of the most important investments for your camera system. A good lens is an investment that will outlast your camera by many years. Because Nikon has removed the Anti-Aliasing/ Optical Low Pass Filter from the sensor on the D3300, increasing the acuity of the sensor, the right lens can mean the difference between a good image and a stunning image.

The lenses that you attach to your camera affect not only sharpness, but also color and contrast. Additionally, the interchangeability of lenses on the D3300 allows you to use lenses to achieve visual effects. You can use a wide-angle lens to distort spatial relations and lines, a telephoto to make far-off objects appear closer, or a macro lens to get close up and show detail that can't be perceived unaided by the human eye.

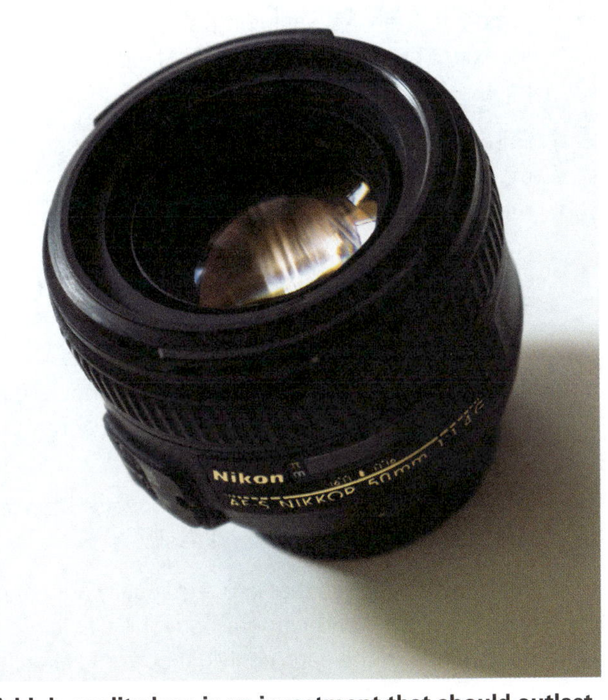

A high-quality lens is an investment that should outlast many dSLR camera bodies.

Deciphering Nikon Lens Codes

If you're a relative newcomer to the world of interchangeable-lens cameras, then you may notice when shopping for lenses that there are a lot of different codes and letters on these lenses. For example, the D3300 kit lens in Nikon nomenclature is AF-S DX NIKKOR 18–55 f/3.5–5.6G VR II. So, what do all of these letters mean? Here's a simple list to help you decipher them:

- **AI/AI-S.** These are Auto Indexing lenses. Lens apertures are held wide open by a mechanism in the camera so that the most light can get through the viewfinder to make viewing bright and easy. The camera automatically adjusts the aperture diaphragm down to the selected setting when you press the shutter-release button. All lenses, including autofocus (AF) lenses made after 1977, are Auto Indexing, but when referring to AI lenses, most people generally mean the older, manual-focus (MF) lenses.

- **E.** These were the budget series of manual focus lenses from Nikon. They were made to be used with lower-end film cameras such as the EM, FG, and FG-20. Although these lenses are compact and often constructed with plastic parts, some of them — especially the 50mm f/1.8 — are of good quality. These lenses are also manual focus only. E lenses are not to be confused with Nikon Perspective Control (PC-E) lenses.

CAUTION AI/AI-S and Series E lenses do not allow for auto-exposure or metering because they don't have a CPU to communicate data with the camera body.

- **D.** Lenses with this designation convey distance information to the camera to aid in metering for exposure and flash.

- **G.** These are lenses that lack a manually adjustable aperture ring, so you must set the aperture on the camera body. Like D lenses, G lenses also convey distance information to the camera. Most current Nikon lenses in production are G lenses.

- **AF, AF-D, AF-I, and AF-S.** All of these codes denote that the lens is an autofocus (AF) lens. The AF-D code represents a distance encoder for distance information; AF-I indicates an internal focusing motor; and AF-S represents an internal Silent Wave Motor.

- **DX.** This code lets you know that the lens is optimized for use with the Nikon DX-format sensor.

NOTE Full-frame lenses do not carry an FX designation, and you can use them effectively on DX cameras, albeit with a smaller angle of view than on an FX camera.

- ▶ **VR.** This code tells you that the lens is equipped with the Nikon Vibration Reduction (VR) image-stabilization system. The latest lenses from Nikon employ a technology known as VR-III, which is capable of detecting both side-to-side and up-and-down motion, and Nikon claims that you can handhold your lens at up to 5 stops slower than a non-VR lens. All of the Nikon Vibration Reduction technology (VR, VR-II, and VR-III) is simply designated as "VR" on the lens.

- ▶ **ED.** This code indicates that some of the glass in the lens is Nikon Extra-Low Dispersion glass, which is less prone to lens flare and chromatic aberrations.

- ▶ **Micro-NIKKOR.** This is the designation for the line of Nikon macro lenses.

- ▶ **IF.** This stands for *Internal Focus.* The focusing mechanism is inside the lens, so the front of the lens doesn't rotate when focusing. This feature is useful when you don't want the front of the lens element to move, such as when using a polarizing filter. The internal focus mechanism also allows for faster focusing.

- ▶ **DC.** This stands for *Defocus Control.* Nikon offers only a couple of lenses with this designation. They make the out-of-focus areas in the image appear softer by using special lens elements to add spherical aberration. The parts of the image that are in focus aren't affected. Currently, the only Nikon lenses with this feature are the 135mm and the 105mm f/2. Both of these are considered portrait lenses.

- ▶ **N.** On some of the higher-end Nikon lenses, you may see a large golden N. This means the lens has Nikon Nano-Crystal Coating, which is designed to reduce flare and ghosting.

- ▶ **PC-E.** This is the designation for Nikon Perspective Control lenses. The E means that it has an electromagnetic Auto Indexing aperture control instead of the typical mechanical one found in all other AI lenses.

Lens Compatibility

Nikon has been manufacturing lenses since about 1937 and is well known for making some of the highest-quality lenses in the industry. You can use almost every Nikon lens made since about 1977 on your D3300, although some lenses will have limited functionality. In 1977, Nikon introduced the Auto Indexing (AI) lens. Auto Indexing allows the aperture diaphragm on the lens to stay wide open until the shutter is released; the diaphragm then closes down to the desired f-stop. This allows maximum light to enter the camera, which makes focusing easier. You can also use some of the earlier lenses, now referred to as *pre-AI,* but the camera's auto-exposure functions and metering will not work. All exposure settings must be calculated and set manually.

> **TIP** There are a number of apps that allow you to take exposure readings with your phone. I use a free one called LightMeter Free.

In the 1980s, Nikon started manufacturing autofocus (AF) lenses. Many of these lenses are very high quality and can be found at a much lower cost than their 1990s counterparts, the AF-D lenses. The main difference between AF lenses and AF-D lenses is that the AF-D lenses provide the camera with distance information based on how far away the subject is when you focus on it. Both types of lenses are focused with a screw-type drive motor inside the camera body. Unfortunately, to reduce the size and weight of the D3300, the camera body isn't equipped with a built-in focus motor. You can only use AF/AF-D lenses for manual focusing, although metering and auto-exposure work perfectly.

CAUTION Although these older lenses offer a great way to save money, I no longer recommend them as highly as I used to because of the high-resolution sensors in the newer cameras such as the D3300. These lenses are optimized for film cameras and can show more flare due to inferior lens coatings as well as reduced contrast and less-accurate color rendition.

The current Nikon line is the AF-S lens. AF-S lenses have a Silent Wave Motor built in to the lens. The AF-S is an ultrasonic motor that allows lenses to focus much more quickly than traditional, screw-type lenses. It also makes focusing very quiet. Most of these lenses are also known as G-type lenses. These lenses lack a manual aperture ring; you control the aperture by using the Command dial on the camera body. Nikon offers a full complement of AF-S lenses for the D3300, ranging from the ultrawide 10–24mm f/3.5–5.6G to the super-telephoto 600mm f/4G.

NOTE The first incarnation of the Silent Wave Motor from Nikon was called AF-I. These are long, expensive telephoto lenses, but they work perfectly with the D3300.

The DX Crop Factor

You may often hear or read about something called the *crop factor*. This concept is often confusing to newer photographers, especially those who are unfamiliar with 35mm film photography. The crop factor is a ratio that describes the size of a camera's imaging area as compared to another format; in the case of SLR cameras, the reference format is 35mm film.

SLR camera lenses were initially designed around the 35mm film format. Photographers use lenses of a certain focal length to provide a specific field of view. The field of view, also called the angle of view, is the amount of the scene that's captured in an image.

This is usually described in degrees. For example, when you use a 16mm lens on a 35mm camera, it captures 107 degrees of the scene, which is quite a bit. Conversely, when you use a 300mm focal length, the field of view is reduced to a mere 6.5 degrees, which is a very small part of the scene. The field of view is consistent from camera to camera because all SLRs use 35mm film, which has an image area of 24mm × 36mm.

Autofocus Concerns

The D3300 does not have an autofocus motor built in to the camera body, and so only lenses that have an integrated focus motor can perform autofocus functions with the D3300. This can lead to some confusion as to which lenses can be used with the D3300 with full functionality including autofocus.

As pointed out earlier, there are many letter designations on lenses. Nikon has its own specific designations and third-party companies use their own. This can make shopping for lenses online a daunting task. You don't want to order a lens and have it shipped to you only to find that the lens isn't equipped with an autofocus motor so you're reduced to manual focusing only.

Every company has its own letter designation for lenses with motors built in to the lens for autofocus, and some companies have more than one designation for different types of built-in motors that are included on different lenses.

Here's a list of the acronyms and keywords to look for when shopping for autofocus lenses for your D3300:

▶ **AF-S/AF-I (Nikon).** Nikon uses AF-S to designate that the lens has the ability to autofocus with the D3300. In Nikon literature, you also sometimes see the term *Silent Wave Motor*, or SWM. An older, rarer version is AF-I.

▶ **HSM (Sigma).** Sigma Corporation uses this acronym for its Hyper-Sonic (integrated focus) motor.

▶ **BIM/USD/PZD (Tamron).** BIM stands for Built-in Motor, USD for Ultra Sonic Drive, and PZD for Piezo Drive.

▶ **SD-M (Tokina).** This company's lens designation system is a bit tricky, so close scrutiny is required. I've seen Tokina integrated motors listed as SD-M (Silent Drive Motor), not to be confused with the SD designation, which is for Super-low Distortion glass. In Tokina literature, you also see Silent DC Motor listed as the name of the integrated motor. For DX-format lenses, all Tokina lenses with the DX II designation have integrated motors, while those with a simple DX designation do not.

With the advent of digital SLRs, the sensor was made smaller (15.6mm × 23.5mm) than a frame of 35mm film to keep costs down because full-frame sensors are more expensive to manufacture. This smaller sensor size was called APS-C or, in Nikon terms, the DX-format. When these same lenses are used with DX-format dSLRs, they have the same focal length they've always had, but because the sensor doesn't have the same amount of area as film (or an FX sensor), the field of view is effectively decreased. This causes the lens to provide the field of view of a longer focal length lens when compared to images taken on a camera with an FX sensor or 35mm film.

Fortunately, the DX sensors are a uniform size, thereby supplying consumers with a standard to determine how much the field of view is reduced on a DX-format dSLR with any lens. The digital sensors in Nikon DX cameras have a 1.5X crop factor, which means that to determine the equivalent focal length of a 35mm or FX camera, you simply have to multiply the focal length of the lens by 1.5. Therefore, a 28mm lens provides an angle of coverage similar to a 42mm lens, a 50mm is equivalent to a 75mm, and so on.

> **TIP** An easy way to figure out the DX equivalent focal length is to divide the focal length by 2, and then add the quotient to the original focal length. For example, take a 50mm lens: 50 divided by 2 is 25, and 50 plus 25 equals 75. The equivalent focal length in 35mm (or FX) is 75mm.

Nikon has created specific lenses for dSLRs with DX sensors. These lenses are known as DX-format lenses. The focal length of these lenses was shortened to fill the gap to allow true super-wide-angle lenses. These DX-format lenses were also redesigned to cast a smaller image inside the camera so that the lenses could actually be made smaller and use less glass than conventional lenses. The byproduct of designing a lens to project an image circle to a smaller sensor is that these same lenses can't effectively be used with FX-format and can't be used at all with 35mm film cameras (without severe vignetting) because the image won't completely fill an area the size of the film or FX sensor.

There are some upsides to this crop factor. Lenses with longer focal lengths now provide a bit of extra reach. A lens set at 200mm now provides the same amount of coverage as a 300mm lens, which can offer a great advantage for sports and wildlife photography, or when you can't get close enough to your subject. Also, when using a lens designed for FX cameras, the sensor only records image information from the center of the lens, which is generally sharper.

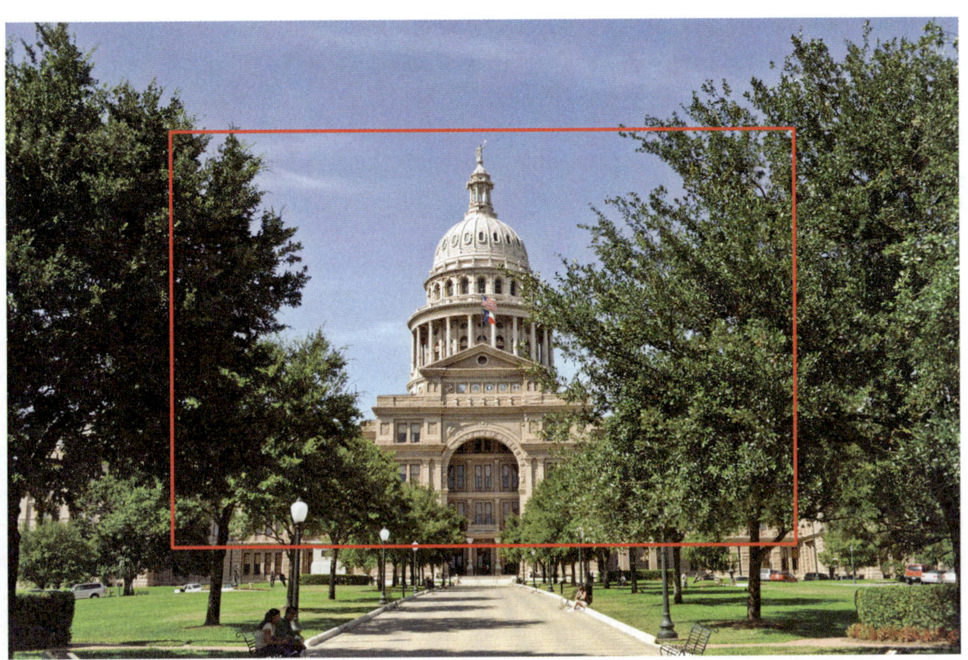

4.1 This image was shot with a 28mm lens on a Nikon FX camera. The area inside the red square is what would be captured with the same lens on a DX camera, like the D3300.

Another advantage of DX lenses is that, because of their relatively small size, they are less expensive to manufacture and, therefore, the lenses are less expensive than their full-frame counterparts.

Third-Party Lenses

Other companies also make lenses for Nikon cameras. These lenses are referred to as *third-party* lenses or sometimes, albeit less frequently, *nonmanufacturer* lenses. What this means is that the company that makes the lenses isn't affiliated with the manufacturer (first-party) or the purchaser (second-party), but is its own entity (third-party).

Previously, third-party lenses were considered inferior substitutes to OEM (Original Equipment Manufacturer) lenses, and in the past that was true. However, in the last 10 years, the digital revolution has brought a huge resurgence in photography, and third-party lens manufacturers have stepped up their game to provide very high-quality lenses at lower prices than those sold by Nikon. While most third-party lenses don't stand up to Nikon professional-grade lenses as far as build quality, third-party lenses are great alternatives to high-end to lower-level Nikon consumer lenses. If you're looking for a relatively inexpensive, fast, constant-aperture zoom with good image quality, then a third-party lens is likely the answer.

There are three major players in the third-party lens game: Sigma, Tokina, and Tamron. You may see other brands such as Vivitar and Promaster, but these lenses are usually made by one of the three and rebranded.

Sigma is a company that has been making lenses for more than 50 years, and was the first lens manufacturer to make a wide-angle zoom lens. Sigma makes excellent, high-quality lenses. Almost all current Sigma lenses are available with what Sigma calls an HSM, or Hyper-Sonic Motor. This is an AF motor built inside the lens. It operates in a similar fashion to the Nikon AF-S, or Silent Wave Motor. This enables almost all current Sigma lenses to autofocus perfectly with the D3300.

Sigma has recently announced some new high-end lenses (called their Global Vision lenses) that can be used with DX cameras such as the D3300. They all have HSM motors and include the 30mm f/1.4; a redesigned 17–70mm f/2.8–4 Macro OS; the pro telephoto 120–300mm f/2.8 OS, an all-in-one zoom; the 18-200 f/3.5-6.3 DC Macro OS; and the groundbreaking 18–35mm f/1.8, the first zoom lens to ever achieve an aperture wider than f/2.8. These are also the first lenses that enable the user to connect the lens to a computer via a USB dock and use proprietary Sigma software to update firmware and make micro-adjustments for focusing. This is an amazing new feature. Sigma is blazing new trails in lens technology. Sigma Global Vision lenses are a viable and affordable alternative to professional offerings from Nikon.

Tokina only offers a few lenses that are fully compatible with cameras that don't have a built-in focus motor, like the D3300. The wide-angle lenses are the 11–16mm f/2.8 Pro DXII, the 12–24mm f/4 Pro DXII, and the 16–28mm f/2.8 Pro FX (this lens also works with full-frame cameras, such as the Nikon D600). Most other current Tokina lenses can be used with the D3300 as manual focus only.

Tamron is another major player in the third-party lens market. The company currently offers about a half dozen lenses that are equipped with a built-in motor to focus with the D3300, with the 17–50mm f/2.8 being the most popular, inexpensive fast zoom lens. Tamron has been working through some problems with its built-in focus motor technology, so there are a few different iterations of its most popular lenses. It has a standard screw-type focus technology, referred to as Built-in-Motor (BIM), that focuses very slowly and loudly with an internal focus motor. It also has the Piezo Drive (PZD) and the Ultrasonic Drive (USD), which are recent additions that are comparable to the Nikon Silent Wave or AF-S lenses. Only lenses with the BIM, PZD, or USD designations will autofocus with the D3300.

Variable-aperture Lenses

One of the issues with less expensive lenses, such as the 18–55mm VRII kit lens, is that they have a *variable aperture*. This means that as you zoom in on something when shooting wide open or closed down to the minimum aperture, the aperture opening effectively gets smaller and allows less light to reach the sensor, causing the need for a slower shutter speed or higher ISO setting. In daylight or brightly lit situations, this may not be a factor, but when shooting in low light, this can be a drawback. Although the VR feature helps when shooting relatively still subjects, moving subjects in low light are blurred.

Higher-end lenses have a constant aperture all the way through the zoom range, which allows you to maintain a consistent exposure setting no matter what focal length you're at.

Types of Lenses

As I mentioned at the beginning of this chapter, one of the most important features of SLR cameras is the ability to use many types of lenses. This allows you to control the aspect in which the image is displayed. Different types of lenses are designed to provide certain effects. The lenses you choose allow you to control the artistic direction of your photography.

Wide-angle lenses

The focal-length range of wide-angle lenses starts at about 10mm (ultrawide) and extends to about 24mm (wide angle). Many of the most common wide-angle lenses on the market today are zoom lenses, although a few prime lenses are available. Wide-angle lenses are typically *rectilinear,* meaning that the lens has molded glass elements to correct the distortion that's common with wide-angle lenses; this keeps the lines near the edges of the frame straight rather than curved. Fisheye lenses, which are also a type of wide-angle lens, are *curvilinear;* the lens elements aren't corrected, resulting in severe optical distortion (which is desirable in a fisheye lens).

Wide-angle lenses have a short focal length, which projects an image onto the sensor that has a wider field of view; this allows you to fit more of the scene into your image. In the past, ultrawide-angle lenses were rare, prohibitively expensive, and out of reach for most nonprofessional photographers. These days, it's easy to find a relatively inexpensive ultrawide-angle lens. The following list includes some of the ultrawide-angle lenses that work best with the D3300:

▶ **AF-S NIKKOR 10–24mm f/3.5–4.5G.** This is a great compact, ultrawide-angle lens. It's nice and sharp, and balances well on the D3300. The only downside is that it is a little pricey compared to third-party lenses of the same caliber.

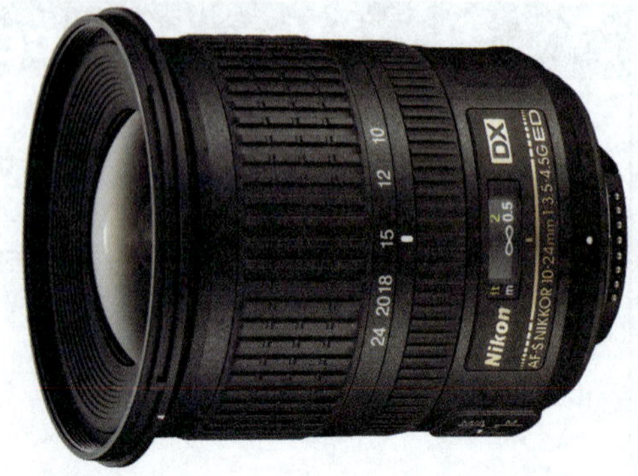

Image courtesy of Nikon, Inc.

4.2 The NIKKOR 10–24mm f/3.5-4.5G lens.

▶ **Tokina 11–16mm f/2.8 Pro DXII.** This is one of the only ultrawide lenses available with a fast, constant, built-in focus motor that allows the D3300 to autofocus. The zoom range is rather small, but when using an ultrawide lens, most photographers tend to stay at the wide end of the range anyway.

▶ **Sigma 10–20mm f/3.5 and f/4–5.6 DC HSM.** Sigma offers two lenses in this range: the f/3.5 constant-aperture version and the variable-aperture f/4–5.6 version. Neither of these is quite as good as the Nikon lens, but they are more affordable. If you do a lot of low-light, handheld shooting, the f/3.5 version is the better option. If you shoot mostly in daylight or photograph landscapes at smaller apertures with a tripod, the cheaper f/4–5.6 lens is a good option.

▶ **Sigma 8-16mm f/4.5-5.6 DC HSM.** For those of you that want the widest angle of view possible (without resorting to a fisheye) this is the widest choice of any lens out there. The difference of 2mm doesn't sound like a lot, but it really makes a big difference.

Wide-angle lenses are perfect for a variety of subjects. The perspective you get from a wide-angle lens isn't like anything that can be seen with the human eye. You can use this lens to create some very bold and interesting images. Once you get used to seeing the world through a wide-angle lens, you may find that you look at your subjects and the world in general in a different way.

I always try to find interesting lines and angles for use with my wide-angle lenses. There are many factors to consider when you use a wide-angle lens. Here are a few:

▶ **Deeper depth of field.** Wide-angle lenses allow you to get more of the scene in focus than you can with a midrange or telephoto lens at the same aperture and distance from the subject.

▶ **Wider field of view.** Wide-angle lenses allow you to fit more of your subject into your images. The shorter the focal length is, the more of the subject you can fit into a shot. This can be especially beneficial when you shoot landscape photos and want to fit an immense scene into your photo, or when photographing a large group of people.

▶ **Perspective distortion.** Using wide-angle lenses causes things that are closer to the lens to look disproportionately larger than things that are farther away. You can use perspective distortion to your advantage to emphasize objects in the foreground if you want the subject to stand out in the frame.

▶ **Handheld shooting.** At shorter focal lengths, it's possible to hold the camera steadier than you can at longer focal lengths. At 14mm, it's entirely possible to handhold your camera at 1/15 second without worrying about camera shake.

▶ **Environmental portraits.** Although using a wide-angle lens isn't the best choice for standard close-up portraits, wide-angle lenses work great for environmental portraits where you want to show a person in his or her surroundings.

Wide-angle lenses can also help pull you into a subject. With most wide-angle lenses, you can focus very close on a subject while creating the perspective distortion for which wide-angle lenses are known. Don't be afraid to get close to your subject to make a more dynamic image. The worst wide-angle images are the ones that have a tiny subject in the middle of an empty area.

Zoom Lenses versus Prime Lenses

Some photographers prefer primes, and some prefer zooms. It's largely a personal choice, and each type has its advantages. One of the main advantages of the zoom lens is its versatility. You can attach one lens to your camera and use it in a wide variety of situations, which reduces how often you need to change your lenses. This is a very good feature because every time you take the lens off your camera, the sensor is vulnerable to dust and debris. In addition, in the time it takes to change from one lens to another, you may miss the shot.

One of the most important features of prime lenses is that they can have a faster maximum aperture than zoom lenses due to their smaller size. Primes also require fewer lens elements and moving parts, so the weight is considerably reduced as compared to a fast zoom. Fast DX primes like the Nikon 35mm f/1.8 are also relatively inexpensive and are some of the best Nikon lenses.

Wide-angle lenses are very distinctive in the way they portray your subjects, but they also have some limitations that you may not find in lenses with longer focal lengths. Here are some pitfalls that you need to be aware of when using wide-angle lenses:

- ▶ **Soft corners.** The most common problem with wide-angle lenses, especially zooms, is that they soften the images in the corners. This is most prevalent at wide apertures, such as f/2.8 and f/4.0; the corners usually sharpen up by f/8.0 (depending on the lens). This problem is most noticeable in lower-priced lenses. The high resolution of the D3300 can really magnify these flaws.

- ▶ **Vignetting.** This is the darkening of the corners in an image. Vignetting occurs because the light necessary to capture such a wide angle of view must come in at a very sharp angle. When the light comes in at such an angle, the aperture is effectively smaller. The aperture opening no longer appears as a circle, but more like a cat's eye (you can see this effect in the bokeh at the edges of very fast lenses). Stopping down the aperture reduces this effect, and reducing the aperture by three stops usually eliminates any vignetting.

- ▶ **Perspective distortion.** Perspective distortion is a double-edged sword: it can make your images look either very interesting or very terrible. One of the reasons that a wide-angle lens isn't recommended for close-up portraits is that it distorts faces, making the nose look too big and the ears too small. This can make for a very unflattering portrait.

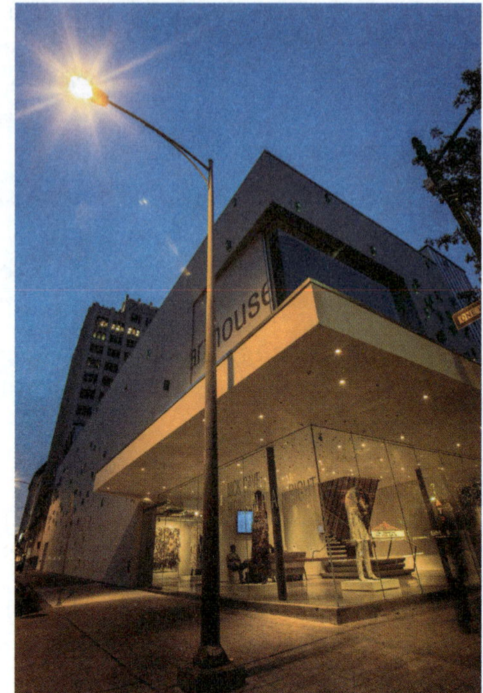

4.3 A wide-angle shot taken with a Nikon 10–24mm f/3.5–4.5G wide-angle lens at 12mm. Exposure: ISO 400, f/11, 1 second.

Focal Length and Depth of Field

Although focal length seems to be a factor in depth of field, technically speaking, this isn't true. Telephoto lenses appear to have a shallower depth of field due to a higher magnification factor, but if the subject stays the same size in the frame, the depth of field is consistent at any given aperture, regardless of the focal length.

What *does* change is the distribution of the zone of acceptable sharpness. At shorter focal lengths, most of the zone is behind the focal point or subject. At longer focal lengths, the zone of acceptable sharpness falls more in front of the focal point. This means that, although mathematically the depth of field is consistent at all focal lengths, the distribution of the zone of sharpness is different.

Wide-angle lenses have a more gradual fall-off of sharpness, which makes the depth of field appear deeper. Telephoto lenses appear to have a shallower depth of field because the zone of sharpness falls off more quickly behind the focal point, and the background is magnified due to compression distortion. This causes the background to appear much larger in relation to the subject than when using a short focal length.

▶ **Barrel distortion.** Wide-angle, and even rectilinear lenses, are often plagued with this specific type of distortion, which causes straight lines outside the image center to appear to bend outward (similar to a barrel). This can be undesirable when doing architectural photography. Fortunately, Photoshop and other image-editing applications enable you to fix this problem relatively easily.

Standard zoom lenses

Standard (or midrange) zoom lenses fall in the middle of the focal-length scale. Zoom lenses of this type usually start at a moderately wide angle of around 16mm to 18mm and zoom in to a short telephoto range between 50mm and 85mm. These lenses are perfect for most general photography applications. In fact, they can be used successfully for everything from architectural to portrait photography. This type of lens covers the most useful focal lengths and will probably spend the most time on your camera. For this reason, I recommend buying the best quality lens you can afford. Here are some options for midrange lenses:

▶ **Sigma 18–35mm f/1.8 DC HSM | A.** This is a new technological marvel of a lens from Sigma. Although it covers a relatively short range, this is the fastest zoom lens ever created. It allows for shutter speeds as fast as a fast prime lens, but with the versatility of a zoom lens. The fast aperture also allows a shallower depth of field than you can get with any zoom lens of the same focal length, for creative use of depth of field for more artistic shots. Although this lens has a very short range, which some people may find limiting, it spends a lot of time on my camera.

▶ **Tamron 17–50mm f/2.8 Di II.** This is a very popular alternative to the Nikon lens for a fast aperture zoom. There are two versions of the Di II lens: the VC (Vibration Compensation) and non-VC. However, you should be aware that there is also an earlier Di version that doesn't have a built-in focus motor and won't autofocus with the D3300.

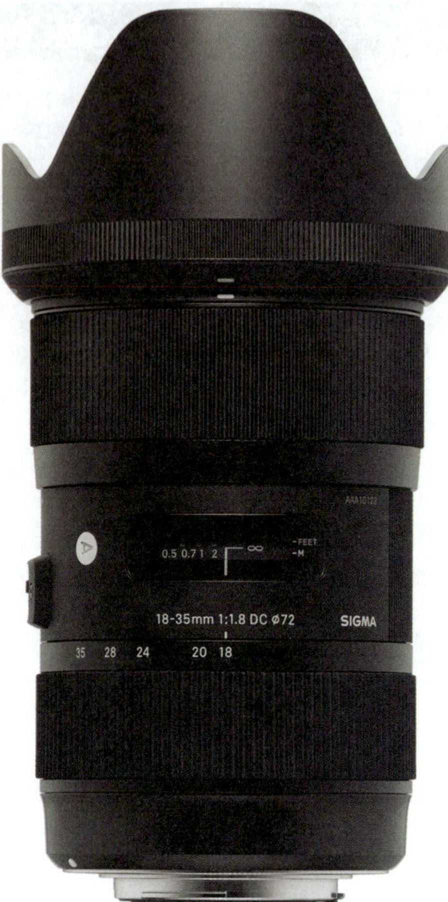

Image courtesy of Sigma, Inc.

4.4 The Sigma 18–35mm f/1.8 DC HSM | A lens.

▶ **Sigma 17–70mm f/2.8–4 HSM OS Macro | C.** This is one of my favorite lenses for DX cameras, and it's easily the most versatile lens I've ever owned. It's relatively fast and good for low-light shooting with Optical Stabilization. It's also very sharp and, although not a true macro lens, it gets you close enough. The best part is that it's not overly expensive. I recommend this lens over all other standard lenses in its class.

In the standard range for primes, the most popular are the 30–35mm normal lenses. They are referred to as *normal* because they approximate the same field of view as the human eye. The Nikon 35mm f/1.8G is a competent, inexpensive, fast normal lens, as is the even faster Sigma 30mm f/1.4. I recommend that every photographer carry a fast prime lens in his camera bag.

CAUTION Nikon now offers two versions of the 35mm f/1.8G. One is made for DX and the other can be used on FX or DX cameras. The newer FX version is about $400 more than the DX model. Keep this in mind when shopping for a Nikon 35mm f/1.8G lens. The DX version is the AF-S DX 35mm f/1.8G.

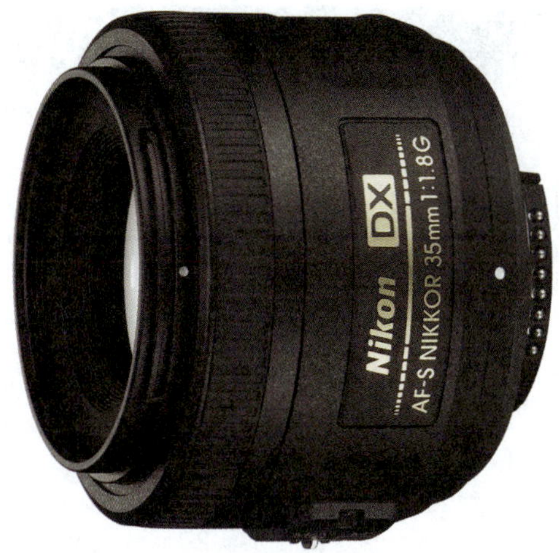

Image courtesy of Nikon, Inc.

4.5 The Nikon 35mm f/1.8G DX lens is a favorite of many photographers.

Telephoto lenses

Telephoto lenses have very long focal lengths that are used to get a closer view of distant subjects. They provide a very narrow field of view and are handy when you're trying to focus on the details of a far-off subject. Telephoto lenses appear to have a much shallower depth of field than wide-angle and midrange lenses, and you can use them to blur out background details to isolate a subject. Telephoto lenses are commonly used for sports and wildlife photography. The shallow depth of field also makes them one of the top choices for photographing portraits.

Like wide-angle lenses, telephoto lenses also have their quirks, such as perspective distortion. As you may have guessed, telephoto perspective distortion is the opposite of wide-angle distortion. Because everything in the photo is so far away with a telephoto lens, the lens tends to *compress* the image. Compression causes the background to look closer to the subject than it actually is. Of course, you can use this effect creatively. For example, compression can flatten out the features of a model, resulting in a pleasing effect. Compression is one of the main reasons photographers often use a telephoto lens for portrait photography.

Using Vibration Reduction Lenses

Nikon has an impressive list of lenses that offer Vibration Reduction (VR). This technology is used to combat image blur caused by camera shake, especially when handholding the camera at long focal lengths. The VR function works by detecting the motion of the lens and shifting the internal lens elements. This allows you to shoot at slower shutter speeds than you normally use while still getting sharp images.

An old rule of thumb is that to get a reasonably sharp photo when handholding the camera, you should use a shutter speed that corresponds to the reciprocal of the lens's focal length. In simpler terms, when shooting at a 200mm zoom setting, your shutter speed should be at least 1/200 second. When shooting with a wider setting, such as 28mm, you can safely handhold at around 1/30 second. Nikon has updated the VR mechanism a few times and refers to it as VR-II and VR-III. They claim that with the original VR, you can shoot up to three stops slower, while the newer VR-II enables you to shoot four stops slower. The brand-new VR-III ups that claim to five stops of reduction. Although the VR feature provides some extra latitude when shooting with low light, it's not made to replace a fast shutter speed. To get a good, sharp photo when shooting action, you need a fast shutter speed to freeze the motion. No matter how good the VR is, nothing can freeze a moving subject but a fast shutter speed.

Some third-party lens manufacturers offer their own version of VR: for example, Sigma has Optical Stabilization (OS) and Tamron has Vibration Control (VC). Tokina doesn't currently include image stabilization on any of its lenses.

A standard telephoto zoom lens usually has a range of about 70 to 200mm. If you want to zoom in close to a subject that's very far away, you may need an even longer lens. These super-telephoto lenses can act like telescopes, really bringing the subject in close. They range from about 300mm up to about 800mm. Almost all super-telephoto lenses are prime lenses, and they're very heavy, bulky, and expensive. To keep costs lower (and in many cases due to size and weight constraints), some super-telephoto lenses have a slower aperture of f/4.0.

There are quite a few telephoto prime lenses available. Most of them, especially the longer ones (105mm and longer), are expensive, although you can sometimes find older Nikon primes that are discontinued or used — and at decent prices — such as the NIKKOR 300mm f/4.0.

The following list covers some of the most common telephoto lenses:

▶ **NIKKOR 70–200mm f/4G VR III.** This is the latest affordable professional grade Nikon alternative to the 70–200mm f/2.8G VR lens. It is sharp and has a constant f/4.0 aperture. This makes for a smaller, lighter lens when speed isn't a necessity. Its relatively small size makes it a great high-quality lens for the D3300. This lens is designed for FX use, but is still a great fit for a DX camera like the D3300 due to its smaller size as compared to other pro telephoto lenses.

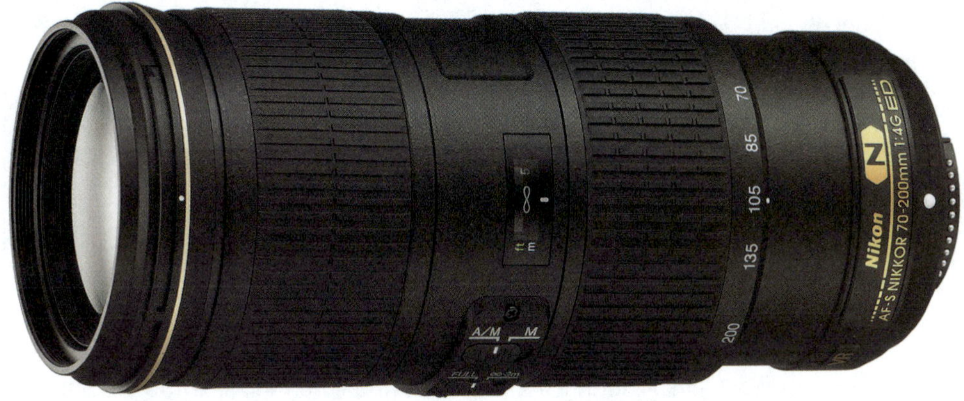

Image courtesy of Nikon, Inc.
4.6 The NIKKOR 70–200mm f/4G VR III lens.

▶ **NIKKOR 55–300mm f/4–5.6G VR.** If you need a lot of reach, but don't have a lot of money, this lens gives you the best results in its price range. It's a stop slower than the 70–200mm f/4 at the long end, but it's smaller, lighter, and much less expensive. The image quality is acceptable for the price, but it's not necessarily the best option for maximum resolving power. This is a great lens to get started with.

▶ **NIKKOR 80–400mm f/4.5–5.6G AF-S ED VR.** This newly redesigned high-power, VR image-stabilization zoom lens gives you a lot of reach. Its versatile zoom range makes it especially useful for wildlife photography when the subject is far away. As with most lenses with a very broad focal-length range, you make concessions with fast apertures and a moderately lower image quality when compared to the 70–200mm constant-aperture lenses. This lens is relatively expensive, but if you need a lot of reach, it is one of the few options for zoom lenses. This lens can also be used with FX cameras.

Super-zoom Lenses

Most lens manufacturers, Nikon included, offer what's commonly called a *super-zoom*, or sometimes a *hyper-zoom*. Super-zooms are lenses that encompass a very broad focal length, from wide angle to telephoto. The most popular of the DX super-zooms is the Nikon 18–200mm f/3.5–5.6 VR. Nikon's DX 18–140mm f/3.5–5.6G VR lens borders on the super-zoom range as well. Very recently Nikon announced the 18–300mm f/3.5–6.3 that covers the widest range of any other lens.

These lenses have a large focal-length range that you can use in a wide variety of shooting situations without having to switch out lenses. This would come in handy if, for example, you were photographing a night landscape scene out in Roswell, New Mexico, using a wide-angle setting, and suddenly an alien space-craft went flying by. You could quickly zoom in with the super-telephoto setting and get a good close-up shot of ALF peeping out the window without having to fumble around in your camera bag to grab a telephoto and switch out lenses, possibly causing you to miss the shot of a lifetime.

Super-zooms come with a price (figuratively and literally). To achieve the great ranges in focal length, concessions must be made with regard to image quality. These lenses are usually less sharp than lenses with a shorter zoom range and are more often plagued with optical distortions and chromatic aberration. Super-zooms often show pronounced barrel distortion at the wide end and can have moderate to severe pincushion distortion at the long end of the range. Luckily, these distortions can be fixed in Photoshop or other image-editing software.

Another caveat to using these lenses is that they usually have appreciably smaller maximum apertures than zoom lenses with shorter ranges. This can be a problem, especially because larger apertures are generally needed at the long end to allow a high enough shutter speed to avoid blurring that results from camera shake when handholding. Of course, some manufacturers include some sort of stabilization technology to help control this problem.

Close-up/macro lenses

A macro lens is a special-purpose lens used in macro and close-up photography. It allows you to have a closer focusing distance than regular lenses, which in turn allows you to get more magnification of your subject, revealing small details that would otherwise be lost. True macro lenses offer a magnification ratio of 1:1; that is, the image projected onto the sensor through the lens is the exact same size as the object being photo-graphed. Some lower-priced macro lenses offer a 1:2 or even a 1:4 magnification ratio, which is one-half to one-quarter of the size of the original object. Although lens manufac-turers refer to these lenses as macro, strictly speaking, they are not.

One major concern with a macro lens is the depth of field; when you focus at such a close distance, the depth of field becomes very shallow. As a result, it's often advisable to use a small aperture to maximize your depth of field and ensure everything is in focus. Of course, as with any downside, there's also an upside: You can also use the shallow depth of field creatively. For example, you can use it to isolate a detail in a subject.

Macro lenses come in a variety of focal lengths, with the most common being 60mm. Some macro lenses have substantially longer focal lengths that allow more distance between the lens and the subject. This comes in handy when the subject needs to be lit with an additional light source. A lens that's very close to the subject while focusing can get in the way of the light source, casting a shadow.

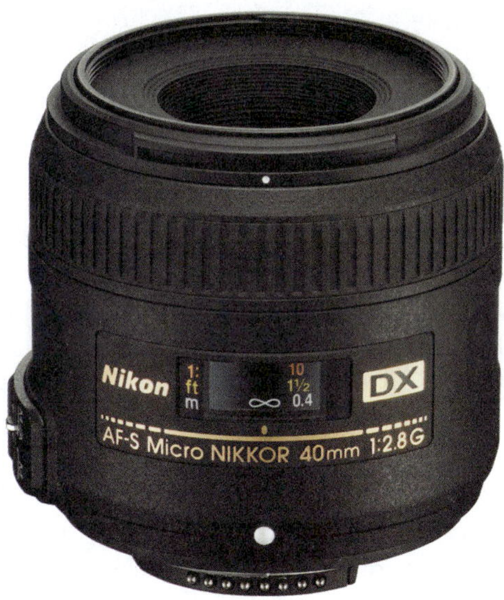

Image courtesy of Nikon, Inc.

4.7 The Micro-NIKKOR 40mm f/2.8G macro lens.

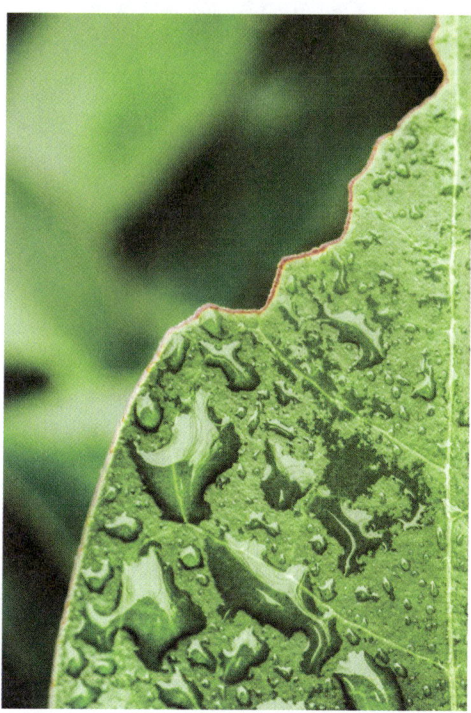

4.8 I shot this macro photo of a leaf covered with raindrops using a Nikon 60mm f/2.8G macro lens. Exposure: ISO 450, f/8, 1/250 second.

When buying a macro lens, you should consider a few things: How often are you going to use the lens? Can you use it for other purposes? Do you need AF? Because newer dedicated macro lenses can be pricey, you may want to consider some less expensive alternatives.

It's not absolutely necessary to have an autofocus lens. When shooting very close up, the depth of focus is very small, so all you need to do is move slightly closer or farther away to achieve focus. This makes an autofocus lens a bit unnecessary. You can find plenty of older manual focus (MF) macro lenses that are very inexpensive, but that have superb lens quality and sharpness.

Nikon has a very strong lineup of macro lenses that offer full functionality with the D3300. They range from normal to telephoto in both VR and non-VR versions and at all price points. The choices include the 40mm f/2.8G, 60mm f/2.8G, 85mm f/3.5G VR, and the 105mm f/2.8G VR when you need some extra reach.

Fisheye lenses

Fisheye lenses are ultrawide-angle lenses that aren't corrected for distortion like standard rectilinear wide-angle lenses. These lenses are known as *curvilinear,* meaning that straight lines in your image, especially near the edge of the frame, are curved. Fisheye lenses have extreme barrel distortion. What makes fisheye lenses appealing is the very thing we try to get rid of in other wide-angle lenses.

Fisheye lenses cover a full 180-degree area, allowing you to see everything that's immediately to the left and right of you in the frame. You need to take special care so that you don't get your feet in the frame, which often happens when you use a lens with a field of view this extreme.

Fisheye lenses aren't made for everyday shooting, but with their extreme perspective distortion, you can achieve interesting, and sometimes wacky, results. You can also *de-fish* or correct for the extreme fisheye by using image-editing software such as Photoshop, Capture NX or NX 2, and DxO Optics. The result of de-fishing your image is that you get a reduced field of view. This is akin to using a rectilinear wide-angle lens, but it often yields a slightly wider field of view than a standard wide-angle lens.

Two types of fisheye lenses are available: circular and full frame. Circular fisheye lenses project a complete 180-degree round image onto the frame, resulting in a circular image surrounded by black in the rest of the frame. A full-frame fisheye completely covers the frame with an image. The 16mm NIKKOR fisheye is a full-frame fisheye on an FX-format dSLR. Sigma also makes a few fisheye lenses in both the circular and full-frame variety. A couple of companies that were initially founded in the former Soviet Union (Zenitar and Peleng) still manufacture relatively high-quality but affordable manual-focus, fisheye lenses. Autofocus is not really necessary on fisheye lenses, given their extreme depth of field and short focusing distance.

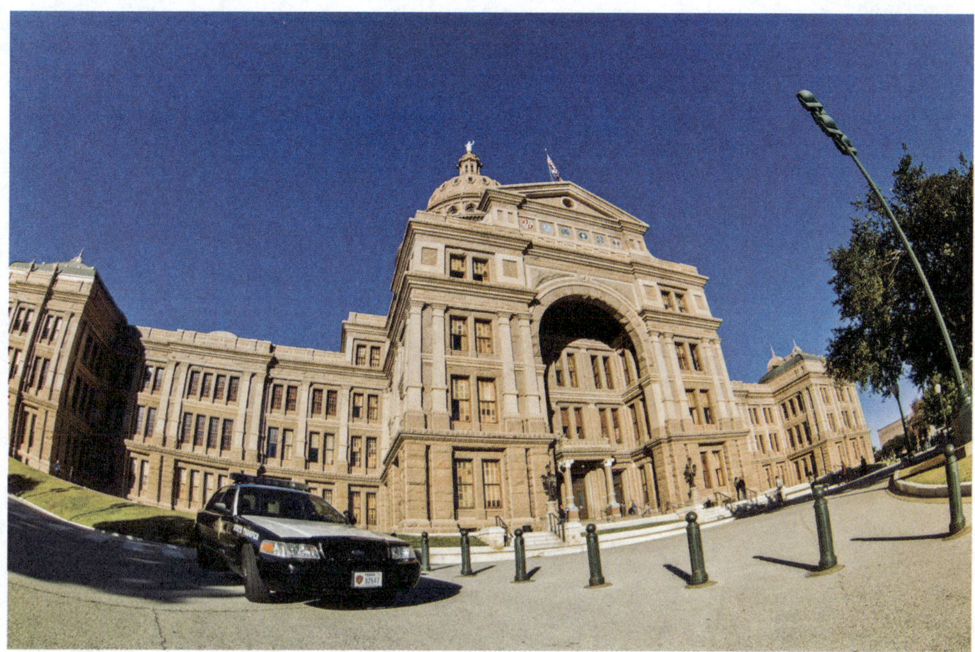

4.9 An image of the Texas State Capitol taken with a Nikon 10.5mm fisheye lens. Notice the pronounced curving distortion at the horizon line. Exposure: ISO 100, f/16, 1/125 second.

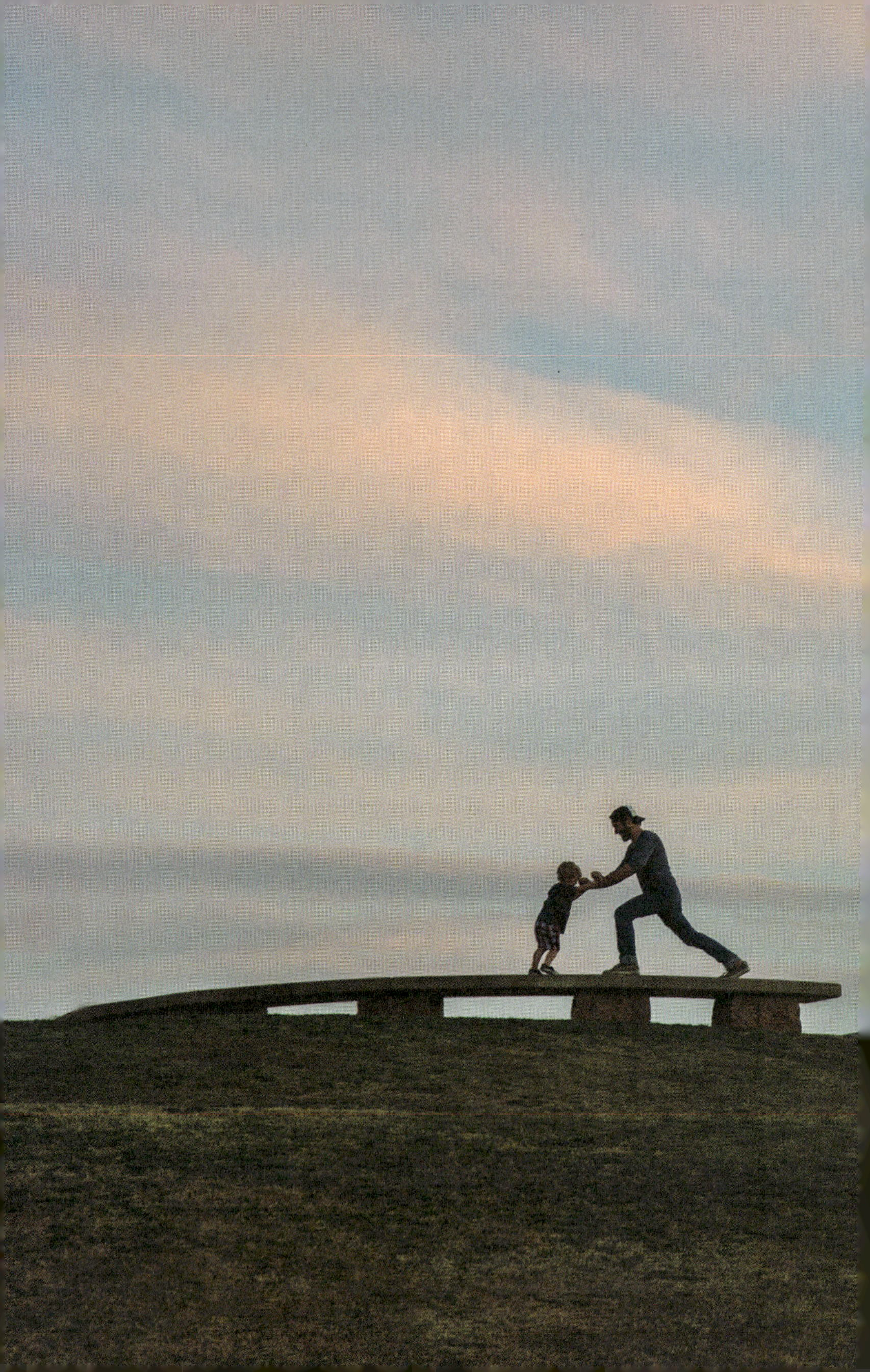

CHAPTER 5

Controlling Exposure

The fact that you bought a book to learn about what your camera is capable of shows that you are interested in more than taking simple snapshots. Understanding the fundamentals of exposure is very important when taking up the hobby of photography. While the scene modes are a starting point for taking photographs of different subjects, if you want to achieve predictable results, then learning about exposure is where you need to start.

Exposure isn't exceedingly difficult to master, but at first, it can seem technical and confusing, especially if you're new to the world of dSLR cameras. In this chapter, I introduce the basic concepts, explain what they are, and cover the different uses that they have for creating artistic photographs.

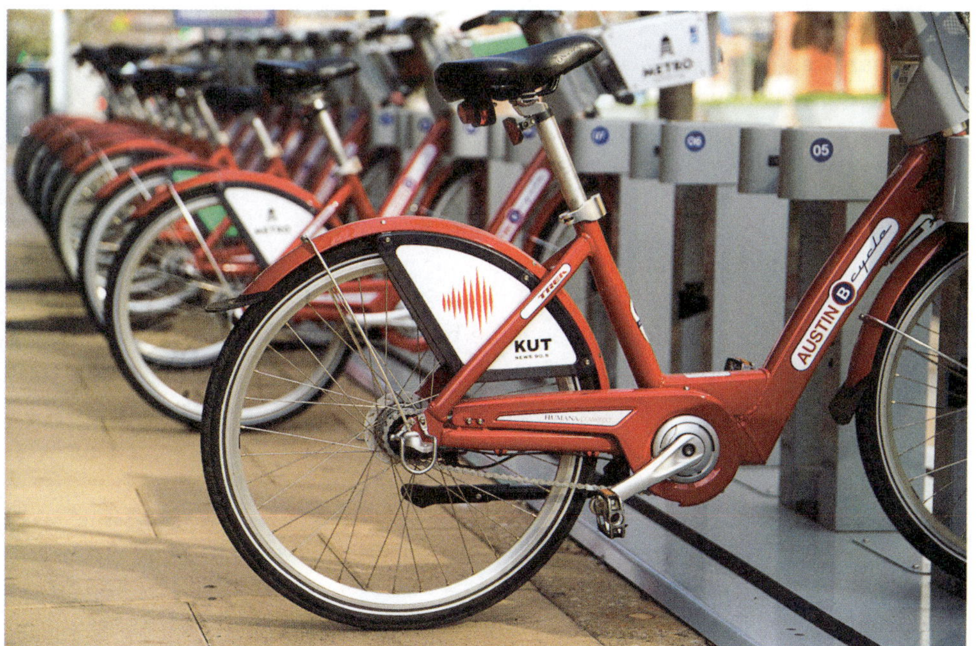

Knowing which modes and features to use in any given situation allows you to get a good exposure, no matter what you're shooting.

Defining Exposure

Exposure is the amount of light that reaches the camera sensor during a single shutter cycle. A *shutter cycle* occurs when the shutter-release button is fully depressed, the reflex mirror flips up, the shutter opens and closes, the mirror flips back down into place, and the shutter resets. While that sounds like a lot, in reality it all happens in a fraction of a second (unless you're using a long shutter speed, of course).

Three things determine how much light reaches the sensor of your D3300 during each shutter cycle. Each of these three elements must be set to a specific value to achieve a proper exposure for the amount of light that exists in the scene that you are photographing. If one of the three elements is changed, one or both of the remaining elements must be adjusted accordingly to get an equivalent exposure.

The three elements of exposure are

▶ **Shutter speed.** The *shutter speed* simply determines the length of time the shutter is open, exposing the sensor to light.

▶ **ISO sensitivity.** The *ISO setting* you choose influences the camera sensor's sensitivity to light — or more correctly, how much the signal from the sensor is amplified.

▶ **Aperture.** The *aperture* (also known as the *f-stop)* is the opening inside the lens that controls the amount of light that reaches the sensor of your camera. Each lens has an adjustable opening. As you change the size of the aperture, you allow more or less light to reach the sensor.

If you've spent any time around photographers or photography forums, you may have heard the word *stop.* All three of the aforementioned elements are measured in *stops.* The term *stop* relates to each of these three elements because they represent the same amount of light. Closing the aperture by 1 stop is the same as reducing your shutter speed by 1 stop or decreasing the ISO sensitivity by 1 stop.

> **NOTE** In current photography lingo, the fine adjustments that you can apply to the ISO, shutter speed, and aperture settings are referred to as steps. A step represents each of the settings between 1 stop increments. The D3300 allows you to set the shutter speed and aperture in 1/3 steps, but the ISO only in 1 stop increments

To clarify, a stop isn't a quantity of light. A stop is the doubling or halving of the amount of light in any given exposure. In short, each whole setting of these three elements of exposure is equivalent to 1 stop of light, and you can use these settings to double or halve the amount of light to which you expose the sensor.

As covered in Chapter 2, the D3300 has a number of exposure modes that can give you a correct exposure. However, keep in mind that there is actually not a single correct exposure setting for any one scene. Depending on the situation, the camera can choose any number of settings that add up to a correct exposure.

As mentioned previously, changing one aspect of the exposure setting requires changing one of the other elements to allow the same amount of light to reach the sensor. This is referred to as *equivalent exposure,* meaning that although some of the settings have been altered, the quantity of light reaching the sensor remains the same. This means that for any given scene, there can be seven or more correct exposures at a specific ISO setting. If you add in ISO sensitivity, you can have more than 14 separate exposure settings that give you the same exposure. If you consider that the D3300 is set by default to work in 1/3-stop settings, that number triples.

Now, when I say there isn't any one correct exposure setting that works for any given scene, this statement comes with a caveat. There is *one* exposure setting that is correct, and that is the one that *you* choose. You can look at the exposure meter in the camera and adjust the settings until the meter shows that you have the right settings to get the right amount of light to make a nice, even exposure, but that doesn't mean that the image will come out exactly as you envision it. You may want the photo slightly overexposed to brighten it, or underexposed to get deeper shadows. This means that you select the appropriate settings to create an artistic image, an *expressive* exposure setting, if you will.

In the following sections, I discuss the basics of the different elements in the exposure trio and how you can use them to express yourself creatively not only to make good exposures but also to use them to create effects that add interest to your images.

ISO

The ISO sensitivity number indicates how sensitive to light the medium is; in the case of the D3300, that medium is the CMOS sensor. The higher the ISO number, the more sensitive it is and the less light you need to take a photograph. For example, you might choose an ISO setting of 100 on a bright, sunny day when you are photographing outside because you have plenty of light. However, on a cloudy day you may want to consider an ISO of 400 or higher to make sure your camera captures enough available light.

NOTE Technically, in digital photography, the ISO sensitivity setting controls how much amplification the signal from the sensor receives.

ISO sensitivity settings on the D3300, in 1-stop increments, are 100, 200, 400, 800, 1600, 3200, 6400, and 12,800. Each ISO setting is twice as sensitive to light as the previous setting. For example, at ISO 400, your camera is twice as sensitive to light as it is at ISO 200. This means it needs only half the light at ISO 400 that it needs at ISO 200 to achieve the same exposure.

Keep in mind, however, that when using Auto ISO (**ISO-A**), the camera uses 1/3-step ISO settings at all times.

In an artistic context, you can use the ISO to control either the aperture or the shutter speed; for example, if you need a faster shutter speed or smaller aperture to get a desired effect, then you can raise the ISO sensitivity setting.

Shutter speed

Shutter speed is the amount of time that the shutter exposes the sensor to light. Shutter speeds are indicated in seconds, with long shutter speeds in whole seconds and short shutter speeds in fractions of a second. Common shutter speeds (from slow to fast) in 1-stop increments include 1 second, 1/2, 1/4, 1/8, 1/15, 1/30, 1/60, 1/125, 1/500, 1/1000, and so on. Increasing or decreasing shutter speed by one setting halves or doubles the exposure, respectively.

The D3300 shutter speed is controlled in 1/3 steps, so it uses the following numbers: 1 second, 1/1.3, 1/1.6, 1/2, 1/2.5, 1/3, 1/4, 1/5, 1/6, 1/8, and so on. Shutter speeds play various roles in creating expressive exposures. They allow the photographer to portray motion in a still photograph in different ways. Although you can use various techniques to portray motion creatively, there are ultimately two types of exposures: fast (or short) exposures and slow (or long) exposures.

For general daytime photography with a still or moderately moving subject, 1/30 second or slower is considered a slow shutter speed, while 1/60 second or faster is considered a fast shutter speed. That being said, there are no hard and fast rules about what a fast or slow exposure is; that depends solely on the subject. For example, for most general photography, 1/250 second is a fast exposure, but if you're photographing speeding cars, 1/250 second is a slow exposure. On the opposite end, if you're photographing the night sky, 1/8 second is a relatively fast exposure, whereas in the daytime, 1/8 second would be very slow. Ultimately, the speed of the shutter is relative to the speed of the subject.

Fast shutter speeds

Fast shutter speeds are used to freeze motion. This stops the movement of the subject and captures the moment with every minute detail intact for that tiny slice of time when the shutter is open. This allows you and your viewers to examine a moment frozen in time forever. This is one of the reasons photography is such an enduring form of art; it allows us to examine, in detail, something that occurred for only a fraction of a second. Fast shutter speeds portray movement by stopping the movement, as counterintuitive as that may seem.

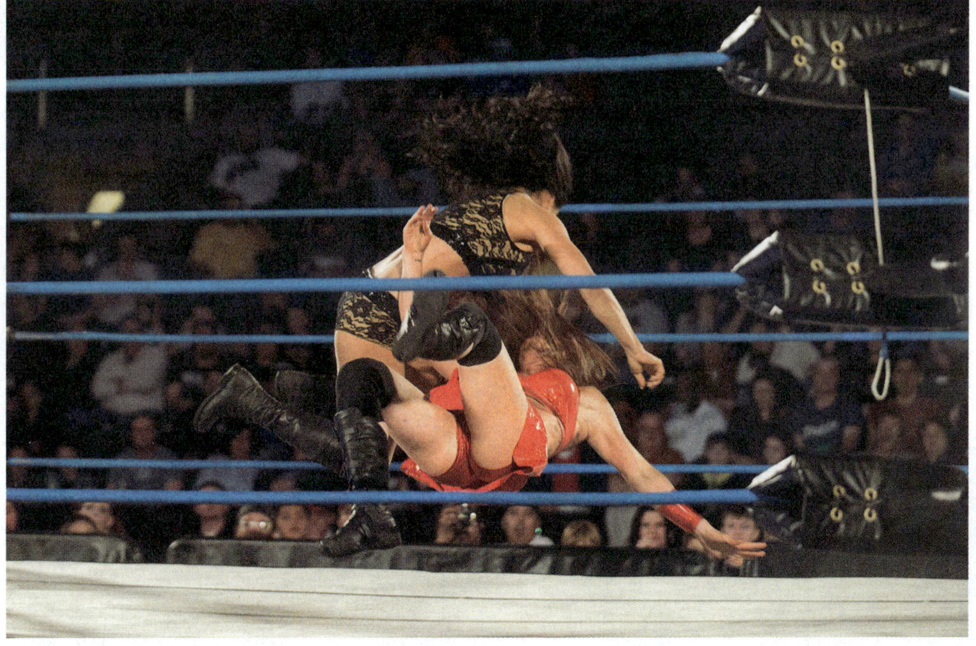

5.1 A fast shutter speed allowed me to freeze the motion of these female wrestlers flying through the air. Exposure: ISO 6400, f/4, 1/400 second, with a Nikon 70–200mm f/4G VR.

Slow shutter speeds

Photographing an image using a slow shutter speed adds another dimension to the image, almost like time travel. You capture the subject moving through time and space.

Even when you shoot quick action, you may sometimes want to use a slower shutter speed. If you use a slow shutter speed while panning (following the subject with the camera lens) on a moving subject, it blurs the background while keeping the subject in relatively sharp focus. A blurred background is an extremely effective way of portraying motion in a still photograph. When using a slow shutter speed, you often need to use a tripod, or in the case of most sports a monopod, to keep some elements of the image sharp. Although blur can be a great way to show motion, you usually don't want the whole image to be a blurry mess.

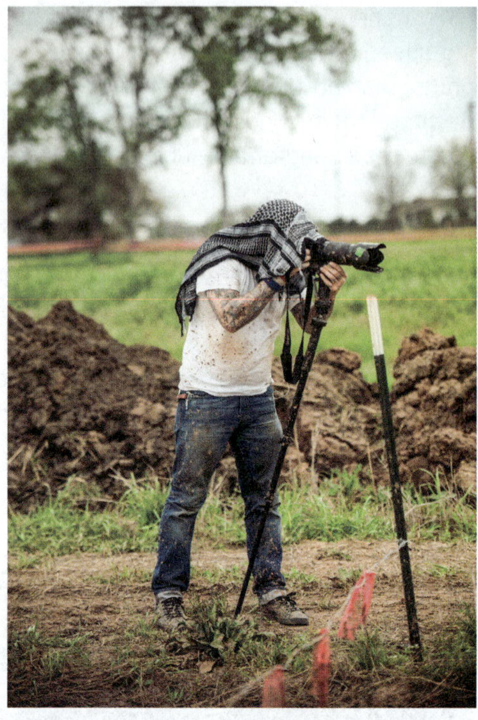

5.2 Here you can see me using a monopod to keep my camera steady and level as I pan along with the subject to keep it nice and sharp while adding a nice motion blur to the background. Photo by David Savoie.

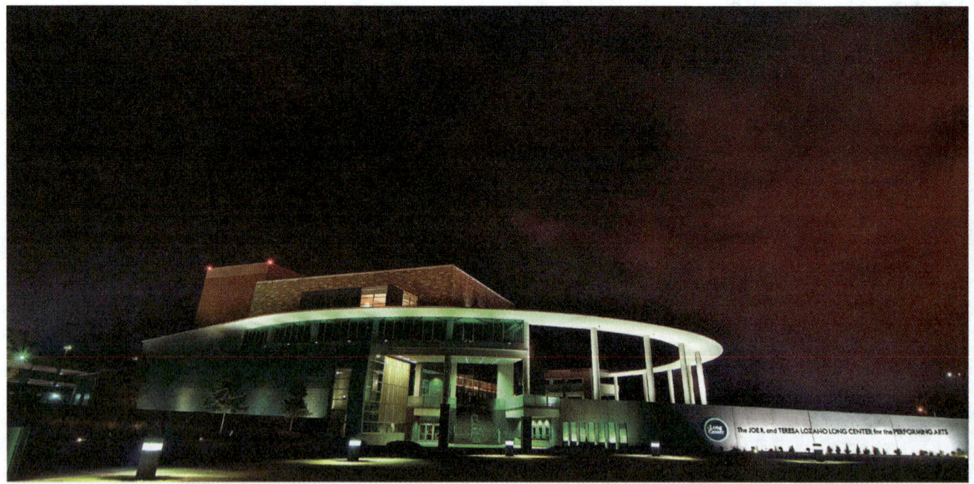

5.3 A very long exposure allowed me to capture the glow of the city lights being reflected from the clouds over this building. Exposure: ISO 200, f/22, 3 seconds, with a Nikon 10–24mm f/3.5–5.6G.

Aperture or f-stop

In my opinion, the aperture is the most important aspect of creative and expressive photography. With the aperture, you can control how much and what part of an image is in focus, which controls the area to which the viewer's attention is drawn. The aperture is the size of the opening in the lens that determines the amount of light that reaches the image sensor. The aperture is controlled by a metal diaphragm that operates in a similar fashion to the iris of your eye. Aperture is expressed as an f-stop number. Here are the most common f-stops in 1/3-step increments, the full stop apertures are in bold type: **f/1.4**, f/1.6, f/1.8, **f/2**, f/2.2, f/2.5, **f/2.8**, f/3.2, f/3.5, **f/4**, f/4.5, f/5, **f/5.6**, f/6.3, f/7.1, **f/8**, f/9, f/10, **f/11**, f/13, f/14, **f/16**, f/18, f/20, and **f/22**.

Here are two important things to know about aperture:

- **Smaller f-numbers equal wider apertures.** A small f-number, such as f/2.8, means the lens aperture is open wide so that more light reaches the sensor. If you have a wide aperture (opening), the amount of time the shutter needs to stay open to let light into the camera decreases.

- **Larger f-numbers equal narrower apertures.** A large f-number, such as f/16, means the lens opening is smaller so that less light reaches the sensor. If you have a narrow aperture (opening), the amount of time the shutter needs to stay open to let light into the camera increases.

NOTE The terms *aperture* and *f-stop* are interchangeable.

One commonly asked question is why the numbers of the aperture seem counterintuitive. The answer is relatively simple: The numbers are actually derived from ratios, which translate into fractions. The f-number is defined by the focal length of the lens divided by the actual diameter of the aperture opening. The simplest way to look at it is to put a 1 on top of the f-number as the numerator. For the easiest example, take a 50mm f/2 lens (okay, Nikon doesn't actually make a 50mm f/2, but pretend for a minute). Take the aperture number, f/2. If you add the 1 as the numerator, you get 1/2. This indicates that the aperture opening is half the diameter of the focal length, which equals 25mm. Therefore, at f/4, the effective diameter of the aperture is 12.5mm. It's a pretty simple concept once you break it down.

As with ISO and shutter speed, there are standard settings for aperture, each of which has a 1-stop difference from the next. The standard f-numbers (f/1.4, f/2.0, f/2.8, f/4.0, f/5.6, f/8.0, f/11, f/16, and f/22) may appear to be random, but they aren't. Upon closer inspection, you notice that every other number is a multiple of 2. Broken down even further, each stop is a multiple of 1.4 (which is the square root of 2). If you start with f/1.0 and multiply by 1.4, you get f/1.4; multiply this by 1.4 again and you get 2 (rounded up from 1.96); multiply 2 by 1.4 and you get 2.8, and so on. As it does with the ISO and shutter speed settings, the Nikon D3300 allows you to set the aperture in 1/3-stop increments.

NOTE In photographic vernacular, *opening up* refers to going from a smaller to larger aperture. *Stopping down* refers to going from a larger to smaller aperture.

Now that you know a little more about apertures, you can begin to see why different aperture settings are used, and the effect that they have on your images. The most common reason why a certain aperture is selected is to control the depth of field, or how much of the image is in focus. Quite simply, using a wider aperture (f/1.4 through f/4.0) gives you a shallow depth of field. This allows you to exercise *selective focus* — that is, focusing on a certain subject and allowing the rest of the image to fall out of focus.

Conversely, using a small aperture (f/11 to f/32) maximizes your depth of field, allowing you to get more of the scene in focus. Using a wider aperture is generally preferable when shooting portraits because it blurs out the background and draws attention to the subject; a smaller aperture is generally used when photographing landscapes to ensure that a larger range of the scene is in focus.

Another way that the aperture setting is used is to control the shutter speed. You can use a wide aperture to allow a lot of light in so that you can use a faster shutter speed to freeze action. Conversely, you can use a smaller aperture if you want to be sure that your shutter speed is slow.

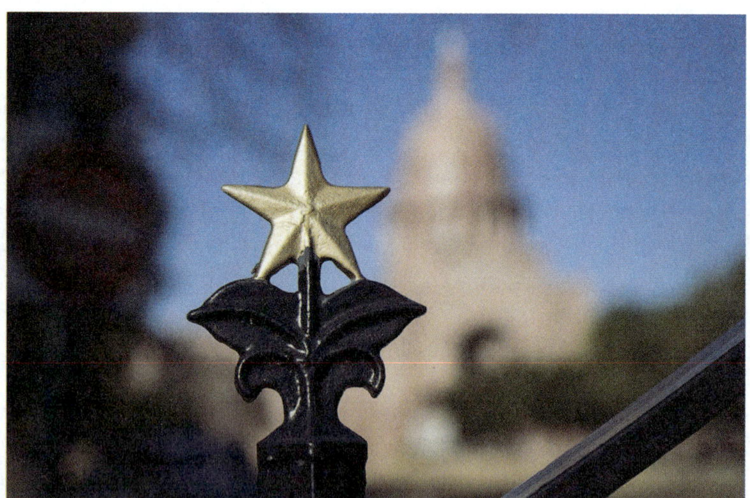

5.4 A shallow depth of field draws your eye directly to the subject. This gives the shot an artistic appearance. Exposure: ISO 100, f/3.8, 1/1600 second, with the kit lens at 35mm.

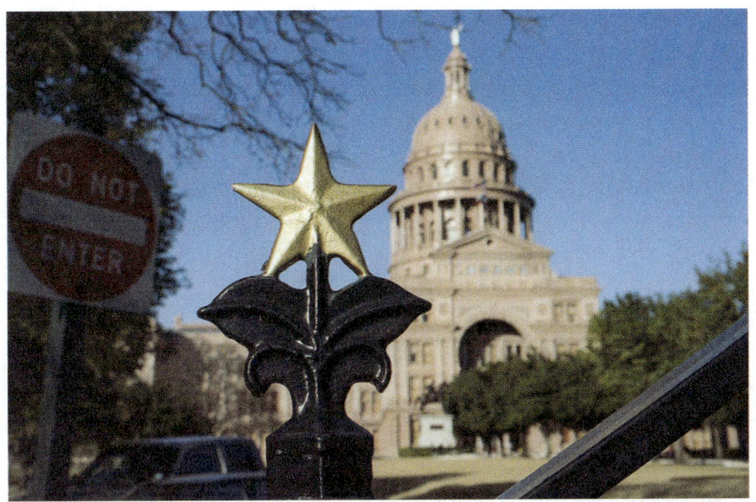

5.5 This is the same subject as in figure 5.4, but as you can see, the smaller aperture allows elements in the background to become clearer. This can be good if you want to place the subject in a certain context. Exposure: ISO 125, f/22, 1/60 second, with the kit lens at 35mm.

Fine-tuning Your Exposure

Now that you know the basics of exposure, you can start fine-tuning to suit your needs. Knowing when you need to adjust the exposure isn't a skill that you acquire overnight — it's knowledge you gain with experience. The more time you spend shooting, the better you will be at judging how your camera and the light meter inside the camera works. Luckily in the digital era we have instant feedback via the monitor rather than having to wait to develop the film.

You can't always rely on your camera's meter to give you the most accurate reading. It is, after all, a computer and does not know what your intentions are for your image. As a result, it can be tricked into under- or overexposing your images by areas of extreme brightness or darkness in the scene. This often occurs when shooting at the beach or in a snowy area. The camera meter detects all of this brightness and tries to control the highlights; however, it ends up underexposing the image, causing the sand or snow to appear a dirty gray instead of a brilliant white, as it should be. The quick fix here is to add a stop or two of exposure compensation, which I talk about in the next section.

Exposure compensation

Exposure compensation is a D3300 feature that allows you to fine-tune the automatic exposure setting supplied by the camera's exposure meter. Although you can adjust the exposure of the image in your image-editing software (especially if you shoot RAW), it's best to get the exposure right in the camera to be sure that you have the highest image quality. If, after taking the photograph, you review it and it's too dark or too light, you can adjust the exposure compensation and retake the picture to get a better exposure.

Exposure compensation is adjusted in increments called *exposure value* (EV); 1 EV is equal to 1 stop of light. You adjust exposure compensation by pressing the Exposure compensation button (⊞), next to the shutter-release button, and rotating the Main Command dial to the left for more exposure (+EV) or to the right for less exposure (–EV). The exposure compensation is adjusted in either 1/3 steps.

You can adjust the exposure compensation up to +5 EV and down to –5 EV, which is a large range of 10 stops. To remind you that exposure compensation has been set, the Exposure compensation indicator (⊞) appears in the viewfinder display. It also appears on the LCD screen when the shooting information displays.

> **CAUTION** Exposure compensation can only be used in Programmed Auto (**P**), Shutter priority auto (**S**), Aperture priority auto (**A**) Panorama and Night Vision modes.

> **CAUTION** Be sure to reset the Exposure compensation (⊞) to 0 after you finish shooting to avoid unwanted over- or underexposed images later.

Using histograms

The easiest way to determine if you need to adjust the exposure compensation is to preview your image. If it looks too dark, adjust the exposure compensation up; if it's too bright, adjust the exposure compensation down. This, however, is not the most accurate method of determining how much exposure compensation to use because the LCD isn't necessarily indicative of the actual exposure because the LCD brightness can be adjusted. One of the most important tools you have to evaluate exposure is the histogram. To determine accurately how much exposure compensation to add or subtract, look at the histogram. The histogram is a visual representation of the tonal values in your image. Think of it as a bar graph that charts the lights, darks, and midtones in your picture.

The histogram's range is divided into 256 brightness levels from 0 (absolute black) to 255 (absolute white). The black levels (or shadows) are represented on the left side of the histogram, and the white levels (or highlights) are represented on the right. The more pixels there are at any given brightness value, the higher the bar. If there are no bars, then the image has no pixels in that brightness range. A typical histogram for an overexposed image is shown in figure 5.6, and a typical histogram for an underexposed image is shown in figure 5.7. The histogram of a properly exposed image is shown in figure 5.8.

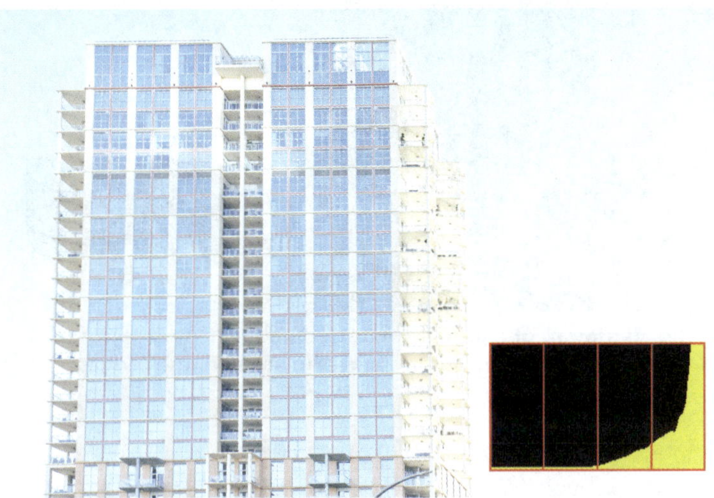

5.6 An example of a histogram from an overexposed image (no highlight detail). Notice that the histogram information is spiking at the far-right side of the graph.

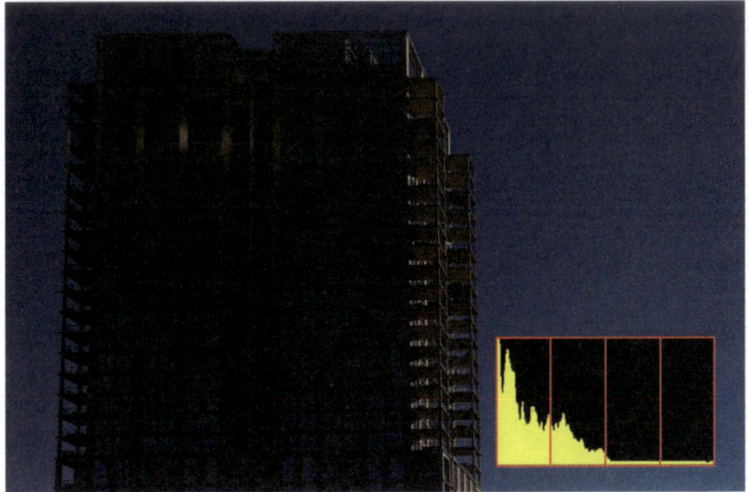

5.7 An example of a histogram from an underexposed image (no shadow detail). Notice the spikes at the far-left side of the graph.

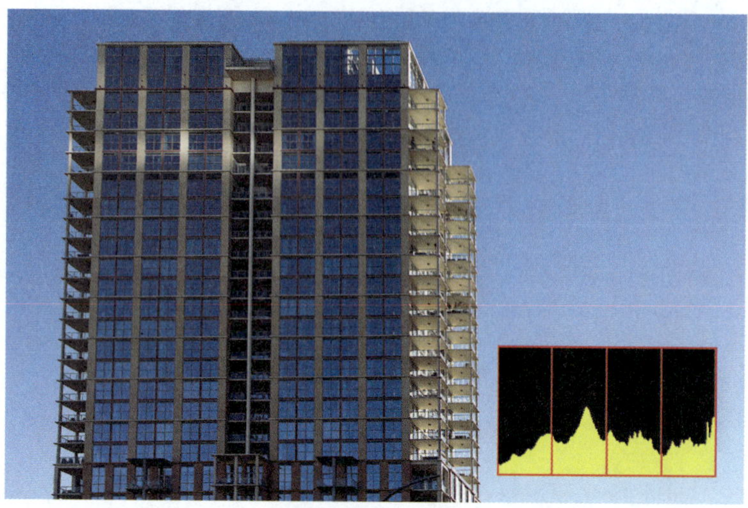

5.8 The histogram of a properly exposed image. Notice that the graph touches, but does not spike at, the left and right edges.

NOTE The histogram displayed on the LCD screen is based on an 8-bit image. When you work with 12- or 14-bit files using editing software, the histogram may be displayed with 4,096 brightness levels for 12-bit or 16,384 brightness levels for 14-bit.

The D3300 offers four histogram views: luminance, which shows the brightness levels of the entire image; and separate histograms for the Red, Green, and Blue color channels.

The most useful histogram for determining if your exposure needs adjusting is the luminance histogram. To display the luminance histogram without the color channel histograms, simply press the multi-selector up (▲) while viewing the image on the LCD screen. This displays a thumbnail of the current image, the shooting information, and a small luminance histogram.

Theoretically, you want to expose your subject so that it falls approximately in the middle of the tonal range. If your histogram graph has most of the information on the left side, then your image is probably underexposed; if it's mostly on the right side, then your image is probably overexposed. Ideally, with most average subjects that aren't bright white or extremely dark, you want to try to get your histogram to have most of the tones in the middle range, tapering off as they get to the dark and light ends of the graph.

However, this is only for most average types of images that would not be too light or too dark, with little contrast. As with almost everything in photography, there are exceptions to the rule. If you take a photo of a dark subject on a dark background (that is, a *low-key* image), then naturally your histogram will have most of the tones on the left side of the graph, as shown in figure 5.9. Conversely, when you take a photograph of a light subject on a light background (that is, a *high-key* image), the histogram will have most of the tones skewing to the right, as shown in figure 5.10.

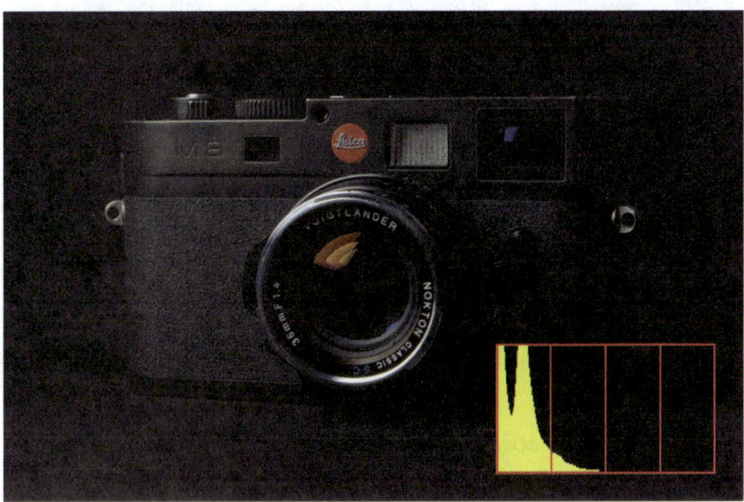

5.9 An example of a histogram from a low-key image. Notice that most of the tones are to the left. Because this image is so dark, this is to be expected.

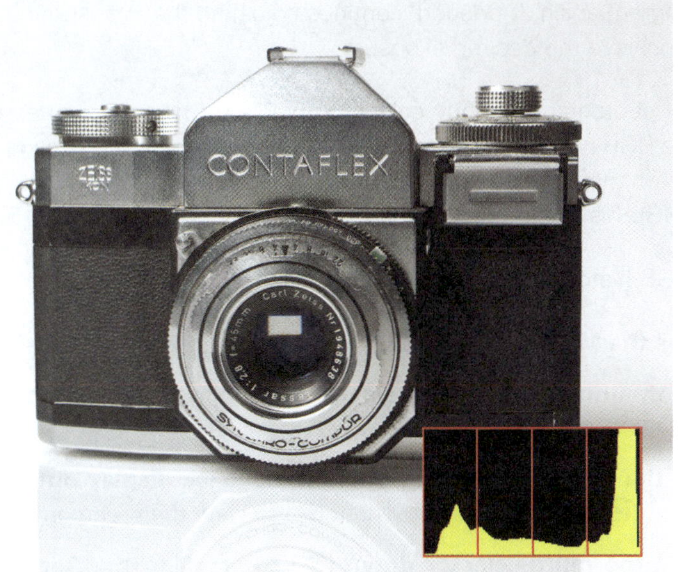

5.10 An example of a histogram from a high-key image.

The most important thing to remember is that the histogram is just a factual representation of the tones in the image and there is no such thing as a perfect histogram. Also remember that although it's okay for the graph to be near one side or the other, you usually don't want your histogram to have spikes bumping up against the edge of the graph; this indicates that your image has blown-out highlights (completely white, with no detail) or blocked-up shadow areas (completely black, with no detail).

Now that you know a little about histograms, you can use them to adjust exposure compensation. Follow these steps when using a histogram as a tool to evaluate your photos:

1. **After taking your picture, review its histogram on the LCD screen.** To view the histogram in the image preview, press the Playback button (▶) to view the image. Press the multi-selector up (▲), and the histogram appears directly to the right of the image preview.

2. **Look at the histogram.** Note if it indicates that the image is properly exposed (see figure 5.8).

3. **Adjust the exposure compensation.** To move the tones to the right, add a little exposure compensation by pressing the Exposure compensation button (⧩), and then rotating the Command dial to the right. To move the tones to the left, press the Exposure compensation button (⧩), and then rotate the Command dial to the left.

4. **Retake the photograph if necessary.** After taking another picture, review the histogram again. If needed, continue adjusting the exposure compensation until you achieve the desired exposure.

When you photograph brightly colored subjects, it may sometimes be necessary to refer to the RGB histograms. It's also possible to overexpose an image in only one color channel, even though the rest of the image looks like it is properly exposed. To view the separate RGB histograms, you need to set the display mode in the Playback menu.

To view RGB histograms, follow these steps:

1. **Press the Menu button (MENU).**

2. **Use the multi-selector to select the Playback menu.** Press the multi-selector right (▶).

3. **Use the multi-selector to highlight Playback display options.** Press the OK button (OK) or multi-selector right (▶) to view the menu options.

4. **Press the multi-selector down (▼) to scroll to the Additional photo info menu option.**

5. **Press the multi-selector down (▼) to scroll down to the RGB histogram menu option.** Press the multi-selector right (▶) to set the option to On; this is confirmed by a small check mark in a box next to the option.

6. **When the option is set, press the OK button (OK).**

It is possible for any one of the color channels to become overexposed — or blown out, as most photographers call it — although the most commonly blown-out channel is the Red channel. Digital camera sensors are more prone to overexposing the Red channel because they are generally more sensitive to red colors. When one of these color channels is overexposed, the histogram for that particular color channel looks similar to the luminance histogram of a typical overexposed image.

Usually, the best way to deal with an image that has an overexposed color channel is to reduce exposure by using exposure compensation. Although this is a quick fix, reducing the exposure can also introduce blocked-up shadows; you can deal with this by shooting RAW or, to a lesser extent when shooting JPEGs, by using Active D-Lighting, which is a proprietary Nikon camera feature that preserves shadow and highlight detail.

5

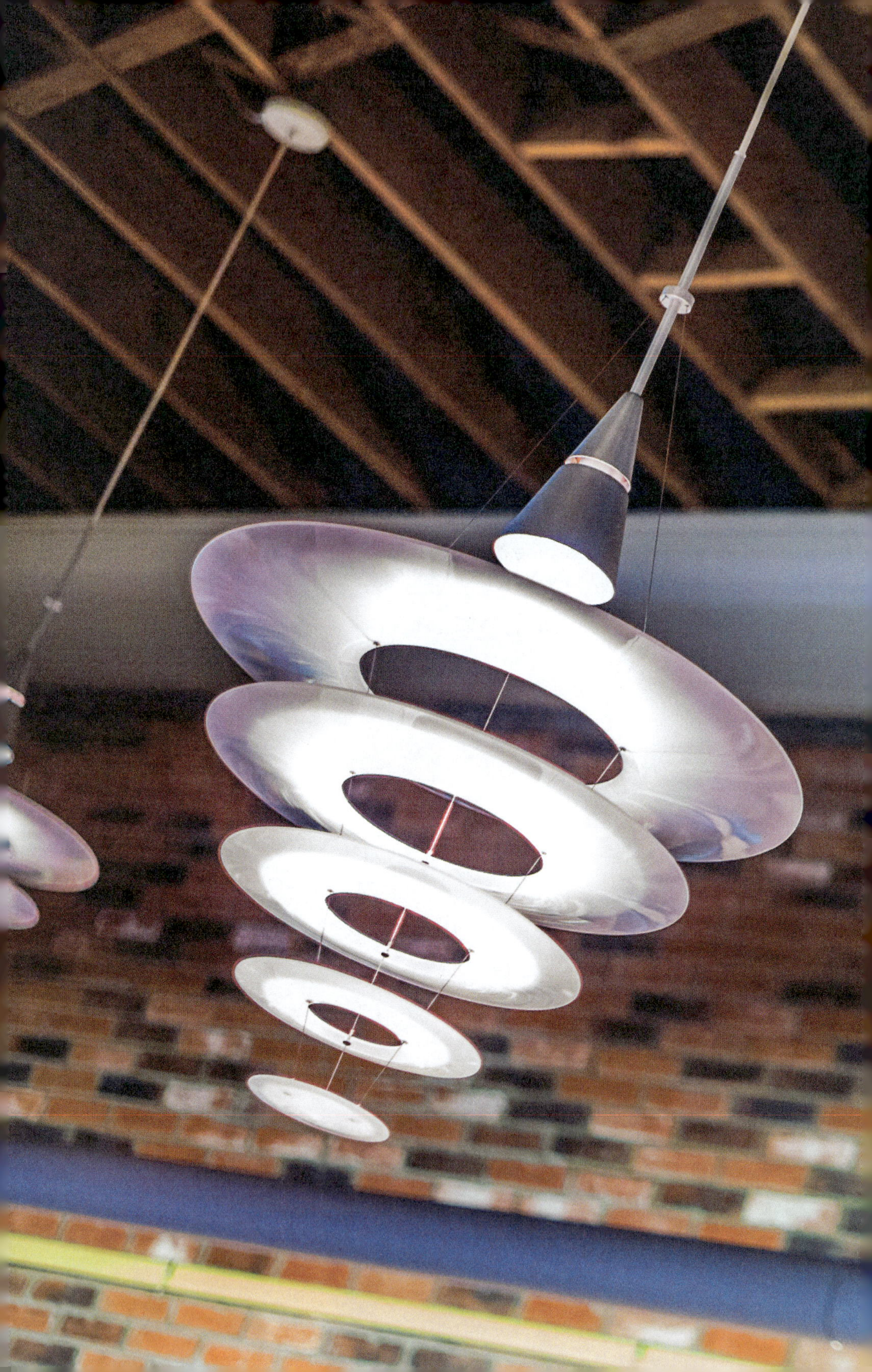

CHAPTER 6

Working with Light

Light is the key to photography; indeed, the first part of the word, *photos,* means 'light' in Greek. This should tell you how important it is. Without light you cannot create an image, but in photography, light involves so much more than simply creating an image. The quantity and quality of light are also extremely important in influencing how your images appear.

Your job as a photographer is to learn how to see the light — the way it interacts with the subject and how it interacts with the camera settings. It's important to learn how to control and shape the light if it doesn't suit your needs. You must acquire the skill of controlling light and not letting the light control your shots.

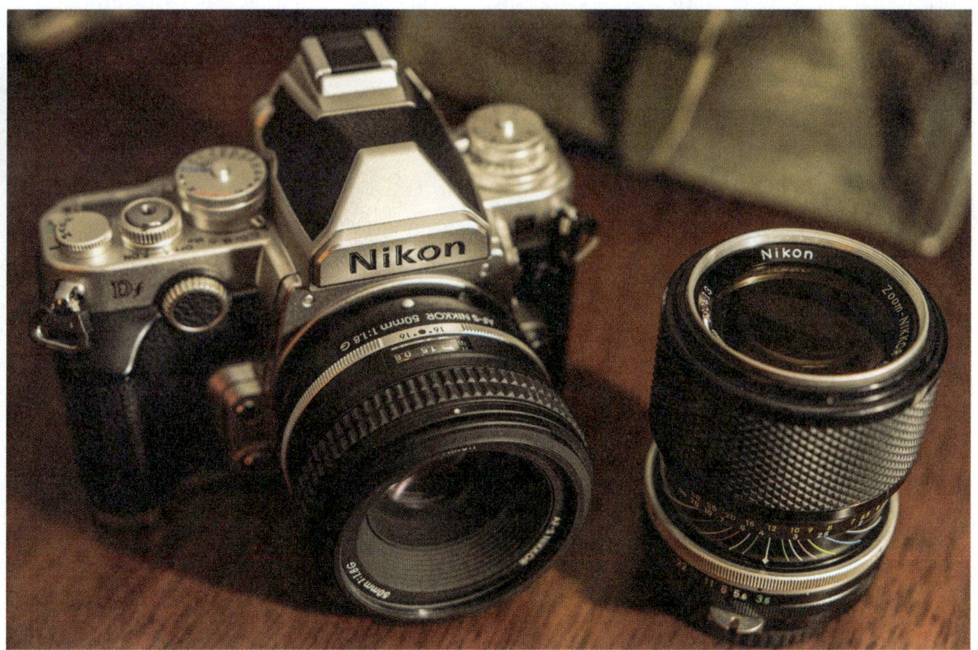

Controlling light is the key to setting the tone of your images.

Lighting Essentials

The angle and direction from which the light comes, as well as the color of the light source and the quality of the light, all work together to play a part in the way the image materializes on the sensor. All of these things combined affect the mood, tone, and feeling of an image, so it's important to grasp the basic tenets behind using light for photography. This section covers the two main types of lighting used by photographers and filmmakers today: soft and hard light.

The quality of light

Photographers and filmmakers use the term *quality of light* to describe the way that light interacts with a scene. The term is somewhat misleading in that *quality* doesn't reflect whether the light is good or bad, but rather how it is rendered when it strikes the subject.

The first thing a photographer should consider when planning an image concept or assessing an existing light scene is the quality of light. For example, if you're planning to shoot a portrait, you need to decide how you want to portray the person. If you're shooting a landscape, think about what time of day the lighting is best for that particular terrain. In the following sections, I cover the different qualities of light and how they affect your subjects.

Soft lighting

Soft light is distributed evenly across the scene and appears to wrap around the subject. It comes from a large light source, and the shadows fade gradually from dark to light, which results in a subtle shadow edge transfer. This is a very desirable type of light to use in many types of photography, especially in portraiture. You can also create soft light by placing a light source close to the subject or by diffusing the light source, thereby mimicking a larger light source.

> **NOTE** The term *shadow edge transfer* is used to describe how abruptly the shadows in images go from light to dark. This is the determining factor in whether light is soft or hard. Soft light has a smooth transition and hard light has a well-defined shadow edge transfer.

Soft light is very flattering to most subjects. It is used to soften hard edges and smooth out the features of a subject. Soft lighting can be advantageous for almost any type of photography, although in some instances it can lack the depth that you get from using a more direct light source.

To achieve soft lighting naturally, you can place the subject in an area that isn't receiving direct sunlight, such as under a porch, overhang, or tree. Cloudy (especially partly cloudy) days are also ideal for soft, diffused lighting.

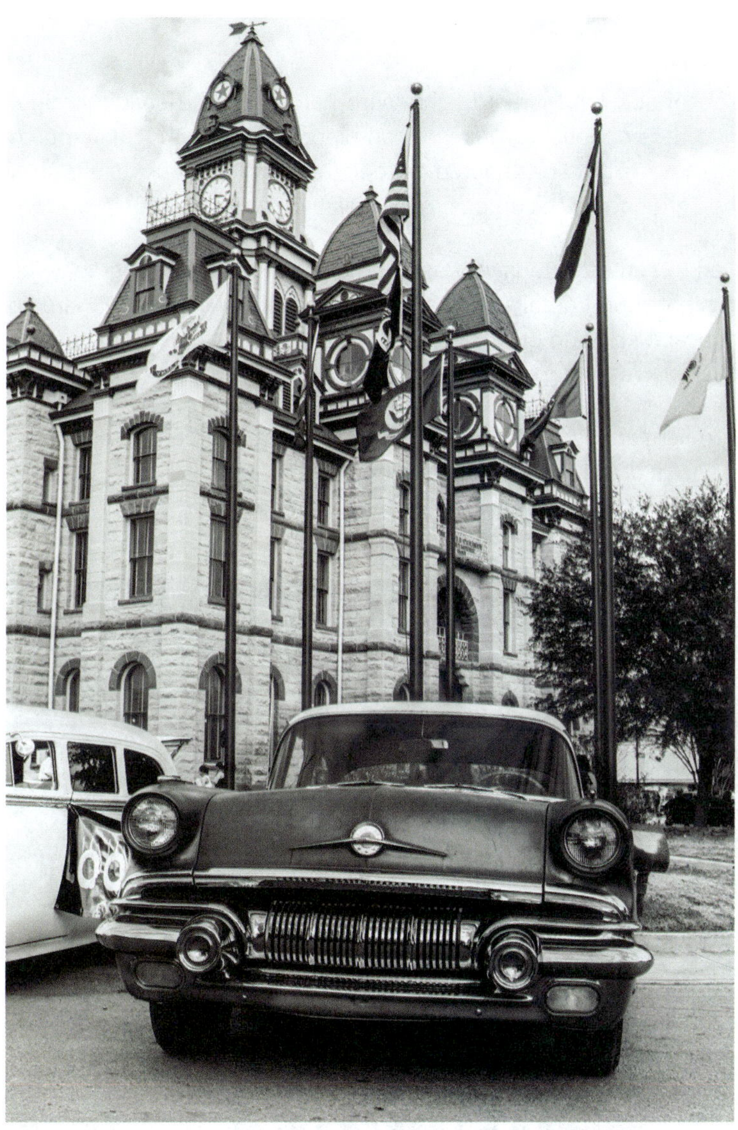

6.1 This photo was taken on a cloudy day, giving the scene a shadowless, soft light appearance. Exposure: ISO 100, f/11, 1/125 second with a NIKKOR 18–55mm f/3.5–5.6G VRII at 24mm.

When artificial light is the source of your subject's illumination, you usually need to modify the light in some way to make it soft. Redirecting or bouncing the light off a wall or some other reflective material softens the light; aiming the light source through diffusion material is also a good way to soften the light.

Hard lighting

The opposite of soft light is hard light. With hard light, the shadow edge transfer is more defined. It is directional, and you can pinpoint where the light source is located very easily. Moving the light source farther from the subject results in harder light because the light source becomes smaller relative to the subject.

Hard light isn't used as extensively as soft light in general photography, but it is very effective in highlighting details and textures in almost any subject. Hard light is often used in landscape shots to bring attention to details in natural formations. Hard light is also effective for creating gritty or realistic portraits.

Artificial hard light is easily achieved with a bare light source. You can also use accessories, such as grids or snoots, to make the light more directional. The bright, midday sun is an excellent example of a natural, hard light source.

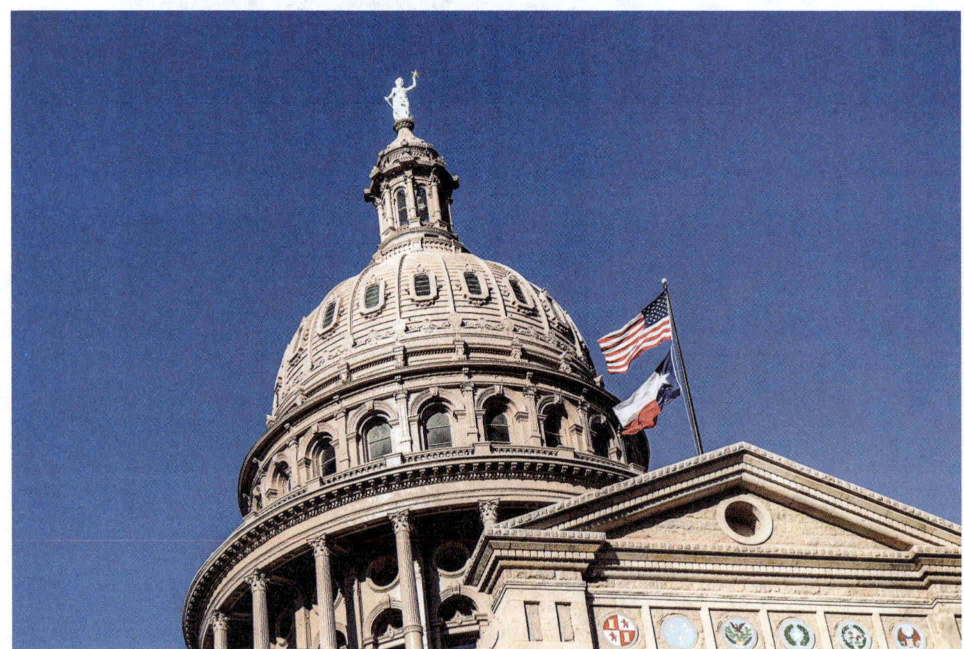

6.2 This hard-light photo was taken using direct sunlight to highlight texture and detail. Exposure: ISO 100, f/8, 1/500 second with the kit lens at 48mm.

Lighting direction

The direction from which light strikes your subject has a major impact on how your images appear. When using an artificial light source, you can easily control the direction of the lighting by moving the light source relative to the subject. When using natural lighting, moving the subject relative to the light source is the key to controlling the lighting direction. I cover the three major types of lighting direction in the following sections.

Frontlighting

Frontlighting comes from directly in front of the subject, following the old photographer's adage to keep the sun at your back. This is a good general rule; however, sometimes frontlighting produces flat results lacking in depth and dimension. In Figures 6.3 and 6.4, you can see the difference that changing the direction of the light can have on a subject. When the light is aimed straight ahead, as shown in Figure 6.3, more of it reflects from the background, which brightens the background significantly, as well.

Frontlighting works pretty well for portraits, and many fashion photographers swear by it, especially for highlighting hair and makeup. Frontlighting flattens out facial features and also hides blemishes and wrinkles very well. Be aware that using frontlighting with a continuous light source, like the sun, can cause your subject to squint.

NOTE Lighting direction is relative to camera position, not subject position, so if you light the front of the subject, but are photographing it from the side, you're using sidelighting.

Sidelighting

Although sidelighting comes in from the side, it doesn't necessarily have to come in from a 90-degree angle. It usually comes in from a shallower angle, such as 45 to 60 degrees.

Lighting the subject from the side increases the shadow contrast and causes the details to become more pronounced. This is what gives two-dimensional photographs a three-dimensional feel. Sidelighting is equally effective when using either hard or soft light, and it works for just about any subject.

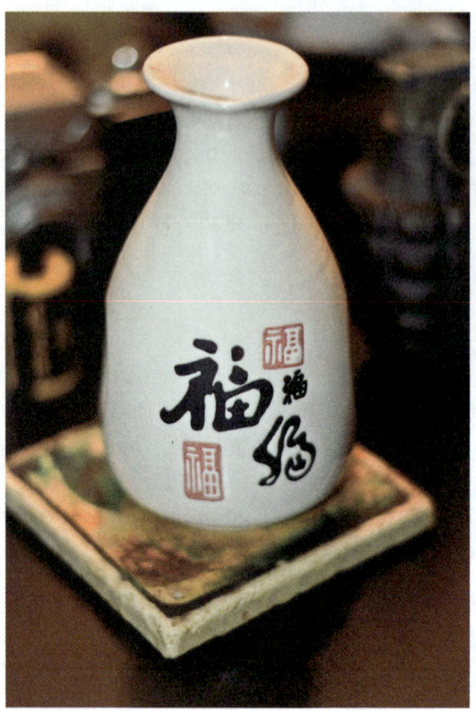

6.3 This Japanese takurri was lit using frontlighting from the built-in flash. Notice that the lighting is flat and even. It's not necessarily unattractive, but it could definitely be improved upon. Exposure: ISO 400, f/1.8, 1/60 second with a Nikon 50mmf/1.8G Special Edition.

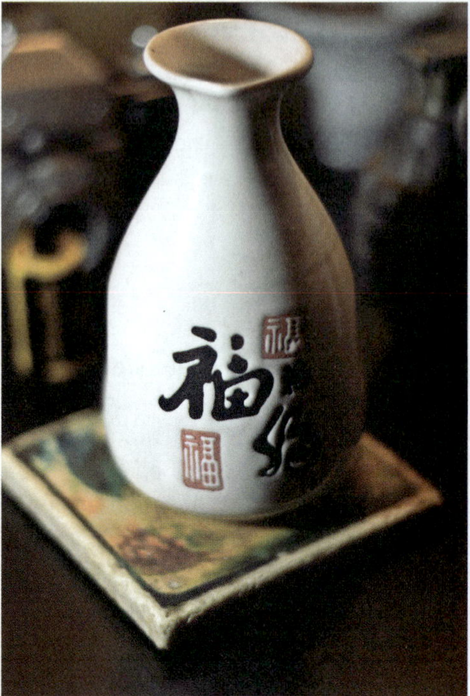

6.4 I used an inexpensive TTL flash cable (Nikon SC-28) to hold the flash off to the side of the microphone. Notice that the takkuri has more texture, depth, and form, giving it more dimensionality and making the photo more interesting and pleasing. Exposure: ISO 400, f/1.8, 1/60 second with a Nikon 50mmf/1.8G Special Edition.

Backlighting

Backlighting involves placing the light source behind the subject. Although it's not as common as front- and sidelighting, it does have its uses. Backlighting is often used in conjunction with other types of lighting to add highlights to the subject.

Backlighting has often received a bad rap in photography, but more photographers are now using it to add artistic flair to their images. Backlight introduces effects that were once perceived as undesirable in classical photography, such as lens flare and decreased contrast. Photographers today are discovering that, when used correctly, backlighting can create interesting images.

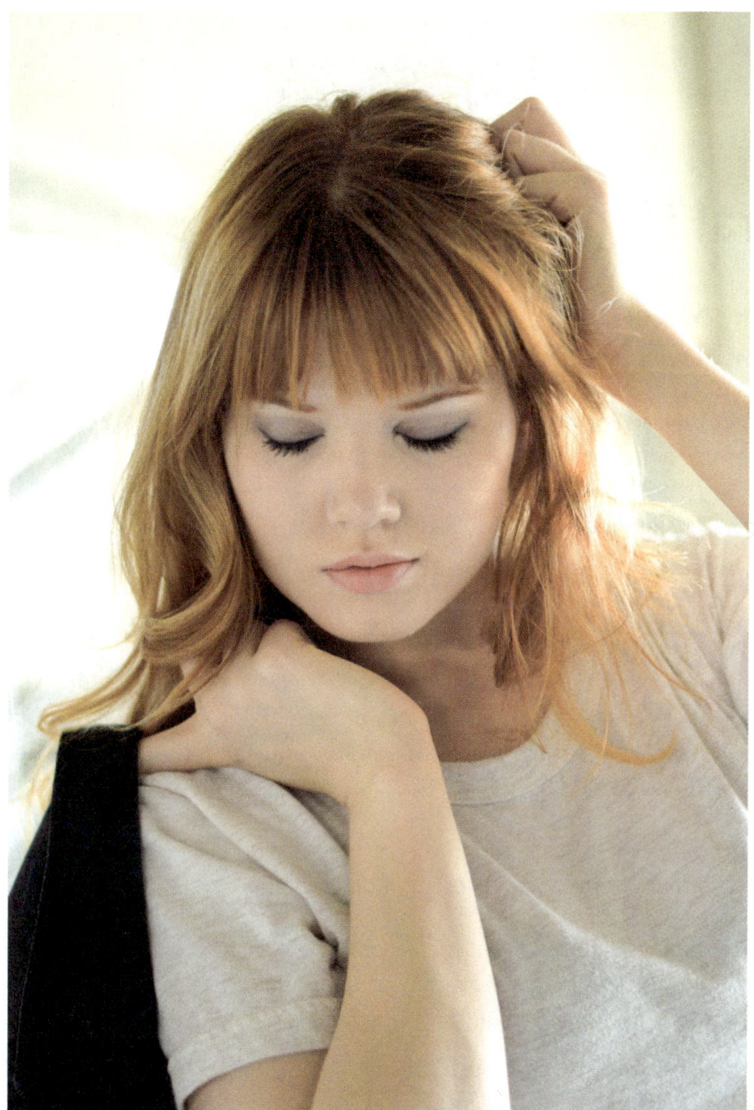

6.5 Backlighting can add a rim of light to your image, giving it a dramatic effect. Exposure: ISO 100, f/1.8, 1/100 second, using a Nikon 50mm f/1.8G Special Edition

TIP Using backlighting and lens flare creates a classic, cinematic effect.

Backlighting can make portraits more dynamic, incorporate silhouettes into landscape photos, or make translucent subjects seem to glow.

> **TIP** The key to making backlighting work is to use the Spot metering mode (⊡). When shooting portraits, meter on the subject; for silhouettes, meter on the brightest area in the scene.

Natural Light

Natural light is probably the easiest light source to find simply because it's all around you, as the sun is the source of all natural light. Some people confuse available light with natural light. To make it clear, all natural light is available light, but not all available light is natural light. Available light is light that exists in a scene and that isn't augmented by the photographer. For example, when you walk into a room that is solely lit with an overhead lamp, the overhead lamp provides the available light, but it is not natural light.

> **NOTE** Early in the morning and late in the evening when the sun is rising or setting are the best times to take photographs. These times are known as the *Golden Hour*.

That being said, natural light can be the most difficult light to work with. It can be too harsh on a bright sunny day, it can be too unpredictable on a partly cloudy day, and although an overcast day can provide beautiful soft lighting, it can sometimes lack definition, which leads to flat images.

Natural light often benefits from some sort of modification to make it softer and less directional. Here are a few examples of natural lighting techniques:

- **Use fill flash.** As contrary as it sounds, using flash to augment natural light can really help. You can use the flash as a secondary light source (not as your main light) to fill in the shadows and reduce contrast.

- **Try to use window lighting.** Like fill flash, this technique is one of the best ways to use natural light, even though it seems contrary. Go indoors and place your model next to a window, as you see in figure 6.6. This provides a beautiful soft light that is very flattering. Many professional portrait and food photographers use window light. It can be used to light almost any subject softly and evenly, yet it still provides directionality. This is definitely the quickest, and often the nicest, light source you can find.

- **Find some shade.** The shade of a tree or the overhang of an awning or porch can block the bright sunlight while still providing plenty of diffuse light with which to light your subject.

▶ **Take advantage of clouds.** A cloudy day softens the light, allowing you to take portraits outside without worrying about harsh shadows and too much contrast. If it's only partly cloudy, you can wait for a cloud to pass over the sun before taking your shot.

▶ **Use a modifier.** Use a reflector to reduce the shadows, or a diffusion panel to block the direct sunlight from your subject.

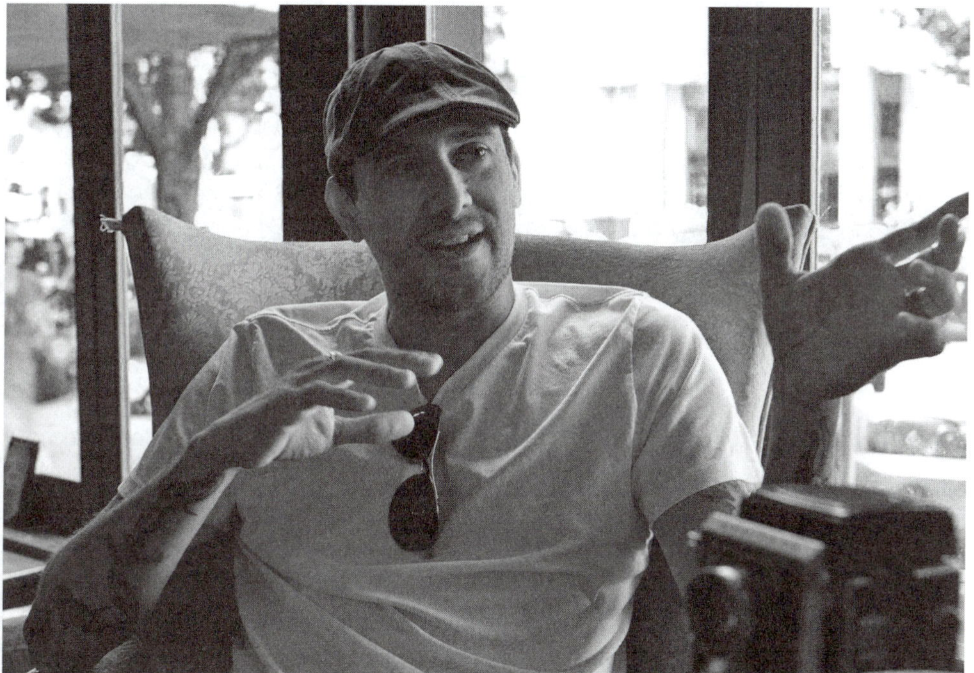

6.6 Natural outdoor lighting diffused by the glass of the window was all that was necessary for this candid shot of photographer Destry Jaimes. Exposure: ISO 200, f/5, 1/15 second, using a Sigma 35mm f/1.4 | A.

Continuous Light

Continuous lighting is a constant light source. It has a *what you see is what you get* effect, and is therefore the easiest type of lighting to use. You can set up the lights and see what effect they have on your subject before you even pick up your D3300. Continuous lights are an affordable option for beginners, and the learning curve isn't too steep.

Continuous Lighting versus Flash

Incandescent lights appear to be very bright to you and your subject, but they actually produce less light than a standard flash unit. For example, a 200-watt tungsten light and a 200-watt-second strobe use the same amount of electricity per second, so they should be equally bright, right? Wrong. Because the flash discharges all 200 watts of energy in a fraction of a second, the flash is actually much, much brighter.

Why does this matter? Because when you need a fast shutter speed and a small aperture, the strobe can give you more light in a shorter time. An SB-700 Speedlight gives you about 30-watt-seconds of light at full power. To get an equivalent amount of light at the maximum sync speed of 1/250 second from a continuous light, you would need a 7500-watt lamp! Of course, if your subject is static, you don't need to use a fast shutter speed; in this case, you can use one 30-watt light bulb for a 1-second exposure or a 60-watt light bulb for a 1/2-second exposure.

As with other lighting systems, you have many continuous lighting options. Here are two of the most common:

- ▶ **Incandescent.** Incandescent, or tungsten, lights are presently the most common type of lights (a standard light bulb is a tungsten lamp). With tungsten lamps, an electrical current runs through a tungsten filament, heating it and causing it to emit light. This type of continuous lighting is the origin of the term *hot lights*. These lights are being phased out and will ultimately be replaced with compact fluorescents or in some cases LEDs.

- ▶ **Fluorescent.** In a fluorescent lamp, electrical energy changes a small amount of mercury into a gas. The electrons collide with the mercury gas atoms, causing them to release photons, which in turn cause the phosphor coating inside the lamp to glow. Because this reaction doesn't create much heat, fluorescent lamps are much cooler and more energy efficient than tungsten and halogen lamps. This energy efficiency is the reason why compact fluorescents are replacing typical tungsten bulbs. These days, there are many different types of color-balanced fluorescent lamps.

If you're serious about continuous lighting, you may want to invest in a photographic light kit. These kits are widely available from any photography or video store. They usually include both the lights and light stands. Some kits also include light modifiers (such as umbrellas or softboxes) to diffuse the light and create a softer look. The kits can be relatively inexpensive, with two lights, two stands, and two umbrellas costing around $100. You can buy much more elaborate setups that cost all the way up to $2,000.

The D3300 Built-in Flash

The Nikon D3300 has a built-in flash that pops up for quick use in low-light situations. Although this little flash is fine for snapshots, it's not always the best option for portraying your subject in a flattering light.

> **TIP** Even when you're using the pop-up flash for snapshots, I recommend using a pop-up flash diffuser. There are a number of brands and types, but I use a LumiQuest Soft Screen. It folds up flat to fit in your pocket and costs a little over $10.

Built-in flash exposure modes

The built-in flash of the D3300 has a few exposure modes that control the way the flash calculates exposure, flash output, and brightness, and a couple of modes for using some advanced flash techniques.

i-TTL and i-TTL BL

The D3300 determines the proper flash exposure automatically using the Nikon proprietary *i-TTL* (Intelligent-Through-the-Lens) flash metering system. The theory behind i-TTL is the same as for standard exposure metering, except that with i-TTL, the camera gets most of the metering information from monitor preflashes emitted from the flash. These preflashes emit almost simultaneously with the main flash, so it almost appears as if the flash only fires once. The camera also uses data from the lens, such as distance information and f-stop values, to help determine the proper flash exposure.

Additionally, the D3300 employs two types of i-TTL flash metering: Standard i-TTL flash and i-TTL BL (short for Balanced Fill-Flash). With Standard i-TTL flash mode, the camera determines the exposure for the subject only and doesn't consider the background lighting. With i-TTL Balanced Fill-Flash mode, the camera attempts to balance the light from the flash with the ambient light to produce a more natural-looking image.

When you use the built-in flash on the D3300, the default mode is i-TTL Balanced Fill-Flash when using the Matrix (▨) or Center-weighted (◉) metering modes. When the D3300 is set to Spot metering (▫), the flash defaults to i-TTL automatically.

<table>
<tr><td>**NOTE**</td><td>When using a Nikon Speedlight such as the SB-300 or SB-700, all the information regarding the iTTL flash settings, sync modes, and Flash Compensation is applicable. Some of the high-end Speedlights, such as the SB-700 and up, also have extra exposure modes. See your flash manual or the *Nikon Creative Lighting System Digital Field Guide* (also from Wiley) for more information.</td></tr>
</table>

Manual

The built-in flash power is set by fractions in Manual mode (**M**), with 1/1 being full power. The output is halved for each setting (which is equal to 1 stop of light). The settings are 1/1, 1/2, 1/4, 1/8, 1/16, and 1/32.

The Guide Number (GN) for the built-in flash is 39 when measuring distance in feet, or 12 when using meters at full power (1/1) set to ISO 100. To determine the GN at higher ISO settings, multiply the GN by 1.4 for each stop that the ISO increases. For example, doubling the ISO setting to 200 increases the GN by a factor of 1.4, so GN 39×1.4 = GN 54.6.

Similarly, when reducing the flash power by 1 stop, you divide the GN by a factor of 1.4, so at 1/2 power, the GN is about 28 (GN $39 \div 1.4$ = GN 27.8).

Guide Number/Distance = Aperture

The equation that photographers use to calculate flash exposure manually is GN/D = A. The Guide Number (GN) is the power of the flash. Distance (D) is the range between the subject and the flash. Aperture (A) is the lens opening that determines how much light comes into the lens. You can change this equation in the following ways to find the information you need to know:

▶ **GN/D = A.** If you know the GN of the flash and the distance of the flash from the subject, you can determine the aperture you need to use to achieve the proper exposure.

▶ **A/GN = D.** If you know the aperture you want to use and the GN of the flash, you can determine the distance to place your flash from the subject.

▶ **A × D = GN.** If you already have the right exposure, you can take your aperture setting and multiply it by the distance of the flash from the subject to determine the approximate GN of the flash.

Flash sync modes

Flash sync modes control how the flash operates in conjunction with your D3300. These modes work with both the built-in Speedlight and accessory Speedlights, such as the SB-910, SB-700, SB-400, and so on. These modes allow you to choose when the flash fires, either at the beginning of the exposure or at the end, and they also allow you to keep the shutter open for longer periods, enabling you to capture more ambient light in low-light situations.

Front-curtain sync

Front-curtain sync flash mode (⚡) is the default for your camera when you use the built-in flash or one of the dedicated Nikon Speedlights. In Front-curtain sync flash mode (⚡), the flash fires as soon as the shutter's front curtain fully opens. This mode works well with most general flash applications.

When you set the Shooting mode to Programmed auto (**P**) or Aperture-priority auto (**A**), the shutter speed is set to 1/60 second automatically.

Front-curtain sync flash mode (⚡) works well when you use relatively fast shutter speeds. However, if you use Shutter-priority auto mode (**S**) and the shutter speed is slowed down to 1/30 second or slower (also known as *dragging the shutter* in flash photography), Front-curtain sync flash mode (⚡) causes your images to have an unnatural-looking blur in front of them. This often occurs when photographing a moving subject because the ambient light reflects off of it.

During flash photography, your camera actually records two exposures concurrently: the flash exposure and the ambient light. When you use a faster shutter speed in lower light, the ambient light usually isn't bright enough to have an effect on the image. When you slow down the shutter speed substantially, it allows the ambient light to be recorded to the sensor, causing *ghosting*. Ghosting is a partial exposure that usually appears transparent on the image.

Ghosting causes a trail to appear in front of the subject because the flash freezes the initial movement of the subject. Because the subject is still moving, the ambient light records it as a blur that appears in front of the subject, creating the illusion that it's moving backward. To counteract this problem, you can use Rear-curtain sync flash mode (⚡ REAR), which I explain later.

Slow sync

When capturing flash photography at night, your subject is often lit well, but the background appears completely dark. Slow flash mode (⚡ slow) helps take care of this problem because it allows you to set a longer shutter speed (up to 30 seconds) to capture some of the ambient light of the background. This allows the subject and the background to be more evenly lit, and you can achieve a more natural-looking photograph.

When using slow sync flash, you may need a tripod if you are using shutter speeds slower than about 1/2 second, depending on the subject.

> **TIP** To avoid ghosting in Slow flash mode (⚡ slow), be sure that the subject remains still for the whole exposure. With longer exposures, you can use ghosting creatively.

Red-eye reduction

Using on-camera flash, such as the built-in flash, often results in the red-eye effect. This occurs because the subject's pupils are wide open in the dark, and the light from the flash is close to the same axis as the lens, so it's reflected off the retina and directly back to the camera lens. Fortunately, the D3300 offers a Red-eye reduction mode (⚡◉). When you activate this mode, the camera either turns on the AF-assist illuminator (when using the built-in flash) or fires some preflashes (when using an accessory Speedlight), which causes the pupils of the subject's eyes to contract. This reduces the amount of light from the flash that reflects off the retina, thus reducing or eliminating the red-eye effect.

Rear-curtain sync

When using Rear-curtain sync flash mode (⚡ REAR), the camera fires the flash at the end of the exposure just before the rear curtain of the shutter starts moving. This is useful when you're taking flash photographs of moving subjects. Rear-curtain sync flash mode (⚡ REAR) allows you to portray the motion of the subject more accurately by causing a motion blur trail behind the subject rather than in front of it, as is the case with the Front-curtain sync flash mode (⚡). You can also use Rear-curtain sync flash mode (⚡ REAR) in conjunction with the Slow flash mode (⚡ slow) to achieve Slow Rear-curtain sync flash mode (⚡ SLOW REAR).

Rear-curtain sync flash mode (⚡ REAR) is available in all of the exposure modes: Programmed auto (**P**), Shutter-priority auto (**S**), Aperture-priority auto (**A**), and Manual (**M**). Slow Rear-curtain sync flash mode (⚡ SLOW REAR) is available only in the Programmed auto (**P**) or Auto (AUTO) mode.

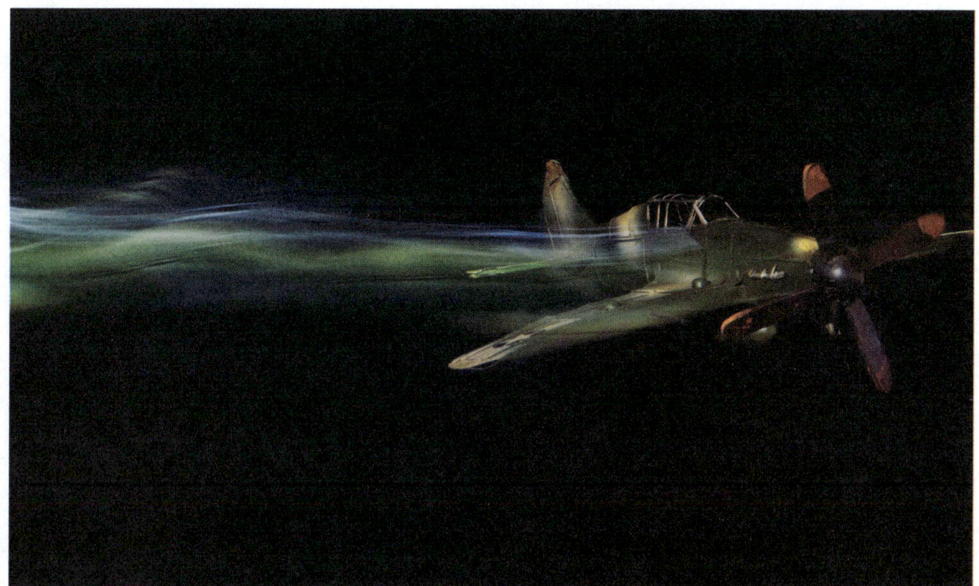

6.7 Rear-curtain sync flash mode gives the image a more natural sense of movement, with the blur following behind the subject. Exposure: ISO 200, f/20, 10 seconds with a Nikon 60mm f/2.8G macro lens.

Flash Compensation

When you photograph subjects using flash, whether you're using the built-in flash on your D3300 or an external Speedlight, there may be times when the flash causes your principal subject to appear too light or too dark. This usually occurs in difficult lighting situations, especially when you use i-TTL metering. Your camera's meter can be fooled into thinking the subject needs more or less light than it actually does. This can happen when the background is very bright or very dark, or when the subject is off in the distance or very small in the frame.

Flash compensation allows you to adjust the flash output manually, while retaining the i-TTL readings so your flash exposure is at least approximately correct. With the D3300, you can vary the output of your built-in flash's TTL setting (or your own manual setting) from –3 Exposure Value (EV) to +1 EV. This means that if your flash exposure is too bright, you can adjust it down three full stops under the original setting. If the image seems underexposed or too dark, you can adjust it to be brighter by one full stop.

Press the Flash compensation (⚡🄴) and Exposure compensation (🄴) buttons simultaneously, and rotate the Command dial to apply flash compensation.

Light Modifiers

When you set up a photographic shot, you are building a scene using light. For some images, you may want a hard light that is very directional; for others, a soft, diffused light works well. Light modifiers allow you to control the light so you can direct it where you need it, give it the quality the image calls for, and even add color or texture to the image. There are many kinds of diffusers, but the following are the most common:

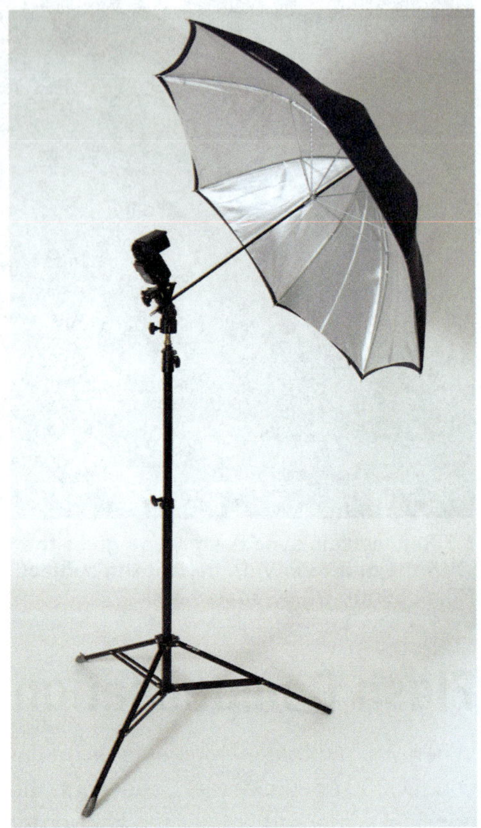

6.8 A Nikon Speedlight with an umbrella.

- ▶ **Umbrella.** The photographic umbrella is used to soften the light. You can either aim the light source through the umbrella or bounce the light from the inside of the umbrella, depending on the type of umbrella you have. Umbrellas are very portable and make a great addition to any Speedlight setup.

- ▶ **Reflector.** These are probably the handiest modifiers you can have. You can use them to reflect natural light onto your subject or to bounce light from your Speedlight onto the subject, making it softer. Some can act as diffusion material to soften direct sunlight. They come in a variety of sizes from 2 to 6 feet and fold up into a small, portable size. I recommend that every photographer have a small reflector in his or her camera bag.

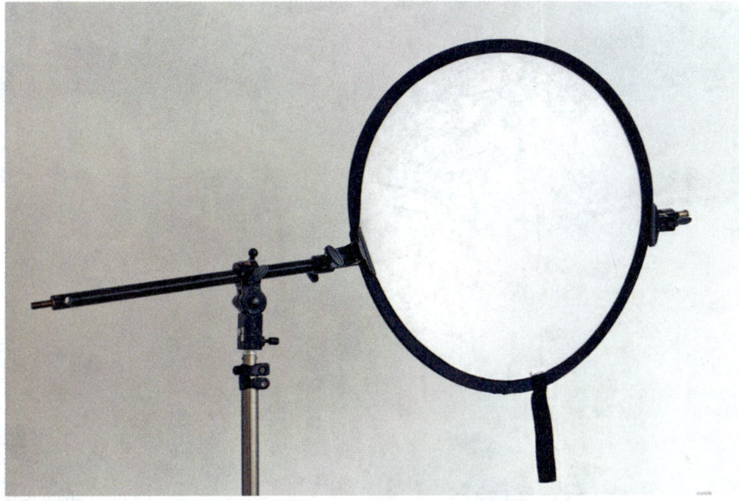

6.9 A small reflector and a reflector holder.

▶ **Softbox.** These also soften the light and come in a variety of sizes, from huge 8-foot softboxes to small 6-inch versions that fit right over your Speedlight mounted on the camera.

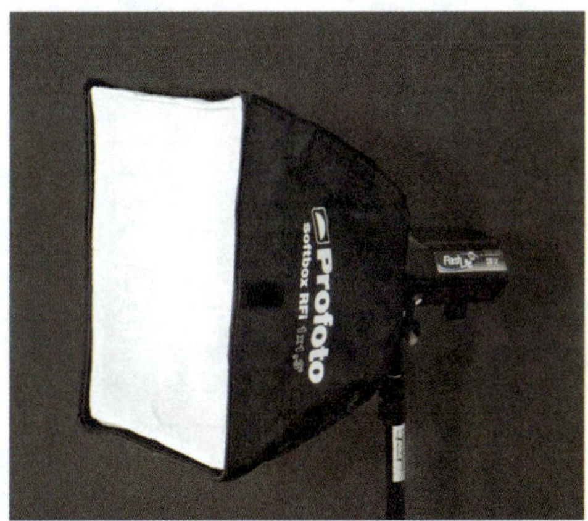

6.10 A medium-sized softbox.

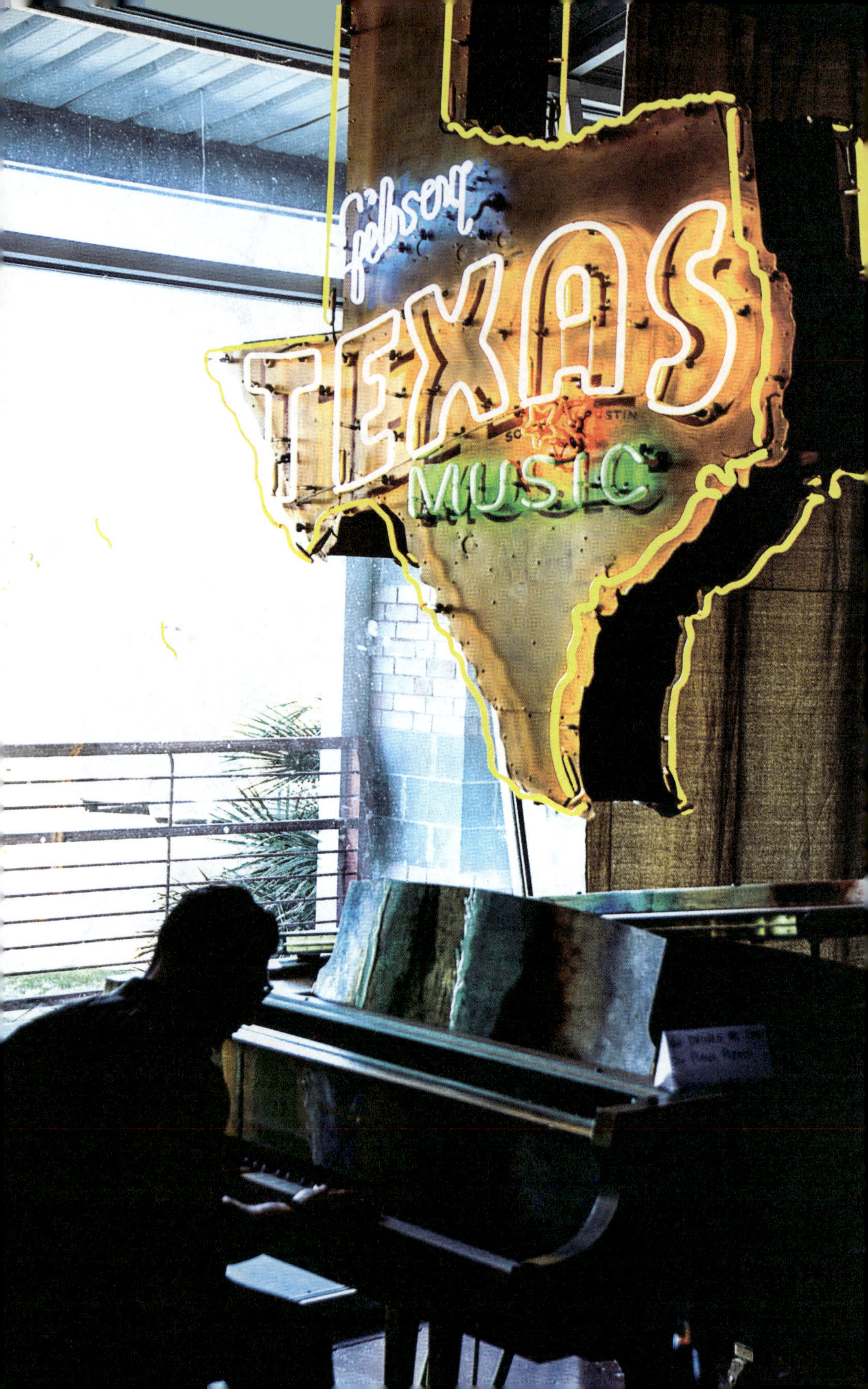
felbson
TEXAS
MUSIC

CHAPTER 7

Working with the Live View and Video Modes

Live View and high-definition (HD) video are standard on all current Nikon dSLRs. When the D3000 was released, the video mode was left out so you had to buy the next model up to capture video, and while the D3100 added video, it was pretty much fully automatic and not truly high-definition. Now with the D3300, the video mode is actually more full featured than with any of the professional models. With the D3300, Nikon adds full 1080p video at 60 frames per second (fps) for seamless integration of slow-motion shots into footage shot at 1080p 30 fps. More importantly, the D3300 allows you to set the exposure manually for full control over the appearance and quality of your videos. As a result, the D3300 is much more viable as a dedicated HD video camera than many of its predecessors.

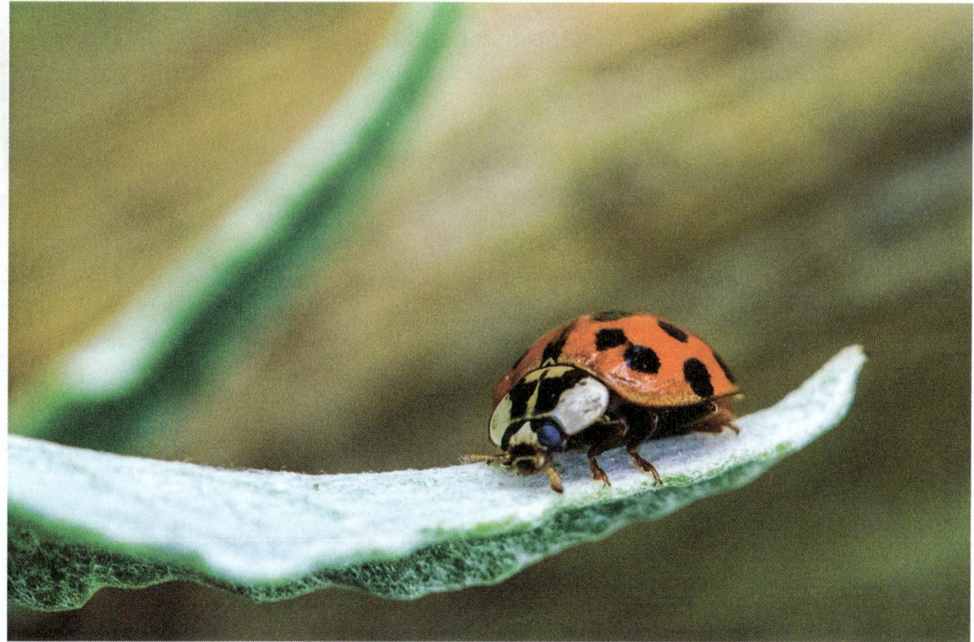

Using Live View mode, you can take your eye away from the viewfinder to compose your images on the 3-inch, high-resolution LCD monitor, which can help make it easier to get more interesting angles.

Live View Mode

Live View mode (**Lv**) is simply a live feed of what is being projected through the lens and onto the sensor. This live feed can also be used to produce a video. To enter Live View mode (**Lv**), press the Live View button (**Lv**) to activate it. The Live View button (**Lv**) is located right above the multi-selector. To shoot still photos, simply half-press the shutter-release button as you normally would to focus when using the viewfinder, and fully press the button to take the picture. To record video, press the movie-record button, which is located just behind and to the left of the shutter-release button.

Automatic Scene Selection

When Live View mode (**Lv**) is activated and you are using one of the two fully automatic exposure modes (Auto [⬛] or Auto flash off [⊛]), the D3300 image processor is able to read the scene and automatically select the appropriate scene mode for you. The camera shows the automatically selected scene mode in the display, with a small icon next to it to indicate that it's an auto scene selection. I admit that when I first read about this feature I was skeptical, but it works surprisingly well. There are six auto scenes:

▶ **Portrait (👤˙).** This mode is selected when the camera detects a face in the scene. It's partial to human faces, but I've noticed it will pick out my dogs once in a while.

▶ **Landscape (🏔˙).** This mode is selected when the camera detects a far-off focus point and an area that is bright across the top half of the frame (sky) and darker across the bottom half (land).

▶ **Close up (🌷˙).** This mode is activated when the camera detects that the focus distance is about 12 inches or less.

▶ **Night portrait (👤˙).** This mode is activated when the camera detects a face and a dark background in the scene.

▶ **Auto (⬛˙).** This is the active mode when the camera detects a scene other than those listed, or if it cannot determine a scene setting.

▶ **Auto flash off (⊛˙).** This mode is the same as the Auto, except that the flash is off.

When you use Live View mode (**Lv**), shooting stills and videos are very similar. Although each feature has some options that the other doesn't have, I'm first going to cover the options they have in common.

7

Focus modes

The D3300 offers three focus modes when using Live View mode (**Lv**). These modes are similar in some ways to those you find when using the traditional, through-the-viewfinder shooting method. When in Live View mode (**Lv**), you change the focus mode by pressing the *i* button (**𝒊**) to enter the Info edit menu.

To select a focus mode, use the multi-selector to navigate to the Focus mode option, and then press the OK button (**OK**). This presents you with three options: Single-servo AF (**AF-S**), Full-time-servo AF (**AF-F**), or Manual focus (**MF**). You can also slide the focus mode switch on the lens to Manual (if the lens features one).

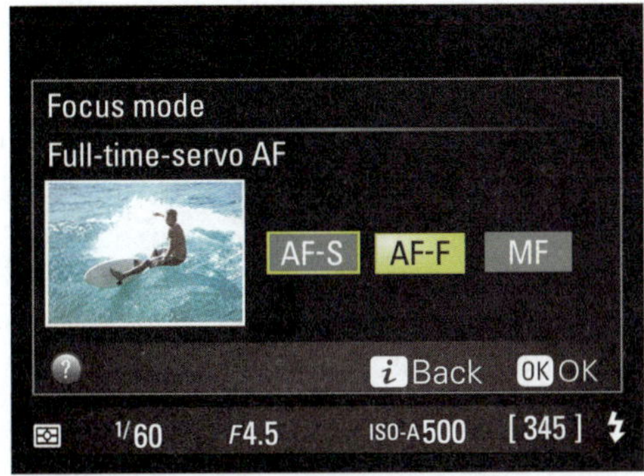

7.1 The focus modes in the Info edit menu.

Single-servo AF

This mode works the same in Live View as when using Single-servo AF (**AF-S**) for shooting stills traditionally with the viewfinder method. Press the multi-selector up (▲), down (▼), right (▶), or left (◀) to move the focus point to your subject, and then press the shutter-release button halfway to focus. Fully press the shutter-release button when the scene is in focus and ready to shoot. Note that the D3300 takes a still photo in Single-servo AF mode (**AF-S**) even if the scene is out of focus when the shutter-release button is fully pressed.

You follow the same procedure for video, except that you press the movie-record button, located just behind and to the left of the shutter-release button, to start recording video. You can do this in two ways: one is to focus first, and then start recording; the other is to start recording out of focus, and then press the shutter-release button halfway to focus in for a cinematic *pull focus* effect (this technique works a lot better in manual focus, however). Once the camera locks focus, it stays focused at that distance unless you press the shutter-release button again.

For still photography, I recommend using Single-servo AF (AF-S) for stationary subjects like portraits, still life, products, and landscapes. For video, you need to be sure that your subject isn't moving backward or forward by a large margin, especially if you're using a wide aperture for a shallow depth of field. Even the slightest change in distance can cause the subject to go out of focus. This setting is good for recording interviews or shooting scenes where there is not much back-and-forth subject movement.

Full-time-servo AF

Full-time-servo AF mode (AF-F) allows the camera to focus continuously, similar to when the shutter-release button is pressed halfway in Continuous-servo AF mode (AF-C).

When using Full-time-servo AF mode (AF-F) while recording video, you should be aware that the camera often hunts for focus, especially if you are moving or panning the camera. This can cause the video to go in and out of focus during your filming, which can cause your videos to look unprofessional (although some mockumentary videos use this for effect).

The Autofocus modes, and the Single-servo AF (AF-S) and Full-time-servo AF (AF-F) modes, operate in conjunction with the AF-area modes, which are covered in the next section.

AF-area modes

To enable you to focus more quickly and easily in Live View mode (Lv), Nikon gives you different options for AF-area modes. The AF-area modes are different from the traditional through-the-viewfinder shooting AF-area modes. When in Live View mode (Lv), you change the focus modes by pressing the *i* button (i) to enter the Info edit menu. Use the multi-selector to navigate to the AF-area mode option, and then press the OK button (OK).

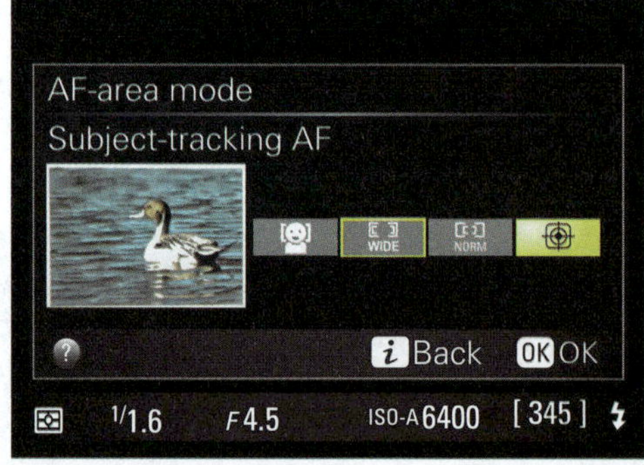

7.2 The AF-area modes in the Info edit menu.

The following options are found under AF-area mode:

▶ **Face-priority AF mode ( ).** Use this mode for shooting portraits or snapshots of the family. You can choose the focus point, but the camera uses face recognition to focus on the face rather than something in the foreground or background. This can really be an asset when shooting in a busy environment, such as when a lot of distracting elements are in the background.

When the camera detects a face in the frame, a double yellow border is displayed around the autofocus area. If the D3300 detects more than one face (the camera can read up to 35 faces), then it chooses the closest face as the primary focus point. You can use the multi-selector to choose a different primary face if you desire. When you use Face-priority AF mode (⊡) to capture group shots, I suggest using an aperture of f/5.6 or smaller to ensure greater depth of field to get all the faces in focus.

NOTE When using Face-priority mode with more than one face in the scene, the primary face is shown with a double border around the AF area.

▶ **Wide-area AF mode (⊞).** This mode makes the area from where the camera determines focus about four times the size of the Normal-area AF mode (⊞). This is good when you don't need to be very critical about the point of focus in your image. For example, when shooting a far-off landscape, you really only need to focus on the horizon line. This is a good general mode for everyday use. You can move the autofocus area anywhere within the image frame.

TIP When using the Face-priority AF (⊡), Normal-area AF (⊞), or Wide-area AF (⊞) modes in Live View mode (**Lv**), press the OK button (**OK**) to quickly return the autofocus area to the center of the frame.

▶ **Normal-area AF mode (⊞).** This mode has a smaller autofocus point than Wide-area AF mode (⊞), and you use it when you need to achieve focus on a very specific or precise area within the frame. This is the preferred mode when shooting with a tripod, or when shooting macros, still life shots, or portraits that require a more precise focus than Face-priority AF mode (⊡) provides (generally, portraits are focused on the eye closest to the camera).

▶ **Subject-tracking AF mode (⊞).** This is an interesting feature, especially when used in conjunction with video. Use the multi-selector to position the autofocus area over the top of the main subject in the image. Focus on the subject, and then press the OK button (**OK**) to start tracking the subject. The autofocus area follows the subject as it moves around within the frame. Be aware, however, that this feature works best with slow to moderately paced subjects that stand out from the background. When using Subject-tracking AF mode (⊞) with a very fast-moving subject, the camera tends to lose the subject and lock onto something of a similar color and brightness within the frame. This mode also becomes less effective as the amount of light decreases. To disable subject tracking, simply press the OK button (**OK**). This resets the autofocus area to the center. To reactivate Subject-tracking AF mode (⊕), press the OK button (**OK**) again.

> **NOTE** All AF-area modes are disabled when you set the camera or lens to Manual focus (**MF**), or when you attach a manual focus or non-AF-S lens to the D3300.

Using Live View mode

As you may already know, the image from the lens is projected to the viewfinder via a mirror that is in front of the sensor. There's a semitransparent area in the mirror that acts as a beam splitter, which the camera uses for its normal phase-detection autofocus. For Live View mode (**Lv**) to work, the mirror must be flipped up, which makes phase-detection autofocus unusable, so the camera uses contrast detection directly from the sensor to determine focus. This makes focusing in Live View mode (**Lv**) a bit slower than focusing normally. In addition, when you're shooting stills, the mirror must flip down and back up, which takes some extra time. This makes Live View mode (**Lv**) a more challenging option to use when shooting moving subjects or events such as sports, where timing is the key element in capturing an image successfully.

That being said, Live View mode (**Lv**) is ideal when shooting in a controlled environment or studio setting, especially when using a tripod. You can move the focus area anywhere within the frame; you're not limited to the 11-point autofocus array. Using Live View mode (**Lv**) also allows you to achieve sharper images when doing long exposures because the mirror is already raised, eliminating any chance of mirror slap, which can sometimes cause images to blur slightly when shooting exposures longer than 1/2 second.

> **TIP** Keep in mind that if you hold the camera at arm's length when it's in Live View mode (**Lv**), you increase the risk of blurry images due to added camera shake. Keep your elbows close to your sides for added stability.

Shooting still photographs in Live View mode (**Lv**) is very simple. Just press the Live View button to activate Live View mode (**Lv**) and you're ready to shoot. Use the multi-selector up (▲), down (▼), right (▶), or left (◀) to position the focus point. When in Single-servo AF mode (**AF-S**), press the shutter-release button halfway to focus; in Full-time-servo AF mode (**AF-F**), wait until the camera achieves focus (you see a green square when the scene is in focus), and then fully press the shutter-release button to take the picture. To shoot video, follow the same procedure, except when you want to start filming, press the movie-record button.

NOTE When using Full-time-servo AF mode (**AF-F**), pressing the shutter-release button causes the camera to refocus before actually taking the photo.

CAUTION When filming video, fully depressing the shutter-release button causes the D3300 to shoot a still frame and ends video recording.

When in Live View mode (**Lv**), the following buttons on top of the camera behave a little differently than they do when in the default viewfinder shooting mode:

▶ **Exposure compensation (☒)/Aperture (⊛) button.** Press this button and rotate the Command dial to adjust the aperture setting when in Manual mode (**M**). It adjusts the exposure compensation when in the Programmed auto (**P**), Shutter-priority auto (**S**), or Aperture-priority auto (**A**) modes.

▶ **Movie-record button.** This button's only function is to start recording video when it's pressed and to stop when it's pressed a second time. Simple. It's located just behind and to the left of the shutter-release button.

▶ **Info button (info).** Pressing this button cycles through a number of options for viewing the information laid over the Live View feed on the LCD monitor. These Live View/Movie Recording Display options are as follows:

  • **Show photo indicators.** As the name suggests, this is the information you need to see when using Live View mode (**Lv**) to shoot still photos (see figure 7.3).

  • **Show movie indicators.** This information display, shown in figure 7.4, shows settings relevant to filming video. This viewing option also has the 16:9 aspect ratio in clear view with the rest of the frame grayed out so you can accurately frame your videos to the correct aspect before you press the movie-record button.

NOTE When the camera is set to record video at 640 × 424, the grayed-out crop area isn't shown, as the aspect ratio is 3:2 like a standard photo.

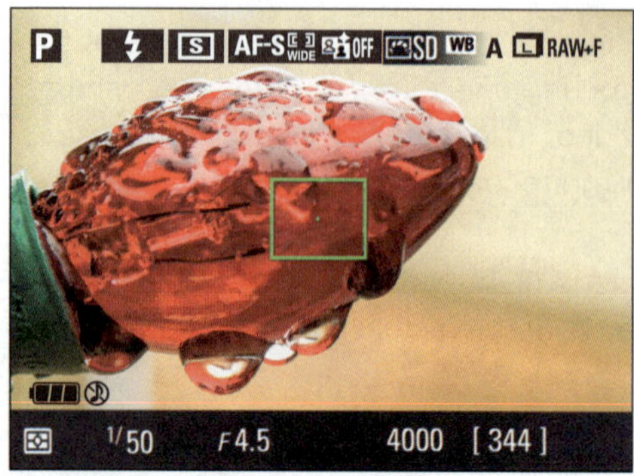

7.3 The Show photo indicators option.

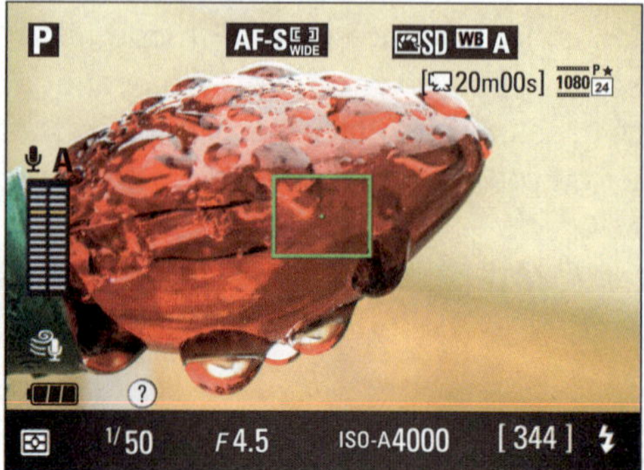

7.4 The Show movie indicators option.

● **Hide indicators.** This option hides all of the extraneous setting indicators in the frame and gives you a clear view so you can frame your shot without distractions. Small brackets are visible for use in lining up the shot to a 16:9 aspect ratio.

● **Framing grid.** This option is similar to Hide indicators, with the addition of a grid, as shown in figure 7.5. The grid is helpful for keeping lines or horizons straight in your compositions, or help- ing to compose with the Rule of Thirds. The shooting information is still displayed on the bottom.

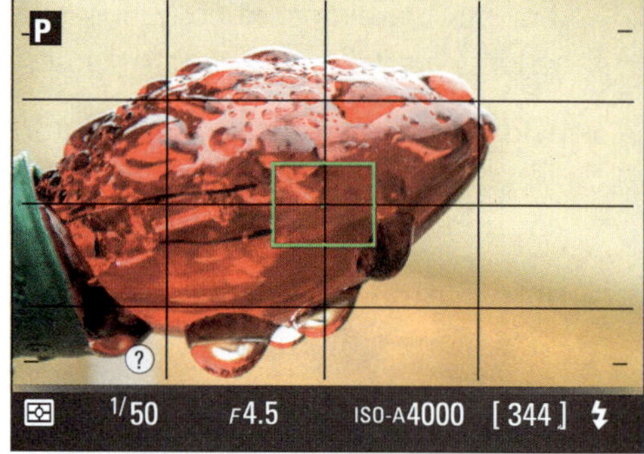

7.5 The Framing grid option displays the same information found in the Hide indicators option with the addition of a grid to aid in composition.

Although you can shoot stills or video when the camera is in any of the Live View/Movie Recording Display options, I recommend setting the display option for your intended recording. For example, set it to Show photo indicators for shooting stills and set it to Show movie indicators for filming video. This may seem like a no-brainer, but it's definitely a good habit to get into.

The buttons on the back of the camera also have some features when using Live View mode (**Lv**). Here are the options:

▶ **Playback button (▶).** Press this button to review your images or videos. Press it again to return to Live View mode (**Lv**).

▶ **Menu button (MENU).** Press this button to access the menu system. Not all options are available. Press the Menu button (MENU) again to return to Live View mode (Lv).

▶ **Zoom in button (🔍).** Press this button to zoom in on your focus point to check focus.

▶ **Thumbnail/Zoom out button (⊞).** Press this button to zoom out when you're back to the standard framing; the shooting information bar reappears at the bottom of the screen.

▶ **i button (ⓘ).** A single press of this button brings up the Info edit menu. Press the *i* button (ⓘ) again to return to Live View mode (Lv).

▶ **AE-L/AF-L button (AE-L/AF-L).** This button functions as assigned in Custom Setting menu (✐) f2 when you press it.

Why Shoot Video with a dSLR?

Not long ago, video in dSLRs was considered by many photographers to be a gimmick — a marketing tactic to get people to buy dSLRs, not only to take pictures, but also to shoot home videos just like a compact camera. However, as the technology has advanced, dSLR videography has become a viable form of filming, not only for family events but also for television shows and even feature-length films meant for the big screen. This is because smaller dSLR cameras have features that outweigh some advantages of a dedicated video camera. Here are some of the major advantages:

▶ **Price.** dSLR cameras are much cheaper than a mid- to pro-level HD video camera.

▶ **Image quality.** The larger CMOS sensors allow the camera to record video with less noise at high sensitivities than most consumer video cameras can.

▶ **Interchangeable lenses.** You can use almost every Nikon lens on the D3300. Additionally, while some HD video cameras take Nikon lenses, you need an expensive adapter, and you lose some resolution and the ability to get a very shallow depth of field.

▶ **Depth of field.** You can get a much shallower depth of field with dSLRs than you can with standard video cameras when using a lens with a fast aperture, such as a 50mm f/1.4. Most video cameras have sensors that are much smaller than the sensor of the D3300, which gives them a much deeper depth of field. A shallow depth of field gives videos a more professional, cinematic look.

Shooting and Editing Video

Using the video feature on the D3300 is quite simple: press the Live View button (**Lv**), focus, and then press the movie-record button. Easy now, Tarantino. Before you hit that Record button, you need to set up the camera.

First, press the Menu button (**MENU**) to enter the menu system. Use the multi-selector to navigate to the Shooting menu (📷), press the OK button (**OK**), and then navigate to the Movie settings option. This is the very last menu item. Press the OK button (**OK**) and you're faced with the following options:

▶ **Frame size/frame rate.** Choose the image size based on your intended output and preferred frame rate (covered later in this chapter). You have the following choices:

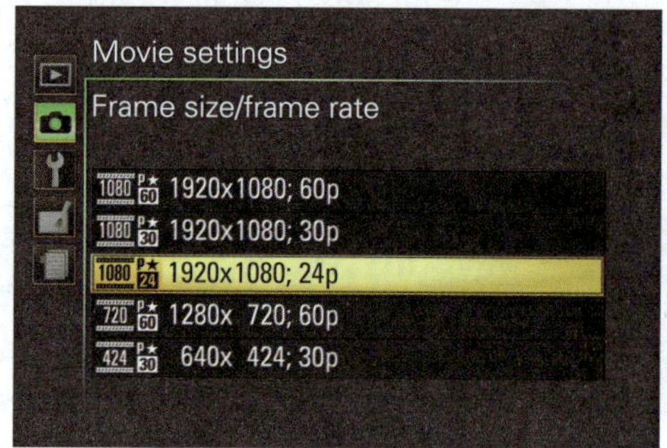

7.6 **The Frame size/frame rate screen.**

- 1920 × 1080; 60p (1080 / 1080)

- 1920 × 1080; 30p (1080 / 1080)

- 1920 × 1080; 24p (1080 / 1080)

- 1280 × 720; 60p (720 / 720)

- 640 × 424; 30p (424 / 424)

▶ **Movie quality.** You have two choices: High and Normal. The difference comes down to bit rate. At higher bit rates, more information is being recorded, resulting in better color rendition and dynamic range; of course, higher bit rates also mean more data and larger file sizes. Keep in mind that High quality movie clips are limited to 20 minutes and Normal quality clips can be up to 29 minutes and 59 seconds. Again, your choice comes down to your intended output. For the web, Normal quality is fine; for viewing on HDTVs, stick with High quality. Notice that when the quality is set to High, a small star appears in the Frame size/frame rate icon.

▶ **Microphone.** The three microphone settings are Auto sensitivity, Manual sensitivity, and Microphone off. Auto works for most general filming, but for a more consistent sound in a controlled environment, you can set the microphone sensitivity manually. You can monitor the levels when filming. When recording sound to an external source, you may want to turn the microphone off. Most professional filmmakers prefer to record the audio to a separate file using a dedicated sound recording system for higher audio quality. The video and sound files are later synced in postproduction.

▶ **Manual movie settings.** When this option is set to the default (which is Off), the camera completely controls the shutter speed and ISO setting, no matter what the settings say in the information display. Set this option to On if you want to set the shutter speed and ISO manually when in Manual exposure mode (M).

CAUTION When you set the Manual movie settings to On, Auto ISO (AUTO) is disabled for video.

Now that the Movie settings are taken care of, you should set the following options:

▶ **Picture Control.** As it does with your still images, the D3300 applies Picture Control settings to your movie. You can also create and use Custom Picture Controls that fit your specific application. One of my favorites is a Custom Picture Control that I created called Raging Bull; it uses the Monochrome Picture Control (MC) with added contrast and the yellow filter option. This gives me a black-and-white scene that's reminiscent of the Martin Scorsese film of the same name. Before you start recording your video, decide which Picture Control you want to use for your movie.

▶ **Exposure mode.** If you set the Manual movie settings to On, this is a *very* important setting. The exposure mode you select determines whether you or the camera will be choosing the settings. Select one of the following options:

- **Programmed auto (P) and Shutter-priority auto (S) modes.** These modes let the camera make all the exposure choices for you. When you press the Live View button (Lv), the camera sets the shutter speed, aperture, and ISO sensitivity. While you're filming, if the lighting changes, the camera adjusts the exposure by adjusting the ISO sensitivity. If the scene becomes too bright, the shutter speed is raised to keep a good exposure unless you lock the exposure by pressing the AE-L/AF-L button (AE-L/AF-L). The only control you have over the exposure is that you can adjust the Exposure compensation (±).

CAUTION It's important to note that when the camera is set to Shutter Priority auto (S), the shutter speed is automatically overridden by the camera as soon as the movie-record button is pressed.

- **Aperture-priority auto mode (A).** This mode allows you a little more control. You can set the aperture to control the depth of field, but the camera automatically controls the shutter speed and the ISO sensitivity. You can also use Exposure compensation (⊠) to brighten or darken the image.

- **Manual mode (M).** If you're serious about video, you should be using this exposure mode. This mode lets you control the exposure by adjusting the aperture, shutter speed, and ISO setting yourself. It takes a little more time to set up, but this allows you to control not only the depth of field but also the amount of noise and the shutter speed effect if you want.

CAUTION When shooting using Manual exposure (M) and Aperture Priority auto (A) mode, the aperture must be set before Live View mode (Lv) is activated.

TIP When shooting in Manual exposure mode (M), set the Function button (Fn) to ISO so you can adjust the ISO settings quickly.

Shutter Speed

In filmmaking, there's a concept called the 180-degree shutter rule. Without getting into why it has this name, the 180-degree shutter rule states that your shutter speed should be about twice your frame rate for natural-looking images. So, for 1080p at 24 fps (1080 24 / 1080 24), you should use a shutter speed of 1/50 second; for 1080p at 30 fps (1080 30 / 1080 30), use a speed of 1/60 second; and at 1080p at 60 fps (1080 60 / 1080 60), shoot at 1/125 second. This gives the video just enough blur to make it look natural to human eyes.

Slower shutter speeds give the video a smeared appearance, although the D3300 avoids this by not allowing you to set the shutter speed slower than the frame rate.

On the opposite end of the spectrum, faster shutter speeds can cause the video to appear slightly jerky. This is because just as when shooting a still image, the action is frozen (remember, videos are just stills played in succession), and as the subject moves through the frame, there is no motion blur to make it look more natural to the eyes. Of course, you can use the jerky, fast shutter speed as an effect as well. Movies such as *Saving Private Ryan, 300,* and *Gladiator* used this effect in the action scenes to get that hyper-real look.

Frame size and frame rate

The D3300 offers a few options for recording video. There are two size settings for HD video with three frame rate options, and one option for shooting smaller videos that are destined directly for the web or e-mail. The high-definition (HD) video sizes are 1920 × 1080 and 1280 × 720. The small size is 640 × 424. When people discuss video frame size, they usually refer to the height number (1080 or 720) because of the way the image is progressively recorded (from top to bottom), but more on that later.

The 1080 video size has more resolution and therefore holds more detail and has less noise in low light. Most professionals prefer to shoot in 1080 and downsize later if necessary. There are, however, some reasons for shooting in 720. For example, the file sizes are smaller and, if you're only shooting videos to post to YouTube or Vimeo or some other online source, you don't really need the higher resolution. If you plan to make DVDs to show on an HDTV, then the extra resolution of 1080p is going to make quite a difference in quality. So, it boils down to your intended output. If you're just planning on e-mailing to friends or just want to shoot a small-size file to be viewed on a laptop or mobile phone, you can use the smallest option of 640 × 424.

An important part of video capture is *frame rate*. This is the rate at which the still images are recorded, and it is expressed in terms of frames per second (fps). At the end of the resolution number (1080 or 720), there is another number in subscript (24, 25, 30, 50, or 60). This subscript number is the frame rate. Video capture involves recording still images, linking them together, and then playing them back one after another in sequence. This allows the still images to appear as if they're moving. Most video cameras capture video at 30 or 60 fps. A rate of 30 fps is generally considered the best for smooth-looking video. Shooting at 24 fps is the minimum rate required to fool the human eye into seeing seamless motion. This is the frame rate that film-based motion pictures use, so 24 fps gives HD video a cinema-like quality.

The frame rate you select depends on a few factors. Most seasoned videographers prefer 30 fps for the smooth video look and the way that it portrays motion more naturally. Some videographers like to use 60 fps as well. This frame rate is generally used when shooting fast action or doing many quick pans, as the faster minimum shutter speed allows the camera to eliminate artifacts such as *skew* (where the subjects appear to slant as the camera pans) that can occur when doing a fast pan. When shooting fast action such as sports, most videographers will recommend 60 fps. Shooting at 60 fps is also a way in which videographers can create smooth slow motion by slowing the 60 fps footage down to 30 fps and using it with the regular footage that was shot at 30 fps.

Some filmmakers who started out using film and have recently transitioned to HDSLR video prefer the 24 fps film look. This is also the preferred frame rate if the footage is going to be intercut with footage that was digitized from actual film stock.

In-camera video editing

You can make simple edits to your videos in-camera. However, for more serious edits, you should consider third-party software such as iMovie for Mac or Adobe Premiere Elements for Mac or PC. These are affordable, entry-level editing programs. As you progress, though, you may need to step up to more powerful programs, such as Final Cut Pro X from Apple or Adobe Premiere Pro. In-camera, you have three options: choose the Start frame, choose the End frame, and grab a still image from the video. Each edit you make is saved as a new file, so there's no need to worry about making any permanent changes to your original file. To edit a video, follow these steps:

1. **Press the Menu button (MENU) and use the multi-selector to select the Retouch menu (✎).**

   > **TIP** You can also press the Playback button (▶), select the video using the multi-selector, and then press the *i* button (ⓘ) and select the Edit movie option.

2. **Select Edit Movie, and then press the OK button (OK) or the multi-selector right (▶) to view the menu options.** Use the multi-selector to choose the movies. You can also use the Playback zoom-in button (🔍) to get a closer look at the initial still frame. Press the OK (OK) button to select the movie you want to edit.

3. **Choose the type of edit that you want to make, and then press the OK button (OK) or the multi-selector right (▶).** The options are Choose start point / end point, or Save selected frame. A menu appears with all videos that are saved to the current memory card (when the movie is selected directly from the Playback screen, this option doesn't appear).

4. **Use the multi-selector to scroll through the available videos until the one you want is highlighted in yellow, and then press the OK button (OK).**

5. **Press the OK button (OK) to begin playback, and then press the multi-selector up (▲) at the point in the video where you want to make the edit.** You can press the multi-selector down (▼) to stop playback, and multi-selector left (◀) or right (▶) to go back or forward in the video clip.

6. **Press the multi-selector up (▲) to make the edit.** I prefer to pause the movie by pressing the multi-selector down (▼) so I can be absolutely sure it is where I want the edit to be. I then make the edit and the movie saves automatically.

> **TIP** When playing back a movie file, you can use the Command dial to jump ahead in 10-second increments. If the clip is less than 10 seconds long, it jumps to the end of the clip.

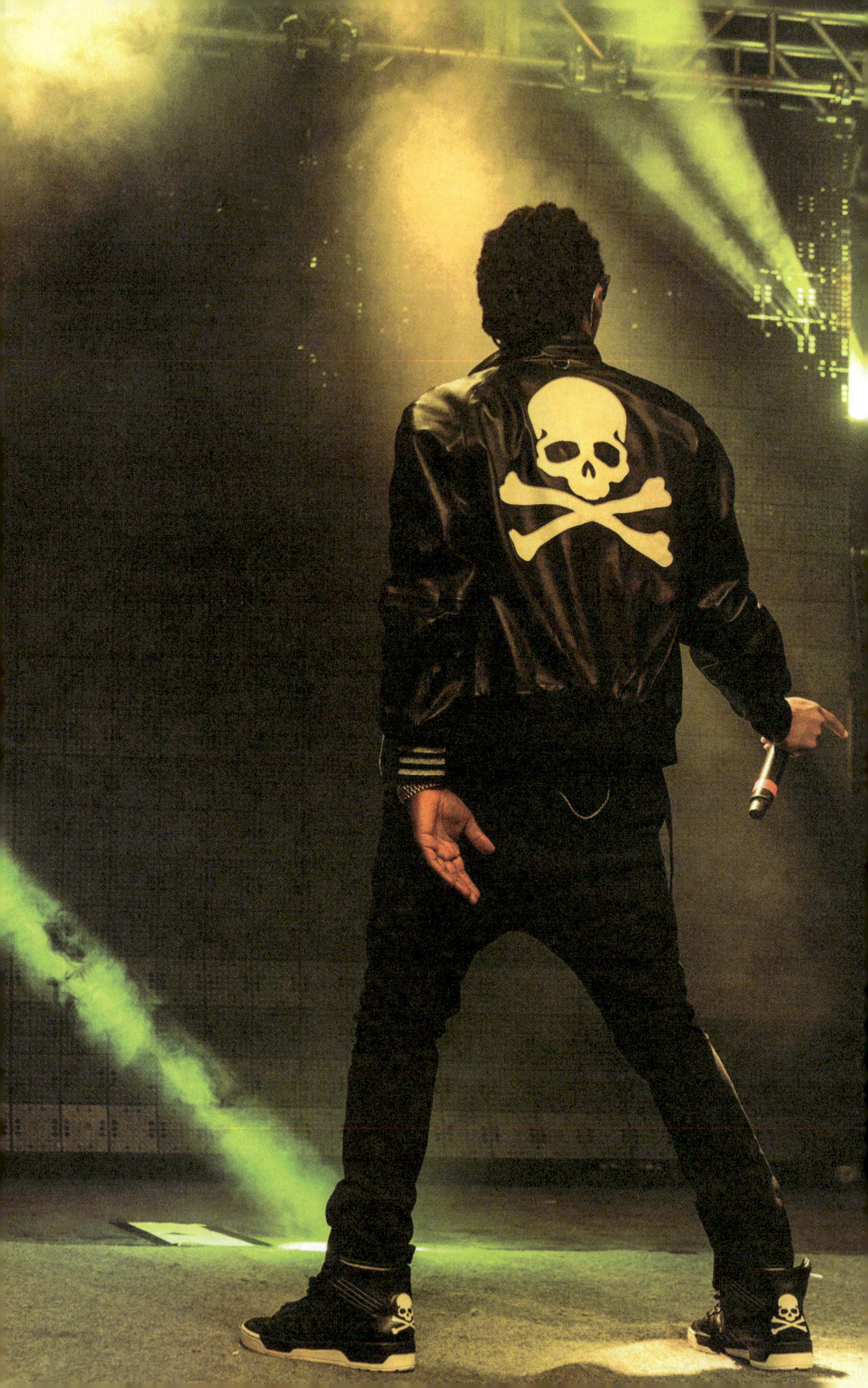

CHAPTER 8

Real-World Applications

Although the D3300 has a lot of modes that you can set to achieve specific effects for many types of photography, the key to becoming a really successful photographer is learning which settings to use in different situations to achieve the results you desire. Once you learn how your camera works, you can get predictable results, even in difficult lighting.

This chapter is meant to help you get past the scene modes and learn which settings and what gear to use for different types of photography. Moving past the scene modes allows you to flex your creative muscles and begin creating photographs rather than just taking pictures.

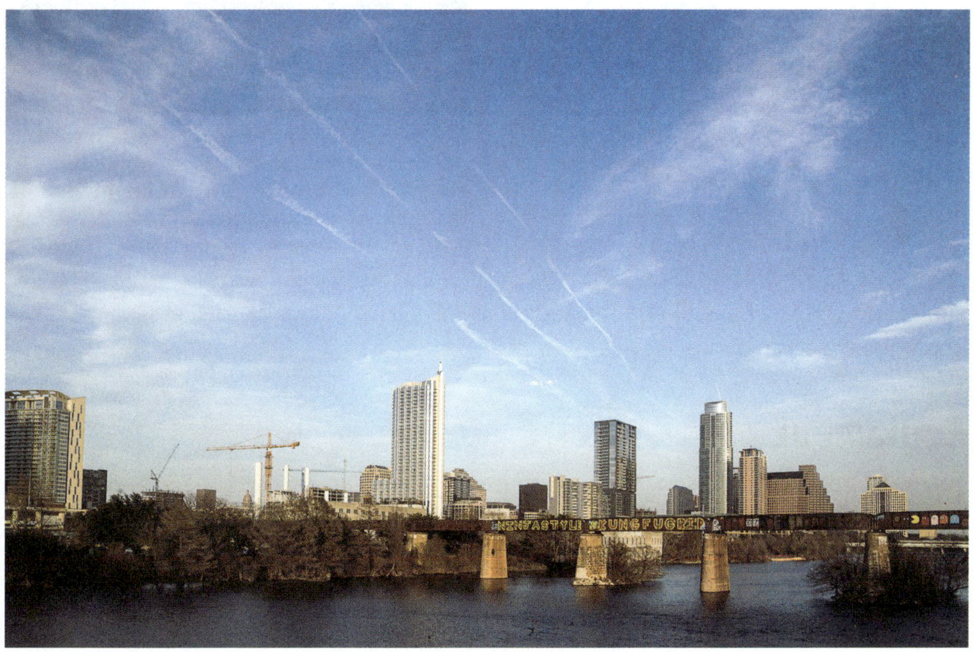

Exposure, composition, camera setting, and equipment choice are all factors in creating an image. The key is to know how to put it all together and make it work in any situation.

Abstract Photography

A common, but incorrect, assumption is that photography is an art form that represents subjects in a realistic way. While this is somewhat true, in reality photography is an abstract art because it takes three-dimensional subjects and depicts them in two dimensions. That in and of itself is an abstraction of reality.

A photographer can further stretch the limits of visual reality by using different tools to create even more abstract concepts. This includes the use of wide-angle lenses to distort spatial relations and long exposures to show a subject as it moves through time and space.

There are two distinct types of abstract photography: *objective* and *nonobjective*. Objective abstract photography takes a subject and depicts it in an unorthodox way. The subject is generally recognizable, but takes on a strange or unique look. Nonobjective abstract photography takes a subject and renders it unrecognizable. Breaking the subject down to its base elements, such as lines, forms, colors, or textures, can result in photographic abstractions.

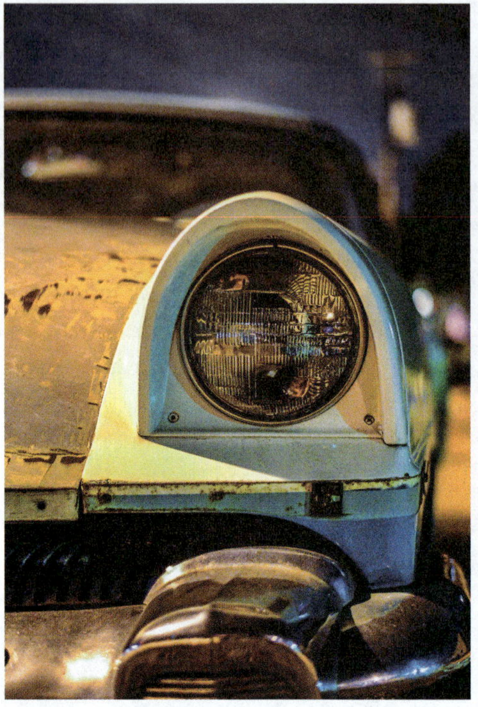

8.1 Here, I closed in and focused on this old car's headlight. This is an objective abstraction because you can identify what the subject is. Exposure: ISO 100, f/1.8, 1/30 second using a Nikon 35mm f/1.8G.

Equipment

You don't need a lot of fancy gear to create photographic abstractions. All you need is a creative vision and an eye for details. You can easily create abstract photography using the kit lens that comes with your D3300.

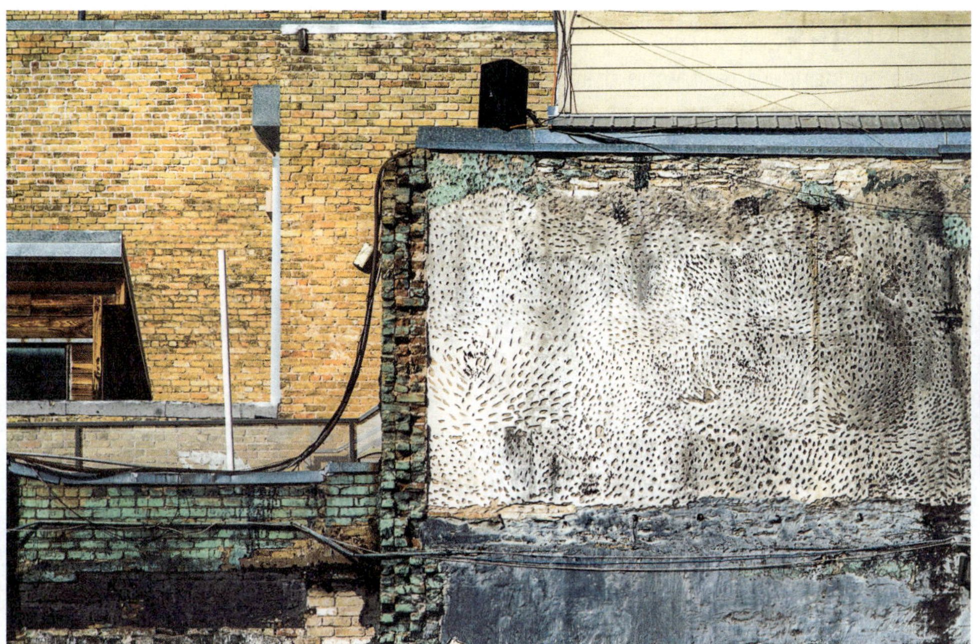

8.2 For this photo, I used a telephoto lens and zoomed in on these neighboring buildings. The compression that the long focal lengths gives the image allows all of the different colors, textures, and patterns to appear flattened as if they are all on one surface. Exposure: ISO 100, f/11, 1/1000 second using a Nikon 70–200mm f/4G VR at 105mm.

That being said, you can also use special lenses, like macros or close-up filters to get extreme close-ups, wide-angle or telephoto lenses to distort the subject, off-camera Speedlights to highlight texture, or color filters to add colorful effects.

You can also use different settings to create abstract effects. For example, you can change the white balance to create unnatural colors, use exposure compensation (⊞) to purposely under- or overexpose your images, or use the Slow-sync (⚡ SLOW) or Rear-curtain sync (⚡ REAR) flash modes.

Technique

There's no standard technique that you can embrace to create abstract images. The best one is to keep your eyes and mind open to abstractions. Interesting lines, bright colors, interesting patterns, and odd textures are things to look for when creating abstract images. I don't typically set out to capture abstract images; they generally appear in unexpected places.

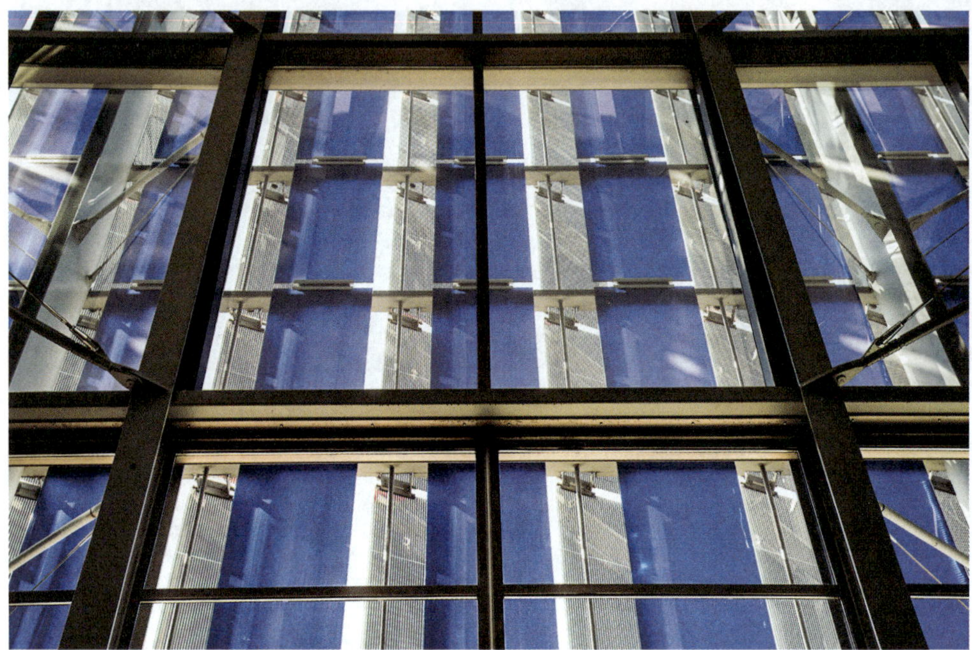

8.3 For this abstract shot, I used the framework and glass windows of a building along with the blue sky to make a composition based on color, line, and form. Exposure: ISO 200, f/8, 1/200 second using a Sigma 35mm f/1.4 | A.

While there is not a foolproof method, there are some techniques that work well for making abstract photographs:

- ▶ Get close up with a wide-angle lens to emphasize spatial relations and accentuate and distort lines in your images.

- ▶ Use a telephoto lens to photograph the detail of a far-off subject or use compression distortion to reduce the apparent distance between faraway objects.

- ▶ Use a macro lens to focus on minute details of a much larger subject; this is great for highlighting texture or individual features.

Action and Sports Photography

Action and sports photography is an entertaining and often exciting endeavor that is popular with many photographers. The D3300 is well suited to this type of photography, with its proven 11-point AF system as well as its 3-D tracking and quick 5-frame-per-second capture rate in Continuous high-speed shooting mode (⧉H). These features all combine to create a good sports camera.

The attraction that people have to action and sports photography stems from the ability to capture a fraction of a second during an event, which allows the viewer the time to examine the motion of the action in great detail. This is something that is impossible to do with any other art form.

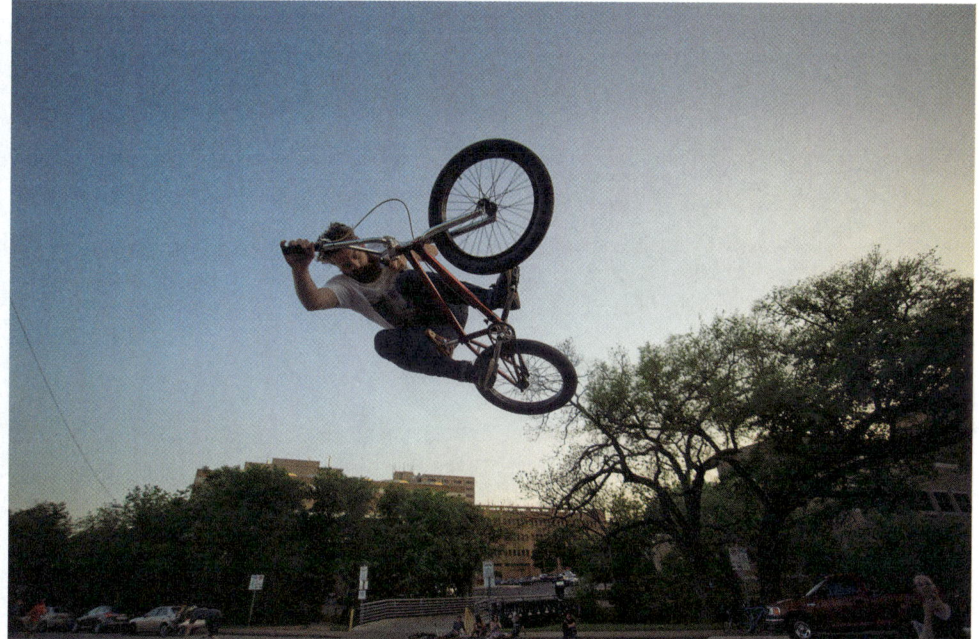

8.4 Using Shutter-priority auto mode and a fast shutter speed, I was able to freeze the motion of this BMX rider as he performed an invert on a ramp. Exposure: ISO 100, f/4, 1/1000 second using a Sigma 17–70mm f/2.8–4 | C at 17mm.

NOTE Keep in mind that action photography doesn't necessarily encompass only sporting events. Action scenes can include nearly any subject — just ask a parent. Capturing a photo of a toddler is more akin to action than portrait photography.

Equipment

Most action and sports photography requires some special equipment. If you're pho-tographing an organized sporting event such as football, soccer, basketball, or volley-ball, it's pretty much a given that you won't be allowed on the court or field with the athletes. As a result, a telephoto lens is often a necessary piece of equipment to get great close-up shots from the sidelines.

While a long lens is a necessity for most sports photographers, another aspect to con-sider is the maximum aperture, or speed, of the lens. For just about any indoor sport such as basketball, hockey, volleyball, or night football, a lens with an aperture of f/2.8 is a necessity. When shooting outdoor sports on sunlit days, you may be able use a slower telephoto zoom lens such as the Nikon 55–200mm f/4–5.6, but on cloudy days you may be pushing the limits of your camera settings.

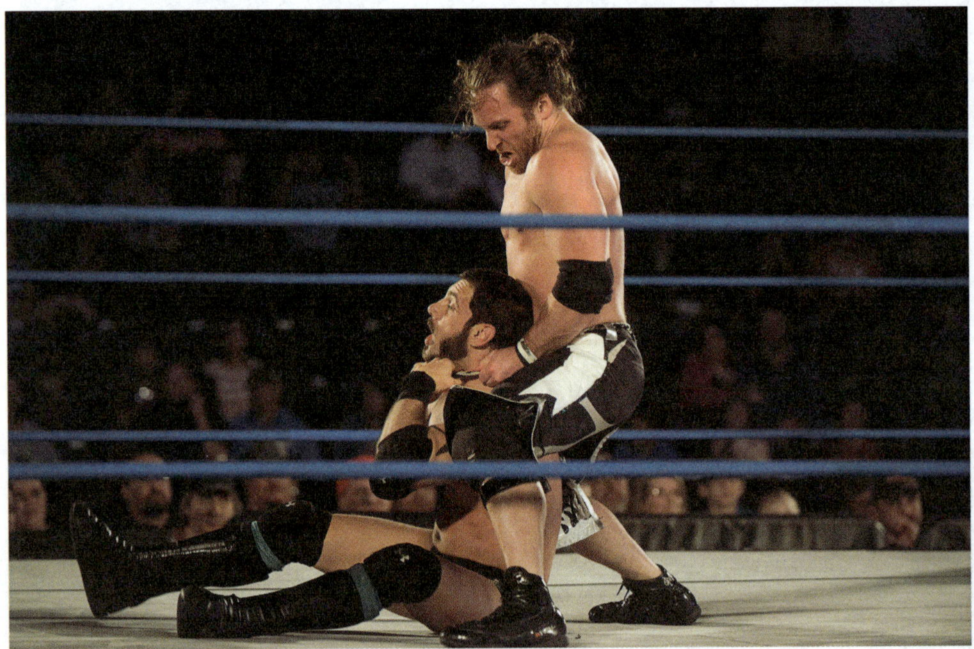

8.5 I used a telephoto lens to photograph these professional wrestlers because I couldn't get up close to the ring. Exposure: ISO 6400, f/2.8, 1/400 second, using a 70–200mm f/2.8G.

When shooting individual action sports such as BMX, skateboarding, freestyle moto-cross, or skiing and snowboarding, you can often use a wide-angle lens to create a more dramatic shot. To make good use of a wide-angle lens, you typically need to get close to the action, so you need to coordinate with the athlete before you jump in and start shooting. You don't want to hop in and startle the athlete, causing an accident. You must also understand that the closer you get to an athlete who is performing stunts on a wheeled device, the greater the likelihood of you or your camera getting hurt or damaged. When attempting this type of action shot, it's important to be completely aware of your surroundings and the actions of the athlete. Being able to dodge a flying skateboard or duck under an out-of-control BMX bike is useful. And when it comes to motocross, well, an out-of-control motorcycle could be potentially fatal.

Finally, another good, if not essential, piece of equipment for most sports photographers is the *monopod*. The monopod reduces camera shake by providing support for the camera and lens, but it doesn't restrict movement like a tripod can.

Technique

Shooting sports sometimes requires skill sets that are completely different from each other, depending on the way you want to portray the scene. The lens choices are vastly different depending on the technique you use. Either you are far away from the action and you use a telephoto lens to bring the action closer, or you are close to the action and you use a wide-angle lens to add some distortion to accentuate the movement. It's rare that a sports photographer would need a midrange focal-length lens.

Photographing action to capture movement can be done in two opposing ways. The first, and probably the easiest and most common, is to use a fast shutter speed to freeze the motion and capture the action in sharp detail. Typically, a shutter speed of 1/500 second or faster is required to capture most mid- to fast-paced subjects. The second way to portray speed and motion in an action photograph is to use a slow shutter speed to introduce motion blur. There are a couple of easy ways to do this. One way is to simply keep the camera stationary and use a fast enough shutter speed to freeze the motion of any slow-moving elements in the frame, but not fast enough to freeze the motion of the fast-moving subject. Another way is to use a technique called *panning*. This is a very common approach that sports photographers use, and it involves following the subject motion with the camera. Moving the camera along with the subject slows down the motion of the subject relative to the camera, which allows you to capture it in focus while making the background a blur that shows that the subject is moving.

> **TIP** You can use a Nikon SC-28 or SC-29 TTL Remote Cord to use a Speedlight off-camera. This creates more dramatic lighting for action shots, while retaining full Through-the-Lens (TTL) metering for easy exposure.

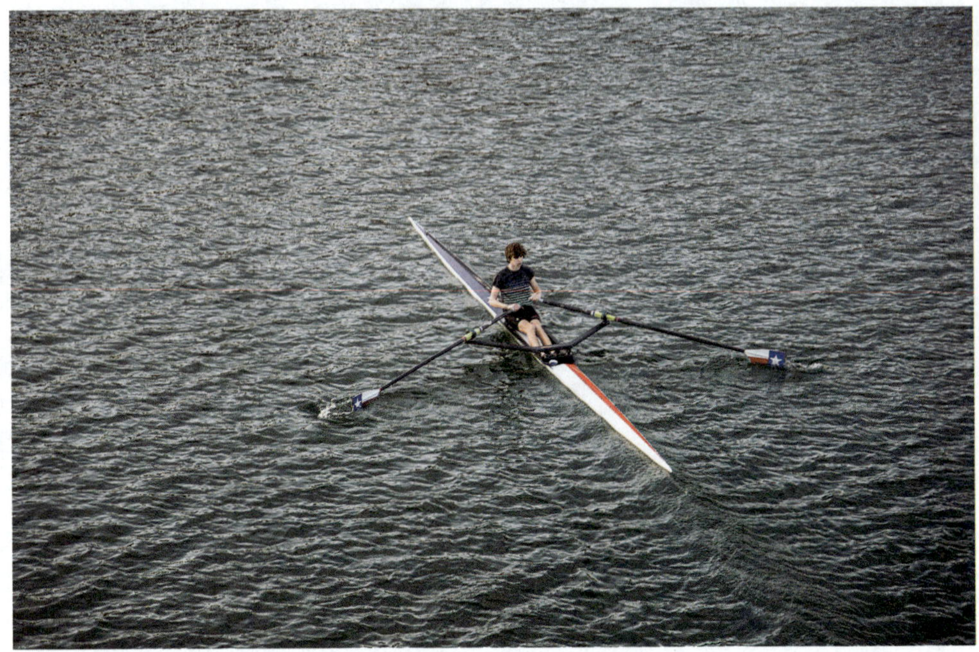

8.6 Not all sports are extremely fast. Taking a photograph of this sculler was more about making the composition interesting than about capturing the action. Exposure: ISO 200, f/5.6, 1/200 second using a Nikon 55–300mm f/4–5.6G.

The speedy 5-fps speed in Continuous high-speed shooting mode (⊒H) is great for firing off rapid shots or creating an action sequence, but the real key to successful action and sports photography is knowing when to take the shot. Every sport has key moments and every motion has a peak. Capturing an athlete at the peak of the motion is the deciding factor in whether your shot is good or great.

TIP Becoming familiar with the sport you are photographing is the best way to figure out when the key moments occur. Before you start shooting, stand back for a few minutes and simply *watch* the action.

Knowing where the action is going to take place is obviously a benefit. You don't have to have a sixth sense to know where the action is — it's really down to common sense. For example, at a baseball game, there's nearly always some action at first base, and if there's a runner on third, you can bet that home plate will see some action. For basketball, the key shots are going to be near the hoop about 90 percent of the time. Some events have action occurring at more than one place, and if you can't cover all spots from one angle, you need to make a judgment call. For example, you can cover sprinters springing from the starting block, or you can catch them at the end of the line breaking the tape, but you can't get both. Decide which shot you think makes a more exciting image.

Concert and Live Music Photography

This is probably one of the fastest-growing genres of photography. It seems just about everyone who has an interest in music and photography wants to capture images of his or her favorite performers at work.

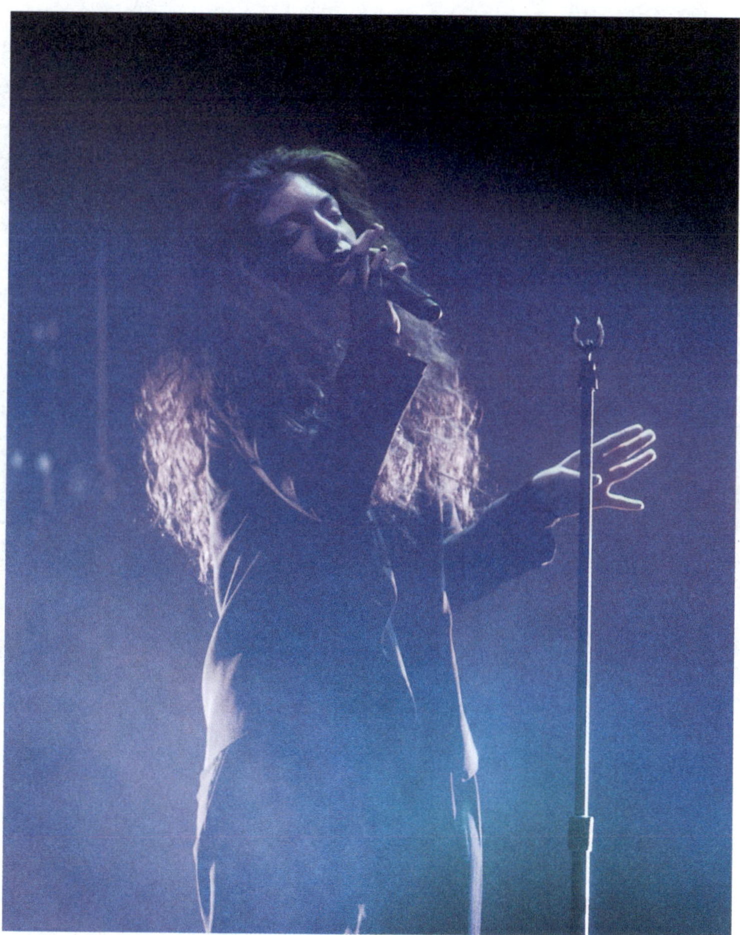

8.7 Sometimes, you won't be able to get close to the performer, so you need an extra-long lens, like the one I used to get this shot of pop singer Lorde in Austin, Texas. Check with the venue beforehand so you know what to bring. Exposure: ISO 6400, f/4.0, 1/400 second using a 300mm f/4 AF-S and a monopod.

Concert photography is generally done in little to no light, especially when starting out in small venues. When there is light, it is usually sporadic — blinking, flashing, strobe, and moving lights are the norm. When you couple the low light with performers who often move quickly and erratically, you have the recipe for a demanding shoot.

Many photographers, myself included, love the challenge of confronting these obstacles and still capturing the shot at the perfect moment when everything comes together — the lights, the performer, and the photographer — in unison. I think it's the dream of everyone who photographs music to capture that iconic moment: Kurt Cobain crashing into the drums, Keith Richards with a cigarette dangling from his lips, or Johnny Cash defiantly flipping the bird at the camera.

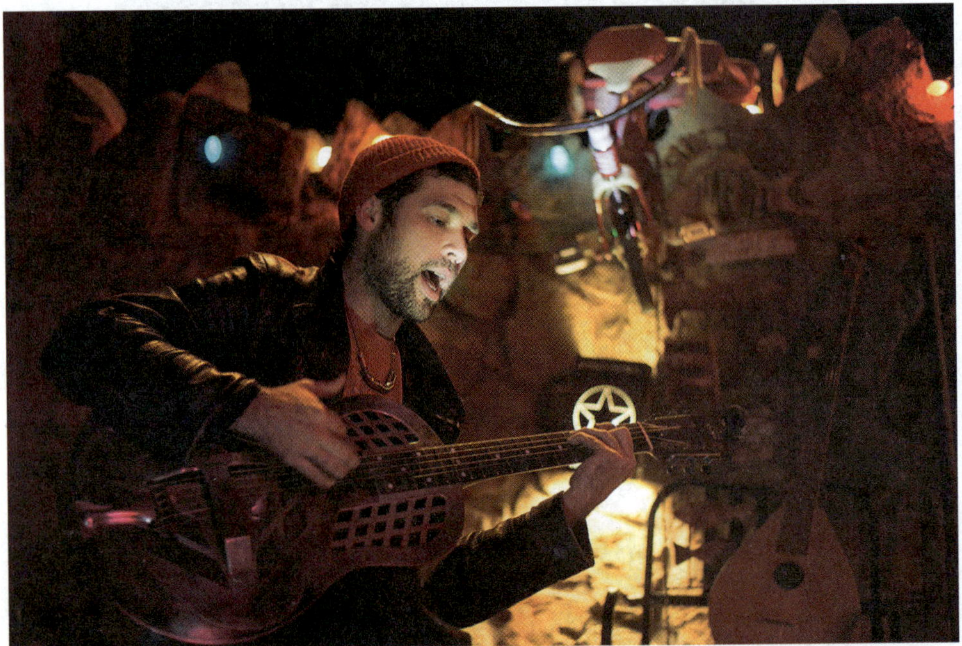

8.8 Small local gigs are the best place to start out with music photography. Smaller venues are more intimate and can have cool backgrounds like the one shown here. Exposure: ISO 6400, f/1.8, 1/50 second using a Sigma 18–35mm f/1.8 | A at 35mm.

Equipment

One of the most important pieces of equipment for concert photography is a camera that has good low-light capabilities. Although the D3300 is not the best camera for this type of photography, it is definitely very capable, as shown in the images in this chapter.

Gaining Access

One of the most common questions I'm asked is how to gain access to photograph famous bands. There really isn't an easy answer; it's mostly hard work and partly luck. You won't start out photographing Lady Gaga. The best place to start is the local music scene. Start shooting local acts in bars and small venues and build up a portfolio. Find a local magazine or website to shoot for. Make friends with other established concert photographers in your city and on the web. Many (but not all) are happy to give some friendly advice.

Making contacts is important in this business because some people may not be able to shoot an assignment and will refer the photo editor to other photographers, which is exactly how I was able to start shooting bigger names. I shot live music for the better part of a decade and a half before I received any assignments from *Rolling Stone* or *SPIN*. Perseverance and patience are key, and you have to *love* what you do.

One piece of equipment that I find essential is a fast, standard wide-angle-to-short telephoto lens with a constant aperture of f/2.8. Lately, my favorite lens on the D3300 for concerts is the Sigma 18–35mm f/1.8. It's an expensive option, costing as much as the D3300 itself, but I find the extra stop is really helpful. However, if you are on a tighter budget, Sigma and Tamron both make fast f/2.8 lenses that won't break the bank. Having a fast telephoto lens for close-up shots is also nice, but is often not necessary. An ultrawide lens is great for full band shots and special effects, but is more of an option than a necessity.

I often see people on Internet forums insisting that a fast prime lens is the way to go, but from my experience photographing hundreds of shows over the years, the compositional limitations that are imposed by the prime lens are more of a hindrance than the benefit you gain with an extra stop of light, especially considering the incredible low-light capability of today's cameras. I'd rather have a well-composed shot with a little more high-ISO noise than a clean, badly composed shot. If I know the venue has particularly bad lighting, I'll bring along a fast prime lens, but this is usually an exception.

That being said, if you can't afford a fast f/2.8 zoom lens, an inexpensive, fast prime lens like the Nikon 35mm f/1.8 may be the best option for you. The bottom line is that for most concert photography, you're going to find that the kit lens isn't practical and a wider lens gets better results. With a wider lens, you can compose loosely and crop in to get a good composition, rather than be stuck with a composition that is too tight from the onset. In fact, assuming that you're close enough to the performer, if you have to choose between a 50mm f/1.8 or a 35mm f/1.8, the 35mm would be the better option.

> **CAUTION** One thing you should always have with you when photographing concerts is a set of earplugs. If you enjoy music, protect your ears so that you can continue to enjoy it for the rest of your life.

Technique

The last thing you want when shooting a concert is to hear the first chords of a song and realize that your camera isn't ready to shoot. Always make sure your camera is set up and ready to go *before* the band starts. Before I even set foot in a venue, my camera is set to the following:

- **Metering mode.** For a typical concert setting, I use Spot metering (⊡), because the most important part of the scene is your focus point. Setting the camera to meter from this point ensures the focus point is properly exposed. At outdoor concert events during the day, I may use Matrix metering mode (▤).

- **Single-point AF (⊡).** With all the flashing lights and movement, you can't trust the camera's autofocus system to make the right choice. You must actively decide where to place the focus point while shooting.

- **Continuous-servo AF (AF-C).** Rarely does a performer stand still during a show. When shooting wide open, even the slightest movement of a performer can cause a missed focus. This setting ensures that the camera is focusing constantly with every move.

- **Manual mode (M).** Depending on the lighting and how much the performers are moving, I usually start with 1/125 second at f/2.8 and adjust from there. During fast numbers, 1/125 second is usually enough to freeze the action. If there is little movement, you can slow the shutter speed; if it's a punk or metal band, you may need to speed it up to 1/250 or even 1/500 second to avoid blur.

- **Auto ISO (AUTO).** This feature is so well implemented, I almost always use it unless I'm shooting outdoors in the daytime. For the D3300, I set the ISO limit to 3200.

Using Flash

As a rule, flash photography isn't allowed when shooting more popular touring bands at large venues. However, you can often use it in the bar and club scene. I don't recommend going with this method, but if you must, use a slower shutter speed or Slow flash mode (⚡ SLOW) to capture some ambient light and bounce the flash to avoid that direct flash look.

If you decide to use the flash, use it sparingly. As a professional musician and photographer, I understand why flash isn't appreciated: it's blinding and very distracting. Yes, I have asked photographers to stop using flash while I was performing.

One factor in concert photography that is often overlooked is composition. Most photographers aren't musicians and as such aren't aware of some of the subtle nuances that come with composing for music photography. I often see many photographers composing shots like they are shooting a portrait — tight head-and-shoulders compositions. While this may be great for a singer, framing a guitar player in this way isn't ideal. When shooting a person performing with an instrument, be it a guitar, bass guitar, banjo, or even a ukulele, the instrument should be treated as if it is a part of the performer. Think of it as an arm or a leg and try to keep the whole thing in the frame. Pay particular attention to the guitar headstock. This is where the brand name usually is, and you can't sell a photo of a guitar player to a guitar magazine or manufacturer if the brand isn't recognizable.

Getting the right shot when photographing music depends greatly on timing. Fortunately, all music is based on timing and is generally rhythmic. Musicians usually make predictable movements when they are in a groove. This is especially true of drummers (who are the most often overlooked musicians). Guitar, bass, and keyboard players are a little less predictable, but they are still very rhythmic. Lead singers are often the most erratic, but also the most fun to shoot. Stop shooting for a second, listen to the beat, and watch the movements. It only takes a few seconds to get a good idea of what kind of movement is happening. Listening for gradual increases in the loudness and intensity of the music can also help you anticipate some kind of action.

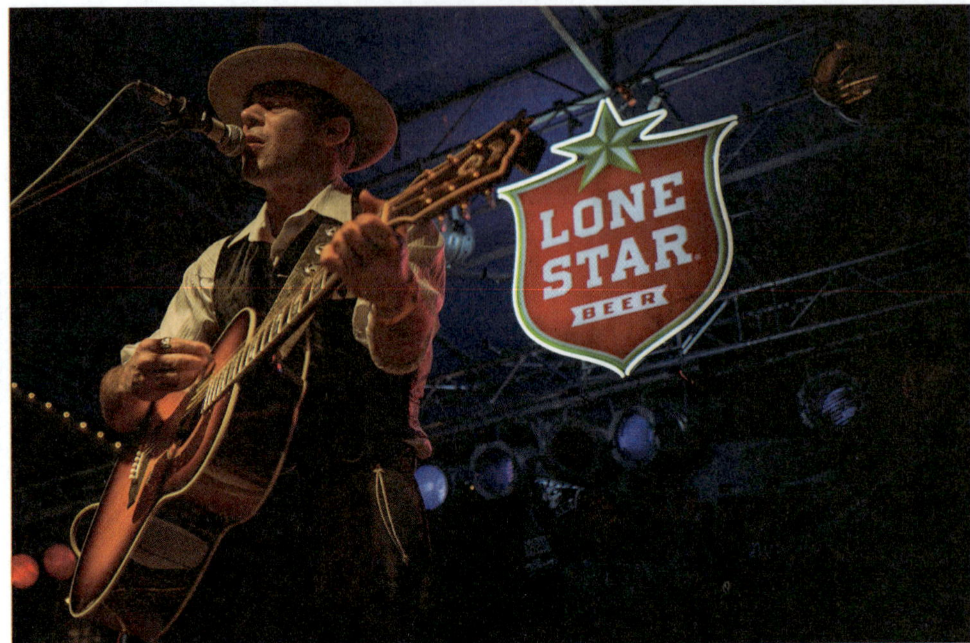

8.9 Including some of the background in the shot is great for adding interest and is also good practice for shooting professionally because event sponsors like to see their brands in the shot. Exposure: ISO 3200, f/4.0, 1/125 second using a Sigma 17–70mm f/2.8–4 | C at 50mm.

Macro Photography

Macro photography (sometimes referred to as close-up photography) involves photographing a subject on a level that is extremely close. It allows the photographer to portray a subject in a way that can't be seen with the unaided eye. It gives you the ability to show different subjects in an elemental way by breaking them down into minute details.

Because most people don't get a chance to see subjects such as insects on this level, macro photography is extremely popular, not only with viewers, but also among photographers.

Macro photography relies on the ability to focus close enough on a subject that the image the lens projects onto the camera sensor is the same size as the subject. The relative size of the actual subject to the projected image is defined in terms of a ratio. For example, if your image size is the same as the subject size, you have a ratio of 1:1.

Strictly speaking, the true definition of a macro image is one that has a ratio of 1:1 or better. These days, however, the marketing gurus at the camera and lens manufacturing companies have broadened the definition of macro lenses to encompass any lens that allows you to get a ratio of 1:2, or even a little less.

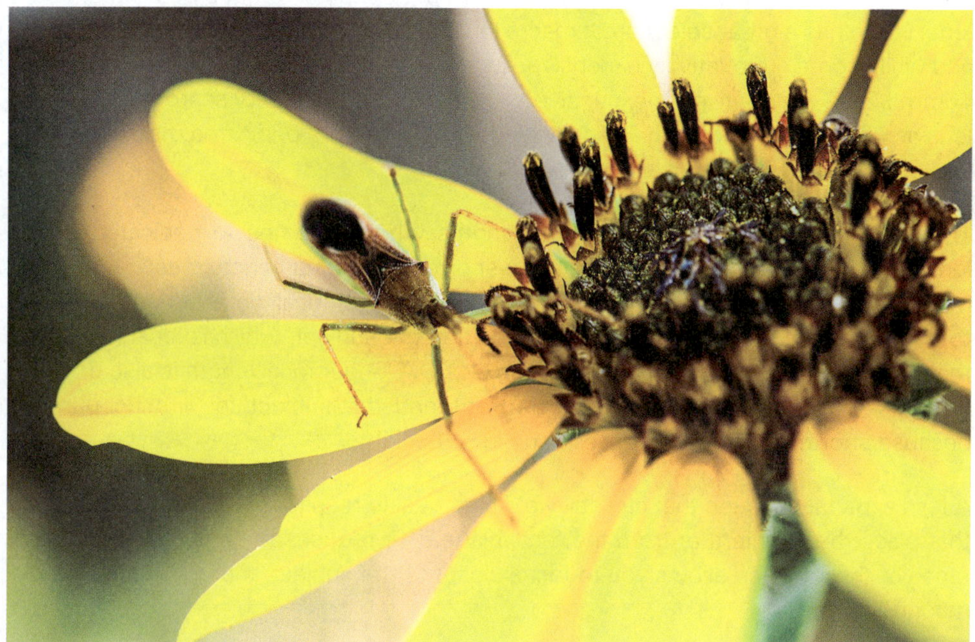

8.10 I just happened to catch this tiny bug as I was photographing this flower. Exposure: ISO 800, f/8, 1/160 second using a Nikon 60mm f/2.8G Macro lens.

Equipment

Starting out in macro photography doesn't require a lot of equipment, but it does require specialized equipment to do it and get good results. As I mentioned previously, some manufacturers market lenses as macro when they are actually close-focus lenses. Generally, these are telephoto or inexpensive, standard zooms that are mid-range in price. This is not meant to disparage these lenses — you can get some great images with them, and some of them are actually more versatile than a dedicated macro lens. For example, one of my favorite lenses is the Sigma 17–70mm f/2.8–4 DC HSM OS Macro (quite a mouthful of a name). While the lens name contains the term *macro*, it only gets to about 1:2.7 (about one-third the actual size). For close-up photography, this is good, and it also allows you the versatility of a wide-angle to telephoto range, which makes it a great all-around lens.

NOTE Nikon calls its macro lenses *micro* lenses.

If you want to get the best results and take advantage of the high resolution of the D3300 sensor to capture the most detail, the best option is to get a dedicated macro lens. Nikon has a great selection of macro lenses (Micro-NIKKOR in the Nikon lexicon), and while some are relatively expensive, such as the 105mm f/2.8G VR, others like the 40mm f/2.8G are relatively inexpensive and can be used as a very sharp normal prime lens as well. Sigma and Tokina also have a few options for a dedicated macro lens that you might want to look into.

There are a number of different focal lengths when it comes to dedicated macro lenses. Shorter focal length lenses have a shorter working distance, meaning that you must be closer to the subject to get to a 1:1 ratio. Longer focal length lenses allow you to get a bit more distance between the lens and the subject, which is ideal for critters that may be scared off by a lens that is too close. A longer focal length is also good for subjects that need space between the lens and the subject for lighting purpose because shorter focal length lenses can block the light.

A less expensive option that can still yield high-quality results is using extension tubes that place the lens farther from the focal plane. This reduces the minimum focus distance of the lens and allows you to focus closer to the subject, thereby increasing the magnification.

The least expensive option is to use close-up filters that screw onto the end of your lens and act like magnifying glasses. This option doesn't typically yield the best results but is an inexpensive way to get started in macro photography.

CROSS REF For more information on macro lenses and accessories, see Chapter 4.

Reversing Ring

One option you may have heard of is a reversing ring. This screws into the front of the lens and allows you to attach the lens to the camera with the rear element facing outward. There are no CPU contacts, so all exposure calculations must be done manually, and if you use a G lens, the aperture stops down completely making the viewfinder dim and difficult to focus. In the end, for the D3300, I find a reversing ring to be more time consuming and likely to be extremely frustrating to anyone just starting out.

A tripod is a very essential piece of equipment for a macro photographer. Unless you're working with live or moving subjects, there's no reason not to use a tripod. As you magnify the subject using a macro lens, camera shake is also magnified exponentially. The *1-over-focal length* rule doesn't apply when using close focus. Sometimes you may need to use a shutter speed up to four times faster than normal to compensate for camera shake when handholding the camera. When you combine these fast shutter speeds with the tiny apertures that are required to get a substantial depth of field, you need a lot of light. Using a tripod allows you to use slower shutter speeds.

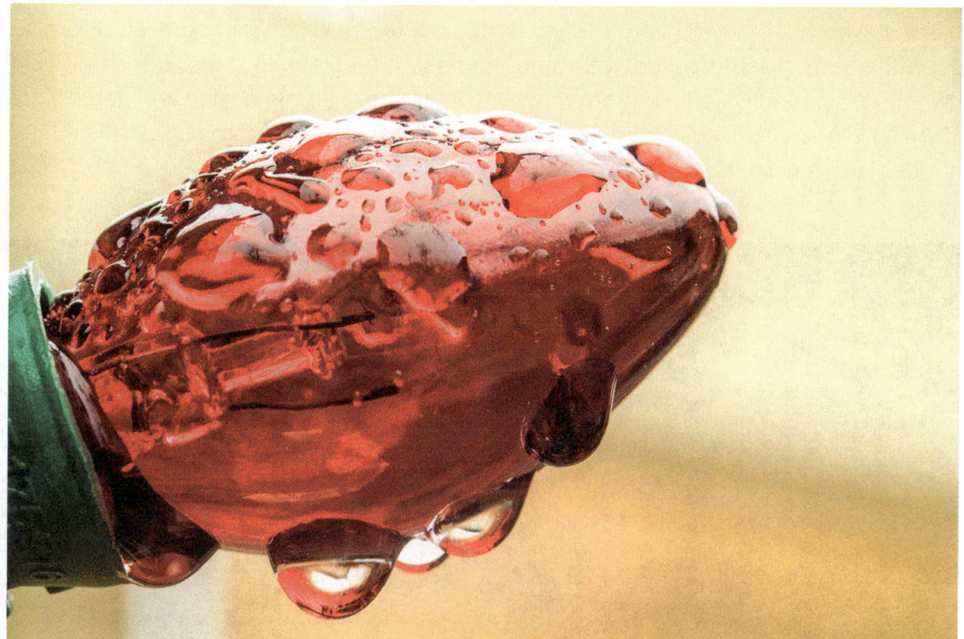

8.11 Stopping down allows you to get the subject completely in focus, but still allows a shallow depth of field for background separation. Exposure: ISO 1600, f/14, 1/80 second using a 60mm f/2.8G Macro lens.

NOTE Some macro lenses include a stabilization feature, but at higher magnifications this technology is much less effective.

Of course, using a tripod isn't always an option, especially when photographing living creatures, such as insects, or even flowers or foliage outdoors in a breeze. In this case, you sometimes need to introduce more light into the scene by using a flash.

When shooting close up, the built-in flash is all but useless because it is blocked by the close proximity of the lens to the subject, and an on-camera Speedlight is too far off axis to be of any use. There are, however, a number of flash systems you can use to provide on-axis lighting to your close-up subject. One is the Nikon R1C1 wireless flash kit. The R1C1 can wirelessly control a number of flashes that attach to a bracket, which then mounts to the lens. However, this kit is rather expensive, so unless you are very serious about macro photography, you probably don't need it.

The most convenient option is known as a *ring flash*. These also attach to the end of the lens to provide on-axis light. There are a number of inexpensive, bare-bones ring flashes available. I have a very cheap (around $100) Phoenix 46N ring flash (I've also seen the same flash branded with other names). It works with the Nikon iTTL (flash metering) system. For a little more money, you can step up the quality and get a Metz 15 MS-1 digital ring-form macro flash or a Sigma EM-140 DG macro flash. These units are of higher quality and also work with the Nikon iTTL flash system.

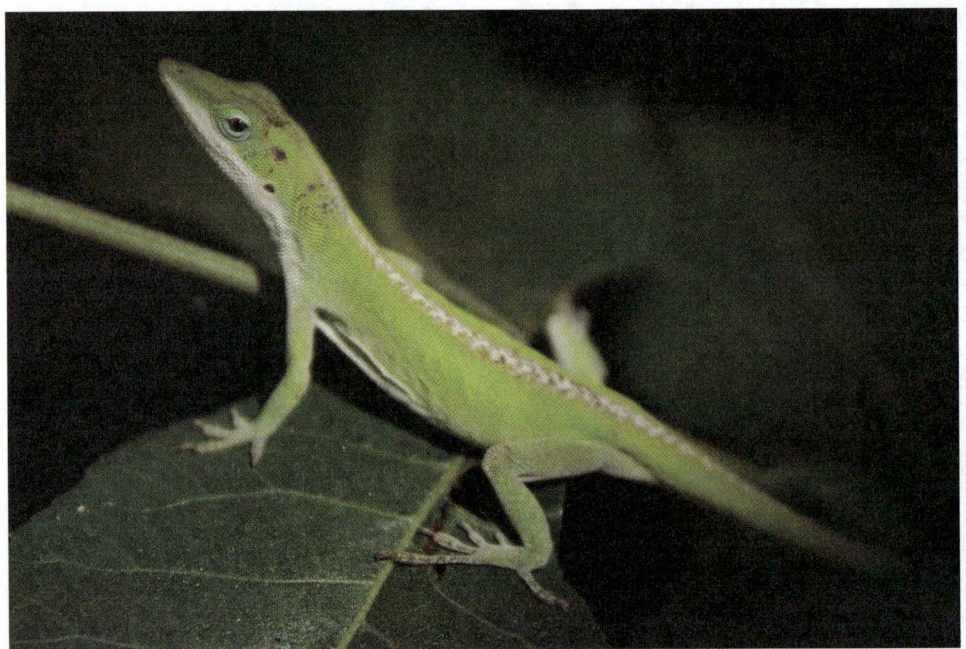

8.12 I held an off-camera Speedlight to the left side of the lens to illuminate this macro shot of a green anole. Exposure: ISO 100, f/4, 1/200 second using a Sigma 17–70mm f/2.8–4 | C at 70mm.

Instead of a ring flash, I often use one of the standard Nikon Speedlights, such as the SB-910, SB-700, or even the SB-400. I use a Nikon SC-28 TTL cable to get the Speedlight off-camera and hold the Speedlight next to the front of the lens. This provides simple, on-axis macro lighting, with the additional benefit of more texture and contour because the lighting only comes from one direction.

Technique

Typically, the most challenging aspect of macro photography is getting enough depth of field to capture the most important aspects of the subject in sharp detail. As you focus closer to the subject and increase the magnification, the depth of field is reduced exponentially. When your lens is less than an inch away from a subject, just breathing in and out, and even the natural movement of your body, are enough to throw off the plane of focus, causing you to miss focus. This is why using a small aperture is usually a necessity to increase the depth of field to workable limits. I say *usually* because sometimes you may want to use a wide aperture and a shallow depth of field to draw attention to a very specific detail in the subject.

Unfortunately, using a small aperture to increase the depth of field for sharpness is a double-edged sword. Once you stop down to a certain aperture, diffraction limits the sharpness, and stopping down further decreases sharpness and starts to soften the image. The diffraction limit for most lenses is about f/16, and even though this is a small aperture, at close focus the depth of field at this aperture is relatively shallow.

If you find it necessary to handhold your macro shot, I recommend using Continuous-servo AF (AF-C). This allows the camera to focus continuously on the autofocus point because even the smallest movements can shift focus. Point of focus is extremely important when capturing macro photography. For example, when photographing an insect's face, if the point of focus is just a little bit off, the eyes will be out of focus but the area behind the subject will be sharp. As with any portrait (even those of nonhumans), the eyes should be sharp.

When shooting inanimate or nonmoving subjects (especially in the studio), I recommend using Single-servo AF (AF-S) and, for the most accuracy, Live View mode (Lv).

Manual Focus with Macro Photography

Although autofocus is a great help in most photography, there are times when it's beneficial to focus manually. Many photographers insist that manual focus is the only way to capture macro photography. Personally, I find that autofocus is a great benefit with macro photography, especially when trying to catch small, fleeting critters, but there are instances where only manual focus will do.

When photographing up close, it's best to focus on the spot that you feel is the most important to the image (such as the eyes). When using autofocus, the best way to do this is to use a single point, but even then, you are relying on the autofocus module, which may not always be exact. Simply switching to Manual focus (**MF**) and using your own eyes to determine if the point of focus is exact can be the best method to ensure that your image comes out exactly as you want.

Another option for inexpensive macro photography is a manual focus lens. Nikon has a few older MF micro lenses that are very sharp, and much less expensive than the newer AF-S versions. You can also look into other options. I have an excellent Pentax M-42 screw-mount macro lens (Macro-Takumar 50mm f/4) that I found for next to nothing. With an inexpensive M-42-to-Nikon F-mount adapter that I purchased on eBay, I have a great macro setup that gives me a 4:1 ratio.

Don't overlook the benefits of taking control and focusing manually. After all, the camera is your tool; make it work *for* you, not against you.

Nature and Landscape Photography

One of my favorite things about photography is that it gives me a great excuse to get outside and shoot in nature. There are so many opportunities that can present themselves in the outdoors, with vast numbers of subjects out there waiting to be explored. From verdant landscapes to flowers and plants as well as wildlife, if you can't find something to photograph when you are out in nature, you might have your eyes closed!

Taking a vacation to an exotic locale might be a great way to find some amazing subjects, but for most of us this just isn't feasible. The good news is you don't necessarily need to venture out of your own backyard to create interesting nature photos. You can find landscape scenes just down the road at your local park or possibly at the outskirts of town. You can photograph wildlife that is native to your locale such as deer, squirrels, birds, and insects, or you can even go to a zoo and, with some creative framing and depth of field, you can take photos of exotic animals that appear to be out in nature. Even in greater metropolitan areas, there are usually parks or greenbelts that allow you to get into nature in the middle of the city.

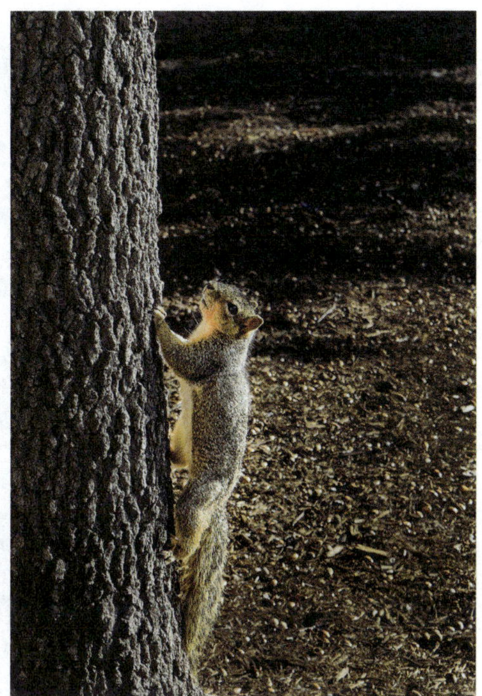

8.13 This "wildlife" shot was taken in the middle of downtown Austin at the Texas State Capitol. Exposure: ISO 140, f/8, 1/100 second using the kit lens at 55mm.

Equipment

The equipment used for nature and wildlife photography is as varied as the subject matter. Just about any type of lens can be employed, and there are many other accessories that may be helpful in some situations, but not in others. If you know what you intend to photograph, packing the right gear is much easier. Think about the type of photography on which you're likely to focus. If you're interested in shooting mostly landscapes, you may find a wide-angle lens and tripod are both necessary.

TIP If you go on an extended trip or long hike, try to pack lenses that can pull double duty, such as a 200mm macro. This lens can capture both distant wildlife and a close-up of a flower.

If your goal is to photograph wildlife and birds, you need a long telephoto lens, a monopod, and possibly a teleconverter. If you shoot a wide variety of subjects, then you may want to get a good, all-in-one super-zoom like the Nikon 18–300mm. It will have you covered for just about anything of interest.

CAUTION Don't forget to pack some protection for your camera in case you are caught in inclement weather. You can get two Optech rain sleeves for less than $10. There's no reason not to have at least one of these in your bag at all times.

Technique

As with the equipment that you may need for nature and landscape photography, the techniques that you use will depend on the subject matter. A common theme in landscape and nature photography is to *take your time.* Stop what you're doing and really look at your subject — not just through the viewfinder, but actually *look.* Don't get so caught up in the technical aspects that you don't take the time to enjoy your surroundings and the actual experience of being out in nature.

Here are a few more tips for shooting landscape and nature photos:

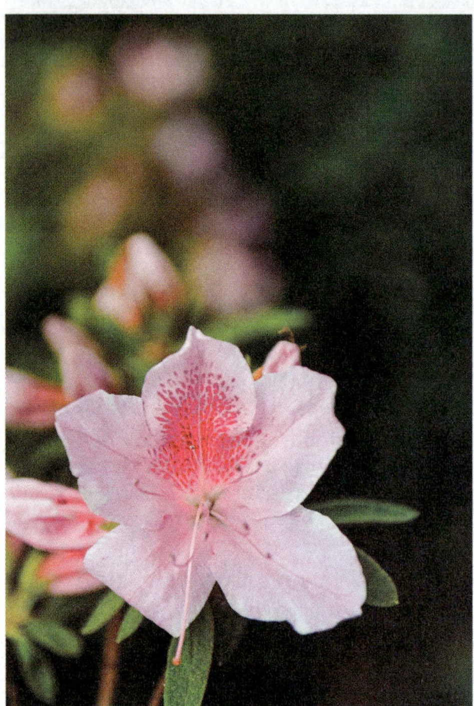

8.14 Be sure to photograph local flora when you're traveling. This Azalea is indicative of the southern Louisiana area. Exposure: ISO 100, f/2.8, 1/640 second using a Sigma 18–35mm f/1.8 | A.

- ▶ **Shoot during the Golden Hour.** The *Golden Hour* is immediately after sunrise or before sunset, when the sun is low in the sky. These are the perfect times of day to shoot just about any outdoor subject, from landscapes and flowers to wildlife. The light is soft and golden, and the shadows are long.

- ▶ **Experiment with backlighting.** Backlight is a good way to add a different quality to your images. It can make plants glow and add a cool lens flare to your landscapes. Backlighting is also essential if you want to create a silhouette.

- ▶ **Shoot smaller apertures for landscapes.** When shooting landscapes you want to create a deep depth of field and capture the sharpest images you can. I recommended shooting in the *sweet spot* of your lens, which is usually between f/5.6 and f/11.

- ▶ **Shoot wider apertures for wildlife.** When photographing wildlife, using a wide aperture helps to separate it from the background. Most animals blend into their habitat, and a busy, sharp background makes it harder to separate the creature from its surroundings.

- ▶ **Try creative compositions.** Shoot landscape images in portrait orientation and vice versa. Most of my favorite landscape shots weren't taken in landscape orientation.

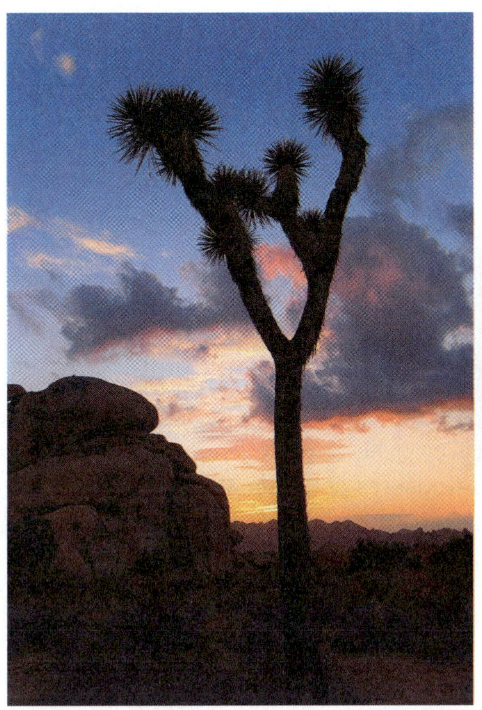

8.15 Shooting this landscape shot of a Joshua tree in portrait orientation adds a little interest to the shot. Exposure: ISO 400, f/11, 1/100 second using a Nikon 10.5mm f/2.8D fisheye.

Night and Low-light Photography

You need light to create a photograph, but sometimes the best photography happens when there is little light. A whole new world opens up for you to capture when the sun goes down. Shooting in the dark enables you to dabble in techniques that can't be used in the daytime.

Just about any type of photography can be done at night or in low light, from land- and cityscapes to portraits, and more. The ultimate goal of low-light photography is to capture the delicate interplay between light and dark, and highlight and shadow to create brightness where there is little illumination.

When confronted by darkness, the first thing most beginning photographers are tempted to do is pop up the flash to add some light to the scene. After all, that's what the flash is for, isn't it? Yes, but the problem is that flash kills any ambience that exists in a scene. It's best to use the flash sparingly. Instead, increase the ISO setting, open the aperture, or experiment with long exposures.

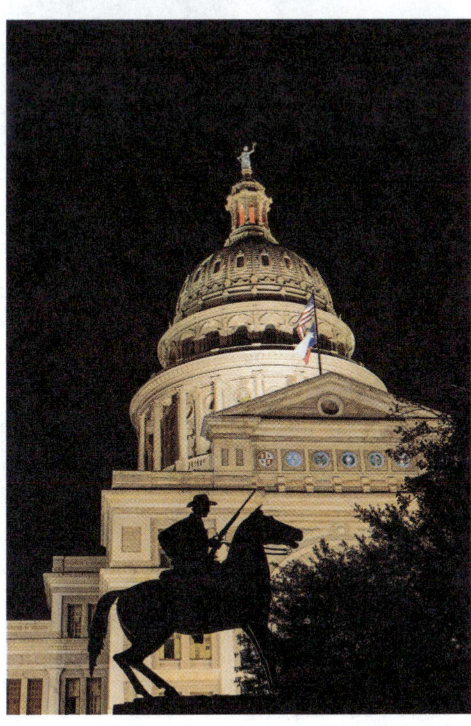

8.16 Not having a tripod handy, I used a wide aperture and higher ISO to capture this low-light image of the Texas State Capitol. Exposure: ISO 3200, f/1.8, 1/30 second using a Sigma 18–35mm f/1.8 | A at 35mm.

Equipment

If you bought your D3300 with one of the kit lenses, you already have a good piece of equipment for low-light photography. The 18–55mm Vibration Reduction (VR) lens is ideal for shooting in low light. Even though it doesn't have the fast aperture of a pro zoom, the VR lens allows you to handhold the camera at slower shutter speeds so you can capture more of the ambient light without worrying about camera shake. Of course, VR only compensates for camera shake — it can't freeze moving subjects, but sometimes that's a good thing. One cool effect is to have a sharp background with a subtle blur in moving subjects within the image.

Of course, Vibration Reduction and handholding your camera only get you so far. I'd say the outside limit for handheld photography with a VR lens at a wide-angle setting is probably about 1/2 second, maybe a bit longer if you're *really* steady. To capture long exposures successfully, you need a decent tripod. The tripod holds the camera completely still so that you can capture enough light to make a good exposure without your picture being a blurry mess.

CAUTION VR should be turned off when using a tripod.

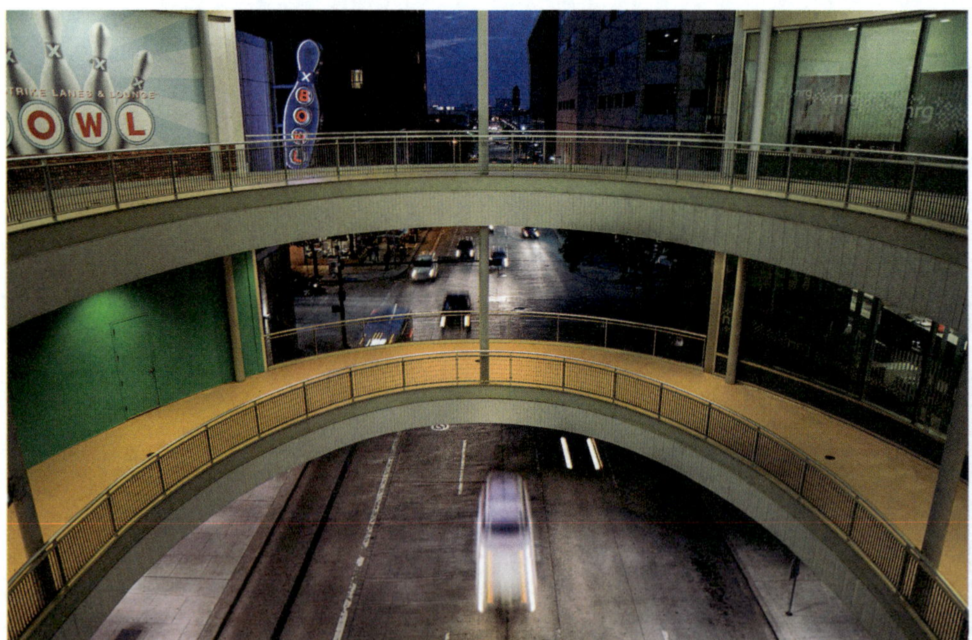

8.17 For this shot, I relied on the VR to get a sharp exposure of the buildings while using a relatively long exposure to capture the blur of the moving vehicles. Exposure: ISO 1600, f/4, 1/2 second using the kit lens at 18mm.

Another option for shooting in low light and at night is to use a fast lens with an aperture of at least f/2.8 or better. Ideally, the faster a lens is, the better, so if you can afford a lens with an f/1.4 aperture, you may want to invest in one if you like to shoot in low light. A number of options are available; probably the best one for the price is the 35mm f/1.8G (DX version). It's about $200 and offers excellent image quality. The newest and most versatile fast lens for shooting at night is probably the new Sigma 18–35mm f/1.8 | A; while it's an expensive lens for low-light photography, it can't be beat.

Another piece of equipment that I find to be a real necessity for long exposures is a remote release. This accessory allows you to trigger the shutter release without touching the camera and causing it to vibrate, because even the slightest movement can cause some blur in your image. The Nikon ML-L3 is an inexpensive wireless remote designed to work perfectly with the D3300, and it's very simple to operate.

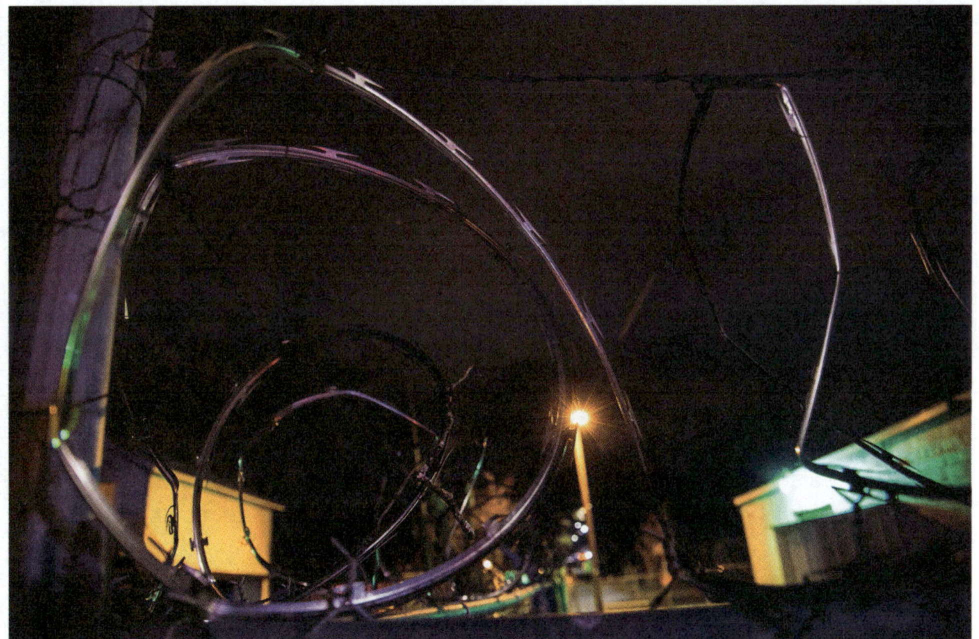

8.18 When shooting at night I look for scenes that have different types of light sources, which cast a myriad of colors into the image. There are no fewer than four different types of light in this scene, giving the photo an almost iridescent look. Exposure: ISO 6400, f/4, 1/10 second using a Sigma 17–70mm f/2.8–4 | C at 17mm.

Choosing a Tripod

Tripods come in a great variety of sizes with many features. You can get a small, lightweight one for about $20, or you can spend a lot more ($300–$500) for a heavy-duty, carbon-fiber tripod with an optional fluid or ball head. For a small camera like the D3300, it's unnecessary to go overboard and buy the most expensive tripod, but I highly recommend buying a *good* one.

A $20 tripod isn't very sturdy and will tend to break, so you'll eventually have to replace it. Buying a good tripod is like investing in a good lens: You will use it for years and be glad that you spent the extra money. During my first few years as a photographer, I went the cheap route on tripods. When I finally spent the money for a good one (about $350 altogether), I was kicking myself for not doing so earlier.

Technique

The techniques for night and low-light exposures are quite simple: Use a long shutter speed or crank up the ISO setting. While these are both sound approaches, each one comes with its own benefits and drawbacks. The most obvious solution is to increase the ISO until you get the exposure settings that are the best for your subject. This is usually the best way to go if your subject is moving, or if you must handhold the camera for a specific reason (such as when you don't have a tripod handy).

In these situations, a great setting to use is Auto ISO (AUTO). Using this feature and setting the minimum shutter speed to *Auto* allows the camera to automatically keep the shutter speed fast enough to avoid camera shake at the given focal length. The only real downside to this is that you will see some increased noise and a loss of resolution as the ISO sensitivity is increased. You can always apply some noise reduction in post-processing. I also find that reducing the image size reduces the size of the noise structure, making it less noticeable. If you don't need the full 24MP size, you can resize the image and make it a little cleaner.

CAUTION Resizing an image isn't the same as cropping. Although both techniques reduce the height and width of the image, cropping doesn't reduce the size of the noise grain whereas making the dimensions of the original image smaller reduces the size of the noise grain.

If you're going for a more artistic approach, you can try using longer shutter speeds. You can use longer shutter speeds while holding the camera, but most of your image is going to be blurry. This isn't always a bad thing — you can produce some cool effects if you handhold the camera during a long exposure. However, your results will be more consistent if you use a tripod.

There are many advantages to using a tripod. First, your camera is (obviously) going to be more stable, allowing you to use much longer shutter speeds and get sharper images than if you handhold the camera. Second, in seeming contrast to the preceding statement, you can get sharper background images while also achieving motion blur in anything that is moving. Some cool examples of this would be a city scene in which you create blurs of people, trails from car headlights moving through sharp scenery, moving water, or stars traveling across the sky.

Longer shutter speeds capture more motion than shorter ones. Try experimenting with shutter speeds of varying lengths to see the different effects they can produce. For example, if you're shooting in a busy city and use a shutter speed that's too long, you won't capture people effectively because they move through the frame too quickly to be adequately recorded. At the opposite end of the spectrum, if you're photographing stars, a shutter speed that is too short won't allow sufficient time for them to move through the scene and leave a trail.

Generally, when doing this type of photography, I use Manual mode (**M**) and bracket my exposures. Bracketing allows me to get the exact exposure that I want and, if necessary, I can combine elements of different exposures. For my base exposure, I set the metering mode to Matrix (▨) and look at the light meter in the viewfinder. I generally start my exposure settings where the meter says that it's 1 stop underexposed. I find that this is generally pretty close to the right exposure. I bracket five frames at 1-stop intervals from my base exposure. You can use smaller (1/3) stops or bracket more frames if you want more or less latitude in your exposures.

> **TIP** A smaller aperture not only increases your exposure time, but also creates a starburst from points of light in the scene due to diffraction from the aperture blades. The smaller the aperture setting, the more pronounced the points of the starburst.

Portrait Photography

By simple definition, a portrait captures (or portrays) the likeness of a person. While the definition of a portrait is straightforward, what makes a great portrait is more elusive. A great portrait isn't necessarily a photograph of a beautiful or handsome model with perfect skin, flawless hair and makeup, and just the right lighting and exposure. While these elements can all go into making a portrait, they don't necessarily make it great.

A portrait, in addition to its primary function of simply showing what a person looks like, should ideally go a little deeper. It should give the viewer a glimpse of the essence (or soul, if you prefer) of the subject. Of course, you can't capture the *complete* essence of a person in just a fraction of a second, but you can capture the essence of the person in *that* fraction of a second.

This involves quite a bit of semantics because, although you can capture a very deep and emotional portrait of someone — whether that emotion is happiness, melancholy, anger, or indifference — you can only capture what the subject projects. As a photographer, though, you can also direct what emotion you want portrayed and a good model, like an actor, can convince the viewer that that emotion is real. Such is the dichotomy of the portrait: It should connect the viewer with the subject and project a sort of reality, but the reality is what you make it.

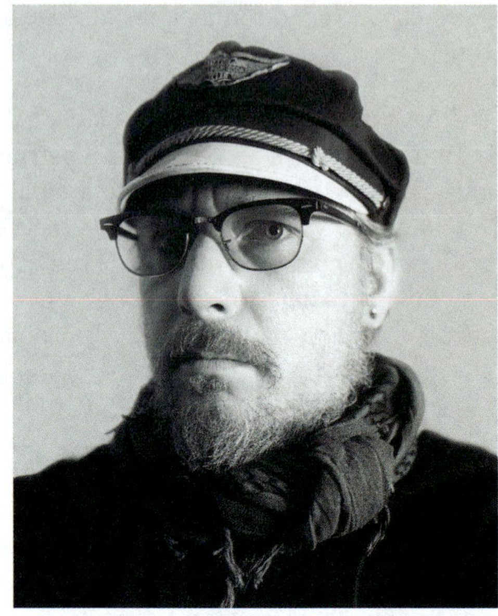

8.19 I used an unmodified, off-camera Nikon SB-900 Speedlight connected with a Nikon SC-27 TTL cable to get this hard-light portrait. Exposure: ISO 400, f/2.8, 1/60 second using a 50mm f/1.8G.

NOTE I'd like to differentiate a subset of portrait photography — the headshot. While the headshot is, indeed, a portrait, the purpose is not to portray emotion on any deep level, but rather, to show a person's face in a generally pleasing manner.

Equipment

The D3300, as it turns out, is an ideal camera for portraiture. The high-resolution, 24MP sensor captures great detail. It also has a very impressive dynamic range for capturing subtle tones. A big pro camera like the Nikon D4s with an 85mm f/1.4 lens can be like looking down the barrel of a cannon for most people, so I find the small size of the D3300 is less intimidating for my subjects, especially if they aren't used to having a camera pointed at them.

Much of how portraiture is conveyed depends on lens choice. There are general guidelines that most people follow when selecting lenses for customary portraits. The general rule is to use short to medium telephoto lenses. For a DX camera like the D3300, lenses with a focal length from about 50mm to 105mm are ideal. This is because wide-angle lenses create unflattering perspective distortion with facial structures, causing noses to appear too large, ears to appear too small, and just making faces generally appear strange (there are situations in which you can use a wide-angle lens, which I cover shortly). Longer lenses tend to flatten the facial features, which is one reason why telephotos are recommended. However, a lens that is too long can flatten the facial features so much that your portraits might lack depth, not to mention the fact that you start gaining a lot of distance between yourself and the model, which can be a hindrance because you end up being too far to communicate with your subject.

Wide-angle lenses are effective for portraits that show more of the background. These are known as *environmental portraits.* The key to making a wide-angle lens work with a portrait is to put some distance between you and the subject or to go all the way and make it look intentionally wacky. If you try to be in the middle, the portrait will just look odd, and not in a good way.

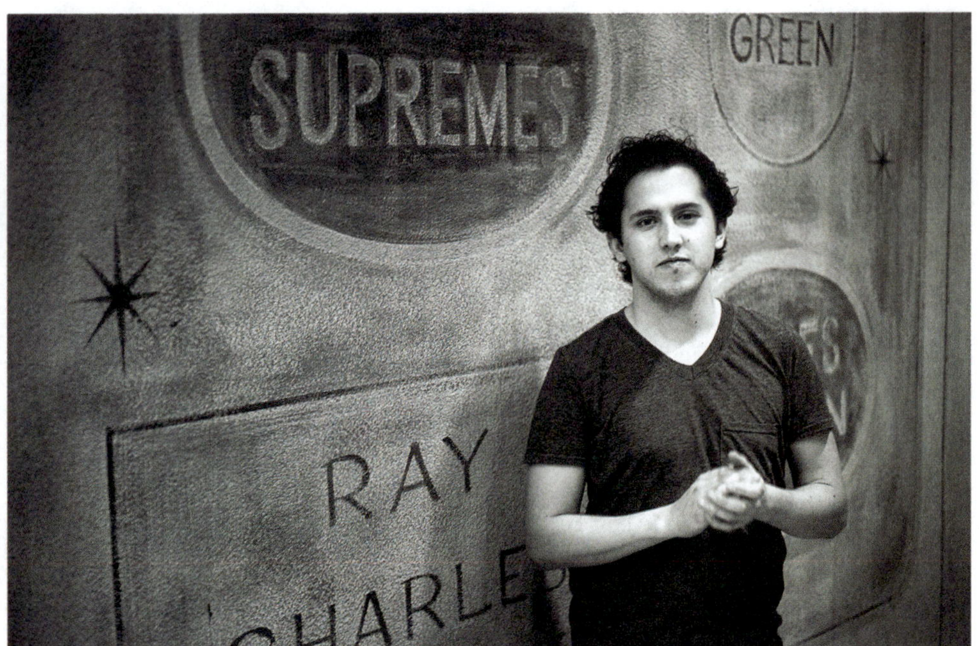

8.20 I used a wide field of view to take this environmental portrait of musician Bennett Jackson. Exposure: ISO 1600, f/1.4, 1/60 second using a Sigma 35mm f/1.4 | A.

Most portrait photographers like to use prime lenses for their more compact size and sharpness. Luckily, Nikon has a plethora of prime lenses from which to choose, and a few of them are very affordable. The 50mm f/1.8G is an inexpensive lens that is often used by photographers who are just getting started with portraiture. One of the best and sharpest lenses (although it's more expensive than the 50mm f/1.8G) is the 85mm f/1.8G. Some photographers like to use the Nikon 105mm f/2.8G VR macro lens, which is my personal favorite for portraits. Its great focal length and near-perfect image quality make this a great, if somewhat expensive, option. Obviously, it also pulls double duty as a macro lens.

Technique

A whole book could be written about portrait techniques and, indeed, quite a few have been, so for simplicity's sake, I only touch on the basics here. In Chapter 6, I cover the *quality of light*, which plays a major role in portrait photography. Essentially, there are two types of portraits: hard light and soft light. For most practical purposes, soft light is preferred for portraits. It's smooth and generally flattering to just about any facial structure. People just tend to look good in soft light. Women, in general, almost always benefit from it. The downside of soft light is that it can lack the depth and drama that harder directional light can lend to a subject.

The following are some of the ways with which you can create a soft-light portrait:

▶ **Window light.** This is by far the easiest way to get great light for just about any subject. Window light has been (and is still) used by photojournalists and fashion photographers alike. Windows act as natural diffusers and filter the sunlight, turning it into pleasing, soft light. There's simply no easier way to get great portrait lighting than by sitting your model close to a window.

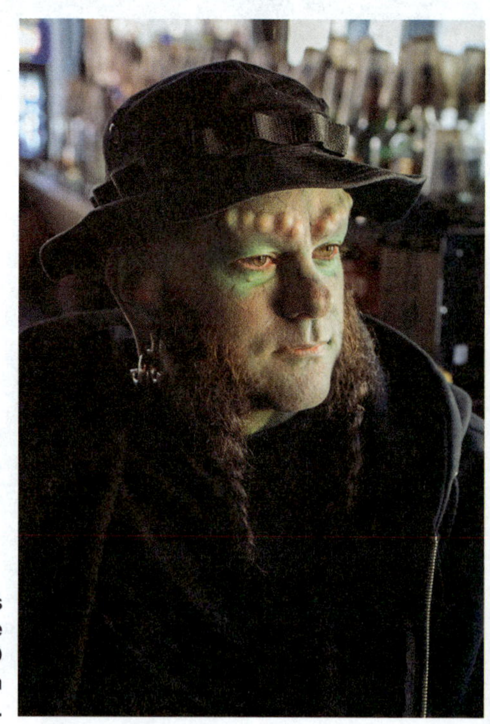

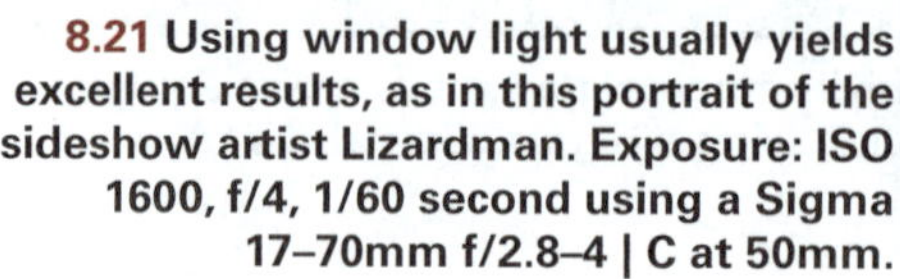

8.21 Using window light usually yields excellent results, as in this portrait of the sideshow artist Lizardman. Exposure: ISO 1600, f/4, 1/60 second using a Sigma 17–70mm f/2.8–4 | C at 50mm.

- ▶ **Bounce flash.** If you're stuck indoors and don't have access to a window, or if it's dark and there's no window light available, you can quickly achieve a decent, soft light effect by using an external Speedlight such as the Nikon SB-400 or SB-700. The key is not to aim the flash directly at your subject, but to tilt or swivel the head and bounce the light from the ceiling or an adjacent wall. Bouncing scatters the light, which softens and diffuses it.

- ▶ **Shade.** If you find yourself shooting portraits outside, you'll notice that the bright overhead sun really isn't the optimum light source for portraits. Move your subject under the shade of a tree or porch overhang. You can also take advantage of the shade provided by clouds on a partly sunny or overcast day.

Soft light isn't always the best option for portraits. Sometimes, a more directional light source is necessary. This adds depth to a portrait, and it is often used to portray strength and character. Hard light accentuates lines and gives definition, whereas soft light plays down these attributes. Hard light is perfect for accentuating textures. Hard light is used more often on men than women because the definition it provides creates a more masculine effect.

CAUTION Pay extra-close attention to where shadows fall when shooting hard-light portraits. Errant shadows can ruin a portrait.

- ▶ **Use off-camera flash.** If you use a Speedlight off-camera with a TTL cable or the Nikon Creative Lighting System, it is much easier to get directional light. Of course, you can also use off-camera flash for soft light, but that requires modifiers such as umbrellas or softboxes. For hard light, you can use a Speedlight pointed directly at the subject with no diffusion. The farther away a light source is, the harder the light will be.

- ▶ **Use a dark background.** Hard-light portraits are, by their nature, high in contrast. A dark background creates a more distinct separation between the subject and background. This gives your portrait a stark, moody look.

TIP Try converting your hard-light images to black and white for a more classic look.

Still-life, Product, and Food Photography

The subjects of still-life, product, and food photography are similar in that they are all inanimate objects and relatively static. As a result, these subjects are easy to work with, and knowing how to photograph them is a very good skill to develop.

One difference about photographing this type of subject is that, as the photographer, you have almost complete control over the setup. For the most part, you can shoot at your leisure (although, food usually photographs best when it's fresh). You can change the lighting, composition, and camera settings without being under pressure.

Some people may find shooting inanimate objects unimaginative or boring, but it can actually be as challenging as you want to make it. As with any other type of photography, you can use lens and lighting choice to portray a certain feeling. You can use the techniques covered in this section to create a version of an old master-style still life, photograph a well-prepared meal, or create professional-looking shots for online auctions.

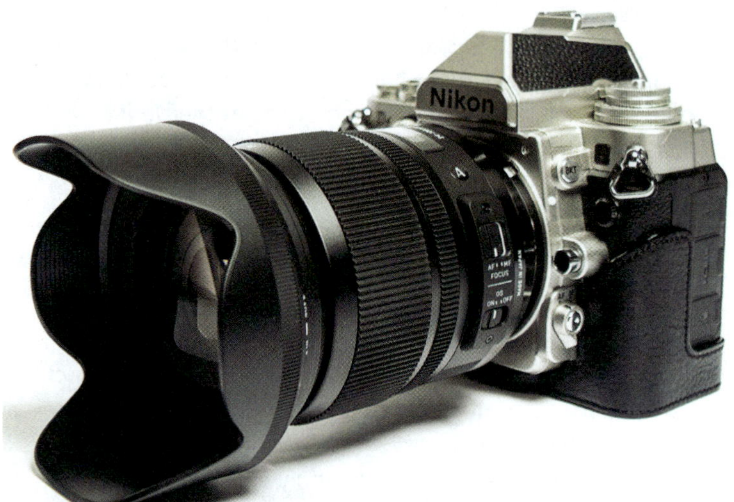

8.22 I used a TTL cord to fire an off-camera SB-600 Speedlight to light this still life of my Nikon Df and Sigma 24–105mm f/4 | A. Exposure: ISO 100, f/5.6, 1/60 second using a Sigma 17–70mm f/2.8–4 at 70mm.

Equipment

The type of equipment you need changes, depending on the scope of what you're doing. At the very least, a good midrange zoom (like the 18–55mm kit lens) works, but a good macro lens (like the Nikon 40mm f/2.8G, 60mm f/2.8G, or 85mm f/3.5GVR) is best. I tend to avoid wide-angle lenses because of the perspective distortion that occurs when I get close to the subject to fill the frame. If you have plenty of working distance, a telephoto lens is also a good choice. This is also one of the few types of photography where you don't really need to have a fast lens because more often than not, you will be shooting in the f/5.6–11 range to get a good, sharp image throughout.

I prefer to shoot most products using a tripod. This frees my hands so I can move the subject or lights, or adjust the background without constantly picking up and putting down my camera.

Lights are also very handy — whether it's an inexpensive set of hot lights, a wireless Speedlight setup, or even studio strobes. Controlled lighting is the best way to give your images a professional look. Along with lights, another necessity is a reflector. This is probably the most essential piece of equipment that I can think of for this type of photography. A small reflector is inexpensive and folds up compactly (a 36-inch reflector folds down to roughly 13 inches). Reflectors can bounce flash, redirect continuous light to brighten shadows, and reflect available light onto the subject to brighten it.

Technique

There are three basic elements that are important for any still-life photograph: background, composition, and lighting. All three must work together if the image is to be successful.

Selecting a background is one of the first things to do (after selecting the subject, of course). Usually, the best background is a simple one that allows the subject to stand out. Some options for backgrounds include seamless paper, poster board, cloth, and black velvet (often used when shooting jewelry to reduce reflections). The main option you're going to be looking at when choosing a background is the color. Two very simple choices are black or white. Either of these works well with almost any subject. Of course, you can use any color in the rainbow. A dark background gives you a *low-key* image, while using a white or light-colored background gives you a *high-key* image. High-key images tend to evoke a lighter feeling. A low-key image is dark with a lot of shadows and contrast. These images tend to be moody and evocative.

> **TIP** Stop at your local fabric store and visit the remnants section to find a lot of great options for background materials for relatively little money.

When using a colored background, remember that it should add to the image, not subtract from, or draw attention away from, the subject. Using complementary colors to set off your subject is a great way to make the subject pop from the background, while using a background with a similar color can add a pleasing monochromatic theme.

> **TIP** Use the D3300 High key (Hi) or Low key (Lo) Effects modes (EFFECTS) to shoot these types of scenes.

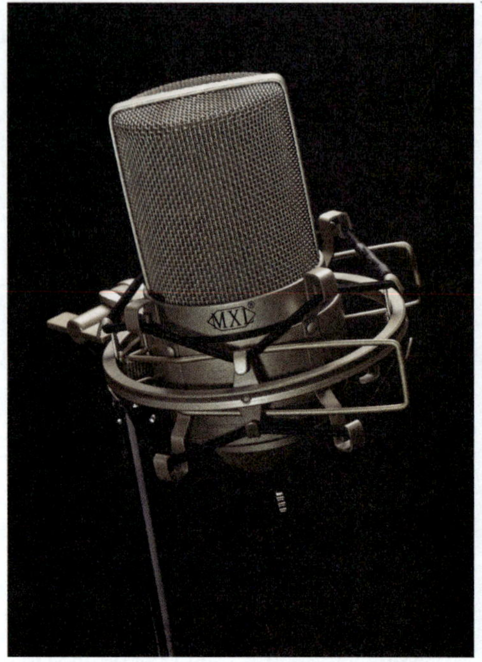

8.23 I used two Speedlights to highlight the fin detail of this microphone. The Speedlights were controlled by a Nikon SU-800 Wireless Infrared Commander. Exposure: ISO 200, f/16, 1/60 second using a Nikon 60mm f/2.8G macro lens.

Often when shooting still-life subjects rather than products, it's fun to build a scene or use props. For example, you could use a cutting board and knife as a background for a shot with fruit, or a burlap sack with coffee beans for a shot depicting a cup of coffee. The key to building a background is to be sure your background props match your subject. You should also be careful not to add too many pieces to the background — you don't want to draw attention away from the subject.

When considering lighting, I find that the best approach is to keep it simple, especially when you're just starting out. Even if you're using flash, try to make the lighting look natural. Window lighting is always an option, especially for food. However, some photographers like to take it a step further and move the dish to a more brightly lit, but relatively shaded, outside area to get a little more directionality. Using a reflector can sometimes help soften the edges if the shadows start to get too hard.

TIP The easiest way to light still life is with window lighting. This is the preferred method of many food photographers.

Using Wireless Flash with the D3300

Unlike the D7100, the D3300 doesn't have the capability to take advantage of the Advanced Wireless Lighting feature of the Nikon Creative Lighting System using the built-in flash. To use the full features of this function, you need at least two Speedlights: one to act as a Commander flash and one to act as a remote.

I have discovered a workaround that can be used effectively if you don't mind setting the flash manually, and a little trial and error with your exposures. Although the built-in flash of the D3300 can't emit the pulse modulation that the Speedlights need to receive to perform iTTL metering, the built-in flash can trigger other flashes with an optical sensor to fire wirelessly.

The flagship flashes from Nikon have an optical sensor built in and can be used in what Nikon calls SU-4 mode (SU-4 is the Nikon code word for *optical sensor*). The Nikon SB-800, SB-900, and SB-910 all feature SU-4 mode, and you can also use them on-camera with full functionality. This is the more expensive route, but you can get started if you can afford one good Speedlight. Nikon has a few older Speedlights designed for film and early digital cameras that also have SU-4 mode: the SB-26, SB-50DX, and SB-80DX. These are less expensive than the newer models, and they can be used on-camera with limited capabilities, as well.

The key is to set the D3300 flash to Manual in Shooting menu (📷), and then set the output to the lowest setting, of 1/32. This reduces the chance of exposure from the built-in flash on the subject. There's also a little gadget called the Nikon SG-3IR that slips into the hot shoe and dangles an infrared filter in front of the built-in flash to reduce actual flash exposure (however, these are difficult to find). You *must* use Manual flash (M⚡) because iTTL flash (TTL⚡) emits preflashes for metering purposes, which trigger the remote flash before the shutter opens. This results in little or no flash on the subject while the exposure is made.

When using flash, whether Speedlights or larger studio strobes, I usually modify the flash by bouncing it from a reflector or an umbrella. On location, I sometimes use whatever is on hand. I've used everything from a wall to a drink menu. Once you learn the basics of lighting a shot, you can start exploring other possibilities and more advanced techniques. However, you'll find that, about 80 percent of the time, a simple lighting setup goes a long way.

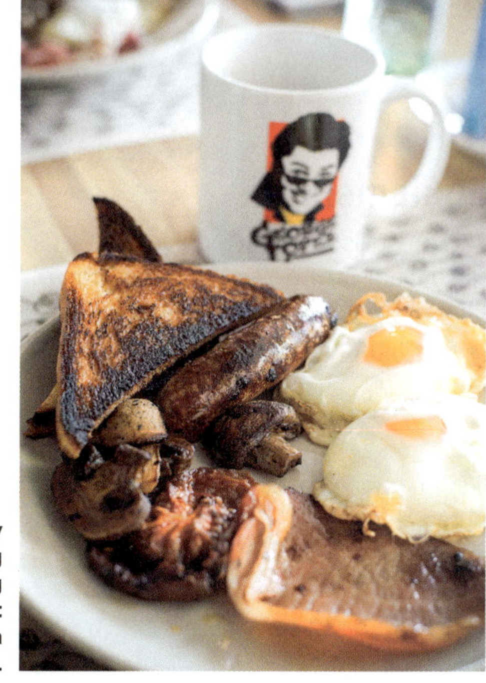

8.24 **This full English breakfast was lit by nothing more than window light, proving once again that it is the easiest lighting to work with and it looks great. Exposure: ISO 100, f/1.8, 1/250 second using a Nikon 35mm f/1.8G.**

CROSS REF See Chapter 6 for more information about calculating manual flash exposures.

Street Photography

This type of photography has seen a big resurgence in the past couple of years. Street photography is a type of candid photography that, as its name implies, often takes place out in the streets, from the inner city to the suburbs to the rural areas.

There are many opinions on what street photography is and isn't, but one thing that can be agreed on is that the ultimate goal of street photography is to capture the essence of everyday life and do it in an interesting way. Street photography is a way for photographers to document society and culture with an impartial eye.

Many street photographs feature people going about their mundane, everyday business or doing interesting things, but street photographs don't always have to have people in them. Quite often, the subjects in street photos are unaware of the camera, but the key is to catch people doing what they do naturally, not to make it look like a spy photo taken by a private eye. On the other hand, many photographers, including myself, do "street portraits," where you approach subjects and ask them if you can take a photo of them. If I see someone interesting, I generally stop and talk to them for a few minutes and create a rapport before taking their photos. This makes both the photographer and subject more at ease because the ice has been broken. I have never been turned down when I've asked to take someone's photo, and I've met many great new people this way.

Equipment

There's no list of 'right' equipment that a street photographer should have. Many photographers like to use certain pieces of gear because of what other famous street photographers used before them. I don't adhere to any hard rules, but as an example, many photographers swear by using prime lenses only, generally a fast 35 or 50mm prime. I find that primes work well, but I typically have a midrange zoom lens on my camera so that I can be better equipped for any situation that I encounter. But if I specifically go out to capture street photography, sometimes I will use a prime lens to lighten the camera and make it less conspicuous. Typically, I find a moderate, wide-to-normal focal length (from about 18 to 35mm) is ideal for most street photography.

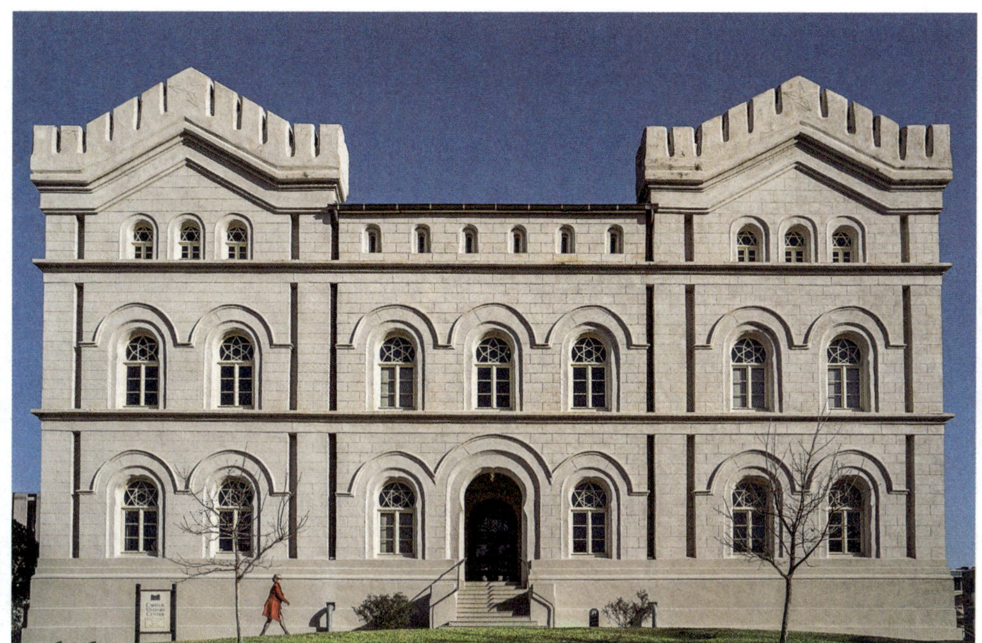

8.25 In street photography, I try to look for odd or eye-catching juxtapositions, such as this lone woman in a bright-red dress walking in front of this enormous, rather dull-colored building. Exposure: ISO 100, f/9, 1/500 second using a Sigma 17–70mm f/2.8–4 at 20mm.

CAUTION There are some photographers who use flash and surprise as a technique to get street photographs. I don't recommend this approach, as it is rude and invasive as well as potentially dangerous. In this day and age, people are already wary of anyone pointing a camera in their direction, and being a nuisance photographer doesn't do any good.

Technique

There are as many techniques for street photography as there are street photographers, and what works for some people won't work for others. I will say this: street photography isn't for shy or nervous photographers. On the other hand, if you are shy around strangers, you can use street photography as a confidence-building exercise. Before I started doing street photography, I almost never talked to strangers, and now I talk to random people all the time.

The most common technique is to use a lens with a slightly wide focal length and to get relatively close to your subject. Again, this technique isn't for the timid but generally makes for the best photos.

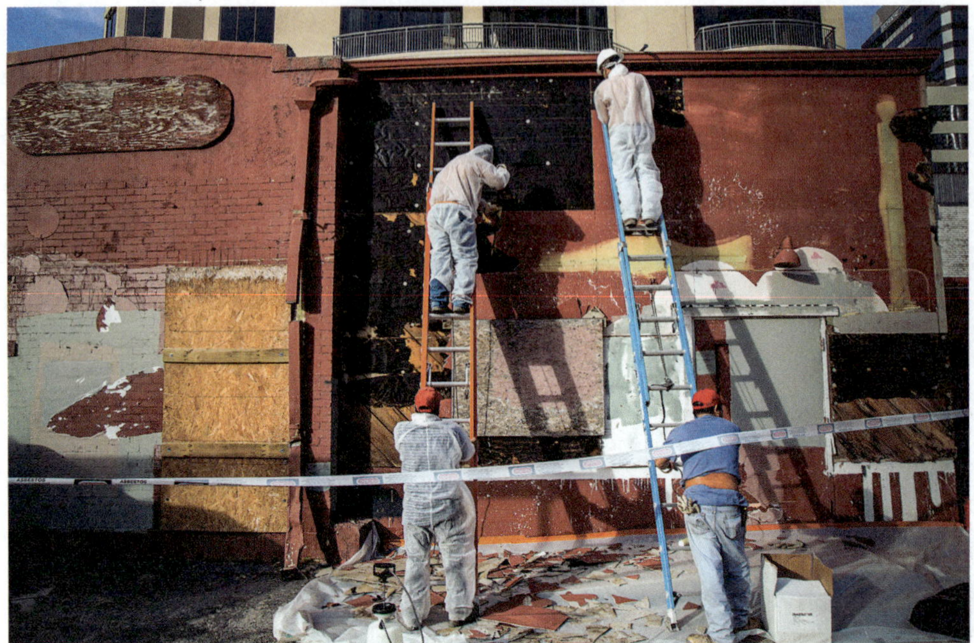

8.26 Sometimes photographing people doing their everyday jobs can create an interesting image. If you are looking too hard, you may miss it when interesting subjects are right in front of you. Exposure: ISO 100, f/16, 1/125 second using the kit lens at 35mm.

One technique that a lot of newcomers to street photography start out with is using a telephoto lens and shooting from afar. This is usually because of timidity. This is a bad habit to get into. Images taken from far away have a voyeuristic, spy-like quality to them that's not indicative of true street photography. If you want to be a street photographer, the best thing to do is to face your fears and jump right in.

Many street photographers like to be inconspicuous so that they can catch the candid moments that make up daily life, but the key to being successfully inconspicuous is not to look sneaky. This is a difficult hurdle for many to overcome. Being hesitant makes you look suspicious and can cause you to miss out on interesting photographs. Being assertive and owning the moment by picking up your camera and pressing the shutter-release button is important. You have to look, act, and most importantly, feel like you know what you're doing. Some people may object to having their photos taken, especially if you look guilty when you do it. If you are confronted, simply explain to the person that you are photographing interesting slices of life, and offer to send them a copy of the photo or a link to the photo. I've never been personally confronted, but typically, if I take a photo of someone who looks up, I'll simply take the initiative and go to that person first.

CAUTION Use your better judgment when choosing your subject. If you see some-one who you think might pose a threat or become easily angered, just don't take the photo. It's not worth risking your safety to get a picture.

Perhaps the most difficult part of the street photography technique is psychological. The camera settings are pretty easy. In the early days, many street photographers used manual focus lenses and a technique called *zone focusing*, where the lens is set to a certain aperture and you set the focus of the lens to be within a certain zone by using depth of field. Zone focusing allows a photographer to simply raise the camera and snap when the subject is in the zone without having to focus. The smaller the aperture, the easier it is. Most manual-focus lenses have depth of field scales that allow you to quickly calculate the focus zone.

Autofocus is fast enough and nearly silent, so using autofocus is generally what I sug-gest when shooting street photos with a D3300. I recommend using the Continuous-servo AF (AF-C) and Dynamic-area AF modes for the focus points.

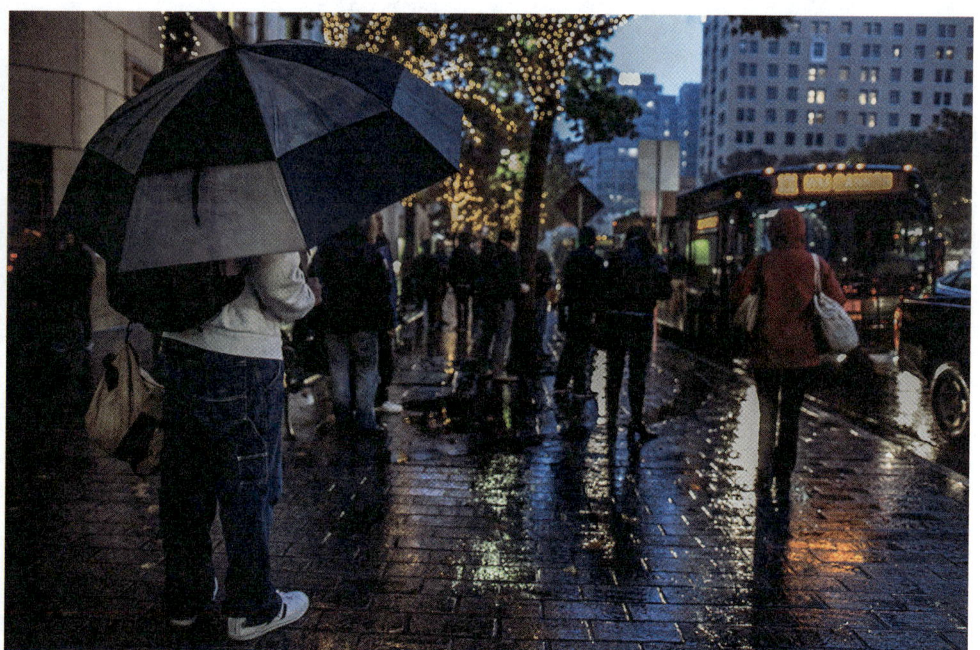

8.27 A great time to shoot street photography is when the weather is less than ideal. People are often too busy to notice you, and wet or cold weather adds something special to the scene. Exposure: ISO 400, f/1.8, 1/30 second using a Sigma 18–35mm f/1.8 | A at 18mm.

When choosing an exposure setting, there isn't a right one; it depends on what you're most comfortable using. If I'm just out and about with my camera, I often set it to Programmed Auto (**P**) for spur-of-the-moment shots. If I'm out specifically to shoot street photographs, I use Manual exposure mode (**M**) so I can decide how I want to freeze the motion and control the depth of field. When using Manual exposure mode (**M**), I typically set Auto ISO (**ISO-A**) to On. If you're comfortable that you have enough light to get a fast enough shutter speed for your needs, you can use Aperture-priority auto mode (**A**) to determine the depth of field. If you want to use a fast or slow shutter speed for effect, but aren't concerned about the depth of field, you can use Shutter-priority auto mode (**S**).

CHAPTER 9

After Capture

Your photographic experience with the D3300 doesn't end once you press the Shutter Release button and capture the image. For many photographers this is just the start of an in-depth process of creating an image. To get started, you can play back the images on the LCD screen to review them. You can use the D3300 to create a slide show, and you can plug the camera into an HDTV and share them with your friends and family. At some point you need to transfer your images to your computer hard drive for more permanent storage.

You may also find that your images may need a little tweaking, and this chapter discusses a few of the better options for making minor adjustments to your images.

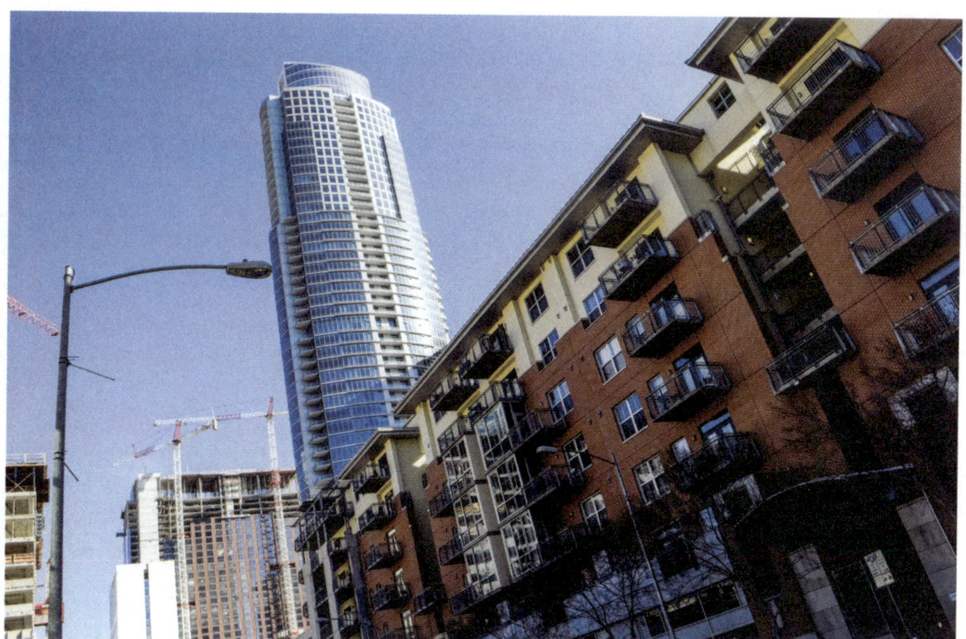

Taking the photo is just the beginning of the photographic process.

Viewing Your Images

The D3300 offers two ways to view your images: You can simply press the Playback button (▶) and view them directly on the LCD monitor, or you can connect the camera to a television and view your pictures on the screen. You can connect to an HDTV using the HDMI out port, or you can connect to the RCA inputs on a standard-definition TV with the EG-CP14 A/V cable supplied with the D3300. If your HDTV also has standard RCA inputs, you can connect it there as well, but the output will not be high definition.

To play back and review your images, press the Playback button (▶). This displays the current image. You can then use the multi-selector left (◄) and right (►) to scroll through the images on the memory card. Press the multi-selector up (▲) or down (▼) to display the photo information. How much information is displayed depends on the settings that you specify in the Playback display options in the Playback menu (▶).

> **TIP** If you prefer, you can also use the Command dial to scroll through images in playback.

You can also use the following buttons and options during playback:

- ▶ *i button* (ⓘ). Pressing this button brings up a dialog box with a few different options for your playback images:

  - **Rating.** This allows you to rate your images and applies the rating so that you can see them in Nikon ViewNX 2, Adobe Lightroom, and some other programs. You can rate the images from zero to five stars by pressing the multi-selector left (◄) or right (►). There's also an option that allows you to select a rating to mark it for deletion.

  - **Retouch.** When you press the *i* button, this is the default option that is highlighted. Pressing the multi-selector right (►) or the OK button (**OK**) takes you to the Retouch menu (✎).

  - **Select to send to smart device/deselect.** You can use this option to select the image to automatically transfer to your smartphone when the optional WU-1a Wi-Fi is enabled and connected with the Wireless Mobile Utility app. Alternately, you can also use this option to deselect images that you have already set for transfer.

- ▶ **Delete button (🗑).** Press this button to display a confirmation dialog box asking if you want to delete the current image. Press the Delete button (🗑) again to erase the photo permanently.

▶ **OK button (OK).** Pressing the OK button (OK) quickly changes the view from full screen image playback to a 4-up thumbnail display. You can use the multi-selector up (▲) or down (▼) to scroll through the images. Pressing the OK button again returns you to full screen playback.

▶ **Protect button (🔒).** You may notice that above the AE-L/AF-L button (AE-L/AF-L), there is a key icon (🔒); this is the Protect button. Press this button to mark an image as protected and prevent it from being deleted accidentally. Once the image is protected, you can simply press the button again to remove the protection status.

CAUTION Protecting an image may also lock the file and prevent you from making changes to it on some computers and software.

▶ **Zoom in button (🔍).** Press this button to zoom in on an image for a closer look to check for focus, sharpness, and so on. After you zoom in on an image, you can use the multi-selector to navigate to different areas of the image. If faces are detected in the image, you can press the *i* button (*i*) once, and then use the multi-selector to center on the face (or faces) in the scene. Rotate the Main Command dial to scroll through the other images on the memory card at the same magnification ratio.

▶ **Zoom out/Thumbnail button (🔍).** In the default full-frame playback mode, press this button to switch to thumbnail playback, and display numerous thumbnails of the images. Press the Zoom out/Thumbnail button (🔍) once to display four thumbnails, press it twice to display 12 thumbnails, and press it three times to view 80 thumbnails. If you press the Zoom out/Thumbnail button (🔍) a fourth time, a calendar appears in which you can choose to view images taken on a particular date. When playback is in Thumbnail mode, you can use the multi-selector to highlight an image. You can then zoom in, delete, retouch, or protect the image. To exit Thumbnail view, press the Zoom in button (🔍) until the camera returns to full-frame playback.

As mentioned previously, you can connect your D3300 to your TV. It functions exactly the same as it does in Playback mode when viewing images on the camera's LCD monitor.

Being able to view your images and videos straight from the camera on your high-definition or standard television is a handy feature. You can set up a slide show to show all your friends the photos you shot that day, or you can edit your photos using the Retouch menu (✎) straight from the camera while being able to view the images larger than life. If your HDTV is device-control compatible (HDMI-CEC), you can also use your television's remote control to browse the images and camera menus. Isn't technology great?

This brings up an important issue regarding connecting the camera to an HDTV that is CEC compatible. By default, when you connect the camera to a CEC-compatible HDTV, the camera will *only* function in Playback mode.

> **NOTE** If your HDTV is HDMI-CEC compatible, the camera displays CEC in place of the number of remaining frames.

If you want to use your CEC-compatible HDTV to show the same view as the camera's LCD monitor, you must go into the Setup menu (Y), select the HDMI option, and then select Device control and set it to Off.

Follow these steps to attach the D3300 to your HDTV:

1. **Turn the camera off.** This helps prevent static electricity from damaging your camera.

2. **Open the connector cover.** The connector cover is on the left side of the camera when the lens is facing away from you.

3. **Plug in the Type C mini-pin HDMI cable.** The cable is available separately from almost any electronics or camera store. Plug the cable into the HDMI out jack. This connection is clearly labeled, and located just below the USB port.

4. **Connect the HDMI cable to the input jack of your HDTV.**

5. **Set your HDTV to the HDMI input setting.** This may differ depending on your TV. See the owner's manual if you are unsure.

6. **Turn on the camera, and then press the Playback button (▶).** Playback functions the same as if you were looking at the LCD monitor.

Downloading Your Images

While viewing your images on the LCD monitor is great, and plugging the camera in and enjoying them in high resolution on your HDTV is even better, there will come a time when you're going to want to get those images into your computer and off of the memory card in the camera. Once they're downloaded to your computer, you can edit them, post them to your social media accounts, e-mail them to friends and family, print them, and so on.

You can approach the downloading process in any of the following ways:

▶ **Camera to computer.** Probably one of the easiest ways is to use the USB cable supplied with the D3300. First, make sure the camera is off, then plug the smaller end (Type B mini) into the USB output port on the camera, and then plug the larger end (Type A) of the USB cable into your computer. While this may be the most convenient option, there are a couple of drawbacks. The transfer usually takes a long time and the process is energy intensive. As a result, you need a charged battery because if the battery dies midtransfer, you run the risk of losing some or all of the images and possibly damaging the memory card, which could render it unusable.

▶ **Card reader.** A card reader is a device that accepts the memory card into it (just like the card fits into the camera) and connects to your computer, usually via a USB port. A card reader transfers data at a much faster rate than the camera does, and the card reader doesn't require a power supply like the camera does. A lot of computers these days have SD memory card slots built in. My MacBook Pro does, and it's so handy not having to worry about whether I packed my reader or not. I have a collection of card readers because I've had to buy them numerous times while on location shooting or on vacation because I forgot to grab one. Card readers are relatively inexpensive. Some readers transfer data faster than others, so if you're using a faster card, make sure your reader supports a fast transfer rate.

▶ **Eye-Fi.** The Eye-Fi is an SD card like any other, but it has Wi-Fi built in. This allows you to upload your images from your camera right to your computer's hard drive wirelessly. The Eye-Fi cards have different features for different models. Check out the Eye-Fi site for more information.

CAUTION Eye-Fi cards cannot be used to transfer information if the optional WU-1a Wi-Fi accessory is enabled.

File Management and Workflow

File management is a very important part of digital photography but it's often overlooked. One thing I can guarantee is that if you didn't have a good workflow system before you got your D3300, you will realize after a few weeks that you need one. The 24MP sensor of the D3300 has the ability to generate a lot of image information. The file sizes are huge. If you're shooting in RAW (as you should be), you will notice very quickly that you are using up more and more drive space faster and faster.

Having a good system for managing files is very important. The thing is, after a while, you'll discover that you can't find the images you're looking for if you haven't developed a good file management and workflow plan. When you start losing track of your files, you will wish you had a better system in place. The best thing to do is to get into the habit of a good workflow early and save yourself a headache later on.

While my workflow may not be perfect for you, in time you will develop your own system. I offer a brief overview of the key elements of a solid workflow in the following sections.

Folder structure

To download your images, you need a place where you can save them to. Many software options, such as Adobe Lightroom, Adobe Photoshop Elements, Windows Photo Gallery, and Apple iPhoto, can help you with this process. While most of these applications can do this for you automatically, I prefer to download images to my hard drive manually so I can place them exactly where I want them. Because I put the files there manually, it helps me remember where they are.

I have separate folders for different types of photography: Concert, Wedding, Event, Commercial, Personal, and so on. From there I go into subcategories. For concerts, I simply use the band name, and within that folder I create another with a date where I store the originals. If I shoot the band again, I create a second folder with another date, and so on. For weddings, I use the couple's last names (Smith/Jones), and for events, the name of the event. For personal work, I name the type of photography: Landscape, Macro, Portrait, and so on. Be specific so you know exactly what you're looking for when you want it. Once you have created your folder system, when you download your images, you just drag and drop them where you want them.

Editing

I suggest starting with a quick edit where you find the images you want to keep and delete any of the duplicates or unusable ones. This process prevents your hard drive from filling up with terabytes of images that you will never use. You can use Adobe Lightroom, Adobe Photoshop Elements, Windows Photo Gallery, or Apple iPhoto to view images and quickly delete the ones that are obviously unusable. Images to delete include highly over- or underexposed images, images that are completely out of focus, and images from a series for which you captured a number of similar shots (pick the best one or two, and then trash the rest).

Don't throw away all of the images that you aren't attracted to straight away because you can always revisit an image later; you may find that you see something in it that you didn't see before, or maybe a different crop will make it work.

Filenames and metadata

Because the default filename that the camera assigns uses a finite numbering system, every 9,999 images will have the same filename. I suggest renaming files right away. There's no set way you should go about it, but I recommended using a system that keeps the filenames distinct. My personal naming convention is a pretty simple one: the subject name, my initials, and numbers. For example, a musician would be TomWaits_JDT_001.NEF or an event might be Xmas2013_JDT_001.NEF. The filename should indicate the subject matter so that it is easier to find in a search.

One thing that I don't think a lot of newer photographers use (maybe because they aren't aware of it, or possibly don't fully understand it) is metadata. Metadata is simply data about data. The following types of metadata are all stored in a single file:

▶ **EXIF.** EXIF stands for Exchangeable Image File Format. This metadata is written and fixed at the time the file is created and can't be easily changed without special software. EXIF data contains the information about your camera, the make and model, serial number, the number of shutter releases, lens focal length and maximum aperture, as well as the shooting data such as the exposure settings, metering mode, and more.

▶ **IPTC.** IPTC stands for International Press Telecommunications Council. It is editable metadata that allows you to embed captions, descriptions, keywords, copyright information, locations, GPS positioning, and more. I add IPTC data to all my images. It makes them easier to find in a search, both on your own computer and online. Keywords are especially helpful. I can shoot a landscape and tag it with a number of keywords, such as landscape, mountain, pine tree, river, Allegheny, Pennsylvania, and so on. If I (or a photo editor) need a specific image, say one with a pine tree in Pennsylvania, a quick search pulls up this image.

▶ **XMP.** XMP stands for Extensible Metadata Platform. These are also known as *sidecar* files because they "ride along" with the image files, and tell software and programs how to interpret some of the data. XMP data is created in the camera and is usually found with RAW files. This is what tells the RAW converter how to initially process the data. It contains information for exposure data, the white balance, proprietary noise reduction, and information of that nature. Once the RAW file has been edited by a RAW converter, additional XMP data is added to reflect changes to the file, but the changes do not affect the RAW data.

Tonal Adjustments and Color Corrections

After you work out a file management system, you can go through and select the images that you want to edit. Some people opt to edit images one at a time, and some do them in batches. I do them both ways depending on the scope of the assignment. If it's a concert or a wedding, I often take a more generalized approach and work in batches, then go back and do individual tweaks.

I almost always shoot in RAW because an image is rarely perfect straight out of the camera. Images usually need minor adjustments, either to make them better or simply to get them to look the way that you want. It may just need a minor white balance adjustment, or maybe sweeping tonal adjustments to recover lost detail in the shadows or highlights.

For the most part, I tend to use Adobe Lightroom because it is a good tool for making simple corrections. It is also one of the most powerful programs you can get at a relatively affordable price. Lightroom is an all-in-one image organizer, RAW file converter, and photo editor. The learning curve is a little steep, but once you master it, you can do nearly all the image editing for most of your photographs provided they don't need extensive retouching.

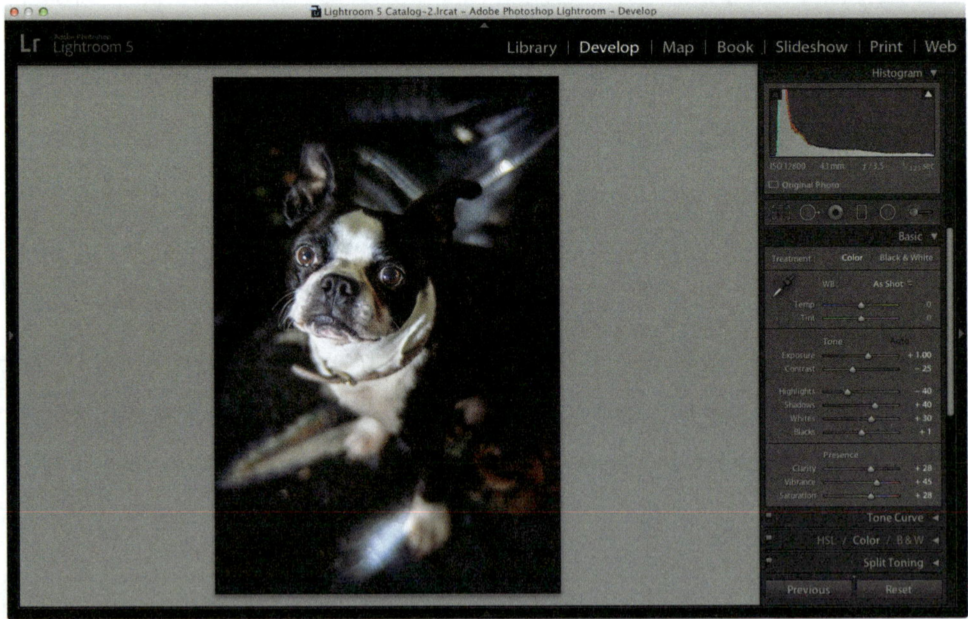

9.1 Adobe Lightroom is a powerful tool for making image adjustments.

The Lightroom Map module also allows you to use GPS data if you used an accessory GPS unit like the Nikon GP-1a with your D3300. This is a very cool feature that enables you to use Google Maps to view the locations where your photos were shot.

For simplicity, and the most features for the least amount of money, I recommend Adobe Photoshop Elements 12. This is actually two programs rolled into one: Elements 12 Organizer and Photo Editor. Organizer offers a very intuitive, fast way to keep your images arranged. The Smart Events feature puts images in order based on the date they were shot, and the Places feature allows you to view images tagged with GPS information on a map.

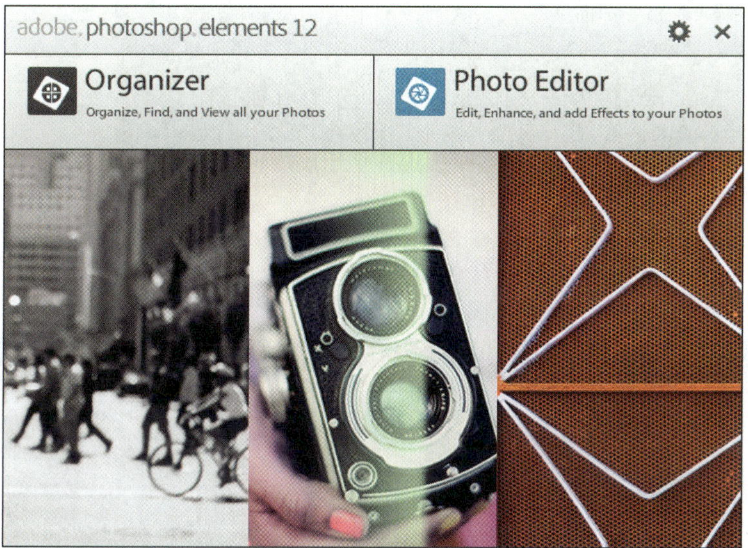

9.2 The Organizer component in Adobe Photoshop Elements 12 helps you keep your images arranged logically.

Photo Editor has some of the same features that make Adobe Photoshop CS6 the de facto software for many imaging professionals, but is much simpler to use. You can make tonal and color corrections, crop, retouch, and a whole lot more. This program has Adobe Camera RAW built right in so that you can make all tonal and color adjustments to the RAW file, which ensures that you are making the most of the RAW data from the camera's imaging sensor.

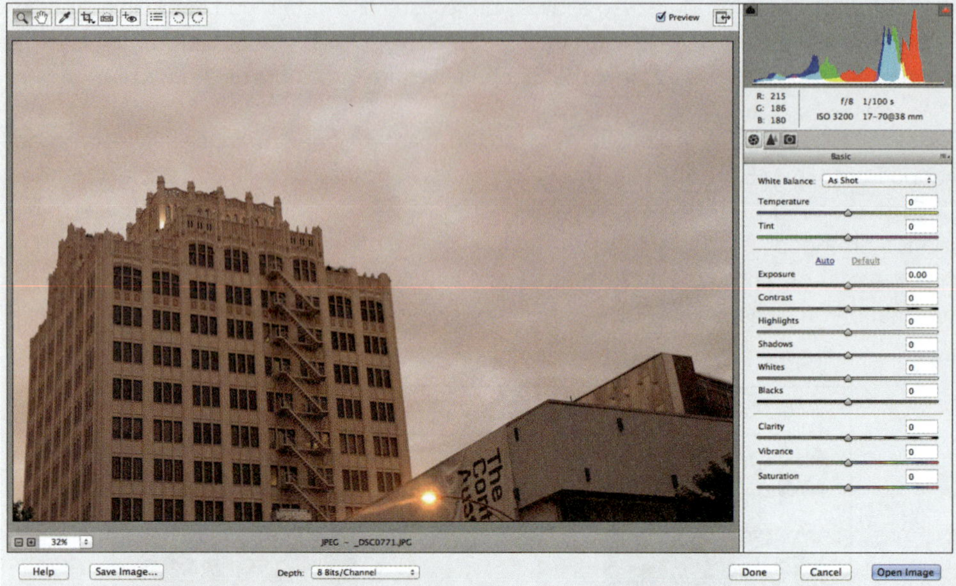

9.3 Adobe Camera RAW is built in to Photoshop CS6 and Photoshop Elements Editor. The application launches automatically when you double-click the file to open it.

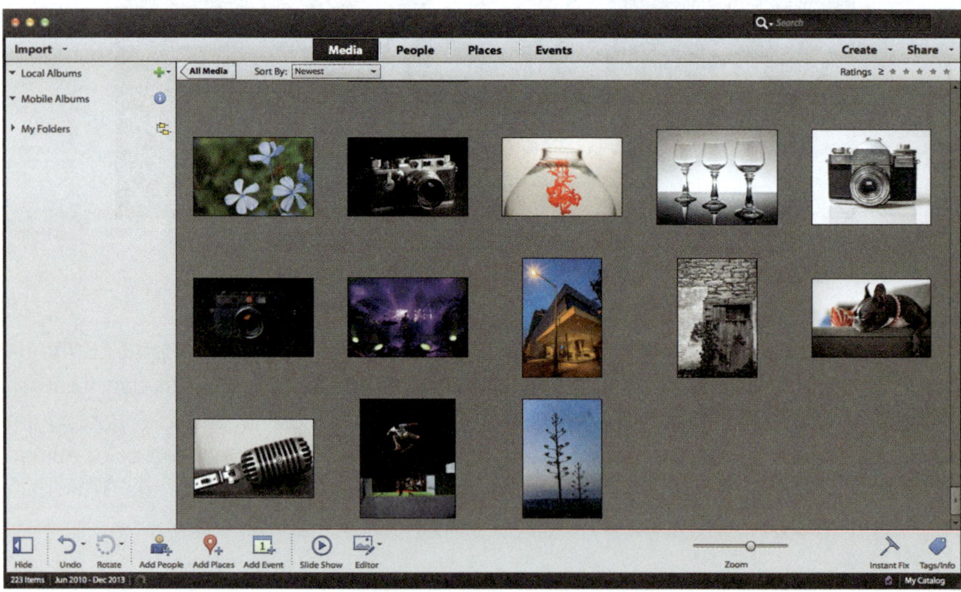

9.4 Adobe Photoshop Elements Editor allows you to do basic tonal and color corrections, as well as retouching.

Many programs enable you to convert RAW files, including Nikon ViewNX 2, which is included with the D3300. A full version of ViewNX 2 also comes bundled with Nikon Transfer 2 to help you transfer your files from the D3300 to your computer. While some programs are more powerful than others, even the most basic RAW file converters, like ViewNX 2, allow you to adjust color, white balance, and tonality.

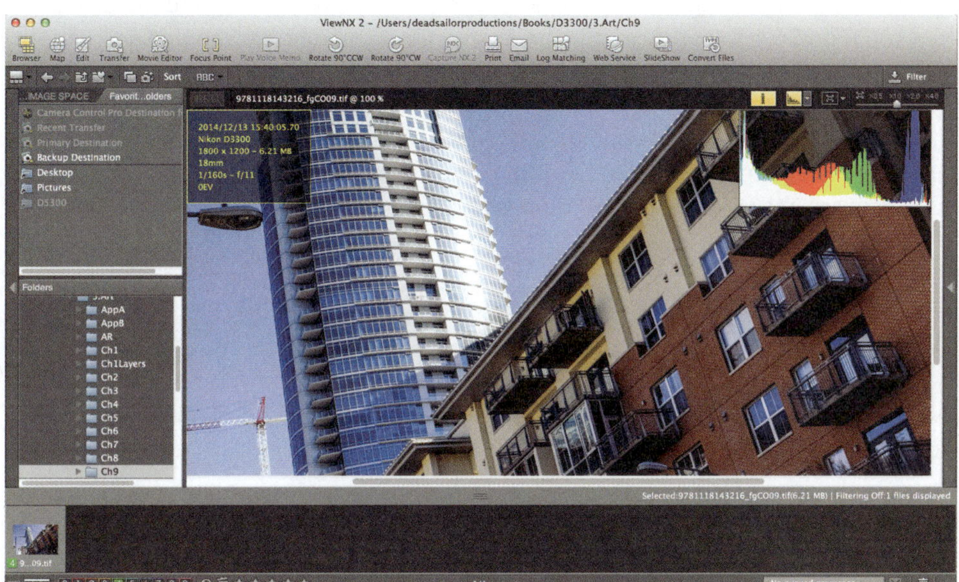

9.5 Nikon ViewNX 2 software comes with your D3300. It allows you to make basic tonal and color corrections.

The first thing to do when making minor adjustments to your image is to assess the white balance. If it's good, leave it alone, but white balance usually needs a little tweak to get it just right. Add a bit of blue to cool the tone, or amber to warm it up. The reason why white balance is the first thing you adjust is because changing the white balance affects the histogram, which can have an impact when you start making tonal adjustments.

Next, you evaluate the exposure. You do this not only by taking a look at the actual image, but also, more importantly, by studying the histogram. The histogram in the RAW editor is likely going to look different than it did on the LCD monitor because the preview on the LCD screen is based on the 8-bit JPEG, while the RAW file has a 14-bit histogram. The histogram will probably change in real time as you move the sliders, so pay close attention.

After analyzing the exposure and histogram, you can determine what (if anything) you should do to adjust it. Most of the time, an image requires a slight contrast boost. To do this, you adjust the Levels or Curves, or use the Exposure or Highlight recovery sliders, depending on what software you're using.

Next, I usually add a bit of saturation to make the image pop, maybe a tiny bit of sharpening or noise reduction, and then I save (or export if I am using Lightroom) as a JPEG to a separate Save folder to keep the adjusted file separate from the original.

This is a simple method of image editing when you're just starting out. You can also make very complex edits to your images. Many filters and borders can be added (similar to the Instagram and Hipstamatic apps). You can also apply effects and conversions, such as black and white or sepia. The possibilities are almost limitless.

General Composition Tips

Photography is an art form, and so follows the same rules of composition as every other form of visual art, such as painting, drawing, and collage. Although they are called "rules," they are really more like guidelines because, obviously, you aren't required to follow them.

Different subjects often require different approaches, and many of the rules of composition often overlap as well, resulting in images that have more than one of these rules in effect.

As I said, you aren't bound to the rules of composition, but when you're just growing accustomed to any visual art, learning these rules and following them will help you learn to create images that are above and beyond general snapshots so you can make professional-looking photographs. Eventually, as you thoughtfully apply the concepts to your photography over and over, you will find yourself intuitively applying them to your compositions.

Keep It Simple

Simplicity is one of the great keys to making a strong image. An image that has a succinctly defined subject commands more attention than a composition in which the viewer must scan the image to determine which part is most important. Images that contain a variety of competing elements can be distracting and cause the viewer to lose interest.

One technique professional photographers use to create simplicity in an image, especially in a busy environment, is to use a wide aperture to create a shallow depth of field, isolating the subject from the background. A shallow depth of field creates blurry, out-of-focus areas in the background that allow the sharp subject to "pop" from the nebulous background.

You can also isolate your subject by changing your angle of approach. For example, you can photograph the subject from down low, aiming up to incorporate the sky as a background. On the opposite side, you can come at your subject from a higher angle and use the ground as the background of your composition.

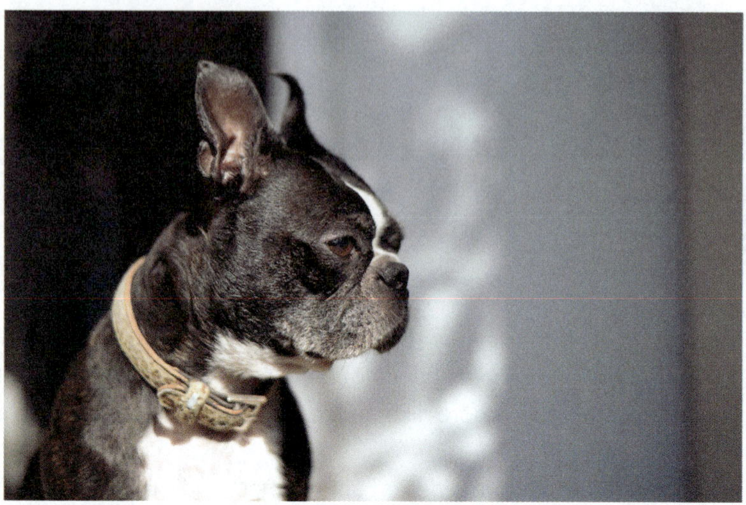

AA.1 A simple image with a definite subject makes for a strong composition. This photo of my dog Henrietta makes it easy to determine the exact subject. The composition also follows the Rule of Thirds. Exposure: ISO 100, f/2.0, 1/1250 second using a Sigma 18–35mm f/1.8 HSM | A at 35mm.

The Rule of Thirds

When starting out, many photographers fall into the trap of placing the subject right in the middle of the frame. It seems to make perfect sense to put the most important part of the image right in the center. However, the truth is that placing your subject off-center creates a more interesting composition by using asymmetrical balance, which introduces diametrically opposing forces that create dynamic tension. When a subject is placed off-center, it can also be balanced by the negative space in the image.

The Rule of Thirds is one of the most useful compositional guides, and artists down through the ages have used it. It involves dividing the image into nine equal parts, using two equally spaced horizontal and vertical lines, kind of like a tic-tac-toe pattern. You want to place the main subject of the image at or near the intersection of one of these lines.

There's another compositional technique that's closely related to the Rule of Thirds because you generally use the Rule of Thirds to take advantage of it. This technique doesn't have a formal name, but you use it when an object is moving through the frame or when a subject is looking at something outside of the frame. It involves leaving space in front of the subject, in the direction the subject is moving or looking.

Leading Lines, S-Curves, and Patterns

Another very helpful technique is to use natural lines that occur in the scene to help draw the eye through the image. Sometimes these lines may be very distinct, such as the lines of railroad tracks leading to a vanishing point. The lines can also be more subtle, like a gentle S-curve in a country road, or a collection of repeating lines that create a pattern. The key is to look for leading lines and incorporate them in your images, either as the main subject, or to bring attention to the main subject.

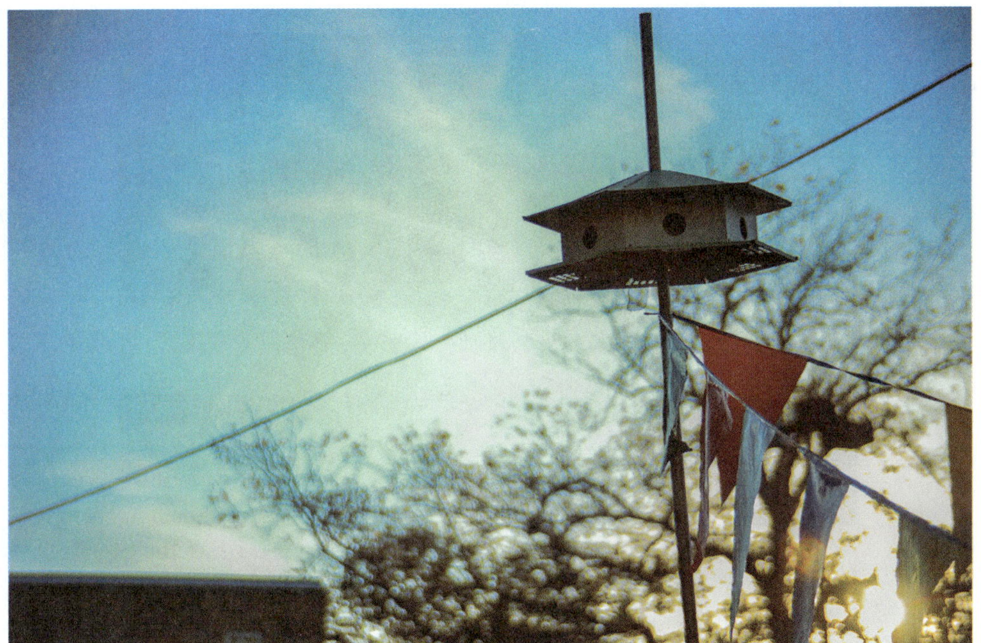

AA.2 Here, I used the wires, flags, and the post of the birdhouse to create leading lines that draw your eye to the subject. This image also uses the Rule of Thirds to create a more dynamic composition. Exposure: ISO 100, f/3.5, 1/400 second using an old Nikon MF lens, NIKKOR 43–86mm f/3.5 43mm.

The Odd Rule

The Odd Rule is a more obscure compositional guideline, and is often used subconsciously. It's not named for using subjects that are *odd* in appearance, but for the number of elements that are included in the picture; the point is that an odd number of elements is more aesthetically pleasing to the eye than an even number of elements (although even numbers can also be used for symmetrical compositions).

The human eye is naturally drawn to the center of a composition when one subject is surrounded by an even number of supporting elements, leaving you with an odd number. An even number of elements tends to cause the brain to divide the composition, leading the viewer to see the image in separate pieces rather than as a whole.

The Odd Rule works best with three elements in the composition. This provides a pleasing triangular shape and can allow two objects to support a third element, creating a stable appearance. Using more than five elements in the composition generally leads to the photograph appearing cluttered.

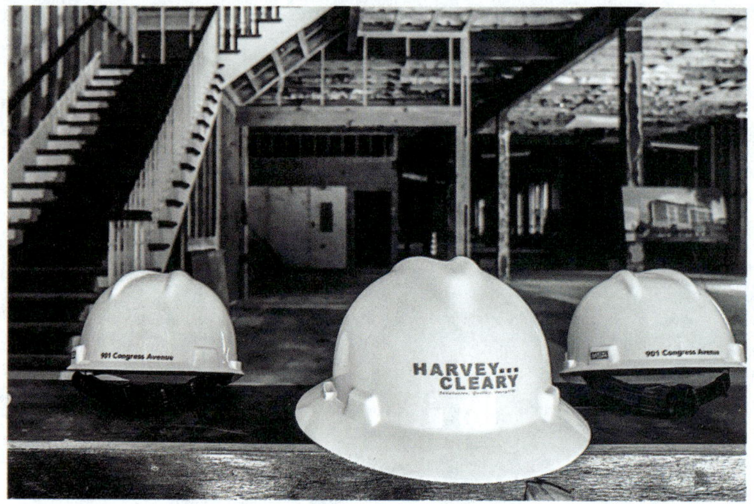

AA.3 These three hardhats follow the Odd Rule. Exposure: ISO 200, f/5.6, 1/320 second, using the 18–55mm kit lens at 55mm.

Using Color

Using color creatively is a great way to make your photographs more interesting. Pay attention to the way the colors in the scene interact with each other and use this as the foundation of your composition. There are some different ways that you can use hues in your images. The most common two are very easy to spot in everyday life or when setting up shots:

▶ **Analogous colors.** These are colors that are similar in tone to one another. This creates a more harmonious composition and also allows you to experiment with images that have definite cool or warm color tones. These colors reside next to each other on the color wheel and can include varying degrees of tones of a similar nature.

AA.4 This photograph of a green-painted wall shows an example of analogous colors. Exposure: ISO 100, f11, 1/80 second, using the 18–55mm kit lens at 18mm.

► **Complementary colors.** These are colors that appear opposite each other on the color wheel, meaning they are opposite, or complementary, colors. These colors are highly contrasting, so using them creates a distinct separation between the elements. Popular complementary color pairings include red/green, orange/blue, and yellow/purple.

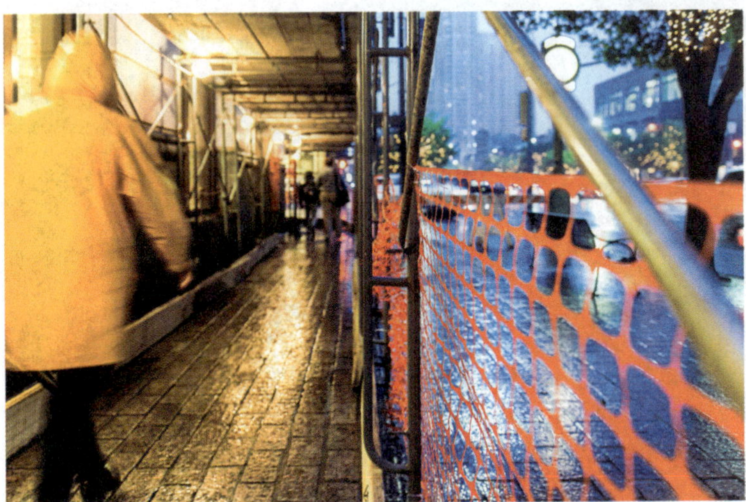

AA.5 This composition contains complementary colors created by the tungsten lights on the left and the twilight of the right side. The orange netting is also a complementary color with the ambient light. In addition, there are plenty of leading lines. Exposure: ISO 500, f/2, 1/13 second, using a Sigma 18–35mm f/1.8 HSM | A at 18mm.

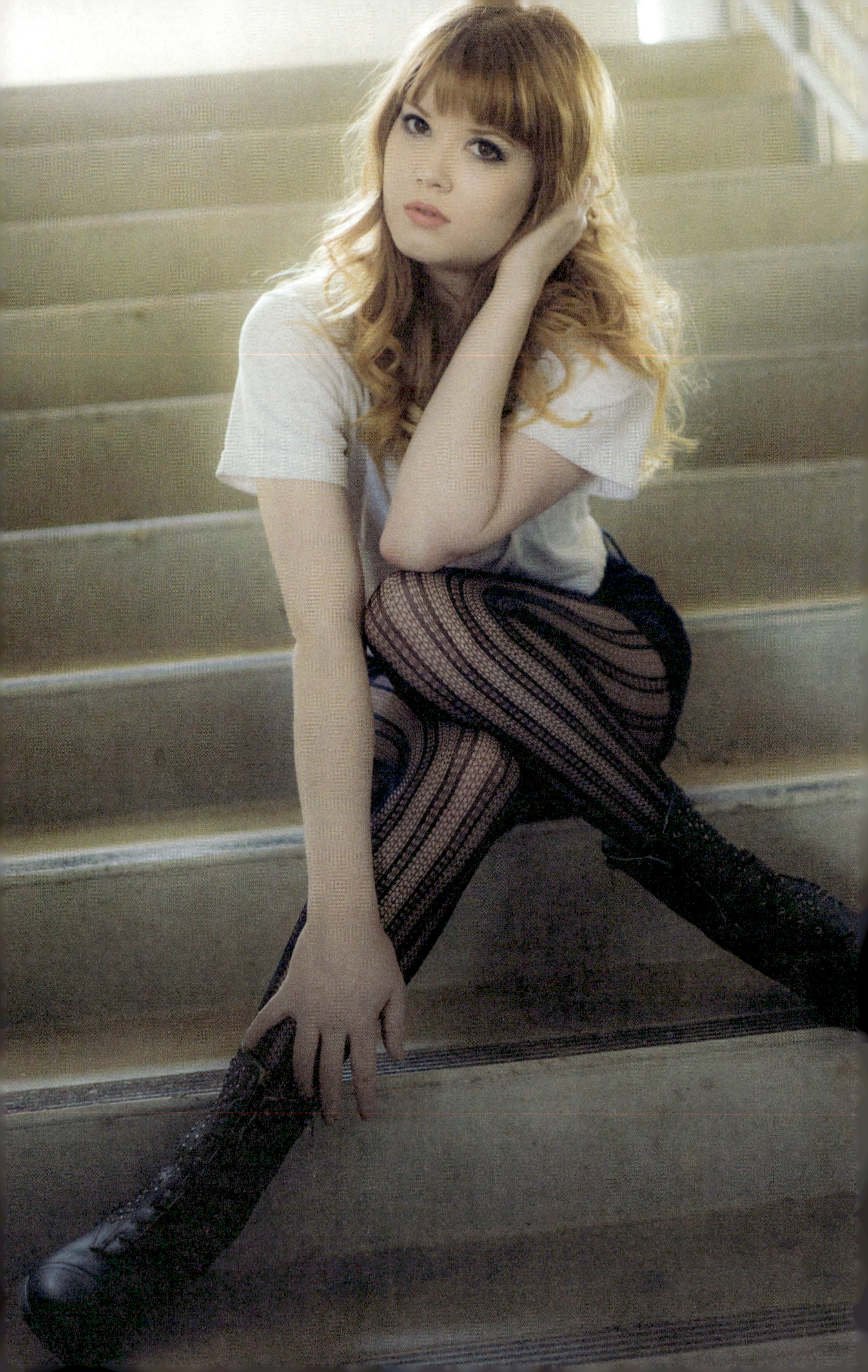

Accessories

The D3300 has a few accessories, which may not be actual necessities, but are just nice to have. These gadgets enhance your picture-taking experiences in different ways, from adding light when you're shooting in dark environments to making it easier to track where you've taken pictures. They also allow you to share your images on your favorite social networking sites, and to control your camera from afar using a smart device.

Speedlights

I've found that having at least one Speedlight is essential if you want to use the D3300 in all types of shooting scenarios. Not only do Speedlights add light when the scene is dark, but you can also use them to create light where it's needed, and you can control the light to make the subject appear exactly as you want it to, as opposed to being at the mercy of existing light. Speedlights give you the power and flexibility of professional lighting at an affordable price. They are compact and can be controlled wirelessly from the D3300 with an additional commander unit (either another Speedlight or the dedicated SU-800 Commander).

Nikon Speedlights operate as part of the Nikon Advanced Wireless Lighting (AWL) system and are part of what is known as the Nikon Creative Lighting System (CLS). AWL allows you to control multiple Speedlights and groups of Speedlights wirelessly while using the

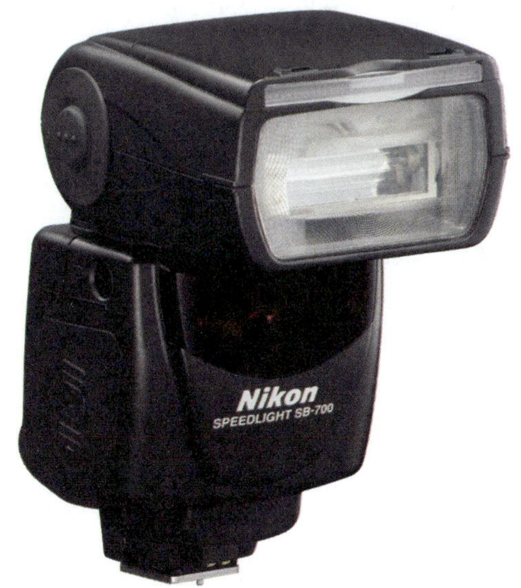

Image courtesy of Nikon, Inc.
AB.1 The Nikon SB-700 Speedlight.

Nikon proprietary i-TTL (Through-the-Lens) flash metering system. This allows you to achieve professional lighting results with a much smaller budget and gear bag.

The D3300 allows you to control up to two groups of additional Speedlights using an SB-700 Commander, and up to three groups of flashes when using an SU-800, SB-800, SB-900, or SB-910 Commander.

The SB-600, SB-700, SB-800, SB-900, and SB-910 can all be used as remote flashes. You can find SB-600, SB-800, and SB-900 units used (and sometimes new), so don't hesitate to buy one if you find it at a good price. They are fully functional with all current Nikon dSLRs and will likely continue to work with future models.

NOTE The SB-400, SB-600, SB-800, and SB-900 Speedlights are discontinued, but still work perfectly with the D3300.

The current lineup of available Nikon Speedlights includes the SB-910 flagship model, the SB-700, SB-300, and SU-800 Commanders, and the R1 or R1C1 Wireless Close-Up Speedlight System.

The ME-1 Stereo Microphone

If you're serious about video, an external microphone is an essential accessory. The Nikon ME-1 is a small stereo microphone that fits into the hot shoe of the D3300. This external microphone records sound much more clearly than the internal microphone.

Also, because it is located farther away from the lens, the ME-1 minimizes the chance of recording noise created by the autofocusing mechanism in the lens. The ME-1 comes with a windscreen to reduce wind noise when shooting outdoors, and also features a low-cut filter to reduce other unwanted low-frequency noises.

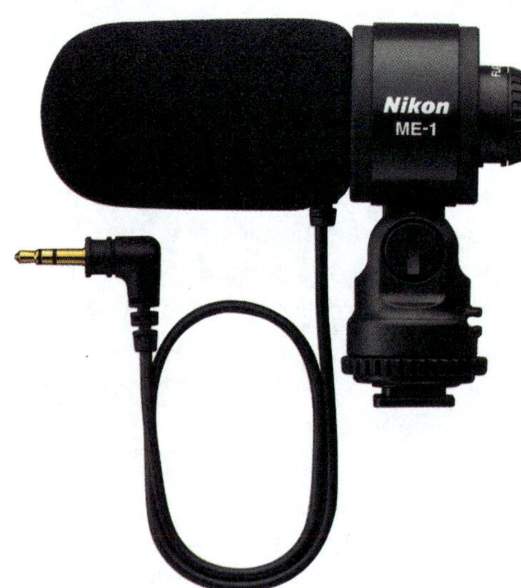

Image courtesy of Nikon, Inc.

AB.2 The Nikon ME-1 stereo microphone.

The ML-L3 Wireless Remote Control

The Nikon D3300 has two infrared receivers (front and back) that allow you to remotely trigger the camera using the ML-L3 infrared remote. This handy accessory is perfect for shooting long exposures, taking self-portraits, or including yourself in a group portrait. The best part about this accessory is that it is very inexpensive. Whereas the infrared remote for higher-end Nikon cameras is over $200, the ML-L3 usually costs less than $20. There's no reason not to own one of these handy little gadgets.

The GP-1 GPS Unit

For traveling photographers, the Nikon GP-1 GPS unit automatically geotags images with latitude, longitude, and specific time information acquired from GPS satellites. This is one of my newest gadgets and I have to say that it works pretty well. Having geotags automatically applied to your images is a great feature, especially for nature and wildlife photographs. The GP-1 can be attached via the hot shoe or to the strap with an included adapter.

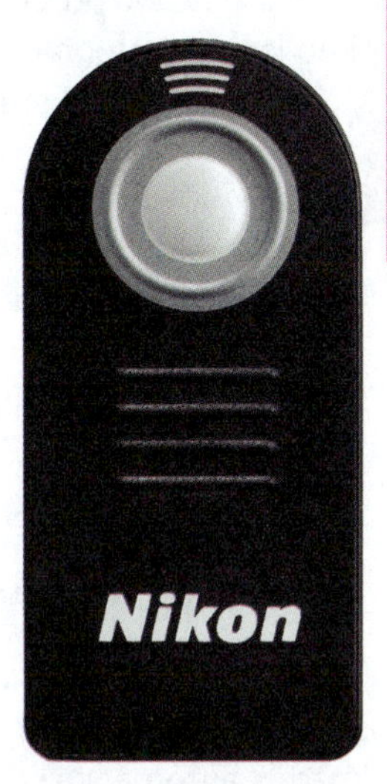

Image courtesy of Nikon, Inc.

AB.3 The Nikon ML-L3 Wireless Remote.

You can use the free Nikon ViewNX 2 software to correlate the images with a map. Adobe Lightroom 5 also supports geotagging map features. I find that geotagging my images makes searching them a snap in Lightroom 5 because I usually remember where a picture was taken, even if I don't remember where I saved it on my hard drive.

Triggertrap

While this isn't a Nikon accessory, it's one of the coolest things I've come across in ages. This is a smartphone app that, when coupled with an inexpensive ($30) dongle, allows you to

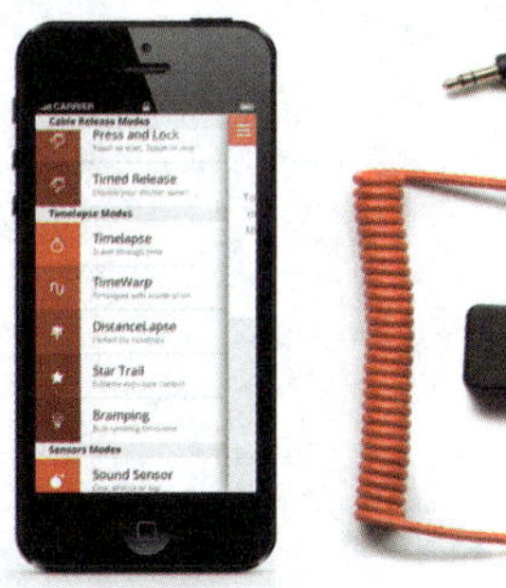

Image courtesy of Triggertrap

AB.4 Screen shot from the Triggertrap App and accessory dongle.

trigger your camera in a number of ways, allowing you to achieve all kinds of interesting effects that would cost a lot more if you had to buy special devices. You can create time-lapse photography, trigger the shutter by sound or vibration, capture long-exposure HDR, easily record star trails, and much more.

Not only does the Triggertrap control your camera, but with another accessory dongle, you can also use it to trigger Speedlights for high-speed flash effects like catching water drops and splashes! Check it out at http://triggertrap.com.

NOTE You can also use this app to control the camera on your phone.

The WU-1a Wireless Mobile Adapter

The latest mobile accessory from Nikon allows you to synchronize the D3300 with smartphones and other devices, such as iPads. You can use the WU-1a to transmit images automatically to your device, so you can share and save them directly to your device as well as to the memory card. This relatively inexpensive wireless adapter also allows you to use your smartphone as a remote release by using the camera's Live View feed, which is visible on your smart device using a free app.

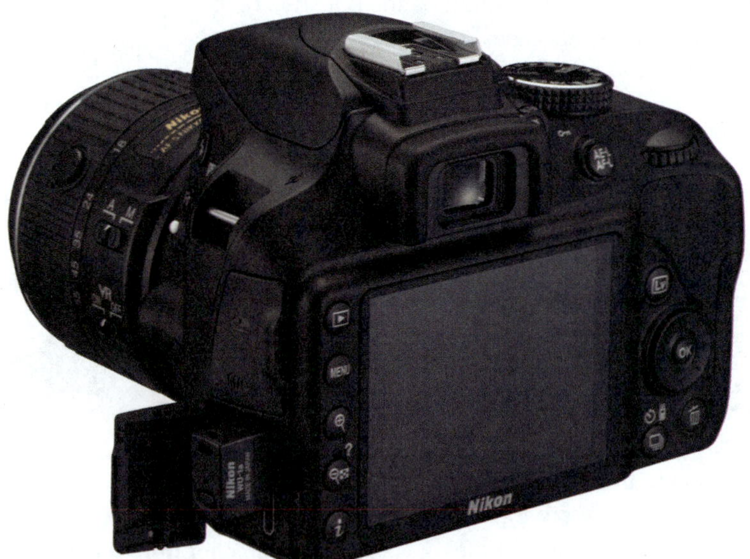

AB.5 The D3300 and the WU-1a.

The only downside to this accessory is that, so far, you cannot adjust exposure settings using the app — any changes to the settings must be made on the camera body. Hopefully, Nikon will add this capability in the near future because it could revolutionize remote shooting in the studio.

Spider Holster

This is a relatively new company that offers a unique alternative to a camera strap. This ingenious device allows you to attach your camera to a belt so that you can quickly grab your camera, and also so that there is no pressure on your neck or shoulders.

This is easily my favorite new camera accessory and has pretty much replaced my using a strap. Spider Holster makes a few different types of camera holsters, from heavy-duty ones complete with a sturdy belt and the ability to carry two full-size pro cameras and optional accessories, down to a small attachment that hooks onto your own belt for smaller camera systems.

The smaller device is called the Black Widow, and that's what I use for my smaller cameras such as the D3300 and Nikon D*f*. You loop your belt through the Black Widow holster and the camera is attached by a locking mechanism to a stud that is threaded into the camera tripod socket (if you use a tripod plate, an adapter is available).

I've done some pretty extensive testing with my Black Widow and I'm not worried one bit about clicking my camera in and riding around town on my motorcycle with it, sometimes quickly grabbing the camera and taking candid street shots at stop lights. Check them out at http://spiderholster.com.

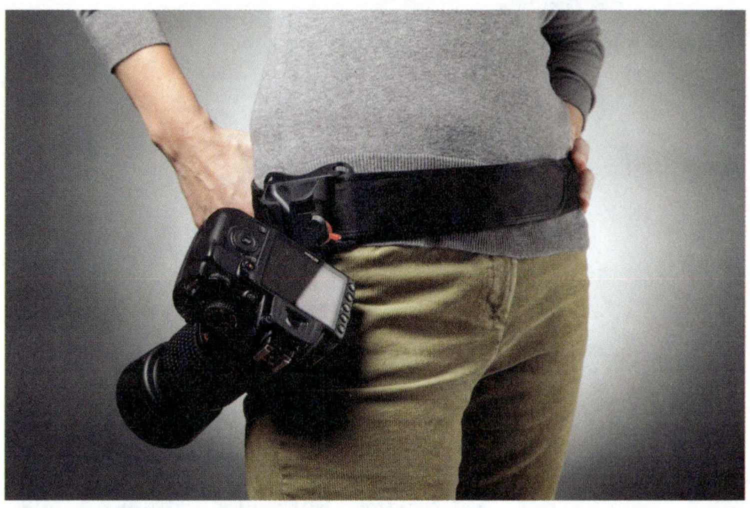

AB.6 **The Black Widow holster.**

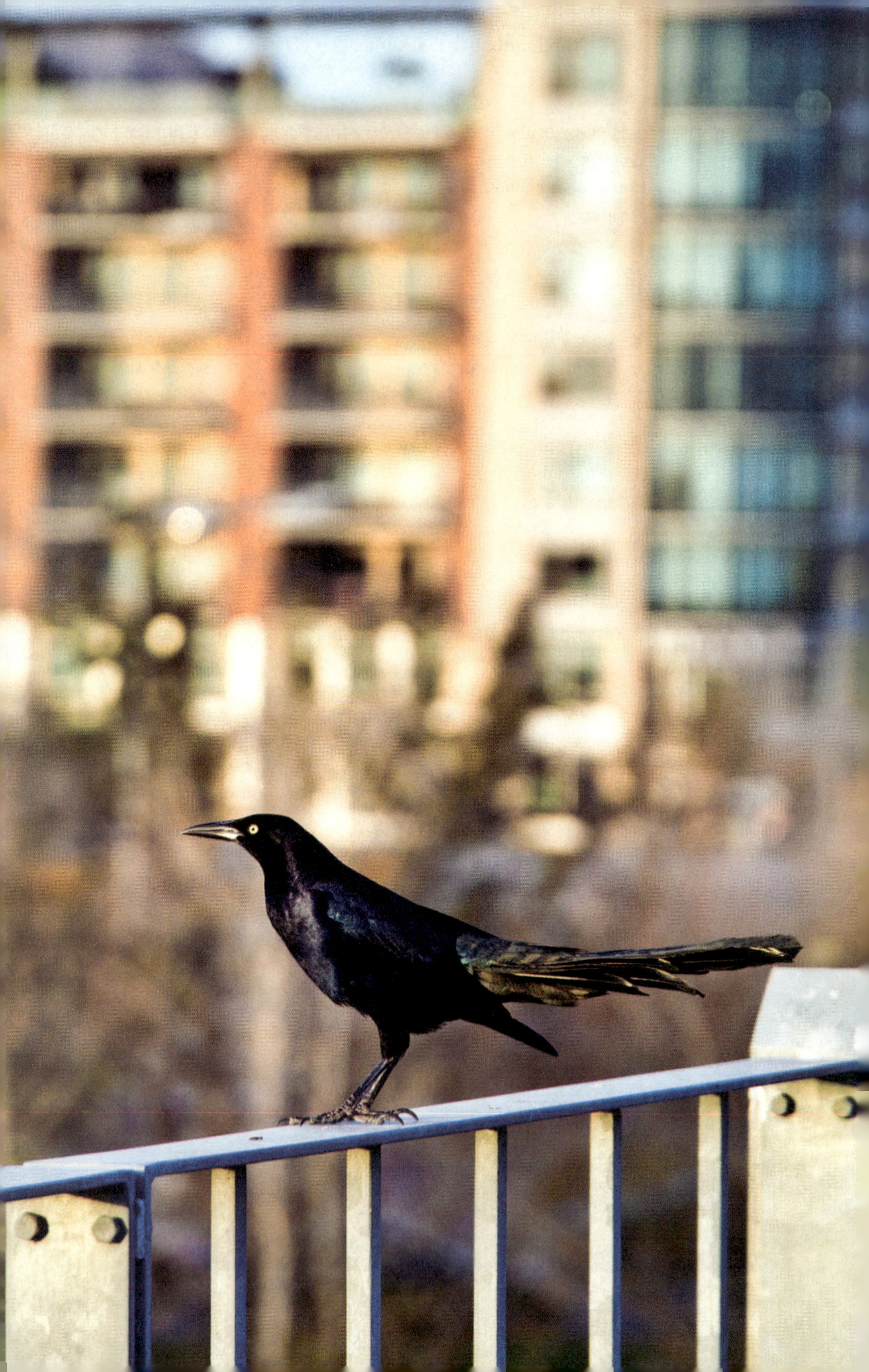

Glossary

Active D-Lighting A camera setting that preserves highlight and shadow details in a high-contrast scene with a wide dynamic range.

AE See *Autoexposure (AE)*.

AF-assist illuminator An LED that emits a beam in low-light or low-contrast situations. The AF-assist illuminator provides enough light for the camera's autofocus to work in low light.

ambient light Lighting that naturally exists in a scene.

angle of view The area of a scene that a lens can capture. The area is determined by the focal length of the lens. Lenses with a shorter focal length have a wider angle of view than lenses with a longer focal length.

aperture The opening of a lens, which is similar to the iris of the eye. The designation for each step in the aperture is called an f-stop. The smaller the f-stop (or f-number), the larger the opening of the aperture; higher f-numbers designate smaller apertures, letting in less light. The f-number is the ratio of the focal length to the aperture diameter.

Aperture-priority auto An exposure mode in which you choose the aperture and the camera automatically adjusts the shutter speed according to the camera's metered readings. Aperture-priority auto is often used to control depth of field. See also *Autoexposure (AE)*, *Programmed auto (P)*, and *Shutter-priority auto*.

aspect ratio The ratio of the long edge of an image to the short edge as printed, displayed on a monitor, or captured by a digital camera. The native ratio for the D3300 is 3:2 for still images and 16:9 for video.

Autoexposure (AE) A camera mode that selects the aperture and/or shutter speed according to the camera's built-in light meter. See also *Aperture-priority auto*, *Programmed auto (P)*, and *Shutter-priority auto*.

Autoexposure/Autofocus (AE/AF) Lock A camera control that lets you lock the current metered exposure and/or autofocus setting prior to taking a photo. This allows you to recompose the shot while retaining the proper focus and/or exposure for the subject. The function of this button can be altered in the Setup menu under the Buttons heading.

Autofocus (AF) A camera mode that determines the proper focus of the subject automatically.

backlighting A lighting effect produced when the main light source is located behind the subject. Backlighting can be used to create a silhouette effect or to illuminate translucent objects. See also *frontlighting* and *sidelighting*.

barrel distortion A lens aberration in which the lines at the horizontal and vertical edges of the image are bowed outward. This distortion is usually found in shorter focal-length (wide-angle) lenses.

bokeh The out-of-focus areas of an image. This term is derived from the Japanese word *boke,* which is loosely translated as *fuzziness*.

bounce flash A technique in which the flash head is pointed upward or toward a wall so that the light bounces off another surface before reaching the subject. Bounce flash softens the light reaching the subject, and often eliminates shadows and provides smoother light for portraits.

bracketing A photographic technique in which you vary the exposure over two or more frames. This ensures a proper exposure in difficult lighting situations in which your camera's meter can be fooled.

camera shake Camera movement (usually at slower shutter speeds) that produces a blurred image.

center-weighted metering A light-measuring algorithm that emphasizes the area in the middle of the frame when calculating the correct exposure for an image.

chromatic aberration A flaw in the design of a lens in which the lens doesn't focus all of the wavelengths of light on the same plane. This is typified by color fringing at the edges of high-contrast areas of the image.

color space This is the palette of colors that is available in any given image. This is also referred to as the gamut. The two most common color spaces are Adobe RGB and sRGB.

colored gel filter A translucent material that is placed over a flash head or light to change the color of the light emitted from the flash. Gels are often used to match the flash output with the ambient light. They are also used to change the color of the background when shooting a portrait or still life, by placing the gel over the flash head and then firing the flash at the background.

compression A technique that reduces the size of a file by digital encoding, which uses fewer bits of information to represent the original subject. Some compression types, such as JPEG, actually discard some image information, while others, such as lossless compressed RAW (NEF), preserve all the details in the original.

Continuous-servo Autofocus (AF-C) A camera setting that allows the camera to focus continuously on a moving subject.

contrast The range between the lightest and darkest tones in an image. In a high-contrast image, the tones extend through the entire range between white and black. In a low-contrast image, the tones are compressed into a smaller range.

curvilinear A term used to describe a lens that does not adjust for the curvature of the lens elements, resulting in an image that appears curved, especially at the edges. Fish-eye lenses are curvilinear.

dedicated flash An electronic flash unit — such as the Nikon SB-910, SB-900, SB-800, SB-700, SB-600, or SB-400 — designed to work with the autoexposure features of a specific camera.

depth of field (DOF) The portion of a scene from foreground to background that appears sharp in the image.

diffuse lighting A soft, low-contrast lighting.

diopter adjustment This is a feature of the optical viewfinder of the camera that allows you to adjust the optics to your own eyesight. This is great for people that wear glasses so you can take them off while shooting and still see everything in the viewfinder sharply.

D-Lighting A camera function that can correct the underexposure that often happens to images that are backlit or in deep shadow. D-Lighting works by adjusting the levels of the image after the image has been captured. This is not to be confused with Active D-Lighting.

dSLR Short for digital single-lens reflex camera. A digital camera design where the light coming from the scene enters through the lens and is reflected by a mirror to a pentaprism; through a series of reflections, this pentaprism rights the image and reflects it to the viewfinder where the photographer can see the exact scene as it is coming through the lens. When the shutter-release button is pressed, the mirror flips up and out of the way, and then flips back down when the exposure is completed.

DX The Nikon designation for dSLRs that use an APS-C–sized (23.6mm × 15.8mm) sensor.

dynamic range The range of brightness or luminosity in any given scene from shadow areas to highlights. Dynamic range can be wide with a lot of contrast or narrow with almost no contrast.

equivalent exposure An exposure with different settings in which the same amount of light reaches the sensor. For example, an exposure of ISO 400 at f/4 for 1/125 second is an equivalent exposure to ISO 200 at f/5.6 for 1/30 second.

equivalent focal length A DX-format digital camera's focal length, which is translated into the corresponding values for 35mm film or the FX format. For example, the 50mm lens on a DX camera gives the same field of view as a 75mm lens on an FX camera.

exposure The amount of light allowed to reach a camera's sensor. Exposure is determined by the ISO setting, the light admitted by the aperture of the lens, and the length of time determined by the shutter speed.

exposure compensation A technique for adjusting the exposure indicated by a photographic exposure meter, in consideration of factors that may cause the indicated exposure to result in a less-than-optimal image.

exposure mode Camera settings that control how the exposure settings are determined. See also *Aperture-priority auto, Programmed auto (P),* and *Shutter-priority auto.*

fill flash A lighting technique in which a flash illuminates the subject just enough to brighten the shadows without overpowering the ambient light. Using a flash for outdoor portraits often brightens the subject in conditions where the camera meters (measures) light from a broader scene.

fill lighting The lighting used to illuminate shadows. Reflectors, additional incandescent lighting, or an electronic flash can be used to brighten shadows (see *fill flash*).

flash An external light source that produces an almost instant flash of light to illuminate a scene. This is also known as *electronic flash.*

flash compensation A feature that adjusts the flash output. If images are too dark (underexposed), you can use flash compensation to increase the flash output. If images are too bright (overexposed), you can use it to reduce the flash output. This is sometimes referred to as Flash Exposure Compensation, or FEC.

flash modes Modes that enable you to control the output of the flash by using different parameters. These modes include Red-eye reduction and Slow sync.

flash output level The output level of the flash as determined by one of the flash modes used.

flash sync speed This is the fastest shutter speed that can be used with a Speedlight due to limitations of the shutter mechanism. The sync speed of the D3300 is 1/200.

focal plane The point at which the lens focuses the image. In a dSLR, the focal plane is where the sensor lies.

frames per second (fps) A term that describes how many images are being recorded per second.

Front-curtain sync A camera setting that causes the flash to fire at the beginning of the period when the shutter is completely open in the instant that the first curtain of the focal plane shutter finishes its movement across the film or sensor plane. This is the default setting. See also *Rear-curtain sync*.

frontlighting The illumination coming from the direction of the camera. See also *backlighting* and *sidelighting*.

f-stop See *aperture*.

FX The Nikon designation for a dSLR that uses a 35mm-sized (36mm × 24mm) sensor.

GPS Short for Global Positioning System. This is a feature that is built in to the D3300 that allows it to connect with a system of satellites to determine the camera's location. This information is then imbedded into the image metadata and can be used to place the image on a map using certain software such as Adobe Lightroom or Nikon Capture NX 2.

High Dynamic Range (HDR) Imaging that allows you to portray a photograph with more tonal range than is possible to capture in a single image, by combining images with two or more exposures. HDR is also a feature on the D3300 that automatically combines two exposures and blends them together.

histogram A graphic representation of the range of tones in an image.

hot shoe The slot located on the top of the camera where the flash connects. The hot shoe is considered hot because it has electronic contacts that allow communication between the flash and the camera.

ISO sensitivity A setting that indicates the light sensitivity of a camera's sensor. In digital cameras, a lower ISO setting provides better-quality images with less image noise; however, a lower ISO setting also requires more exposure. ISO stands for International Organization for Standardization.

JPEG (Joint Photographic Experts Group) An image format that compresses the image data from the camera to achieve a smaller file size. The compression algorithm discards some of the detail when saving the image. The degree of compression can be adjusted, allowing a selectable trade-off between storage size and image quality. JPEG is the most common image format used by digital cameras and other photographic image-capture devices.

kelvin (K) A unit of measurement of color temperature based on a theoretical black body that glows a specific color when heated to a certain temperature. Direct sunlight is approximately 5500K.

lag time The length of time between when the shutter-release button is pressed and the shutter is actually released. The lag time on the D3300 is so short that it is almost imperceptible. Compact digital cameras are notorious for having long lag times, which can cause you to miss important shots.

leading line An element in a composition that leads a viewer's eye toward the subject.

lens flare An effect caused by stray light reflecting off the many glass elements of a lens. Lens shades typically prevent lens flare, but sometimes you can choose to use lens flare creatively by purposely introducing it into your image.

macro lens A lens with the capability to focus at a very close range, enabling extreme close-up photographs. Nikon terminology refers to these as "micro" lenses.

Manual exposure An exposure mode in which the aperture and shutter speed are set by the photographer, not the camera.

Matrix metering A Nikon-exclusive meter that reads the brightness and contrast throughout the entire frame and matches those readings against a database of images (over 30,000 in most Nikon cameras) to determine the best exposure settings for the scene.

metering A technique for measuring the amount of light in the scene by using a light meter.

moiré This is an imaging artifact that is created when two fine patterns are overlapped. In the case of photography a fine repeating pattern such as synthetic material, hair, feathers, or some architectural features like brickwork or rows of windows in a high-rise can cause a moiré pattern due to interference from the Bayer color filter which covers the sensor and allows the camera to determine color. Moiré typically appears as fine banding or a rainbow-like effect (often referred to as false color).

monocoque structure The monocoque structure is a design that uses a single external frame design to provide the main support. The D3200 used an interior chassis to provide stability and strength to the camera body. The D3300's monocoque design allows the camera to dispense with the interior metal chassis resulting in a lighter and stronger design.

Nikon Electronic File (NEF) The name of the Nikon RAW file format. See also *RAW*.

noise The appearance of pixels with randomly distributed color values in a digital image. Noise in digital photographs tends to be more pronounced in shadow areas with low-light conditions and long exposures, particularly when you set your camera to a higher ISO setting.

Noise Reduction (NR) A technology used to decrease the amount of random information in a digital image, often caused by long exposures and/or high ISO settings.

Optical Low Pass Filter (OLPF) Also referred to as an Anti-Aliasing filter, this is a filter that is integrated into the camera's sensor mechanism that gives a slight blur to the image to reduce the optical artifacts of moiré and false color. With the higher resolution sensors of the D3300 the moiré effect is reduced negating the use of the OLPF. The absence of the filter in the D3300 allows for sharper more detailed images. See also *moiré*.

panorama A super wide view of a scene. In photography this is often achieved by taking a number of images and combining them to create a view that is wider than you can capture with a typical lens.

pincushion distortion A lens aberration in which the lines at the horizontal and vertical edges of the image are bowed inward. It is usually found in longer focal-length (telephoto) lenses.

Programmed auto (P) A camera setting in which the shutter speed and aperture are set automatically. See also *Aperture-priority auto, Autoexposure (AE)*, and *Shutter-priority auto*.

RAW An image file format that contains the unprocessed camera data as it was captured. Using this format allows you to change image parameters, such as white balance, saturation, and sharpening. Although you can process RAW files in-camera, the preferred method requires special software, such as Adobe Camera Raw (available in Photoshop), Adobe Lightroom, or Nikon Capture NX 2 or View NX 2. See also *Nikon Electronic File (NEF)*.

Rear-curtain sync A setting that causes the flash to fire at the end of the expo-sure an instant before the second, or rear, curtain of the focal plane shutter begins to move. With slow shutter speeds, this feature can create a blur effect from the ambient light, showing as patterns that follow a moving subject, with the subject shown sharply frozen by the flash at the end of the blur trail. This setting is often used in conjunction with longer shutter speeds. See also *Front-curtain sync*.

rectilinear A term used to describe a design feature that corrects (or rectifies) for the field curvature found in wide-angle lenses. Most wide-angle lenses are rectilinear, whereas a fish-eye lens is not and retains the field curvature. See also *curvilinear*.

red-eye An effect from flash photogra-phy that appears to make a person's eyes glow red or an animal's eyes glow yellow or green. This effect is caused by light bouncing off the retina. It is most noticeable in dimly lit situations (when the irises are wide open), as well as when the electronic flash is close to the lens and, therefore, prone to reflect the light directly back.

Red-eye reduction mode A flash mode used to prevent the subject's eyes from appearing red. Multiple flashes are fired just before the shutter opens, causing the subject's irises to contract, therefore reflecting less light from the retina to the camera.

release mode The release mode deter-mines how the shutter is released when the shutter-release button is pressed. The D3300 offers a few options such as single release, continuous release, and a quiet release mode.

SD This is a type of flash memory card that is used to store the image data collected from the camera's sensor. SD stands for Secure Digital and features a small switch that allows you to lock the card so that data cannot be modified. SD cards can be standard SD (up to 2GB of storage), SDHC (High Capacity from 4 to 32GB), SDXC (Extended Capacity from 64GB to 2TB), or SDHC and SDXC UHS-1 which provides Ultra High Speed read/write speeds for faster transfer of data.

selective focus A camera setting that uses shallow depth of field to isolate the subject and make it more prominent by blurring out the rest of the image.

self-timer A mechanism that delays the opening of the shutter for several seconds after the shutter-release button has been pressed.

shutter A mechanism that allows light to pass to the sensor for a specified amount of time.

Shutter-priority auto A camera mode in which you set the desired shutter speed and the camera automatically sets the aperture for you. It is best used when shooting action shots to freeze the subject's motion by using fast shutter speeds. See also *Aperture-priority auto, Autoexposure (AE),* and *Programmed auto (P).*

shutter speed The length of time the shutter is open to allow light to fall onto the imaging sensor. The shutter speed is measured in seconds or, more commonly, fractions of a second.

sidelighting Lighting that comes directly from the left or right of the subject. See also *backlighting* and *frontlighting.*

Single-servo Autofocus (AF-S) A setting that locks the focus on the subject when the shutter-release button is half-pressed. This allows you to focus on the subject and then recompose the image without losing focus.

Slow sync mode A flash mode that allows the camera's shutter to stay open for a longer time to record ambient light. The background receives more exposure, which gives the image a more natural appearance.

Speedlight A term for Nikon accessory flashes.

spherical aberration A problem with lens design that causes the light coming through the lens not to converge at a single point, resulting in soft or unfocused images. Many lenses on the market today include an aspherical lens element that corrects this problem.

spot meter A metering system in which the exposure is based on a small area of the image. On the D3300, the spot is linked to the AF point.

Through-the-Lens (TTL) A metering system in which the light is measured directly through the lens.

vanishing point The point at which parallel lines converge and seem to disappear.

Vibration Reduction (VR) A function in which lens elements are shifted by a mechanism in the lens to reduce the effects of camera shake. Note that VR is a Nikon proprietary term, and third-party lenses have other designations that mean the same thing, such as Optical Stabilization (OS; Sigma) and Vibration Compensation (VC; Tamron).

White balance A setting used to compensate for the differences in color temperature from different light sources. For example, a typical tungsten light bulb is very yellow-orange, so the camera adds blue to the image to ensure that the light looks like standard white light.

Wi-Fi A technology that is built in to the D3300 that allows you to wirelessly connect, control, and send images to certain devices using the Nikon Wireless Mobile Utility App.

Index

red-eye reduction, 158
slow sync, 158
Built-in flash mode/Speedlight Flash Exposure
compensation, 16, 17

C

camera shake
Auto ISO setting, 204
monopods and, 185
Night portrait mode, 31
Programmed auto mode, 23
Self-timer release mode, 49, 89
tripods and, 195
VR lens and, 122, 202
card reader, 223
Center-weighted metering mode, 42–43
Child flash mode, 10
Child mode, 30–31
Choose a date option, Guide mode, 28
chromatic aberrations, 109, 124
chrominance, 52
Clean at shutdown option, camera, 86
Clean at startup and shutdown option,
camera, 85, 86
Clean at startup option, camera, 86
Clean now option, camera, 85
Cleaning off option, camera, 86
Close up automatic exposure mode, 164
Close-up flash mode, 10, 31
close-up lenses, 124–126, 182
Cloudy white balance setting, 54
CLS (Creative Lighting System), 237
CMOS sensor, 131
color
analogous, 234–235
color corrections, 226–230
color space, 79
color temperature, 53
complementary, 235
Color balance option, Retouch menu, 99
Color matrix metering II option, Matrix metering
mode, 42
Color outline feature, Retouch menu, 103
Color sketch effect, 35, 104
Color toning option, Picture Control feature, 59
colored gel filter. *See* filter effects
Command dial, 5, 6
complementary color, 235
composition
color
analogous, 234–235
complementary, 235

concert and live music photography, 191
leading lines, 233
Odd Rule, 233–234
patterns, 233
Rule of Thirds, 232
S-curves, 233
simplicity, 231–232
compression, 62
concert photography
equipment, 188–190
overview, 187–188
technique, 190–192
Continuous high-speed shooting mode, 49
continuous light, 153–154
Continuous low-speed shooting mode, 49
Continuous-servo AF mode
concert and live music photography, 190
macro photography, 197
overview, 45–46
contrast detection, 44–45
Contrast setting, Picture Control feature, 57
cool colors, 53
Cool white fluorescent option, 76
Creative Lighting System (CLS), 237
Cross screen filter, 98
cross-type autofocus sensors, 44
Current option, Playback folder, 69
curvilinear, 115, 126
Cyanotype color option, 59, 97

D

D lens code, 108
dark frame noise reduction, 52, 80
Date and time option, clock, 88
Date format option, clock, 88
Date imprint, 16, 17
Day white fluorescent option, 76
Daylight fluorescent option, 76
Daylight saving time option, clock, 88
DC lens code, 109
DCT (Discrete Cosine Transform), 62
dedicated flash. *See* built-in flash; flash
Delayed remote mode, 50
Delete button
back of camera, 5, 7
Playback menu, 68–69, 220
Storage folder, 92
Delete photos option, Guide mode, 28
depth of field (DOF)
aperture and, 137
controlling, 24
wide-angle lenses, 116, 119

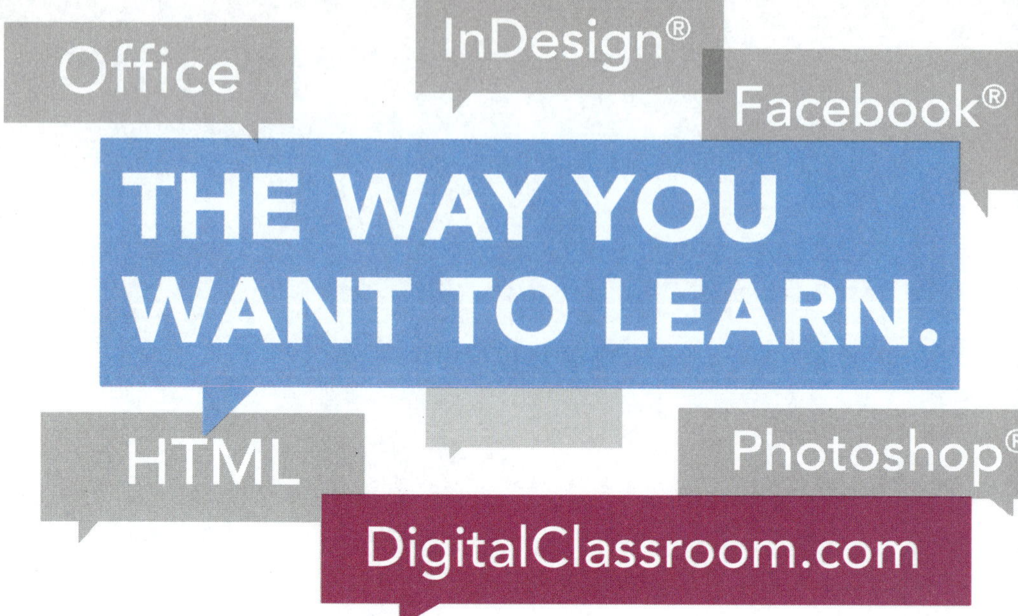

Flexible, fast, and fun, DigitalClassroom.com lets you choose when, where, and how to learn new skills. This subscription-based online learning environment is accessible anytime from your desktop, laptop, tablet, or smartphone. It's easy, efficient learning — on *your* schedule.

- Learn web design and development, Office applications, and new technologies from more than 2,500 video tutorials, e-books, and lesson files
- Master software from Adobe, Apple, and Microsoft
- Interact with other students in forums and groups led by industry pros

Learn more!
Sample DigitalClassroom.com for free, now!

We're social. Connect with us!

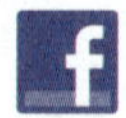  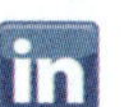 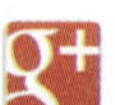 

facebook.com/digitalclassroom
@digitalclassrm

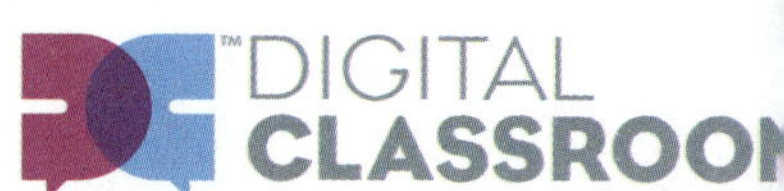